श्री चाणक्यनीति

Śrī Cāṇakya-nīti

Ancient Sense for Modern Success

Based upon the teachings of

His Divine Grace
A. C. Bhaktivedanta Swami Prabhupāda

Founder-*Ācārya* of the
International Society for Krishna Consciousness

With extensive commentary by
Patita Pāvana Dāsa Adhikārī

Translation: Paṇḍita V. Badarayana Murthy with Patita Pāvana Dāsa Adhikārī
Commentary: Patita Pāvana Dāsa Adhikārī
Sanskrit editing, proofreading, research: Kiśora Dāsa Adhikārī and Ananta-sarovara Dāsī
Formatting, illustration and cover: Abhaya Mudrā Dāsī

ISBN 978-93-82109-32-7

Previous Printings: 6,000 copies
Third Printing of the Second Edition (2019): 3,000 copies

Web: books.bvks.com
Email: books@bvks.com
Whatsapp: +(91) 70168 11202

Abhaya Ashram Publishing
New Gauda Mandala Bhumi
Blagoevgrad, Bulgaria

Published by Bhakti Vikas Trust, Surat, India

श्री चाणक्यनीति
Śrī Cāṇakya-nīti

Ancient Sense for Modern Success

nava nandān dvijaḥ kaścit prapannān uddhariṣyati
teṣāṁ abhāve jagatīṁ mauryā bhokṣyanti vai kalau

sa eva candraguptaṁ vai dvijo rājye 'bhiṣekṣyati
tat-suto vārisāras tu tataś cāśokavardhanaḥ

"A certain *brāhmaṇa* [Cāṇakya] will betray the trust of King Nanda and his eight sons and will destroy their dynasty. In their absence the Mauryas will rule the world as the age of Kali continues. This *brāhmaṇa* will enthrone Candragupta, whose son will be named Vārisāra. The son of Vārisāra will be Aśokavardhana."

(*Śrīmad-Bhāgavatam* 12.1.11–12)

DEDICATION

Humbly bowing before my Śrī Sad-Gurudeva Mahārāja,
I offer this book at the lotus feet of the *jagad-guru:*

Śrī Śrīmad (108) Abhaya Caraṇāravinda
Bhaktivedanta Swami Prabhupāda

Who enjoyed quoting
Cāṇakya Paṇḍita on every occasion.

Contents

Foreword.. xv

Preface to the First Edition.................................. xvii

Preface to the Second Edition xxi

Chapter One.. 1

Invocatory prayers to the Supreme Lord; benefits of studying *nīti-śāstra;* what makes even a learned *paṇḍita* suffer; causes of death; save your soul; put aside some wealth; where one should not reside; how one's associates are tested; who is a true friend; do not lose the eternal; marriage between persons of equal status; whom to not trust; accept what is valuable disregarding its origin; women compared to men.

Chapter Two.. 33

The seven flaws of women; the fruits of austerities; heaven on earth; qualities expected of relatives and friends; reject a so-called friend; do not entrust secrets even to friends; keep plans to yourself; what is painful; the rarity of *sādhus;* how to educate and discipline one's offspring; always study and memorize śāstric knowledge; six kinds of evil; swift destruction; strength of each *varṇa;* everyone in the world sees only one's own benefit; quick ruination in the company of rogues; friendship between equals.

Chapter Three.. 60

No one is free of blemish and suffering; how to discern a person's qualities; what to do with one's children, friends and enemies; difference between a rascal and a snake; kings prefer good assistants; *sādhus* never change; do not associate with fools; persons devoid of learning; what is real beauty; renounce the world for your spiritual benefit; fruits of endeavor; avoid extremes; there are no impediments for the strong; on good and bad sons; how to discipline a son; how to protect one's life; a worthless life; the residence of Lakṣmī.

Chapter Four 87

What is ordained by fate; follow the *sādhu;* saintly devotees look after their associates; advance spiritually while still healthy; learning is like the *kāmadhenu;* one moon is better than many stars; better a still-born son than a fool; six circumstances that burn one like fire; a son who is neither a scholar nor a devotee; shelter from the miseries of material life; what happens only once; what to do alone and what in the company of others; a true wife; all is void to a poor man; four kinds of poison; what should be abandoned; four kinds of weariness; constantly think about your circumstances; different visions of God.

Chapter Five 112

Four *gurus;* four ways of testing a person; how to get rid of fear; no two people are the same; one who is honest cannot deceive; envy; what becomes ruined; learning is retained through practice; what preserves what; blasphemers come to grief; what destroys what; no happiness is higher than spiritual knowledge; one is born alone and dies alone; Svarga is but a straw; *dharma* is the only friend; rain upon the sea; no wealth is dearer than stored food grains; the poor crave riches; all things rest upon truth; religious merit alone is steady; barber is cunning; five fathers; five mothers.

Chapter Six 43

The importance of hearing; who is a *cāṇḍāla;* what cleanses what; traveling; the man of means is respected; everything is controlled by Providence; time is insurmountable; who is blind; the soul is alone in *saṁsāra;* who accepts the sins of others; four enemies at home;

how to appease different characters; better to have no kingdom than a worthless one; who is happy in the kingdom of a wicked king; lessons from animals; a lesson from a lion; a lesson from a crane; four lessons from a cock; five lessons from a crow; six lessons from a dog; three lessons from a donkey; applying these lessons makes one invincible.

Chapter Seven 161

A wise man does not reveal his embarrassment; when to renounce shyness; difference between satisfaction and greed; three things to be satisfied with and three not to; do not pass between two *brāhmaṇas;* do not touch fire with your foot; safe distance; how to control animals and fools; *brāhmaṇas* are satisfied by a fine meal; the art of conciliation; the power of kings, *brāhmaṇas* and women; do not be too upright; one should be steady; wealth is preserved by spending; only one who is wealthy is respected; four heavenly qualities; four hellish qualities; the lion's den and the cave of a jackal; the uselessness of a dog's tail; kinds of purity; how to perceive the soul.

Chapter Eight 180

Honor is the true wealth; what can be ingested before religious rituals; diet determines offspring; offer wealth only to the worthy; the *yavana* is the basest of men; one remains a *cāṇḍāla* until he bathes; water before and after the meal; knowledge is lost without practical application; who is unfortunate; devotional service is the basis of success; the Lord does not reveal Himself unless He is worshipped with devotion; no austerity is equal to a peaceful mind; anger is the god of death; good qualities are an ornament; beauty is spoiled by immorality; what is pure; four persons who are ruined; high birth destitute of scholarship; learning is universally honored; animals in the form of men; an improperly performed *yajña* consumes the kingdom.

Chapter Nine 202

Abandon the objects of sense desire; base men who gossip about the secrets of others; no one has advised Lord Brahmā; the best medicine; one who predicts eclipses must be a *vidvān;* the seven who should be awakened; the seven who should not be awakened; *dvijas* who are like serpents without poison; those who can neither control nor protect; the show of terror; what to discuss over the day; how to be blessed with Indra's opulence; what becomes useful through exertion; how to overcome poverty.

Chapter Ten 216

Who is destitute; perform only deeds that are carefully considered; some value enjoyment and others knowledge; what slips past the observation of a poet; fate makes a beggar a king; who is whose enemy; beasts in the form of men; bamboo will never become sandalwood; a mirror to a blind man; there is no way to reform an evil man; the consequences of offenses; living among relatives when reduced to poverty; the *brāhmaṇa* is like a tree; who is at home in all the three worlds; birds fly off in the morning; one who possesses intelligence is strong; why be concerned for one's maintenance; Sanskrit and other languages; gradations of nutrition; diseases are nourished by sorrow.

Chapter Eleven 244

Inbred qualities; one who abandons his community; elephants are controlled by an *aṅkuśa;* in Kali-yuga, Lord Hari and the Gaṅgā abandon the earth; those engrossed in family affairs cannot acquire knowledge; a neem tree will never become sweet; mental impurities cannot be washed away; an elephant pearl and a *guñjā* berry; eating meals in silence; students should renounce eight flaws; a *vipra* who is called a *ṛṣi;* a *brāhmaṇa* who is called a *dvija;* a *brāhmaṇa* who is actually a *vaiśya;* a *brāhmaṇa* who is actually a *śūdra;* a *brāhmaṇa* who is actually a cat; a *brāhmaṇa* who is actually a *mleccha;* a *brāhmaṇa* who is actually a *cāṇḍāla;* the fame of charitable personalities.

Chapter Twelve.................................. 269

The blessed *gṛhastha;* the glories of charity to a qualified *brāhmaṇa;* who is happy in this world; who pollutes even the jackal; the exclamation of the *mṛdaṅga's* beat; who can erase what Lord Brahmā has ordained; wicked men become saintly in the company of devotees; devotees are holy places personified; as a worm survives in poison; a house which is like a funeral pyre; the kinsmen of a *sādhu;* immediately engage yourself in *dharma;* sources of joy; another's wife as one's mother; praise of Lord Rāma; who to learn from; who is swiftly ruined; the intelligent should be concerned about *dharma;* gradually accumulate knowledge, virtue and wealth; a wicked person never changes.

Chapter Thirteen................................ 295

A life of only a moment is successful; deal only with the present; how to please others; the character of great souls; attachment is the root of all grief; the fatalist is ruined; subjects follow the king; dead though living; nipples on a goat's neck; the hearts of base men burn; the mind alone is responsible for bondage or liberation; shed bodily identification; learn contentment; good or bad deeds follow us; he whose actions are disorganized; how the student acquires knowledge; the wise act after due circumspection; *guru* should be worshipped; a *sādhu* will never swerve from the spiritual path; three gems upon this earth.

Chapter Fourteen 313

Fruits of the tree of sins; the body can never be regained; overcome the enemy; what spreads according to one's nature; the state of mind at the burning *ghāṭa;* intelligence before sinning and during repentance; do not feel proud; he who lives in our mind is near; speak pleasingly if in need of a favor; association from a proper distance; be cautious with six causes of death; he who is virtuous is living; the roaming cow of fifteen faces; who is a *paṇḍita;* a single object seen in three different ways; what the wise should not divulge; the song of the *kokila;* secure and keep these five; leave the wicked and associate with devotees.

Chapter Fifteen.. 330

If the heart melts with compassion; repaying the debt to the *guru;* two ways of dealing with evil-minded men; whom the goddess of fortune forsakes; there is no better relative than wealth; wealth acquired sinfully; powerful men who perform a wrongful deed; definitions of a true meal, friendship, wisdom and *dharma;* glass and gems; learn that which is essential; the host who disregards guests; a ladle does not taste the dish; the "boat" of the qualified *brāhmaṇa;* the moon in the abode of the sun; a bumblebee in a foreign land; Lakṣmī refuses to dwell in the houses of *brāhmaṇas;* the bond of affection; a noble man does not lose his qualities; fame is gained only by sufficient *puṇya.*

Chapter Sixteen 350

An old man's lamentation; the affection of a woman is not one-pointed; a *śakunta* bird tied to a string; who has not become haughty upon attaining riches; intelligence at the time of adversity; a crow cannot become Garuḍa; qualities make a man worthy of respect; he whose glories are sung by others; a gem in a golden ornament; every scholar needs patronage; undesirable kinds of wealth; money should be used; no one has ever been satisfied with these four; acts of charity never perish; the beggar; death preferable to dishonor; there is no poverty in pleasant words; two nectarean fruits; good habits from previous lives; knowledge sitting in books.

Chapter Seventeen 368

Studying innumerable books; repay the favors; nothing can defeat *tapasya;* no vice worse than covetousness; we cannot rely on what was given at birth; he who is devoid of virility becomes a *sādhu;* no offering is equal to food; the wicked are saturated with poison; how a woman becomes holy; water after washing the feet; realized knowledge is the key to salvation; how prosperity is lost; milk restores vigor; he who nurtures benevolence; what enjoyment is there in the world of Indra; men without knowledge are beasts; the bees and the elephant; eight persons who do not understand the suffering of others; searching for the pearl of youth; a single excellence.

Appendix I 391
Appendix II.. 401
Appendix III....................................... 402
Glossary... 404

Abbreviations Found in This Text

Bg—*Bhagavad-gītā As It Is*
Cc—*Śrī Caitanya-caritāmṛta*
CN—*Cāṇakya-nīti*
GP—*Bṛhaspati-nīti-sāra* from the *Garuḍa Purāṇa*
MS—*Manu-saṁhitā*
NS—*Nīti-śataka* of Bhartṛhari
SB—*Śrīmad-Bhāgavatam*
SN— *Śukra-nīti* of Śukrācārya
VN—*Vidura-nīti*

FOREWORD BY BHAKTI VIKĀSA SWAMI

I first met Patita Pāvana Prabhu in 1975, at the intergalactically famous temple of Śrī Śrī Rādhā-Londonīśvara. I was a raw recruit; he, a grand old veteran of seven years. He found in me a ready audience for his large repertoire of stories about Śrīla Prabhupāda and about India, and for his many takedowns of Māyāvāda that he had imbibed from Śrīla Prabhupāda and that he willingly imparted to me. As ordained by fate, our ways soon parted, until about two years ago when we again met (on the internet—where else?). We found ourselves to be still united on the eternal platform of service to Śrīla Prabhupāda and his mission. In the interim, we had both written and published books. Some thirty years before, I had read the English edition of *Śrī Cāṇakya-nīti* which he had produced, and when I learned that he was planning to issue an expanded version, I suggested that he have it edited by my capable disciple Kiśora Dāsa. After Kiśora's work, I further reviewed it, and the final result is what you now hold in your hands.

Cāṇakya was both an accomplished scholar and a practical man of this world. While offering realistic directions for navigating the complexities of life, he yet surpasses the sound advice offered in the many wisdom traditions of the world. Due to his being firmly grounded in Vedic culture, Cāṇakya's realism extends beyond the blip of our present temporary situation and points us toward our eternal spiritual existence, clear knowledge of which is the distinguishing feature of Vedic culture. Unlike his *Artha-śāstra,* which is advice specifically meant for rulers, Cāṇakya's *Nīti-śāstra* is more suitable for those *brāhmaṇas* like himself whose aim is to instruct the rulers of society. Thus *Śrī Cāṇakya-nīti* is most appropriate for ISKCON *brāhmaṇas,* for whom Śrīla Prabhupāda envisaged such a role.

Although Cāṇakya was not a Vaiṣṇava, his guidelines can be valuable for Vaiṣṇavas, as ratified in their having been often quoted by no less a Vaiṣṇava than His Divine Grace A.C. Bhaktivedanta Swami Prabhupāda. As a faithful disciple of Śrīla Prabhupāda, Patita Pāvana Dāsa has given a distinctly Vaiṣṇava perspective on Cāṇakya's teachings, and has also, as did Śrīla Prabhupāda, upheld Cāṇakya's statements concerning Vedic cultural norms (for instance, those concerning the role of women as dutiful and subordinate wives), not withstanding their unpopularity in today's purportedly egalitarian ethos. Patita Pāvana Dāsa has added to all this several of his own insights and perceptions, gleaned from his lifelong practice of Kṛṣṇa consciousness, and the end result is a colorful compendium of behavioral advice, penned for ancient civilization and presented herein as relevant for the more thoughtful among modern humankind.

PREFACE TO THE FIRST EDITION

Shri Chanakya Pandit, also known as Kautilya, or sometimes as Vishnugupta, attained lasting fame some 2300 years ago for two reasons: (1.) his Sanskrit writings on polity, and (2.) the practical and effective counsel he gave to King Chandragupta Maurya who conquered most of India under his guidance. Of his writings, *Artha Shastra* is a well-known work and many editions have come out in English. As implied by its title, *Artha Shastra* is a scripture of economic development for kings and court *pandits*. Some of its topics are: the duties of the king, qualifications of ministers, formation of villages, tax collection, proper punishments for offenders, the training of spies, declaring war and making peace and protection of the citizens.

Chanakya's *Niti Shastra* is this great court *pandit's* most famous work. *Niti* is variously translated as "the science of morality," "common sense," "expediency" or "ethics." Hence *Shri Chanakya Niti Shastra* contains sagacious wisdom that may be applied to our daily affairs with profit. In other words, Chanakya herewith teaches us how to be happy in mundane life. If the devotee can improve his execution of devotional service unto the Supreme Personality of Godhead Lord Shri Krishna by taking practical counsel from Chanakya Pandit, then the value of these proverbs will be increased. Past acharyas have said that just as a woman who has a lover serves her own husband with even greater attention, similarly, the devotee, though always absorbed in thoughts of the Lord, carries out his so-called mundane activities with even greater expertise.

Although many of Chanakya's *shlokas* or aphorisms were borrowed from earlier works, Chanakya's name reverberates through history for his ability to practically apply *shastric* wisdom. It can be said that Chanakya's uncanny proficiency to outguess the enemy at every step and to guide his king to resounding victory has caused his name to stand out as one of history's most profound political thinkers. Today in India's capital city of Delhi, the diplomatic housing enclave bears his name: Chanakya Puri.

The British scholar Dr. J.F. Fleet has written, "Kautilya (Chanakya) is renowned not only as a king-maker, but also for being the greatest Indian exponent of the art of government; the duty of kings, ministers and officials; and the methods of diplomacy." We are told that the East India Company strongly urged its officers to study the writings of Chanakya Pandit if they hoped at all to succeed in ruling India.

In his *Artha Shastra,* Chanakya Pandit identifies himself as being responsible for the overthrow of the corrupt Nanda dynasty of Magadha (present day Bihar State in Northern India). A brief account of how he accomplished this is herewith given:

About 2300 years ago, the Greek conqueror Alexander the Great invaded the Indian sub-continent. His offensive upon the land's patchwork of small Vedic empires proved to be highly successful due to the disunity of the petty rulers. It was Chanakya Pandit who, feeling deeply distressed at heart, searched for and discovered a highly qualified leader in the person of Chandragupta Maurya. Although a mere *dasi-putra,* that is, a son of a maidservant by the Magadha King Nanda, Chandragupta was highly intelligent, courageous, and physically powerful. Chanakya cared little that by birth he should not have dared to approach the throne. A man of acute discretion, Chanakya desired that only a ruler of extraordinary capabilities be raised to the exalted post of King of Magadha so that the offensive launched by the Yavanas (Greeks) could be repressed.[1]

Legend says that Chanakya had been personally offended by King Nanda, and that this powerful *brahmana* had vowed to keep his long *shikha* unknotted until he saw to the demise of the contemptuous ruler and his drunken princes. True to his oath, it was only after Chanakya

1. Chanakya shares his opinion of India's Greek invaders in 8.5.

Pandit engineered the swift demise for the degraded and worthless rulers of the Nanda clan that this great *brahmana* was able to tie up his brahminical tuft of hair. There are several versions relating to the exact way that Chanakya set about eliminating the Nandas, and it appears historians have found it difficult to separate fact from legend as regards to specific details.

After the Nanda downfall, it became easy for Chandragupta Maurya to win the support of the citizens of Magadha, who resounded warmly to their new heroic young ruler. Kings of neighboring states rallied under Chandragupta's suzerainty, and the last of the Greeks headed by Alexander's general Seleucus were defeated.

With the dual obstacles of the Nandas and Alexander's troops out of the way, Chanakya Pandit used every political device and court intrigue to unite the greater portion of the Indian sub-continent. Under the ministry of Chanakya, Chandragupta Maurya conquered all the lands up to Persia in the Northwest and down to the extremities of present-day Karnataka or Mysore in the south. It was by his wits alone that this skinny and ill-clad *brahmana* directed the formation of the greatest Indian empire ever before in history, since the beginning of Kali Yuga. Thus the indigenous Vedic culture and civilization of the sacred land of Bharata was protected and its spiritual practices remained unhampered.

Although the great *pandits* of *niti*—including Brihaspati, Shukracharya, Bhartrihari and Vishnusharma—have echoed many of these instructions in their own celebrated works;[2] it is undoubtedly the way that Chanakya *applied* his teachings of *niti* that has made him stand out as a significant historical figure. The *pandit* teaches us that lofty ideals can become certain reality if we diligently work towards achieving our goals in a determined and practical manner, keeping in mind the instructions of the preceptor.

---

2. *Brihaspati Niti Sara* ("Cream of Niti") of the *Garuda Purana, Shukra Niti, Niti Shataka, and Panchatantra,* respectively.

Preface to the First Edition

Dr. R. Shamashastry, the English translator of *Kautilya's Artha Shastra,* quotes a prediction from the *Vishnu Purana,* fourth canto, twenty-fourth chapter, regarding the appearance of Chanakya Pandit. Incidentally, Vyasa scribed this prediction 2700 years before this political heavyweight and man of destiny was to appear. "(First) Mahapadma, then his sons—only nine in number—will be the lords of the earth for a hundred years. A *brahmana* named Kautilya will slay these Nandas. On their death, the Mauryas will enjoy the earth. Kautilya himself will install Chandragupta on the throne. His son will be Bindusara and his son will be Ashokavardhana." Similar prophecies are also repeated in the *Bhagavata, Vayu* and *Matsya Puranas.*

In presenting this work, I have used as references two old English versions of *Chanakya Niti-shastra* published at the close of the Eighteenth Century.[3] I have also consulted another version, an unedited manuscript from the ISKCON Center in Vrindavana which contained both an English translation and Latinized Sanskrit transliteration. It was, however, the learned Vaishnava Pandit and scholar of Sanskrit Shri V. Badarayana Murthy of the Udipi Madhva School who helped me see the depth and import of these verses from the original Devanagari script.

I have been told that our blessed spiritual master His Divine Grace A. C. Bhaktivedanta Swami Prabhupāda had expressed a desire that *Shri Chanakya Niti Shastra* be properly translated into English. It is hoped that our present rendering will be at least useful if not instructive to the reader. Let us now examine a few words on the science of *niti,* or common sense, from the pen of Shrila Bhaktivinode Thakur, the great nineteenth century devotee-pioneer of the worldwide propagation of Lord Chaitanya's divine message. Taking the words "common sense" right up to the highest level, Shri Bhaktivinode has written:

3. Shri K. Raghunathji's *Vriddha Chanakya – The Maxims of Chanakya* (Family Printing Press, Bombay 1890) was especially helpful.

Man's glory is in common sense,
Dictating him the grace,
That man is made to live and love,
The beauteous heaven's embrace.

In other words, the real goal of *niti,* indeed the goal of life, is to realize one's eternal position of Krishna consciousness. The *Bhagavad Gita* confirms the Thakur's view in the final line of its last *shloka: dhruva nitir matir mama.* The full translation of that verse runs, "(Sanjaya said) Wherever there is Krishna, the Master of all mystics, and wherever there is Arjuna, the supreme archer, there will certainly be opulence, victory, extraordinary power, and morality (*niti*). That is my opinion."

Patit Uddharana Das (Patita Pavana Das Adhikary)
Makara Sankranti Day
Pausha Shukla Navami
Lucknow, India (14 January, 1981)

PREFACE TO THE SECOND EDITION

Cāṇakya Paṇḍita was relatively unknown outside of India until Śrīla Prabhupāda introduced the world to this master politician. Our first edition of *Śrī Cāṇakya-nīti-śāstra* sold out in 1981, but since then the internet has made that edition the widely read version in English. Therefore we are hopeful that this updated version with the added benefit of commentaries, transliterated Sanskrit, cross-references to other sources in *nīti-śāstra* and most importantly Śrīla Prabhupāda's insight into key verses will cause this second edition to be widely welcomed. That Śrīla Prabhupāda wanted the members of his ISKCON to have access to Cāṇakya Paṇḍita's *ślokas* is seen in a letter His Divine Grace wrote to Dayānanda Prabhu in April of 1974 in which he stated, "As for *Cāṇakya-śloka,* I think the best thing is if I translate it myself and send it to you for printing, rather than wait…"

In the first verse Cāṇakya Paṇḍita himself explains that these *ślokas* have been raked from other sources. He says: "I now recite maxims selected from various *śāstras* pertaining to political ethics." This edition annotates for the first time the verses from the *Garuḍa Purāṇa* and elsewhere that are the likely origins of many of these parables for success.

As far as our own personal qualifications for presenting *Śrī Cāṇakya-nīti,* I confess that I have none. Śrīla Prabhupāda has told me, "I am simply praying to Kṛṣṇa to give you intelligence." He clarified this point a few years later when he explained to me in no uncertain terms that I am the greatest fool and rascal and do not even deserve to live. Aside from that, he told me to deliver everyone in the universe. Therefore, since we are without qualifications, we have simply let the verses and Śrīla Prabhupāda's insight into them speak for themselves.

My sincere thanks to my respected Godbrother His Holiness Śrīla Bhakti Vikāsa Mahārāja for kindly arranging for the printing of this volume and for his valuable insight into the text. His disciples Śrīmān Kiśora Dāsa Adhikārī and Śrīmatī Ananta-sarovara Dāsī, a husband-wife team, have brought the work to a higher focus through their expertise of Sanskrit editing, proofreading, insight and generally bringing the text up to the scholastic standard of the Bhaktivedanta Book Trust. I would also like to thank them for composing the table of contents and the glossary. Another proficient disciple of Mahārāja, Śrīmān Vṛndāvana Candra Prabhu, capably handled the final formatting. Thanks also to my companion and better half at Mithuna Twiins Astrological Services Śrīmatī Abhaya Mudrā Dāsī for her suggestions, art work, formatting and cover design. It is our deep regret that our dear mentor in this effort Paṇḍita Śrī V. Badarayana Murthy has departed this planet and will not see this edition. He was a faithful servant of both his Mādhva Vaiṣṇava *sampradāya* and of Śrīla Prabhupāda, and he was like our real father. We pray that he has reached the supreme destination at Śrī Kṛṣṇa's lotus feet.

Śrīla Prabhupāda teaches, "In explaining the glories of the Lord, inexperienced men may compose poetry with many faults, but because it contains glorification of the Lord, great personalities read it, hear it and chant it." (SB 1.5.11) And, "Despite its minute literary discrepancies, one must study poetry on the merit of its subject matter. According to Vaiṣṇava philosophy, any literature that glorifies the Lord, whether properly written or not, is first class. There need be no other considerations." (*Śrī Caitanya-caritāmṛta,* 1.16.102, purport) We therefore pray that we are excused for any errors in this presentation.

Hare Kṛṣṇa.

Patita Pāvana Dāsa Adhikārī
Blagoevgrad, Bulgaria
www.vedicastrologers.org

Monday, 26 January 2015, Aśvinī-*nakṣatra* Māgha-*māsa śukla-saptamī* (corresponding to the 7th day of the waxing moon of the Gauḍīya month of Mādhava)
Appearance Day of Śrī Advaita Ācārya

CHAPTER ONE

ŚLOKA 1.1

प्रणम्य शिरसा विष्णुं त्रैलोक्याधिपतिं प्रभुम् ।
नानाशास्त्रोद्धृतं वक्ष्ये राजनीतिसमुच्चयम् ॥१॥

praṇamya śirasā viṣṇuṁ
trailokyādhipatiṁ prabhum
nānā-śāstroddhṛtaṁ vakṣye
rāja-nīti-samuccayam

Bowing my head before the overlord of the three worlds and master of all, the all-pervasive Viṣṇu, I now recite maxims selected from various śāstras pertaining to political ethics.

Commentary: As stated by our eternal spiritual master, His Divine Grace A. C. Bhaktivedanta Swami Prabhupāda, in his commentary on *Śrīmad-Bhāgavatam* (3.1.10, purport):

> In modern times Cāṇakya Paṇḍita is considered the authority in good counsel and political and moral instruction.

Following the example of all great Vaiṣṇava sages, the renowned *paṇḍita* begins his collection of verses on the subject of common sense with due salutations unto Lord Viṣṇu, the Triloka-pati or "Lord of the three worlds."

Regarding worship of Lord Viṣṇu as transcendent to this material world, Śrīla Prabhupāda gives the following quote in the introduction to the eleventh chapter of the Sixth Canto of *Śrīmad-Bhāgavatam:*

> If one is a devotee of the Supreme Personality of Godhead, Lord Viṣṇu, and depends on Lord Viṣṇu in every respect, then victory, opulence and peace of mind are all inevitably available. Such a person has nothing for which to aspire in the three worlds. The Supreme Lord is so kind that He especially favors such a devotee by not giving him opulence that will hamper his devotional service. Therefore I wish to give up everything for the service of the Lord. I wish always to chant the glories of the Lord and engage in His service. Let me become unattached to my worldly family and make friendships with the devotees of the Lord. I do not desire to be promoted to the higher planetary systems, even to Dhruvaloka or Brahmaloka, nor do I desire an unconquerable position within this material world. I have no need for such things.

Lord Viṣṇu is a four-armed expansion—or plenary portion—of Lord Śrī Kṛṣṇa, the Supreme Personality of Godhead. Lord Kṛṣṇa is identified as the Supreme Lord throughout the Vedic literature, as confirmed by Śrīla Vyāsadeva in *Śrīmad-Bhāgavatam* (1.3.28):

> *ete cāṁśa-kalāḥ puṁsaḥ kṛṣṇas tu bhagavān svayam*
> *indrāri-vyākulaṁ lokaṁ mṛḍayanti yuge yuge*

> All of the above-mentioned incarnations are either plenary portions or portions of the plenary portions of the Lord, but Lord Śrī Kṛṣṇa is the original Personality of Godhead. All of them appear on planets whenever there is a disturbance created by the atheists. The Lord incarnates to protect the theists.

Significantly, the Sanskrit word *tu* (but) lends important emphasis as in, "But—out of all other incarnations and forms of the Lord—Śrī Kṛṣṇa is the self-sufficient Supreme Lord."

Lord Brahmā, the creator demigod (who is born from a lotus springing from the navel of Lord Viṣṇu), sings in his *Śrī Brahma-saṁhitā:*

govindam ādi-puruṣaṁ tam ahaṁ bhajāmi. "I worship Govinda—Kṛṣṇa—the primeval Lord." Govinda (literally, "One who gives pleasure to the cows and the senses") is a popular name of Kṛṣṇa, and the Supreme Lord is twice addressed as such by Arjuna in the *Bhagavad-gītā.* Śrī Kṛṣṇa Himself explains that He personally is the divine origin of Viṣṇu to Arjuna with the words *ādityānām ahaṁ viṣṇuḥ:* "Among Ādityas, I am Viṣṇu." (Bg 10.21) Śrī Kṛṣṇa as the Ādi-puruṣa or original Godhead expands into His various forms of Viṣṇu for the creation and maintenance of this unlimited material universe.

In his *Śrī Govinda-virudāvali* (2) Śrīla Rūpa Gosvāmī, the great Vaiṣṇava *ācārya* in the Gauḍīya *sampradāya* confirms:

> O lotus-eyed Supreme Lord Kṛṣṇa, when You wish to enjoy Your pastimes in this material world, You appoint the demigod Brahmā to create a place for them. Then You appoint the demigod Śiva to eventually remove them.

Here Cāṇakya Paṇḍita invokes all auspiciousness for his *nīti-śāstra* by offering reverence unto Him who is the source of all demigods, as well as the repository of all common sense and morality.

Now, having offered due obeisances to the Personality of Godhead, Cāṇakya Paṇḍita states his purpose, explaining the essence of *nīti. Nīti* does not mean simply "politics" as is often understood. *Cāṇakya-nīti* is replete with common sense advice for living a fuller life here in this material world, while keeping one eye focused upon spiritual development. In a nutshell, it is Cāṇakya Paṇḍita's expressed wish that we seize the situation at hand, assuring future progress in both the here and hereafter. Life's ultimate goal is the achievement of loving service unto the Supreme Lord Śrī Kṛṣṇa through the grace of the bona fide spiritual master. This exalted goal of transcendence may be actively pursued by the devotee even if he lives comfortably in this world, by keeping his needs to a minimum and living in compliance with the laws of both man and God. Cāṇakya Paṇḍita shows us how all this and more can be achieved by treading softly yet deliberately.

The *triloka* (three worlds) mentioned in this verse are a reference to the three levels of the material universe. Śrīla Prabhupāda writes in his purport to *Śrīmad-Bhāgavatam* (2.6.19): "In the material world, the planetary systems are arranged in three spheres, called *triloka,* or Svarga, Martya and Pātāla, and all of them constitute only one fourth of the total *sandhinī* energy."

Since the lifespans of the denizens of Svarga last for many millions of years, those demigods who live there may think of themselves as *amara* (never-dying). The vast array of comforts at their disposal makes sensual enjoyment a priority over the proper quest for spiritual emancipation, which is attained only through service to the highest authority. The ready abundance of sense gratification in those heavenly regions is the cause of forgetfulness of our eternal constitutional position as subordinates of the Supreme Lord Viṣṇu or Kṛṣṇa. In Naraka (the hellish regions), suffering is so acute that liberation becomes impossible as past misdeeds are expunged through painful punishment at the hands of the Yamadūtas. These middle worlds or "earths" are the ideal "launching pads" for the devotee in search of liberation. Therefore, here and now we must undertake a thorough study of *Cāṇakya-nīti* to vouchsafe not only our present happiness but our eternal salvation. This rare opportunity of human birth, the vehicle for going back to home and back to Godhead, may not soon present itself again.

Cāṇakya Paṇḍita scribed his *nīti-śāstra* some twenty-five hundred years ago, well into Kali-yuga, or within the present age of quarrel and discord. As we will find throughout all authorized literatures—the revealed scriptures—worship of Lord Viṣṇu or Kṛṣṇa is the recommended process for freeing the fettered *jīva* soul from the shackles of *karma* in his urgent quest for spiritual awakening. In Kali-yuga, worship of the Absolute Godhead is performed by the chanting of His holy names.

To spread this worship of Kṛṣṇa through the chanting of His holy names, Lord Kṛṣṇa advented Himself in the fifteenth century in the village of Māyāpur, West Bengal, as Śrī Caitanya Mahāprabhu. In this divine appearance the Lord spread the movement of *saṅkīrtana,* the congregational public chanting of the great *mantra* for deliverance, the *mahā-mantra.*

There are many different kinds of *mantras* for different Vedic sacrifices or *yajñas* such as marriage, laying foundations, and other auspicious occasions. Many *mantras* exist also for the propitiation of the *devatās,* resorted to by short-sighted persons in search of material gain. Ultimately, however, all forms of worship are meant for the adoration of the Supreme Personality of Godhead Śrī Kṛṣṇa as indicated by Cāṇakya Paṇḍita here in the first verse.

This Hare Kṛṣṇa *mantra* is known as the *mahā* (great) *mantra* because in one fell swoop it settles the affairs of all other *mantras.* In *The Journey of Self-Discovery* Śrīla Prabhupāda explains:

> The Sanskrit word *mantra* is a combination of two syllables, *man* and *tra. Man* means 'mind,' and *tra* means 'deliverance.' Therefore a *mantra* is that which delivers you from mental concoction, from hovering on the mental plane. So if you chant this *mantra*—
>
> Hare Kṛṣṇa Hare Kṛṣṇa Kṛṣṇa Kṛṣṇa Hare Hare
> Hare Rāma Hare Rāma Rāma Rāma Hare Hare
>
> —very soon you'll find that you are coming from the darkness to the light.

Among all the eighty-four *lakhs* (8,400,000) species of life recorded in the Vedic literature, man alone has a mind which he must use for spiritual liberation. The soul encased in the form of a plant, insect or animal species must wait many millions of painful births to once again achieve this human form of life. Therefore, the blessing of a rational mind means that we should energetically pursue the liberation of Kṛṣṇa consciousness before our inevitable date with the Grim Reaper catches us unaware.

Life is too short to waste in chasing the illusory objects of desire. It is a grave mistake to ruin this rare opportunity of life by submerging the senses in the so-called pleasures of bodily enjoyment that are widely available even to cats and dogs on the street. In the first verse of *Śrī Cāṇakya-nīti,* the wise *paṇḍita* turns us toward the goal of life, worship of the Supreme Lord, before turning his attention to the more mundane aspects of *nīti-śāstra.* He who wishes to become great must serve the greatest and that can be accomplished only through humility. Thus our great *paṇḍita* shows us the way by bowing his head unto the almighty Viṣṇu before stating *vakṣye rāja-nīti-samuccayam:* "I shall now describe political ethics."

ŚLOKA 1.2

अधीत्येदं यथाशास्त्रं नरो जानाति सत्तमः ।
धर्मोपदेशविख्यातं कार्याकार्यं शुभाशुभम् ॥२॥

adhītyedaṁ yathā-śāstraṁ
naro jānāti sattamaḥ
dharmopadeśa-vikhyātaṁ
kāryākāryaṁ śubhāśubham

A person is most excellent who, through a study of these scriptural precepts obtained from various śāstras, acquires an understanding of these principles of dharma, and thereby understands what is to be followed and what is not to be followed.

Commentary: Here Cāṇakya Paṇḍita demonstrates that in order to be rightly called "the *śāstra* of common sense," *nīti-śāstra* must eventually lead to *dharma-śāstra,* pursuance of spiritual goals. It follows therefore that a life void of religious understanding is a life that is bereft of common sense. The second verse underscores the first.

Śrī Kṛṣṇa, the Supreme Personality of Godhead, declares in the *Bhagavad-gītā, cātur-varṇyaṁ mayā sṛṣṭam,* "I alone created the fourfold divisions of society." Certain duties apply to each level of society. *Brāhmaṇas,* who are the head of society, conduct *yajñas* and offer spiritual guidance to the other members. *Kṣatriyas,* the kings and warriors, are the administrators, protectors and enforcers of law and order. *Vaiśyas,* members of the mercantile class, protect cows, run the farms and engage in commerce. *Śūdras* are the working class. Whereas each class has its own regulations that apply to that class alone, *nīti-śāstra* is meant for all classes. From householders to renunciants, it has something for everybody. Hence *nīti-śāstra* being common to all mankind, is "common sense." In this verse Cāṇakya Paṇḍita says that those who master these principles will come to the stage of *dharma,* or Kṛṣṇa consciousness. *Kalau śūdra-sambhavaḥ:* here and now in Kali-yuga when practically everyone is born a *śūdra* and are thus lacking in every form of common sense, the urgency for *Śrī Cāṇakya-nīti* is magnified.

Śrīla Prabhupāda states in the introduction to his *Bhagavad-gītā As It Is* that *dharma* means "that which sustains." He writes:

> Now a particular religious faith may have some beginning in the history of human society, but *sanātana-dharma* lies outside of history, for it belongs to the living beings who have no birth and who never die.
>
> Let us try to understand this eternal religion from the Sanskrit verbal root *dhṛ,* which means 'to sustain.' Therefore *dharma* is that quality which remains always and which cannot be taken away. When we speak of fire it is concluded that light and heat will be there. Otherwise we cannot call it fire. In a similar way, we must find the constant companion of the eternal being: that eternal part or quality is his religion, his *dharma.*

True *dharma,* our loving relationship with God, is our sustenance. To find our relationship with Him is the highest common sense.

Sanātana-dharma is the essence of the soul and, like the soul, is everlasting. Cāṇakya Paṇḍita directs us towards the all-harmonizing "eternal religion" of spirit as distinguished from the material or divisive "religions" created by man. Although our original *dharma* is ever-present within our heart of hearts, our loving link to the Lord has been covered due to *māyā* (illusory material energy) and temporary "*dharmas.*" The eternal religion locked within the spiritual particle or soul is nothing less than the dormant desire to actively engage in loving devotional service unto the Supreme Personality of Godhead Śrī Kṛṣṇa. Our eternal constitutional position is one of loving service to God, yet our present infatuation with temporary sense enjoyment or material *dharmas* has covered the natural function of the soul. Cāṇakya Paṇḍita advises us to learn what is to be done and what is not to be done, keeping in mind that the fruits of our deeds are meant for the pleasure of the Supreme Lord alone. The enlightened devotee's material duties coincide with his eternal *dharma.* Simple for the simple yet complex for the crooked, this plain advice is easy to understand for the humble devotee, but impossible for the atheistic materialist. Although such a person claims to be following doctrines which he mistakes for *dharma,* he is actually an opportunist ready to bend nature to his every whim.

ŚLOKA 1.3

तदहं सम्प्रवक्ष्यामि लोकानां हितकाम्यया ।
येन विज्ञानमात्रेण सर्वज्ञत्वं प्रपद्यते ॥३॥

tad ahaṁ sampravakṣyāmi
lokānāṁ hita-kāmyayā
yena vijñāna-mātreṇa
sarvajñatvaṁ prapadyate

Therefore, with an eye to the public good, I shall speak that which when understood will lead to knowledge of all things in their proper perspective.

Commentary: Cāṇakya Paṇḍita herewith reveals the first qualification for a man to be recognized as knowledgeable: he must understand all things "in their proper perspective." True knowledge is sublime, broad and even. It is neither top-heavy nor cumbersome like the mental burden carried by so-called "men of letters." Here Cāṇakya Paṇḍita promises that his instructions will "make one all-knowing." His compassionate motives for penning his *nīti-śāstra* are also revealed: "to give benefit to the entire world."

Unlike most writers of today, Cāṇakya Paṇḍita did not scribe his *nīti-śāstra* to see his name in print or to earn royalties. As a renounced and threadbare *brāhmaṇa,* the great Cāṇakya Paṇḍita had no desire for fame or riches. His goal was the upliftment and guidance of society, and that is why King Candragupta Maurya respectfully sat at his feet. The spiritual jewels of eternal wisdom are far greater than the baubles of the rich and powerful, while the power of renunciation exceeds the strength of armies.

ŚLOKA 1.4

मूर्खशिष्योपदेशेन दुष्टस्त्रीभरणेन च ।
दुःखितैः सम्प्रयोगेण पण्डितोऽप्यवसीदति ॥४॥

mūrkha-śiṣyopadeśena
duṣṭa-strī-bharaṇena ca
duḥkhitaiḥ samprayogeṇa
paṇḍito 'py avasīdati

Even a learned paṇḍita suffers by instructing a foolish disciple, by maintaining a wicked wife and by association with the wretched.

Commentary: The origin of this *śloka* is *Bṛhaspati-nīti-sāra,* a section of the *Garuḍa Purāṇa.* (GP 1.108.4) This *Bṛhaspati-nīti-sāra* incidentally was conveyed by Bṛhaspati, the priest of the *devas,* to

Lord Indra the king of Svarga, after he defeated an army of demons in battle. The rarity of śāstric lessons should be appreciated. Indra had to emerge victorious from a terrible war to receive this fruit of knowledge which today is freely available thanks to the pioneering efforts of Śrīla Prabhupāda.

The transmission of knowledge from a genuine spiritual master to a proper student is illustrated with the following comparison: If a husband is potent and his wife is fertile, then if there is coition, there will be a pregnancy. Similarly, transmission of knowledge is not the sole responsibility of the *guru.* As Cāṇakya Paṇḍita will demonstrate, a disciple must qualify himself through faithful service to his *guru mahārāja.* Only then will Śrī Guru permit the transmission of knowledge.

The *Manu-saṁhitā* advises:

> A spiritual master should not wholesale his knowledge unasked, nor even convey his learning to those who ask improperly. It is better to remain as a dumb man and die with his knowledge than for a sage to sow seeds in a saline field. (MS 2.110–113)

Today it has become fashionable for many celebrities to keep some self-appointed New Age *guru* around like a trained, well-groomed dog. Cāṇakya Paṇḍita illustrates why such sycophantic relationships are unproductive. He who wants to be cheated will obtain his desire when an imposter *guru* arrives at his door. Was not Rāvaṇa clad in the saffron dress of a *sādhu* when he abducted Sītā? Unless both the disciple and *guru* are genuine, any pretense of following *dharma* will be a farce.

Regarding association with the wretched, Bhartṛhari states in his *Nīti-śataka:*

> A man is like a drop of water. On a stove, the water evaporates. Sitting upon the lotus leaf, it glistens in the sun. But if a drop of water enters an oyster under the influence of the Svātī star, it becomes a pearl. (NS 66)

Similarly one's character is influenced by his associates. Cāṇakya Paṇḍita's advice that we choose our friends wisely should be taken to heart if we want to live happily. The useless society of worldly men destroys all good qualities. Conversely there is no fellowship like the company of genuine *sādhus,* devotees of the Lord.

Regarding Cāṇakya Paṇḍita's tidbit about a wicked wife, Śukrācārya says:

> Begging and death are better than being a householder with a bad wife. (SN 3.288)

ŚLOKA 1.5

दुष्टा भार्या शठं मित्रं भृत्यश्चोत्तरदायकः ।
ससर्पे च गृहे वासो मृत्युरेव न संशयः ॥५॥

duṣṭā bhāryā śaṭhaṁ mitraṁ
bhṛtyaś cottara-dāyakaḥ
sa-sarpe ca gṛhe vāso
mṛtyur eva na saṁśayaḥ

An unchaste wife, a false friend, an insolent servant, and living with a poisonous serpent in the house are nothing but death.

Commentary: He who lays trust in mundane friendship is as foolish as the man from Kerala who died after a month in a cage with cobras while trying to get his name into the *Guinness Book of World Records.* A man is judged by his company, just as a *guru* is judged by the quality of his disciples, or parents by their offspring. Whomsoever we associate with, marry or accept service from hinges upon our power of discrimination. Cāṇakya Paṇḍita repeats this *śloka* from *Bṛhaspati-nīti-sāra.* (GP 1.108.25)

Śrīla Prabhupāda dilated on this verse during a lecture in San Francisco on 16 July 1975 from *Śrīmad-Bhāgavatam* 6.1.31:

So this Ajāmila, he was *dāsī-pati.* He was a husband of a prostitute. So he was not happy. He was attached. Another thing is ... That is also Cāṇakya Paṇḍita. He says, *duṣṭā bhāryā,* means this prostitute. She who is polluted by another man is called *duṣṭā. Strīṣu duṣṭāsu varṇa-saṅkaraḥ abhibhavāt.* Therefore human civilization must be very careful that the women may not become polluted. *Strīṣu duṣṭāsu. Duṣṭā* means she is not satisfied with husband. She wants new, new. That is called *duṣṭā.* So Cāṇakya Paṇḍita says, *duṣṭā bhāryā:* "If the wife is *duṣṭā, duṣṭā bhāryā śaṭhaṁ mitram,* and friend is *śaṭham,* hypocrite, talking very friendly, but he has got something, design ..." That is called *śaṭhaṁ mitram. Śaṭham* means hypocrite. So "If somebody's wife is *duṣṭā* and friend is hypocrite, *duṣṭā bhāryā śaṭhaṁ mitraṁ bhṛtyaś cottara-dāyakaḥ,* and *bhṛtya,* servant, does not obey, he argues with the master ..." Master says, "Why did you not do?" "Oh, I am this ..." No argument. *Bhṛtya* should be very silent. Then he is faithful servant. Sometimes master may be angry, but *bhṛtya* should be silent. Then master becomes kind. But if he replies on equal level, oh, then it is very bad. *Duṣṭā bhāryā śaṭhaṁ mitraṁ bhṛtyaś cottara-dāyakaḥ, sa-sarpe ca gṛhe vāso:* "And you are living in a apartment where there is a snake." So if these four things are there or one of them, not all the fours, then *mṛtyur eva na saṁśayaḥ:* "Then you are doomed. You are doomed. Your life is spoiled."

ŚLOKA 1.6

आपदर्थे धनं रक्षेद्दारान् रक्षेद्धनैरपि ।
आत्मानं सततं रक्षेद्दारैरपि धनैरपि ॥६॥

āpad-arthe dhanaṁ rakṣed
dārān rakṣed dhanair api
ātmānaṁ satataṁ rakṣed
dārair api dhanair api

Save your money against hard times, protect your wife at the sacrifice of riches, but always save your soul even at the cost of your wife and riches.

Commentary: Often a green disciple expresses a desire to sacrifice himself in order to save the entire world. To which the teacher invariably answers that the only way to save others is to first save oneself. Unless one has elevated himself to the platform of transcendence above the three modes of nature, he can do nothing to extricate others trapped by their own desires. The good wishes of a man fallen with us into the same dark well are of little consequence. He must first climb out and obtain a rope with which to pull us to safety.

Cāṇakya Paṇḍita advises us to prepare for life's inevitable turmoils through protecting our wealth and family. But by all means one must first save himself at any cost. A show of renunciation will not save one from the well of material existence. Here and now in Kali-yuga when people are dull-witted and short-lived, we must execute Kṛṣṇa consciousness by chanting the Hare Kṛṣṇa *mantra* and inviting others to do the same. That is the only hope of extricating ourselves and others.

This verse also appears in the *Garuḍa Purāṇa,* 1.109.9.

ŚLOKA 1.7

आपदर्थे धनं रक्षेच्छ्रीमतां कुत आपदः ।
कदाचिच्चलिता लक्ष्मीः सञ्चितं च विनश्यति ॥७॥

āpad-arthe dhanaṁ rakṣec
chrīmatāṁ kuta āpadaḥ
kadācic calitā lakṣmīḥ
sañcitaṁ ca vinaśyati

Put aside some wealth in case of a future calamity. Never ask, "Why should a rich man dread hard times?" If Lakṣmī, the goddess of fortune, decides to go elsewhere, your savings will dwindle.

Commentary: Here Cāṇakya Paṇḍita calls Lakṣmī, the goddess of wealth, by her name Calitā (she who is always moving). Lakṣmī is also called Cañcalā (unsteady), as Cāṇakya Paṇḍita will later write in 5.20. Wealth, which represents her in this world, never stops moving from one hand to the next. Whenever a clever man acquires wealth, others lay schemes for its plunder. Banks through exorbitant interest rates, governments through excessive taxation, thieves through extortion and common citizens through lawsuits all conspire to reduce a rich man's fortune to zero. Viṣṇuśarmā laments in his *Pañca-tantra,* "Coming and going, money is nothing but a headache."

Lakṣmī is the wife of Lord Viṣṇu and His association alone is the source of her happiness. Therefore, the means to keep the goddess who governs riches pleased is to see that at least some portion of one's wealth is engaged in the service of Lord Viṣṇu. There is a modern legend in India about the wealthy Birla family. It is said that three or four generations ago, the grandsire of this family was blessed by a *sādhu.* The sage told him that his future generations would remain wealthy provided whatever they earned was used in the service of the Lord. Birla was instructed to "never allow the mason's trowel to rest."

Today for the sake of public good, as well as their own, the Birla family has constructed many beautiful temples to Lord Viṣṇu throughout India. We have visited several of the magnificent temples built by the Birlas including: the Lakṣmī-Nārāyaṇa Mandir in Delhi, the Gītā Mandir at Kurukṣetra, the Veṅkaṭeśvara Mandir at Hyderabad and the Śrī Kṛṣṇa Mandir on the Mathura-Vrindavan Road. Neither has the trowel rested.

Neither wealth nor personal property are ours to hoard ultimately, so to avoid a miser's fate in Naraka, one's accumulated assets must be engaged for the pleasure and service of the almighty Viṣṇu. Then Calitā may kindly condescend to make her address our very home once we have dedicated everything to her Lord Mādhava (the *dhava* or "husband" of *mā* the "goddess of fortune").

In this all-too-short spot life we will be wise to sing in one voice with the great King Kulaśekhara who prays in his *Mukunda-mālā-stotra* (verse 24):

> O Mādhava, please do not let me even glance at those whose pious credits are so depleted that they have no devotion for Your lotus feet. Please do not let me be distracted from listening to the worthy narrations of Your pastimes and become interested in other topics. Please, O Lord of the universe, let me pay no attention to those who avoid thinking of You. And let me never be unable to serve You in some menial way, birth after birth.

ŚLOKA 1.8

यस्मिन् देशे न सम्मानो न वृत्तिर्न च बान्धवाः ।
न च विद्यागमोऽप्यस्ति वासं तत्र न कारयेत् ॥८॥

yasmin deśe na sammāno
na vṛttir na ca bāndhavāḥ
na ca vidyāgamo 'py asti
vāsaṁ tatra na kārayet

Never live in that land where you are disrespected, cannot earn a living, are friendless or there is nothing to be learned.

Commentary: Cāṇakya Paṇḍita advises not to dwell where *vidyā* (knowledge) cannot be acquired. To sit at the feet of a self-realized soul who can impart real knowledge of Kṛṣṇa consciousness brings greater profit than being tied to a string of postgraduate degrees from every university on earth. Self-realization is the starting point for liberation, whereas material education without a spiritual purpose is an endless entanglement in the web of *māyā.* A *paṇḍita* who lives under the four humiliating conditions outlined in this verse metaphorically resides in a *śmaśāna* (crematorium). Genuine *paṇḍitas* thrive only where Vedic wisdom is honored.

ŚLOKA 1.9

धनिकः श्रोत्रियो राजा नदी वैद्यस्तु पञ्चमः ।
पञ्च यत्र न विद्यन्ते न तत्र दिवसं वसेत् ॥९॥

dhanikaḥ śrotriyo rājā
nadī vaidyas tu pañcamaḥ
pañca yatra na vidyante
na tatra divasaṁ vaset

Do not stay even for a day where you do not find these five: a man of means, a brāhmaṇa learned in the Vedas, a king, a river and a physician.

Commentary: In a word, Cāṇakya Paṇḍita advises us to avoid any place where there is no Vedic civilization and culture. According to the ideals of socialism and communism, the affluent must be forced to share their wealth with the poor. Cāṇakya Paṇḍita's vision for a healthy society is quite the opposite. He advises that the wealthy are ultimately beneficial for society as they are the ones who provide employment and shoulder a tax burden, which is meant to ultimately benefit all members of society.

Brāhmaṇas (spiritually-inclined intellectuals) are urgently required in society because they are the teachers or *mukha* (lit. "head") of society. Without the guidance of duly initiated Vaiṣṇava *brāhmaṇas,* social organization becomes like a headless corpse. The absence of common sense and spiritual leadership results in an infrastructure that disintegrates into chaos which exactly reflects today's world situation. It is ironic that the *yajñas* (spiritual sacrifices) performed by the poor *brāhmaṇas* can be credited with causing the rain of prosperity on the earth, hence the formation of rivers as mentioned in this verse. Though *brāhmaṇas* lead a Spartan existence, their *yajñas* actually create affluence for others. 2,300 years ago Cāṇakya Paṇḍita led a very frugal life—yet he planned and executed the organization of a vast and prosperous kingdom centered in Magadha. As hinted at in this verse, the king is also essential, not least because he maintains the *brāhmaṇas* whose *yajñas* sustain society.

Śrīla Prabhupāda commented on this verse in a lecture on *Śrīmad-Bhāgavatam* (1.8.40) delivered on 20 October 1974 in Māyāpur:

> Cāṇakya Paṇḍita says that "Don't go to a town and city where there is no river and where there is no friend and there is no temple." Don't go to that city. If there is no river, no friend and no temple, then that great city is a great forest. So that is forbidden. So we should be happy with these things. Cities and towns, this does not mean big, big slaughterhouse, cinema, brothel, and factories and all dirty things. Here it is not mentioned.

In that lecture Śrīla Prabhupāda especially drew attention to the purity of the sacred Gaṅgā flowing not far from the temple. He was revealing in part his vision for the spiritual city he was founding, one that has become a reality since that lecture and which fulfills all the criteria of this verse.

From rivers we derive the benefits of health, nourishment and cleanliness, which is why those who contaminate waterways with sewage were punished in Vedic culture. This verse has been taken from the *Bṛhaspati-nīti-sāra.* (GP 1.110.26)

ŚLOKA 1.10

लोकयात्रा भयं लज्जा दाक्षिण्यं त्यागशीलता ।
पञ्च यत्र न विद्यन्ते न कुर्यात् तत्र सङ्गतिम् ॥१०॥

loka-yātrā bhayaṁ lajjā
dākṣiṇyaṁ tyāga-śīlatā
pañca yatra na vidyante
na kuryāt tatra saṅgatim

Do not live in places where there is no means of earning a living, where the citizens have no fear and shame and where they lack expertise and renunciation.

Commentary: Bṛhaspati similarly states:

> Do not dwell where you are not respected, where you have no kinsmen, and where there is no facility for higher education. (GP 1.109.20)

In his offbeat guidebook, *World's Most Dangerous Places,* Robert Young Pelton reveals the shocking chaos that exists in many of the world's darkest corners.[4] In Pelton's discussion of Africa, he describes a recent Liberian dictator, the late Samuel Doe:

> A typical day with Sam Doe was sleeping in, drinking American beer, and then jumping into Jeeps wearing Halloween costumes. People would be shot for fun from the speeding Jeeps, and some hapless victims would be dragged back to the Executive Mansion to be tortured to death and then fed to Doe's two pet lions.

Tragically, several faithful devotees preaching Kṛṣṇa consciousness to the people of Liberia, including our dear Godsister Hlādinī-devī and several African *bhaktas* were unceremoniously abducted from the temple and executed by the order of the country's leader. Sometimes devotees enter such places at great risk to themselves in order to benefit the unfortunate citizens struggling under the rule of asuric despots. As shocking as it sounds, there are indeed many such places on earth, although the media we rely on hardly reports such incidents (in their pretension of fairness and balance). Truth is a rare commodity in this world, yet Vedic *brāhmaṇas,* as seen from the example of Cāṇakya Paṇḍita, are sworn to speak the truth, even when it is socially unpalatable.

---

4. Collins Reference, 5th Revised Edition (2003).

ŚLOKA 1.11

जानीयात् प्रेषणे भृत्यान् बान्धवान् व्यसनागमे ।
मित्रं चापत्तिकालेषु भार्यां च विभवक्षये ॥११॥

jānīyāt preṣaṇe bhṛtyān
bāndhavān vyasanāgame
mitraṁ cāpatti-kāleṣu
bhāryāṁ ca vibhava-kṣaye

The servant is tested in the discharge of his duty and a relative is tested in difficulty. A friend is tested in a time of misfortune and a wife when one's wealth dwindles.

Commentary: A faithful wife is called a *pati-vratā* (she whose only vow is steady devotion to her husband). There is no dearth of *pati-vratās* in the Vedic literatures, including the *Purāṇas, Mahābhārata* and *Rāmāyaṇa.* Therein the narrations of Gāndhārī, Damayantī, Sukanyā, Sītā, Sāvitrī, Anasūyā and a host of other ladies of legendary character inspire *pati-vratās* to this day.

ŚLOKA 1.12

आतुरे व्यसने प्राप्ते दुर्भिक्षे शत्रुसङ्कटे ।
राजद्वारे श्मशाने च यस्तिष्ठति स बान्धवः ॥१२॥

āture vyasane prāpte
durbhikṣe śatru-saṅkaṭe
rāja-dvāre śmaśāne ca
yas tiṣṭhati sa bāndhavaḥ

He alone is your true friend who does not forsake you even when you are ill, in misfortune, famine, when surrounded by enemies, in the court of the king or at the funeral pyre.

Commentary: He is a true friend indeed whose loyalty never lags even at the bitter end. Yet there is a friend who dares to accompany each one of us even beyond the *śmaśāna* (funeral pyre). He is the Lord in the heart, the Soul of all souls, the indwelling friend who has been following each of us life after life since time immemorial. The *Śvetāśvatara Upaniṣad* gives the example of two birds in a tree, one of which is eating the fruits of the tree, and the other who is simply observing. Only when the *jīva* soul relinquishes his false platform of material enjoyment and turns to the Lord of the heart—the friendly "watching bird"—can the opportunity for going back to Godhead arise.

As Lord Brahmā prayed in his *Brahma-saṁhitā* (5.35):

> I adore Govinda, Kṛṣṇa, the primeval Lord. All the universes exist in Him and He is present in every atom scattered throughout the universe.

Because He is all-pervasive, He is also all-seeing. Turning to Him who is our dearest friend in a mood of loving service not only nourishes the seed of devotional service (*bhakti*), but it douses this fiery cycle of death and rebirth which has caused us so much pain on the false platform of so-called enjoyment.

ŚLOKA 1.13

यो ध्रुवाणि परित्यज्य अध्रुवं परिषेवते ।
ध्रुवाणि तस्य नश्यन्ति अध्रुवं नष्टमेव हि ॥१३॥

yo dhruvāṇi parityajya
adhruvaṁ pariṣevate
dhruvāṇi tasya naśyanti
adhruvaṁ naṣṭam eva hi

He who renounces that which is imperishable for that which is perishable, loses that which is imperishable and doubtlessly loses the perishable also.

Commentary: Throughout his *Nīti-śāstra,* Cāṇakya Paṇḍita teaches us how to have it all: to live here as congenially as possible while focusing on the hereafter. Our forgetfulness of God and of our eternal constitutional position as His servants is the root of all misery. This verse goes one step farther than the Biblical admonition, "What of him who gains the world yet loses his eternal soul?" Cāṇakya Paṇḍita teaches that even suzerainty over the entire earth is temporary, and will be lost, just as even the great Indra must someday relinquish his temporary post as king of heaven.

The world is called *mṛtyu-loka* (the place of inevitable death). Having fallen under the spell of *māyā,* the world's deluding energy, all others deceive themselves into believing that they are securely ensconced in whatever situation they have attained by birth and karma. Thinking "I am comfortable, this is who I am," they make untenable plans to enjoy this false, temporary lifestyle forever.

In *Śrīmad-Bhāgavatam* (11.22.45), Lord Śrī Kṛṣṇa describes this folly of misplaced values to His dear friend Uddhava with these words:

> Although the illumination of a lamp consists of innumerable rays of light undergoing constant creation, transformation and destruction, a person with illusory intelligence speaks falsely, saying, "This light is still shining." As one may observe a flowing river, ever-new water passes by and flows far away, but still, observing the same point in the river, a foolish person falsely states, "This is the water of the river." Similarly, although the material body of a human being is constantly undergoing transformation, those who are simply wasting their lives falsely think and say that each particular stage of the body is the real identity of the person.

Apparently the ignorance of today's general mass of people is no different now than when Lord Kṛṣṇa was present over 5,000 years ago.

Likewise, Lord Kṛṣṇa instructs Arjuna:

> Those who are seers of the truth have concluded that of the nonexistent there is no endurance, and of the eternal there is no cessation, for they have seen the nature of both. (Bg 2.16)

Even in the here and now with his mind fixed upon that which is eternal—that is by serving the Supreme Lord's will even with the objects of this material world—the surrendered devotee attains the platform of "that which is imperishable." Full self-realization or Kṛṣṇa consciousness means seeing Kṛṣṇa as the source of this world and treating everything as His property. By acting in that realization Kṛṣṇa's devotee is transferred to the spiritual domain at the end of this life. From there he never again has to return to this perishable world of repeated birth and death.

This instruction of Cāṇakya Paṇḍita has been repeated from its source in the *Bṛhaspati-nīti-sāra* (1.110.1).

ŚLOKA 1.14

वरयेत् कुलजां प्राज्ञो विरूपामपि कन्यकाम् ।
रूपशीलां न नीचस्य विवाहः सदृशे कुले ॥१४॥

varayet kula-jāṁ prājño
virūpām api kanyakām
rūpa-śīlāṁ na nīcasya
vivāhaḥ sadṛśe kule

A wise man should marry a virgin of a respectable family even if she is ugly. He should not marry even a beautiful girl of good character from a lower class. Marriage in a family of equal status is preferable.

Commentary: Regarding marriage, the *Manu-saṁhitā* offers another point of view:

> Receive knowledge even if it is spoken by one of lower caste, learn the highest virtues if displayed by the lowest of society, and accept a *strī-ratna* (jewel of a woman) even if she is from a bad family. (MS 2.238)

Cāṇakya Paṇḍita will concur with this verdict also in verse 1.16. *Nīti-śāstra* teaches that each situation is different and requires a unique judgment pertaining to time and circumstances. An intelligent devotee should consider first and foremost the devotional qualifications of the proposed life partner as the single-most important factor for executing Kṛṣṇa consciousness in the *gṛhastha-āśrama.* For devotees, the purpose of marriage is to spread the chanting of the holy names in all countries of the world. One thing is certain, and that is that a devotee should not be tempted to marry a nondevotee.

In a Vedic marriage, once details such as age, family, education, health, social status and a host of other attributes are settled, the science of Vedic astrology—or *jyotiṣa-śāstra*—is the final factor in determining compatibility. This process, based upon the moon's position among the twenty-seven *nakṣatras* (stars), is still used in India to this day, and is recommended by Śrīla Prabhupāda in his purport to *Śrīmad-Bhāgavatam* 9.18.23. The position of the couple's moon signs in relationship to one another is of vital importance in deciding mutual attraction, the relationship's potential for longevity, prosperity, harmony, children, etc. Certain astrological signs (*rāśis*) exert a certain magnetic attraction that is understood as "love" over each other, while other signs repel like the opposite poles of magnets. Marriage is always a roll of the dice, but through Kṛṣṇa conscious astrology the cards are stacked in favor of the young couple. Thereby the inevitable struggles will be minimized.

The Vedic formula for a happy marriage was given by Śrīla Prabhupāda in his purport to *Śrīmad-Bhāgavatam* (4.27.1):

> The great politician Cāṇakya Paṇḍita has said: *bhāryā rūpavatī śatruḥ*—"a beautiful wife is an enemy." (CN 6.11) Of course every

woman is very beautiful in the eyes of her husband. Others may see her as not very beautiful, but the husband, being very much attracted to her, sees her always as very beautiful. If the husband sees the wife as very beautiful, it is to be assumed that he is too much attracted to her. This attraction is the attraction of sex. The whole world is captivated by the two modes of material nature *rajo-guṇa* and *tamo-guṇa,* passion and ignorance. Generally women are very much passionate and are less intelligent; therefore somehow or other a man should not be under the control of their passion and ignorance. By performing *bhakti-yoga,* or devotional service, a man can be raised to the platform of goodness. If a husband situated in the mode of goodness can control his wife, who is in passion and ignorance, the woman is benefited. Forgetting her natural inclination for passion and ignorance, the woman becomes obedient and faithful to her husband, who is situated in goodness. Such a life becomes very welcome. The intelligence of the man and woman may then work very nicely together, and they can make a progressive march toward spiritual realization. Otherwise, the husband, coming under the control of the wife, sacrifices his quality of goodness and becomes subservient to the qualities of passion and ignorance. In this way the whole situation becomes polluted.

The conclusion is that a household life is better than a sinful life devoid of responsibility, but if in the household life the husband becomes subordinate to the wife, involvement in materialistic life again becomes prominent. In this way a man's material bondage becomes enhanced. Because of this, according to the Vedic system, after a certain age a man is recommended to abandon his family life for the stages of *vānaprastha* and *sannyāsa.*

ŚLOKA 1.15

नदीनां शस्त्रपाणीनां नखीनां शृङ्गिणां तथा ।
विश्वासो नैव कर्तव्यः स्त्रीषु राजकुलेषु च ॥१५॥

nadīnāṁ śastra-pāṇīnāṁ
nakhīnāṁ śṛṅgiṇāṁ tathā

viśvāso naiva kartavyaḥ
strīṣu rāja-kuleṣu ca

Never trust rivers, armed men, beasts with claws or horns, women or politicians.

Commentary: It is said that women, kings and the *guru* are like fire: stay too far away and you cannot avail the benefit you could otherwise obtain from them; get too close and you'll risk a burn. These statements from *nīti-śāstra* are repeated from older sources like *Bṛhaspati-nīti-sāra* (GP 1.109.14) and *Śukra-nīti* (SN 3.142). Bṛhaspati carries this thread a step further with the advice:

> One should not reside in that land where there is no leader, or where there are many leaders, or where the leadership is vested in a woman or a child. (GP 1.115.62)

In the *Anuśāsana-parva,* section 38 of the *Mahābhārata,* Grandfather Bhīṣma on his deathbed describes to King Yudhiṣṭhira the meeting of Śrī Nārada Muni with the Apsarā named Pañcacūḍā:

> King Yudhiṣṭhira said, "O best of the Bhāratas, I wish to hear about the nature of women. Women are said to be fickle and the root of all faults."
>
> Bhīṣma said, "Please hear in this connection the history of the discourse between the celestial *ṛṣi* Nārada and the heavenly courtesan Pañcacūḍā. Once in ancient times, the great sage Nārada, having traveled throughout the universe, met the stunning Apsarā Pañcacūḍā, who resided in Brahmaloka. The ascetic said to her, 'O lady of slender waist, could you please dispel a doubt I have in my mind?'
>
> Bhīṣma continued, "Thus addressed by the *ṛṣi,* the Apsarā replied, 'If the subject is one upon which I am competent to discourse, and if you think that I am qualified to speak on the topic, I shall certainly say what is in my mind.'

"Nārada said, 'O amiable one, I would never ask you to do anything that is beyond your abilities. O beautiful lady, I wish to hear from you about the disposition of women.'

Bhīṣma continued, "Hearing these words of the celestial *ṛṣi,* that foremost of Apsarās replied, 'Being myself a woman I am unable to speak ill of women. You know what women are and with what nature they are endowed. Therefore, O celestial *ṛṣi,* it does not behoove you to ask me to perform such a task.' Unto her the celestial *ṛṣi* said, 'O lady of slender waist, what you say is very true. Although one incurs fault by speaking that which is untrue, there can be no blame for speaking that which is true.' Thus addressed by him, the sweetly-smiling Apsarā Pañcacūḍā consented to answer Nārada's question and agreed to discuss the true and eternal faults of women.

"Pañcacūḍā said, 'Even if they are high-born, blessed with beauty and possessed of protectors, women wish to transgress those restraints that are assigned to them. This fault truly blemishes them, O Nārada. Nothing else is more sinful than women. As you certainly know, women are truly the root of all evils, O Nārada. Even when women have husbands who are famous and wealthy, who are handsome and are completely obedient to them, they are prepared to disregard them once they get the opportunity. O most expert one, this is our immoral disposition. Casting off modesty, we cultivate the companionship of men of sinful habits and intentions. Women like those men who court them and who respectfully serve them even slightly. Only through want of solicitation by persons of the other sex, or through fear of their relatives, women—who naturally shun all restraints—do not transgress those who have been ordained to protect them. For these reasons only do they remain by the side of their husbands.

"'There is no one to whom women are incapable of offering their favors. They never take into consideration the age of the person they are prepared to favor. Whether ugly or handsome, if only the person happens to belong to the opposite sex, women are ready to enjoy his companionship. That women remain faithful to their husbands is due neither to their fear of sin, nor to compassion, nor to wealth, nor to affection springing from their hearts for kinsmen and children. Women from respectable families envy those members of their sex who are young, adorned with jewels and who live freely. Women who are loved by their husbands and treated with great respect have been known to bestow their favors upon even men who are hump-backed, who are blind, who are idiots, or who are dwarfs. Women have been known to enjoy the companionship of even those men who are ugly or who cannot walk. O great *ṛṣi,* there is no man in this world whom women may regard as unfit for companionship.

"'Through their inability to obtain the company of persons of the opposite sex, or through fear of relatives, or through fear of death and imprisonment, women remain within the restraints prescribed for them. They are exceedingly restless, for they always hanker after new companions. In consequence of their indecipherable nature, they are incapable of being kept in obedience by affectionate treatment. Their disposition is such that they cannot be restrained when they are bent upon their transgressions. Women surely fit the descriptions spoken by the wise: just as fire is never satiated with fuel, or the ocean can never be filled with the waters that flow into it from countless rivers, or as Lord Śiva, the destroyer, is never satiated even after slaying all living creatures, women are never satisfied by men. This, O celestial *ṛṣi,* is another of womankind's mysteries. As soon as they see a man of handsome and charming appearance, unfailing signs of desire appear on their persons. They never show sufficient regard for even those husbands who satisfy all their desires, who never fail to do what is agreeable to them and who protect them from want and danger. Women never regard so highly even an abundance of articles of enjoyment, or ornaments, or other possessions—as they do the companionship of men.

"'Yamarāja, wind, death, Pātālaloka, a submarine volcano, the razor's edge, poison, a serpent and fire: all these causes of destruction together are equal to women. From the eternal Supreme Brahman from whom the five great elements have sprung into existence, from whom Lord Brahmā, the creator, has ordained the universe, and indeed from where men have sprung, verily from the same eternal source have women also come into existence. At the very time when women were created these faults that I have enumerated were planted in them, O Nārada.'"[5]

The Supreme Lord Viṣṇu in His form as a woman known as Mohinī-mūrti instructs the demigod descendants of Kaśyapa Muni:

viśvāsaṁ paṇḍito jātu kāminīṣu na yāti hi

Indeed, at no time will a *paṇḍita* ever place his trust in a woman. (SB 8.9.9)

The *Bhāgavatam* gives many such instructions, including this one:

A woman's face is as attractive and beautiful as a blossoming lotus flower during autumn. Her words are very sweet, and they give pleasure to the ear, but if we study a woman's heart, we can understand it to be extremely sharp, like the blade of a razor. In these circumstances, who could understand the dealings of a woman? (SB 6.18.41)

In his Bhaktivedanta purport to this verse, Śrīla Prabhupāda comments:

Women are generally known as the fair sex, and especially in youth, at the age of sixteen or seventeen, women are very attractive to men. Therefore a woman's face is compared to a blooming lotus flower in autumn. Just as a lotus is extremely beautiful in autumn, a woman at the threshold of youthful beauty is extremely attractive. In Sanskrit a woman's voice is called *nārī-svara* because women generally sing and their singing is very attractive. At the present moment, cinema artists, especially female singers, are especially welcome. Some of them earn fabulous amounts of money simply by singing. Therefore, as taught by Śrī Caitanya Mahāprabhu, a woman's singing is dangerous because it can make a *sannyāsī* fall a victim to the woman.

Sannyāsa means giving up the company of women, but if a *sannyāsī* hears the voice of a woman and sees her beautiful face, he certainly becomes attracted and is sure to fall down. There have been many

5. Adapted from the *Mahābhārata,* translated by Kisari Mohan Ganguli.

examples. Even the great sage Viśvāmitra fell victim to Menakā. Therefore a person desiring to advance in spiritual consciousness must be especially careful not to see a woman's face or hear a woman's voice. To see a woman's face and appreciate its beauty or to hear a woman's voice and appreciate her singing as very nice is a subtle falldown for a *brahmacārī* or *sannyāsī.* Thus the description of a woman's features by Kaśyapa Muni is very instructive.

When a woman's bodily features are attractive, when her face is beautiful and when her voice is sweet, she is naturally a trap for a man. The *śāstras* advise that when such a woman comes to serve a man, she should be considered to be like a dark well covered by grass. In the fields there are many such wells, and a man who does not know about them drops through the grass and falls down. Thus there are many such instructions. Since the attraction of the material world is based on attraction for women, Kaśyapa Muni thought, 'Under the circumstances, who can understand the heart of a woman?' Cāṇakya Paṇḍita has also advised, *viśvāso naiva kartavyaḥ strīṣu rāja-kuleṣu ca:* 'There are two persons one should not trust—a politician and a woman.' (CN 1.15) These, of course, are authoritative śāstric injunctions, and we should therefore be very careful in our dealings with women.

Sometimes our Kṛṣṇa consciousness movement is criticized for mingling men and women, but Kṛṣṇa consciousness is meant for anyone. Whether one is a man or woman does not matter. Lord Kṛṣṇa personally says, *striyo vaiśyās tathā śūdrās te 'pi yānti parāṁ gatim:* whether one is a woman, *śūdra* or *vaiśya,* not to speak of being a *brāhmaṇa* or *kṣatriya,* everyone is fit to return home, back to Godhead, if he strictly follows the instructions of the spiritual master and *śāstra.*

ŚLOKA 1.16

विषादप्यमृतं ग्राह्यममेध्यादपि काञ्चनम् ।
नीचादप्युत्तमां विद्यां स्त्रीरत्नं दुष्कुलादपि ॥१६॥

viṣād apy amṛtaṁ grāhyam
amedhyād api kāñcanam
nīcād apy uttamāṁ vidyāṁ
strī-ratnaṁ duṣkulād api

From poison extract nectar. Retrieve gold from an unclean place. Learn the absolute truth from even the low-born. And marry a jewel-like woman even if she is born in a disreputable family.

Commentary: "Love is where you find it." So goes the old song my grandmother used to sing to me. Line four appears to contradict verse 1.14. Yet Cāṇakya Paṇḍita's emphasis is upon the character, not the physical beauty, of the bride. He advises, "Disregard the family's blemish and accept the *strī-ratna,* the jewel among women." Naturally a true jewel of a wife is a devotee of Kṛṣṇa, for such a wife blesses the household with a wonderful sense of spiritual grace that no material adjustment can equal. A lady or gentleman seeking the companionship of a loving partner should look first to the candidate's advancement in Kṛṣṇa consciousness. The potential bride or groom who is interested in excessive sense gratification and material expansion should be rejected.

Regarding the advice *nīcād apy uttamāṁ vidyām,* the acquisition of the highest *vidyā* (knowledge) from one who is *nīca* or "of a lower class," consider this example. When one is injured, does he cross-examine the physician regarding the doctor's familial status and religion? Or does he overlook the physician's status in society and plead with him to save his life? We must seek out and accept the Absolute Truth, regardless of the source that teaches us that truth. The goal is great and life is much too short. Today there are many devotees from every country on earth who were born as Christians, Jews, Buddhists, etc., yet they are preaching the Absolute Truth from the pages of Śrīla Prabhupāda's transcendental *śāstras.* We find even high-born *brāhmaṇas* learning from the mouths of these so-called *śūdra-mahājanas.* Truth spoken honestly does not change because the mouth is different.

Speaking to this point while lecturing on SB 1.3.21 in Los Angeles on 26 September 1972, Śrīla Prabhupāda said:

> Just like Cāṇakya, in his moral lessons, he says that *viṣād apy amṛtaṁ grāhyam.* (CN 1.16) When there is a tub of poison... but, if there is little nectar, then you take it. Don't think that "It is in the poison pot, why shall I take it?" No, you can take it... Suppose in a very filthy place where people pass stool, urine, there is some gold. So you should take it. Don't think that because the gold is in the polluted place, gold has become polluted. No. You take it.

Again, quoting this verse in his *Kṛṣṇa Consciousness: The Matchless Gift,* Śrīla Prabhupāda comments:

> Real civilization is not concerned simply with man's animal needs but with enabling man to understand his relationship with God, the supreme father. One may learn about his relationship with God by any process—through Christianity, through the Vedic literatures or through the *Koran*—but in any case it must be learned. The purpose of this Kṛṣṇa consciousness movement is not to make Christians into Hindus or Hindus into Christians but to inform everyone that the duty of a human being is to understand his relationship with God. One must learn this; otherwise he is simply wasting his time by engaging in animalistic propensities. We must all try to love Kṛṣṇa or God. If one has a process, he should practice it, or he can come and learn this process. One should not begrudge the selection of one process over another.

Here Cāṇakya Paṇḍita's immortal advice was handed down from the priest of the demigods, Bṛhaspati. (GP 1.110.8)

In another version of Cāṇakya's *ślokas* called *Cāṇakya-nīti-darpaṇa,* the last two lines in the verse above are different: *amitrād api sad-vṛttaṁ bālād api subhāṣitam* meaning, "Learn proper conduct even from an enemy and accept good advice even from a child."

ŚLOKA 1.17

स्त्रीणां द्विगुण आहारो लज्जा चापि चतुर्गुणा ।
साहसं षड्गुणं चैव कामश्चाष्टगुणः स्मृतः ॥१७॥

strīṇāṁ dvi-guṇa āhāro
lajjā cāpi catur-guṇā
sāhasaṁ ṣaḍ-guṇaṁ caiva
kāmaś cāṣṭa-guṇaḥ smṛtaḥ

Women have twice the hunger, four times the shyness, six times the daring and eight times the lust as compared to men.

Commentary: *Paṇḍitas* point out that the meaning of *lajjā* runs from modesty or bashfulness to embarrassment and even shame. However, *lajjā* is said to be a lady's "safety valve." Men have declared from time immemorial, "Women! Can't live with them and can't live without them." Nonetheless, a devotee wife can be a valuable asset. The *Satya-saṁhitā* compares a faithful wife to a boat that helps a man cross a dangerous river.[6] Generally, a man should marry and live peacefully in the company of his wife, learning the art of keeping himself satisfied. (See CN 7.4) Renunciation or the fourth stage (*sannyāsa-āśrama*) is for only a rare few detached souls who have truly realized the uselessness of material life.

Sannyāsa is actually meant for the man who has conquered sex desire. Happiness remains elusive for those who blindly rush headlong into marriage. As Ambrose Bierce wryly observes in his *Devil's Dictionary*—"the better half will soon become the bitter half." Cāṇakya's oft-quoted verse has been sourced from *Garuḍa Purāṇa* 1.109.33.

Thus Ends Chapter One

6. *Satya-saṁhitā* is an astrological text by Satyācārya.

CHAPTER TWO

ŚLOKA 2.1

अनृतं साहसं माया मूर्खत्वमतिलोभिता ।
अशौचत्वं निर्दयत्वं स्त्रीणां दोषाः स्वभावजाः ॥१॥

anṛtaṁ sāhasaṁ māyā
mūrkhatvam atilobhitā
aśaucatvaṁ nirdayatvaṁ
strīṇāṁ doṣāḥ svabhāva-jāḥ

Untruthfulness, recklessness, guile, foolishness, avarice, uncleanliness and cruelty: these are a woman's seven natural flaws.

Commentary: He who is born into this material world will have flaws. This material world is predominated over by goddess Durgā, whose name means "insurmountable fort." This world, Durgā's citadel, serves as a prison for the fettered conditioned souls who, in their rebelliousness, have forgotten their relationship with Lord Kṛṣṇa. From the *zamindar* living in a mansion to the beggar in the bazaar, the only difference in the "prisoners" of this world is the quality of the jail cell. As a consequence of our forgetfulness of God, we have fallen into the ocean of *māyā,* illusion, and now we are mistaking lust for the flickering material beauties of this world as love. This body is not our true self, and our spiritual existence has been waylaid by our misidentification with material energy. By becoming attracted to the temporary features of the physical body, we are forced to face the worst elements of nature.

Śrīla Prabhupāda explains that:

> A mundaner: (1) is sure to commit mistakes, (2) is inevitably illusioned, (3) has the tendency to cheat others, and (4) is limited by imperfect senses. (Bg, introduction)[7]

As Śukrācārya states:

> The following persons are considered dead although living: one who falls under the sway of women, one who is always in debt, one who is extremely poor, a beggar, one who has no good qualities and one who is dependent on his enemies. (SN 3.128)

This world is a cruel place, despite the opinions of New Age utopians who blindly hum pseudo-wise parables like, "It's all good" or "Everything is perfect." Indeed, the holy name of God alone can deliver us from *māyā* and we have no other recourse if we are to see that our eternal souls are saved from this terrible ocean of birth and death.

ŚLOKA 2.2

भोज्यं भोजनशक्तिश्च रतिशक्तिर्वराङ्गना ।
विभवो दानशक्तिश्च नाल्पस्य तपसः फलम् ॥२॥

bhojyaṁ bhojana-śaktiś ca
rati-śaktir varāṅganā
vibhavo dāna-śaktiś ca
nālpasya tapasaḥ phalam

To have the power of digestion when the food is ready, to be robust and virile in the company of one's religiously wedded wife, and

7. See Cc 1.2.86.

to be charitably disposed when one is prosperous are the fruits of not slight austerities.

Commentary: Herewith Cāṇakya Paṇḍita hints at the subject of life's "fruits" (*phala*) as results of austerities (*tapasya*) performed in a past life. Each living entity brings into this birth the dormant seeds created by his previous life's deeds, which sprout here and now for better or worse. Those who are born into misery are reaping the result of misdeeds of a prior existence, and those who fit the description of this verse are enjoying the results of *pūrva-puṇya-phala* (fruits of past life piety).

The science of reincarnation is summarized by Lord Kṛṣṇa:

> As a person dons new garments, giving up those he has worn out, similarly the soul accepts new material bodies, giving up the old and useless ones. (Bg 2.22)

The quality and fit of the individual spirit soul's analogous "suit of clothing" hangs in the closet of his past deeds.

As far as *tapasaḥ phalam* (the "fruits of austerity") which an individual soul brings into his present existence, Bhartṛhari observes:

> Whatever small or great amount of wealth is written upon your forehead, that you will surely obtain. Therefore do not needlessly adopt a servile attitude towards the rich. A jar holds the same amount of water whether dipped into the ocean or into the well. (NS 48)

There is a certain irony in this verse, indeed a *sādhu* would read it from quite an opposite perspective. For a devotee, austerities are meant for the pleasure of the Supreme Lord and must not be performed for the acquisition of temporary and illusory pleasures. Lust and gluttony, the strongest impulses in this world of bodily consciousness, are the very urges that a devotee scorns in his search after liberation from rebirth. Such is the irony of this material world that men in the modes of passion and ignorance perform austerities to achieve those very things that bind them to an eternity of misery. Therefore true and lasting austerity should be performed for the satisfaction of the Supreme Lord Śrī Kṛṣṇa. That is the true meaning of *tapasya* in the fourth line.

ŚLOKA 2.3

यस्य पुत्रो वशीभूतो भार्या छन्दानुगामिनी ।
विभवे यश्च सन्तुष्टस्तस्य स्वर्ग इहैव हि ॥३॥

yasya putro vaśī-bhūto
bhāryā chandānugāminī
vibhave yaś ca santuṣṭas
tasya svarga ihaiva hi

He whose son is obedient to him, whose wife's conduct is in accordance with his wishes, and who is content with his riches, has his kingdom-come here on earth.

Commentary: Cāṇakya Paṇḍita herewith praises the quality of satisfaction (*santoṣa*) as the means of achieving Svarga (heaven). Some decades back John D. Rockefeller, then the wealthiest man in America, was asked, "How much money is enough?" "A little more," was the response. He who uncomplainingly counts his blessings and is satisfied with his lot, however meager, is truly rich—not an overstuffed miser racked by greed.

Another way to translate the Sanskrit word *chandānugāminī* is "she who follows the Vedic way of life."

Śrīla Prabhupāda gives Cāṇakya Paṇḍita's formula for happiness:

> **Prabhupāda:** Cāṇakya Paṇḍita says that "Who is happy?" He says, "The man who does not go out of home, and who is not a debtor he is happy." Very simple thing. Who does not go out of home, and he's not a debtor, he's happy. So now we see everyone is out of home, and everyone is a great debtor. So how you can be happy? In America the bank canvasses that "You take money, you purchase

motorcar, you purchase your house, and, as soon as you get your salary, you give me." That's all. Finished. You take the card… American… What is it called? Am-card? Yes.

Śyāmasundara: Bankamericard.

Prabhupāda: 'Bank-card' or something. 'Bank-rupt.' [laughter] You see? So you take the card and you purchase whatever you like. And deposit your money in the bank. Then again, you are without any money. Simply that card. That's all. (Lecture, SB 1.2.18, Vṛndāvana, 29 Oct 1972)

ŚLOKA 2.4

ते पुत्रा ये पितुर्भक्ताः स पिता यस्तु पोषकः ।
तन्मित्रं यत्र विश्वासः सा भार्या यत्र निर्वृतिः ॥४॥

te putrā ye pitur bhaktāḥ
sa pitā yas tu poṣakaḥ
tan mitraṁ yatra viśvāsaḥ
sā bhāryā yatra nirvṛtiḥ

They alone are sons who are devoted to their father. He is a father who maintains his children. He is a friend in whom we can confide, and she only is a wife in whose company the husband feels contented and peaceful.

Commentary: Our Guru Mahārāja used to refer to irresponsible men who, avoiding to enter into responsible, regulated family life procreate here and there like cats and dogs as "bachelor daddies." He would add, "Unless the father is able to give his children the knowledge of liberation from birth and death, he is their enemy." It is the duty of children to serve their parents, not merely to comfortably occupy the same house at their leisure.

Regarding the third line, the true friend (*mitra*) is the one who has your well-being at heart. The last line refers to the wife (*bhāryā*) who invisibly binds her husband with threads of loving service. Such a contented husband will never look elsewhere.

ŚLOKA 2.5

परोक्षे कार्यहन्तारं प्रत्यक्षे प्रियवादिनम् ।
वर्जयेत्तादृशं मित्रं विषकुम्भं पयोमुखम् ॥५॥

parokṣe kārya-hantāraṁ
pratyakṣe priya-vādinam
varjayet tādṛśaṁ mitraṁ
viṣa-kumbhaṁ payo-mukham

You should reject a so-called friend of endearing speech who flatters you on your face and plots your ruin behind your back. He is like a jug of poison with milk on its surface.

Commentary: Although Cāṇakya Paṇḍita chose to stand alone and without any friends, he places much emphasis upon loyal relationships. Friendship can exist only between equals. Cāṇakya Paṇḍita renounced mundane friendship because he was a friend to the entire world, and therefore had no equal.

The *Garuḍa Purāṇa* advises learning the art of body language to determine the level of truth and honesty in an acquaintance:

> The inner workings of a man's mind should be inferred from his facial reflexes, behavior, gestures, movements, speech and the contractions and distortions of his eyes and lips. (GP 1.109.52)

ŚLOKA 2.6

न विश्वसेत् कुमित्रे च मित्रे चापि न विश्वसेत् ।
कदाचित् कुपितं मित्रं सर्वं गुह्यं प्रकाशयेत् ॥६॥

na viśvaset kumitre ca
mitre cāpi na viśvaset
kadācit kupitaṁ mitraṁ
sarvaṁ guhyaṁ prakāśayet

Neither entrust your secrets to a bad friend, nor even to good friends. Should your friend ever grow angry with you, he will bring all your secrets to light.

Commentary: Each of us has "personal issues" that we would loathe to see the light of day. Often the difference between a man of good reputation and a man with a bad one is the former's ability to keep his mouth shut.

Even today in India there are still *sādhus* whose lives are open books, whose characters are so spotless that they have no secrets to keep. For a living example of such a rare *paramahaṁsa,* we need only to dive into the nectarean volumes of *A Transcendental Diary.* In these, Hari Śauri Dāsa's day-by-day account of Śrīla Prabhupāda, we have the rare fortune of glimpsing the life of one who allowed the entire world to scrutinize his every moment. Therefore, the definition of a holy man could be "he whose public and personal lives are the same."

ŚLOKA 2.7

मनसा चिन्तितं कार्यं वाचा नैव प्रकाशयेत् ।
मन्त्रेण रक्षयेद्गूढं कार्ये चापि नियोजयेत् ॥७॥

manasā cintitaṁ kāryaṁ
vācā naiva prakāśayet
mantreṇa rakṣayed gūḍhaṁ
kārye cāpi niyojayet

Whatever is planned mentally should not be disclosed in speech. Quietly, and through wise counsel, bring your plans into execution.

Commentary: Śrīla Prabhupāda states in his purport to *Śrī Upadeśāmṛta* (4):

> For a similar reason, we should not disclose our minds to the serpent Māyāvādīs and *karmīs*. Such disclosures will never help. It is best to avoid association with them completely and never ask them about anything confidential because they cannot give good advice. Nor should we extend invitations to Māyāvādīs and atheists nor accept their invitations, for by such intimate intermingling we may become affected by their atheistic mentality.

A man's ability to reason and to discriminate is that which separates him from the animal's fourfold propensities of (1) mating, (2) eating, (3) sleeping, and (4) defending. Our Guru Mahārāja compared the mind to a blank check, and it is for the thoughtful person to fill in that check with the largest sum possible. As Kṛṣṇa explains to Arjuna (Bg 6.6):

bandhur ātmātmanas tasya yenātmaivātmanā jitaḥ
anātmanas tu śatrutve vartetātmaiva śatru-vat

> For him who has conquered the mind, the mind is the best of friends (*bandhu*), but for one who has failed to do so, his mind will remain the greatest enemy (*śatru*).

The mind of man is a tiny reflection of the mind of God. So vast is the mind of the Lord that the countless spiritual and material universes—all perfectly ordered—have emanated from His mind and by His will. He alone can comprehend His own potencies. Although we will never be able to comprehend the tiniest fraction of the mind of Śrī Kṛṣṇa, if we are to liberate ourselves from *māyā* we must actively engage our minds in contemplating His glories as described by the previous *ācāryas*. This is true meditation, not trying to empty the mind into an imaginary void as recommended by today's misleading fashion *gurus*.

ŚLOKA 2.8

कष्टं च खलु मूर्खत्वं कष्टं च खलु यौवनम् ।
कष्टात्कष्टतरं चैव परगेहनिवासनम् ॥८॥

kaṣṭaṁ ca khalu mūrkhatvaṁ
kaṣṭaṁ ca khalu yauvanam
kaṣṭāt kaṣṭataraṁ caiva
para-geha-nivāsanam

Foolishness is painful and so is youth. But more painful than either is being obliged to reside in another's house.

Commentary: As it is said, youth is wasted on the young; or to state that differently, "Too soon old and too late smart." The final words of the French diva Edith Piaf, who had lived a life of heedless abandon, were: "Every damn fool thing you do in this life, you pay for!"

As far as the second bit of *nīti* from this verse is concerned, one example comes to mind. The moon in daytime loses its glow and luster due to being in the house of the sun. Bṛhaspati counsels:

> One should never blame anyone, take another's possesions, ridicule anyone, enjoy another's wife and live in another's house. (GP 1.108.13)

Cāṇakya Paṇḍita advises that dependency causes a loss of self-respect, while dignity and confidence arise from self-reliance. And no money is sweeter than that which has been earned honestly by one's own hand.

ŚLOKA 2.9

शैले शैले न माणिक्यं मौक्तिकं न गजे गजे ।
साधवो न हि सर्वत्र चन्दनं न वने वने ॥९॥

śaile śaile na māṇikyaṁ
mauktikaṁ na gaje gaje
sādhavo na hi sarvatra
candanaṁ na vane vane

Rubies are not found in every mountain, nor are pearls found in the head of every elephant; neither are saints found everywhere, nor are sandalwood trees found in every forest.

Commentary: The most precious jewel of this world is the association of *sādhus* or devotees of Lord Kṛṣṇa, and this is the only reason Śrīla Prabhupāda formed the International Society for Kṛṣṇa Consciousness. True devotees are very rare. As the Buddhists say, "One seed, ten thousand seeds." From the spotless character of one pure devotee an entire religious movement has blossomed.

ŚLOKA 2.10

पुत्राश्च विविधैः शीलैर्नियोज्याः सततं बुधैः ।
नीतिज्ञाः शीलसम्पन्ना भवन्ति कुलपूजिताः ॥१०॥

putrāś ca vividhaiḥ śīlair
niyojyāḥ satataṁ budhaiḥ
nīti-jñāḥ śīla-sampannā
bhavanti kula-pūjitāḥ

Wise men always educate their sons in the many aspects of good behavior. Well-behaved sons who know nīti-śāstra are worshipped in their own families.

Commentary: The son's activities reflect his upbringing. A student's acumen reflects his teacher's abilities to transmit knowledge. The character of the disciple is the gauge by which society judges his *guru*. Therefore, devotees should be constantly aware of the watchful scrutiny of the public and we must always bear in mind that "example is louder than precept." In many ways, the legacy of the spiritual master rests upon the character of responsible disciples just as Śrīla Prabhupāda became the light of the Gauḍīya Maṭha as the successor *ācārya* to his own Guru Mahārāja.

ŚLOKA 2.11

माता शत्रुः पिता वैरी याभ्यां बाला न पाठिताः ।
सभामध्ये न शोभन्ते हंसमध्ये बको यथा ॥११॥

mātā śatruḥ pitā vairī
yābhyāṁ bālā na pāṭhitāḥ
sabhā-madhye na śobhante
haṁsa-madhye bako yathā

The mother and father who do not teach their children the science of transcendence are their enemies. As a stork among swans, so is an ignorant son in a public assembly.

Commentary: This verse has been quoted from *Garuḍa Purāṇa* 1.115.80. Sometimes the *śāstras* disparage family life while at other times marriage is praised. Everything hinges upon time and circumstances. To set an example for mankind, Lord Kṛṣṇa's father Vasudeva sent his son to the *āśrama* of Śrī Sāndīpani Muni in Avantikā to study the sixty-four Vedic arts and sciences. Śrī Kṛṣṇa's education and relationship with His Guru Mahārāja are described in Śrīla Prabhupāda's *Kṛṣṇa, the Supreme Personality of Godhead,* which contains the complete list of the sixty-four Vedic arts. (ch. 45, "Kṛṣṇa Recovers the Son of His Teacher")

It is said that one can lay any extravagant claim to learning, education and social status as long as he keeps his mouth shut. It is through listening that the wise discern the difference between the poser and the *paṇḍita,* seen in this verse as the stork (*baka*) and the swan (*haṁsa*).

Regarding the role of a proper son, Prince Puru explains to his father King Yayāti: "Who in this world can repay his debt to his father? By the mercy of one's father, one gets the human form of life, which can enable one to become an associate of the Supreme Lord. A son who acts by anticipating what his father wants him to do is first class, one who acts upon receiving his father's order is second class, and one who executes his father's order irreverently is third class. But a son who refuses his father's order is like his father's stool." (SB 9.18.43–44)

ŚLOKA 2.12

लालनाद् बहवो दोषास्ताडने बहवो गुणाः ।
तस्मात्पुत्रं च शिष्यं च ताडयेन्न तु लालयेत् ॥१२॥

lālanād bahavo doṣās
tāḍane bahavo guṇāḥ
tasmāt putraṁ ca śiṣyaṁ ca
tāḍayen na tu lālayet

Many a bad habit is developed through overindulgence, and many a good one by chastisement. Therefore discipline your son as well as your student, for they should never be overindulged.

Commentary: "Spare the rod and spoil the child." There is no pain like that of an over-indulged son or daughter who turns on his or her own parents. It seems some children are born only to bring about the bitter end of their families, and many families have been torn apart by their brats out of control. Bṛhaspati advises:

> The son should be fondled for five years, and then disciplined until he is sixteen. Afterwards, he may be treated like a friend. (GP 1.114.59)

In a lecture (SB 2.9.4) in Japan on 22 April 1972 Śrīla Prabhupāda dilated upon this point:

Therefore, in the first chastisement, Kṛṣṇa was accepted as spiritual master. A spiritual master has the right to chastise. Father, spiritual master, they are advised to chastise. *Putraṁ ca śiṣyaṁ ca tāḍayen na tu lālayet.* So father and teacher are advised by Cāṇakya Paṇḍita that "You should always chastise your son and disciple. Chastise." *Tāḍayet. Tāḍayet* means "Simply chastise. Always find out their mistake." Don't be angry, but it is the business of the teacher and the father simply to find out your mistakes, not to find out your good things. *Tāḍayen na tu lālayet. Lālayet* means patting: "Oh, my dear son, my dear boy, you are so nice." Sometimes it is done, but it is the business of the teacher and the father to chastise. Never recognize the disciple's business or son's business as very good. Then they will spoil. That is the injunction of Cāṇakya Muni.

Lālane bahavo doṣāḥ: If you simply pat, then there will be so many faults. *Doṣāḥ* means faults. *Tāḍane bahavo guṇāḥ.* And if you chastise, oh, they will be very much qualified. *Tāḍane bahavo guṇāḥ, tasmāt.* Therefore, *putraṁ ca śiṣyaṁ ca tāḍayen na tu lālayet,* simply chastise. Don't pat. This is the injunction, moral injunction. So far we are concerned, when our spiritual master used to chastise, we took it as blessing. That was very nice. And he would chastise like anything. "Damn rascal, foolish, stupid," anything, all good words. (laughter)

One day it so happened… That was not my fault. My, another old Godbrother, was… Prabhupāda was speaking. So I was very much fond of hearing. That gentleman, he was a retired doctor. So he wanted to speak something. He should not have done so, but… So naturally I also… And Prabhupāda saw it, and he became so angry. So he knew that my attention was drawn by him. He chastised him like anything. He was old man. Actually almost like his age. So he was paying sixty rupees in those days per month. So he became so angry, that "Do you think that because you pay sixty rupees, you have purchased us? You can do anything and anything?" He said like that. Very strong word he used. "Do you think that I am speaking for others? You have learned everything? You are diverting your attention." So many ways, he was very, very angry. You see? So this is nice, to chastise.

Śrīla Prabhupāda also quoted this verse as it appears in text 2.12 above. He dilated upon "sons and disciples" in a *Śrī Īśopaniṣad* lecture delivered in Los Angeles on 8 July 1971:

> Formerly the spiritual master, the disciplic succession, there are two ways. One is called *śaukra* and another is called *sautra. Śaukra* means succession from the seminal. Just like son. Son is born by the semina, and the disciple is born by Vedic knowledge. So the one familywise is called *śaukra. Śukra* means semina, coming from the *śukra,* and the other is *sautra,* by hearing. So spiritual master… In India still there are *gotras. Gotra* means coming from that great sage. Just like our family belongs to the Gautama-gotra. Gautama Ṛṣi, from him the familywise *gotra,* and similarly disciplic succession is also *gotra.* There is no difference between *putra* and *śiṣya. Putra* means son, and *śiṣya* means disciple. Cāṇakya Paṇḍita said, *putrāṁś ca śiṣyāṁś ca;* they are equally treated. Both of them are equally eligible for hereditary rites from the person, whether he is a son or a disciple. So Brahmā distributed knowledge to some… Practically everyone was his son because he was the first living creature. So later on, disciples also, son's son. So in this way Brahmā distributed this Vedic knowledge.

For more on this subject, please refer to CN 3.18.

ŚLOKA 2.13

श्लोकेन वा तदर्धेन तदर्धार्धाक्षरेण वा ।
अबन्ध्यं दिवसं कुर्याद् दानाध्ययनकर्मभिः ॥१३॥

ślokena vā tad-ardhena
tad-ardhārdhākṣareṇa vā
abandhyaṁ divasaṁ kuryād
dānādhyayana-karmabhiḥ

Learn one śloka daily. Otherwise learn half of it, one line of it or even half a syllable of it. Let not one day pass without study, an act of charity or other pious activity.

Commentary: As dripping water fills a tub overnight, so by gradual study a man becomes learned. Through this gradual process, many *paṇḍitas* and devotees have committed several thousand *ślokas* to memory. Bṛhaspati advises:

> These five should be pursued slowly and cautiously: assimilating knowledge, pursuing wealth, climbing a mountain, learning virtuous conduct and approaching women. (GP 1.109.46)

For the upliftment and support of the world, the ancient Sanskrit *śāstras* were written down by sage Vyāsadeva, "the compiler." Vyāsa divided the *Vedas*, compiled the eighteen *Purāṇas,* wrote the *Vedānta-sūtra* and the world's longest epic poem the *Mahābhārata,* of which the *Bhagavad-gītā* is the essence. Cāṇakya advises that at least one verse must be studied as a daily routine.

The American humorist Ambrose Bierce in his *Devil's Dictionary* defines:

> *Scriptures, n.* the sacred books of our holy religion, as distinguished from the false and profane writings on which all other faiths are based.

Farsighted beyond his times, Bierce was of course taking a back-handed swing at narrow-minded Western religionists who refuse to recognize universal scriptural truths because they appear foreign. The Supreme Absolute Truth is one. All men are brothers because they have the same father. Śrīla Prabhupāda used to say that his books were meant for people everywhere because they freely give the name and address of God. The sacred Vedic *śāstras* of ancient Bhārata do not belong to some particular ism, sect or religious cult. The universal wisdom they teach is meant for world enlightenment.

ŚLOKA 2.14

कान्तावियोगः स्वजनापमानम्
ऋणस्य शेषः कुनृपस्य सेवा ।

दरिद्रभावो विमुखं च मित्रं
विनाग्निना ते प्रदहन्ति कायम् ॥१४॥

kāntā-viyogaḥ sva-janāpamānam
ṛṇasya śeṣaḥ kunṛpasya sevā
daridra-bhāvo vimukhaṁ ca mitraṁ
vināgninā te pradahanti kāyam

Separation from one's wife, disgrace before one's own people, an unpaid debt, service to a wicked king, poverty and a friend who has turned away: these six kinds of evils if afflicting a person burn him like fire.

Commentary: Vedic civilization prescribes marriages, religious celebrations and other events to be timed according to the positions of the planets and proper lunar phase to assure a happy outcome. The art of timing is like birth astrology in reverse: an auspicious moment is selected in advance for the "birth" of some auspicious event. Marriage ceremonies performed under bright stars between an astrologically compatible man and wife are less likely to end in divorce, death of one partner or unfortunate consequences of astrological disharmony. There is no ceremony for divorce prescribed anywhere in the Vedic scriptures; a husband and wife should remain together. The Vedic system of matching horoscopes for the sake of a successful marriage is described by Śrīla Prabhupāda in his purport to SB 9.18.23:

> According to the Vedic system, the parents would consider the horoscopes of the boy and girl who were to be married. If according to astrological calculations the boy and girl were compatible in every respect, the match was called *yoṭaka* and the marriage would be accepted. Even fifty years ago, this system was current in Hindu society. Regardless of the affluence of the boy or the personal beauty of the girl, without this astrological compatibility the marriage would not take place. A person is born in one of three categories, known as *deva-gaṇa, manuṣya-gaṇa* and *rākṣasa-gaṇa.* In different parts of the universe there are demigods and demons,

and in human society also some people resemble demigods whereas others resemble demons. If according to astrological calculations there was conflict between a godly and a demoniac nature, the marriage would not take place.

Similarly, there were calculations of *pratiloma* and *anuloma.* The central idea is that if the boy and girl were on an equal level the marriage would be happy, whereas inequality would lead to unhappiness. Because care is no longer taken in marriage, we now find many divorces. Indeed, divorce has now become a common affair, although formerly one's marriage would continue lifelong, and the affection between husband and wife was so great that the wife would voluntarily die when her husband died or would remain a faithful widow throughout her entire life. Now, of course, this is no longer possible, for human society has fallen to the level of animal society. Marriage now takes place simply by agreement. *Dāmpatye 'bhirucir hetuḥ.* (SB 12.2.3) The word *abhiruci* means "agreement." If the boy and girl simply agree to marry, the marriage takes place. But when the Vedic system is not rigidly observed, marriage frequently ends in divorce.

Regarding "loss of faith before one's own people," Kṛṣṇa says to Arjuna:

sambhāvitasya cākīrtir maraṇād atiricyate

For a respectable man, dishonor is worse than death. (Bg 2.34)

Wise kings always kept one eye upon enemies. Bṛhaspati advises:

Do not neglect even an insignificant enemy. Even a tiny spark, if not extinguished, consumes the entire world. (GP 1.114.72)

Regarding a friend who has become hostile, *vimukhaṁ ca mitram* literally means "a friend who has turned away his face (from our direction)."

ŚLOKA 2.15

नदीतीरे च ये वृक्षाः परगेहेषु कामिनी ।
मन्त्रिहीनाश्च राजानः शीघ्रं नश्यन्त्यसंशयम् ॥१५॥

nadī-tīre ca ye vṛkṣāḥ
para-geheṣu kāminī
mantri-hīnāś ca rājānaḥ
śīghraṁ naśyanty asaṁśayam

A tree on the riverbank, a young lady in another's house, a king without ministers: without doubt all of these soon meet with destruction.

Commentary: Kings were absolutely aware of their need for impartial counsel. This principle is practically demonstrated in *Śrīmad-Bhāgavatam* wherein Lord Kṛṣṇa at Dvārakā asked the advice of his friend Uddhava regarding His attendance at King Yudhiṣṭhira's Rājasūya-yajña in Hastināpura. To which Uddhava replied (SB 10.71.2), "O Lord, as the sage advised, You should help Your cousin fulfill his plan for performing the Rājasūya sacrifice, and You should also protect the kings who are begging for Your shelter." Kṛṣṇa followed Uddhava's advice to the letter, and arranged for the death of Jarāsandha at the hands of Bhīma, and for the release of the 100,000 kings he had held hostage.

Regarding an unprotected lady in the house of another, *Bṛhaspati-nīti-sāra* (GP 1.109.16) also stresses the importance of protecting a woman's chastity and warns against: "... base association, long separation from the husband, flattery, attention shown by a would-be seducer and residence in another man's house." Concerning a man who abandons his wife, Parāśara Muni, the illustrious father of the great Vyāsadeva, is quoted in the *Garuḍa Purāṇa:*

> He who forsakes a chaste wife in the prime of her youth shall be reborn as a woman in his next seven successive births, suffering widowhood each time. (GP 1.107.24)

Regarding a young lady in another's house, the following episode regarding the birth of the demigod Budha or planet Mercury is told in *Śrīmad-Bhāgavatam* (8.9): Tārā, the wife of the priest of the demigods Bṛhaspati, was kidnapped by Soma, the lord of the moon planet. Consequently a great battle broke out in which Śukrācārya and his demon followers took the side of Soma, and Indra the king of heaven, fought for Bṛhaspati. Finally, when Tārā was rescued from the house of Soma, it was discovered that she had become impregnated by Soma the moon god. Thus was born to her the beautiful and golden-colored son of the moon, Budha or Mercury. Hence, Cāṇakya Paṇḍita's instructions apply not only to this world, but are useful throughout the material universe. Even the great demigods in Svargaloka fall prey to the same defects of conditioning that we have.

In his *Vidura-nīti,* sage Vidura advises:

> Praise is meant for that lady who has passed beyond her youth. (VN 3.59)

From this statement we understand that he who praises a comely young lady will be suspected of harboring illicit motivations.

ŚLOKA 2.16

बलं विद्या च विप्राणां राज्ञां सैन्यं बलं तथा ।
बलं वित्तं च वैश्यानां शूद्राणां पारिचर्यकम् ॥१६॥

balaṁ vidyā ca viprāṇāṁ
rājñāṁ sainyaṁ balaṁ tathā
balaṁ vittaṁ ca vaiśyānāṁ
śūdrāṇāṁ pāricaryakam

Realized knowledge is the brāhmaṇa's strength, the king's strength is his army, stored wealth is the vaiśya's strength and the strength of the śūdra is his service attitude.

Commentary: Today's so-called "caste system of India" is a muddled reflection of the original system of social organization called *varṇāśrama.* Kṛṣṇa tells Arjuna:

cātur-varṇyaṁ mayā sṛṣṭaṁ guṇa-karma-vibhāgaśaḥ

> The four *varṇas* have emanated from Me, each according to their personal qualities and type of work. (Bg 4.13)

Kṛṣṇa makes the point clearly that personal qualities and activities are the only determining factor of *varṇa.* Following the verdict of the *Bhagavad-gītā,* this is also the conclusion of Cāṇakya Paṇḍita, as seen from this verse. As Cāṇakya Paṇḍita herewith implies, one who is truly learned may be called a *brāhmaṇa,* but an unlearned "birth *brāhmaṇa*" cannot be considered a *brāhmaṇa.*

In Kali-yuga almost everyone is born into the fourth (*śūdra*) class: *kalau śūdra-sambhavaḥ.* Consider the following example: you are on a jetliner and you notice the pilot cavorting with the young stewardesses. You ask, "Who is flying the plane?" You are told, "The pilot's son. He has no formal training, but being the son of the pilot qualifies him as a pilot." Your next thought is that you have mere seconds left to live. Similarly, polished *śūdras* who claim to be born *brāhmaṇas* have sent society into a tailspin.

According to a prophecy in the *Varāha Purāṇa,* in Kali-yuga many demons take birth as *brāhmaṇas* and preach false and concocted gospels thereby spreading confusion and undermining social structure. The *brāhmaṇa* (teacher) must earn his status through his cleanliness, austerity, penance and learning. Even in the West, which touts a supposed caste-free society, we see that individuals automatically gravitate to their own quality of work. *Varṇāśrama* based upon personal merit is as natural as water seeking its own level.

The best example of "quality as the determining force of caste" was seen in the life and times of Cāṇakya Paṇḍita. He elevated the great Candragupta Maurya to the throne even though by birth he was not qualified to reign as king. Similarly, the great Sikh master Śrī Guru Gobind Singh began his *khālsā* family of warriors with five disciples among whom there were a barber and a washerman. Our illustrious grand spiritual master Śrīla Bhaktisiddhānta Sārasvatī Gosvāmī, founder of India's sixty-four Gauḍīya Maṭhas, offered *sannyāsa* initiation to an ex-*pān-wālā* who surrendered his life to Kṛṣṇa. When our grand Guru Mahārāja toured Vṛndāvana in 1932 along with his saffron-clad *brahmacārīs,* he found many temples had closed their doors due to reluctance on the part of the caste Gosvāmīs to admit "lower class" Kṛṣṇa-*bhaktas* inside. Our own Guru Mahārāja Śrīla Prabhupāda had no hopes of finding *brāhmaṇas* in America, so one by one he created his own army of *brāhmaṇas,* one that is based upon *guṇa* (quality) and not *janma* (birth).

A true *brāhmaṇa* is compared to the mystical *cintāmaṇi* touchstone, which can transform base metal into gold. A genuine *brāhmaṇa* imparts wisdom unto a disciple by which the disciple becomes elevated. It is this logic that Śrīla Prabhupāda followed in offering his own Western disciples the *yajñopavīta* (sacred thread) as the mark of a *dvija.* The entity's first birth is the appearance of the material body from the womb of his mother. The second birth is the spiritual awakening through the touchstone of the bona fide spiritual master.

ŚLOKA 2.17

निर्धनं पुरुषं वेश्या प्रजा भग्नं नृपं त्यजेत् ।
खगा वीतफलं वृक्षं भुक्त्वा चाभ्यागतो गृहम् ॥१७॥

nirdhanaṁ puruṣaṁ veśyā
prajā bhagnaṁ nṛpaṁ tyajet
khagā vīta-phalaṁ vṛkṣaṁ
bhuktvā cābhyāgato gṛham

The harlot abandons her customer when his money is spent; the citizen rejects that king who cannot protect him; birds flee a tree

from which the fruit has been plucked; and the guest leaves the house once he has enjoyed his meal.

ŚLOKA 2.18

गृहीत्वा दक्षिणां विप्रास्त्यजन्ति यजमानकम् ।
प्राप्तविद्या गुरुं शिष्या दग्धारण्यं मृगास्तथा ॥१८॥

gṛhītvā dakṣiṇāṁ viprās
tyajanti yajamānakam
prāpta-vidyā guruṁ śiṣyā
dagdhāraṇyaṁ mṛgās tathā

Brāhmaṇas take leave of the yajamāna once they have received their due alms; disciples depart their gurus when their education is completed; and deer flee burning forests.

Commentary: Cāṇakya Paṇḍita explains in the first verse that he has raked his verses from many different scriptures. A similar verse appears in the *Bṛhaspati-nīti-sāra* (GP 1.109.9):

> Birds abandon a tree when the fruits are exhausted. The *sārasa* birds fly from the lake when it is dry. The courtesan chases away that man whose pockets are empty. Ministers bid adieu to the king who has lost his throne. Honeybees avoid the withered flower. Deer flee a burning forest.

The above two verses can be compared to those from *Śrīmad-Bhāgavatam* (10.47.7–8) wherein the *gopīs* of Vṛndāvana appear to criticize Kṛṣṇa propelled only by their ecstatic love for Him.

niḥsvaṁ tyajanti gaṇikā
akalpaṁ nṛpatiṁ prajāḥ
adhīta-vidyā ācāryam
ṛtvijo datta-dakṣiṇam

khagā vīta-phalaṁ vṛkṣaṁ
bhuktvā cātithayo gṛham
dagdhaṁ mṛgās tathāraṇyaṁ
jārā bhuktvā ratāṁ striyam

Prostitutes abandon a penniless man, subjects an incompetent king, students their teacher once they have finished their education, and priests a man who has remunerated them for a sacrifice. Birds abandon a tree when its fruits are gone, guests a house after they have eaten, animals a forest that has burnt down, and a lover the woman he has enjoyed, even though she remains attached to him.

Regarding the first line, "Prostitutes kick out the client when he is *nirdhana* (penniless)," there was an interesting story entitled "Ex-husband Hits Jackpot" that appeared in the *San Francisco Chronicle,* Nov. 17th 1999. Denise Rossi of Los Angeles never mentioned to her husband Thomas that she won the State Lottery of $1.3 million in December of 1996. Instead she filed for divorce eleven days after hearing of the windfall. Two years later, Thomas learned of his wife's secret serendipity through a letter that was delivered accidentally. Thomas Rossi went to court and sued for a share of the fortune for which his wife of twenty-five years had abandoned him. A sympathetic judge took every penny away from Denise and handed over the entire fortune to Thomas, who cried for joy. Indeed, sometimes divorce of convenience replaces marriage of convenience in Kali-yuga.

ŚLOKA 2.19

दुराचारी दुरादृष्टिर्दुरावासी च दुर्जनः ।
यन्मैत्री क्रियते पुम्भिर्नरः शीघ्रं विनश्यति ॥१९॥

durācārī durādṛṣṭir
durāvāsī ca durjanaḥ
yan maitrī kriyate pumbhir
naraḥ śīghraṁ vinaśyati

He who befriends the following rogues: those of vicious deeds, those of crooked vision, and those who reside in places of utter disrepute—is quickly ruined.

Commentary: Herewith Cāṇakya Paṇḍita warns against the association of three types of *durjanas* or "evil men." These are the *durācārī* (men of evil actions), the *durādṛṣṭi* (men of perverse views), and the *durāvāsī* (men who reside in places of sin). In the First Canto of *Śrīmad-Bhāgavatam,* we find that the mighty King Parīkṣit banished the devil Kali to that place where the following four sins are rampant: (1) illicit sex, (2) animal slaughter, (3) gambling, and (4) intoxication. Today we are more than 5100 years into Kali-yuga (the iron age), a time when abominable activities have generally become socially acceptable or even considered desirable. Today more than ninety per cent of the world's population fit the *dur*-descriptions of this verse.

In a lecture on *Bhagavad-gītā* 2.21–22 delivered in London on 26 August 1973, Śrīla Prabhupāda advised:

> So give up this. Cāṇakya Paṇḍita also says, *tyaja durjana-saṁsargam,* "Give up the association of these rascals." *Bhaja sādhu-samāgamam,* "Only associate with devotees." (CN 14.19) This will be right.

At the end of the Kali-yuga 427,000 years hence, the mass of people will have become too dulled by sinful activities to be reasoned with. At that time Lord Śrī Kṛṣṇa will appear as the Kalki *avatāra* and liberate those miscreants with the cold steel of His terrible swift sword. In the *Garuḍa Purāṇa,* we find the following lamentation:

> Alas, life in the Age of Kali is indeed troublesome! Virtue itself has taken to renunciation. Penance has left for an extended journey. Truth has been exiled to some foreign country. The earth is barren, the citizens are fraudulent, the *brāhmaṇas* are beset by greed, men are overly submissive to domineering wives and women are fickle and loose while rascals of base character are elevated to high positions. (GP 1.115.2)

Welcome to Kali-yuga where the only redeeming quality is the *saṅkīrtana* movement.

When the people are bent upon evil to the extent that they destroy the very arms that maintain them, there must be a reaction. Over the ages the Lord comes personally to rid the earth of dangerous civilizations or at other times material nature reacts in the form of great epidemics and disasters. That is the very reason why Kṛṣṇa ordered Arjuna to do battle with the incorrigible and avaricious sons of the wicked Dhṛtarāṣṭra:

> Arise and fight, O great bowman. Your enemies are already put to death by My arrangement and you can be but an instrument in this fight. (Bg 11.33)

Bad association is like a Pandora's box by which many evil habits are formed thereby opening the door to hell, while the association of devotees is the path to liberation. The famous pilgrim of the *Mahābhārata,* Vidura, an incarnation of Yamarāja, says to the blind King Dhṛtarāṣṭra:

> He who is wise never cultivates friendship with those who are haughty, foolish, fierce, rash or otherwise devoid of virtue. Accept as a friend he who is grateful, virtuous, truthful, noble, a resolute devotee, self-controlled and steadfast in all principles of morality and virtue. (VN 7.36–37)

As noted by Vidura, *sādhu-saṅga* (association with spiritually elevated persons) is the cause of all success. The sixteenth-century Bengali classic *Śrī Caitanya-caritāmṛta* (2.22.54) of Kṛṣṇadāsa Kavirāja Gosvāmī states:

> *'sādhu-saṅga', 'sādhu-saṅga'—sarva-śāstre kaya*
> *lava-mātra sādhu-saṅge sarva-siddhi haya*

> The association of devotees! The association of devotees! All sacred texts declare that every perfection—*sarva-siddhi*—is awakened through even a moment's association with holy saints.

While Kali-yuga is compared to a dark and overcast night, the holy name of God is compared to the full moon, and the messenger of God Śrīla Prabhupāda is the purifying wind that blows away the clouds. To counteract the evils of Kali-yuga described in this verse we are advised to always chant:

Hare Kṛṣṇa Hare Kṛṣṇa Kṛṣṇa Kṛṣṇa Hare Hare
Hare Rāma Hare Rāma Rāma Rāma Hare Hare

ŚLOKA 2.20

समाने शोभते प्रीतिः राज्ञि सेवा च शोभते ।
वाणिज्यं व्यवहारेषु दिव्या स्त्री शोभते गृहे ॥२०॥

samāne śobhate prītiḥ
rājñi sevā ca śobhate
vāṇijyaṁ vyavahāreṣu
divyā strī śobhate gṛhe

Friendship between equals flourishes, service under a king is respectable, business flourishes in social intercourse and a beautiful woman is safe in her own home.

Commentary: Regarding the fourth line, which literally means that "a woman glows or beautifies her own house," Cāṇakya Paṇḍita has portrayed quite an opposite scenario in 2.15. There he states *para-geheṣu kāminī,* "a woman in another's house is ruined." Apparently, this statement holds true all the way up to America's supreme house, the White House. During the tenure of President Bill Clinton (1993–2001) several allegations of sexual misconduct surfaced against the supreme commander from seduction to rape. The President stood trial and admitted his guilt on national television giving new meaning to the phrase "affairs of state." It is a sad fact of life that many men view young women as nothing more than convenient vehicles that were created simply for the satisfaction of their lusty desires. Mere moralizing over the issues of right versus wrong leads to no solution at all, at least as long as the viper-like senses remain uncontrolled.

Kṛṣṇa advises Arjuna:

> *strīṣu duṣṭāsu vārṣṇeya jāyate varṇa-saṅkaraḥ*

> When women become polluted the result is unwanted population. (Bg 1.40)

Manu-saṁhitā, the "law book for mankind" advises:

> A wife is never released from her husband. (MS 9.46)

Bṛhaspati agrees:

> A woman shall not be allowed independence. She is protected by her father in childhood, by her husband in marriage, and by her grown-up sons in old age. (GP 1.115.63)

The *Araṇya-kāṇḍa* of *Śrī Rāmāyaṇa* describes the incident wherein Lord Rāma left Sītā under the care of His younger brother, Lakṣmaṇa, in order to chase Marīca in the form of a golden deer. Though Lakṣmaṇa was the personification of chaste devotion, Sītā did not hesitate to accuse him of sinful desires. Therefore Lakṣmaṇa replied:

> O Princess of Mithilā, you are like a deity to me. Thus I cannot speak harshly in reply. I know that it is the nature of women to create trouble and discord between friends. Indeed, women are so fickle and hard-hearted that when they become obsessed with some desire, they give up all sense of morality. (*Śrī Rāmāyaṇa, Araṇya-kāṇḍa,* 45.28–29)

Maintaining a harmonious social infrastructure through protection of women is at the highest priority of Vedic civilization because it insures that the population overall will be raised properly.

Thus Ends Chapter Two

CHAPTER THREE

ŚLOKA 3.1

कस्य दोषः कुले नास्ति व्याधिना को न पीडितः ।
व्यसनं केन न प्राप्तं कस्य सौख्यं निरन्तरम् ॥१॥

kasya doṣaḥ kule nāsti
vyādhinā ko na pīḍitaḥ
vyasanaṁ kena na prāptaṁ
kasya saukhyaṁ nirantaram

Who was born into a family without blemish? Who is not troubled by diseases? Who hasn't experienced calamities? Who has achieved eternal happiness?

Commentary: Answers: (1.) Nobody. (2.) Nobody. (3.) Nobody (4.) Nobody (with the exception of the Lord's pure devotee).

Regarding the question of eternal happiness, in this world the experiences of happiness (*sukha*) and distress (*duḥkha*) come and go in waves like ocean tides, while the devotee remains equipoised like a rock on the shore. Śrī Kṛṣṇa explains to Arjuna:

mātrā-sparśās tu kaunteya śītoṣṇa-sukha-duḥkha-dāḥ
āgamāpāyino 'nityās tāṁs titikṣasva bhārata

> O son of Kuntī, the nonpermanent appearance of happiness and distress, and their disappearance in due course, are like the appearance and disappearance of winter and summer seasons. They arise from sense perception, O scion of Bharata, and one must learn to tolerate them without being disturbed. (Bg 2.14)

Unless spiritualized, the temporary senses of the material body can do little or nothing in the way of providing permanent enjoyment. Genuine happiness can be found only in spirit since only spirit is everlasting. Therefore one should always chant:

Hare Kṛṣṇa Hare Kṛṣṇa Kṛṣṇa Kṛṣṇa Hare Hare
Hare Rāma Hare Rāma Rāma Rāma Hare Hare

ŚLOKA 3.2

आचारः कुलमाख्याति देशमाख्याति भाषणम् ।
सम्भ्रमः स्नेहमाख्याति वपुराख्याति भोजनम् ॥२॥

ācāraḥ kulam ākhyāti
deśam ākhyāti bhāṣaṇam
sambhramaḥ sneham ākhyāti
vapur ākhyāti bhojanam

One's descent may be discerned by his conduct, his country by his pronunciation of language, his affection by respect he shows, and his capacity to eat by his body.

Commentary: What has come to be known as "body language" speaks volumes about an individual to the observant sage. There are two types of body language: (1) the body itself and (2) its mannerisms and movements. Not only do the cultured speak and articulate differently than the base, but their walk, mannerisms and gestures all serve to reveal their social status. An illiterate blockhead will be betrayed by his walk and other movements even before his mouth opens. Much can be determined through silently observing others. Even Arjuna asked of Kṛṣṇa:

> What are the symptoms of one whose consciousness is thus merged in transcendence? How does he speak, and what is his language? How does he sit, and how does he walk? (Bg 2.56)

And this is why Śrīla Prabhupāda stressed that devotees adorned with *tilaka* and Vaiṣṇava dress must behave and represent their *ācārya* properly, whether alone or through the lens of the critical public eye.

Regarding the second point concerning speech, our Guru Mahārāja related a story that was told by Birbal, King Akbar's advisor. In South India the story is credited to Raman of Tenali, the famous court *paṇḍita* of King Krishnadeva Raya. Once there was a mysterious fellow who spoke many Indian languages with perfect fluency. None could trace his first language. Curious, his associates formed a plan. One day, while the fellow's attention was distracted, one of his friends stole up behind him and struck him from behind. This multilingual man quickly turned and verbally abused his attacker. The group listened carefully, for he had angrily retorted in his native tongue, the Oriya language. Now the secret was out. His family hailed from the state of Odisha. The lesson of this story is that a man reveals his inner nature through his anger.

Himalayan *sādhus* have reported meeting *yogīs* meditating in mountain caves who speak a form of Sanskrit that has not been spoken for hundreds of years. Thus, through the speech of these *yogīs,* it can be discerned that they have extended their lives to centuries through *yoga* practice. There is no better yardstick of measuring another's status and elevation than his speech.

As far as the fourth point of this verse is concerned, *vapur ākhyāti bhojanam* or "one's body depicts his eating habits," we turn again to the sardonic *Devil's Dictionary* of Ambrose Bierce: "*Edible,* adjective. Good to eat, and wholesome to digest, as a worm to a toad, a toad to a snake, a snake to a pig, a pig to a man and a man to a worm!"

ŚLOKA 3.3

सुकुले योजयेत्कन्यां पुत्रं विद्यासु योजयेत् ।
व्यसने योजयेच्छत्रुं मित्रं धर्मे नियोजयेत् ॥३॥

sukule yojayet kanyāṁ
putraṁ vidyāsu yojayet
vyasane yojayec chatruṁ
mitraṁ dharme niyojayet

Give your virgin daughter in marriage to a good family and see that your son becomes educated. Make sure your enemy comes to grief, but engage your friends in spiritual life.

Commentary: Through his judgment of time and circumstance, an intelligent person knows what is to be done to satisfy the moment and what is not to be done. The highest *dharma* is service to Kṛṣṇa. Here Cāṇakya Paṇḍita advises that we bring our friends to *dharma* (Kṛṣṇa consciousness). As far as educating your son is concerned, Bṛhaspati counters with:

> Of what purpose is a son who is neither virtuous nor scholarly? (GP 1.114.55)

Regarding "putting enemies to grief," history gives no better authority on this subject than Cāṇakya Paṇḍita. His plotting the downfall of his powerful royal enemies the Nandas was dramatized in the play of Viśākhadatta (circa sixth to ninth century), the *Mudrā-rākṣasa.* This play's intricate and complicated plot offers a romanticized version of Cāṇakya Paṇḍita's wily schemes to outwit Rākṣasa, the chief minister of the last Nanda king. In the play, as in real life, Cāṇakya Paṇḍita's chessmaster-like plans never failed to unfold in his favor. He was a follower of Bṛhaspati who declares, "I find no fault when a wicked man meets with wickedness."

ŚLOKA 3.4

दुर्जनस्य च सर्पस्य वरं सर्पो न दुर्जनः ।
सर्पो दंशति काले तु दुर्जनस्तु पदे पदे ॥४॥

durjanasya ca sarpasya
varaṁ sarpo na durjanaḥ
sarpo daṁśati kāle tu
durjanas tu pade pade

Of a rascal and a snake, the serpent is the better of the two. The viper strikes only at the time he is destined to kill, whereas the scoundrel inflicts pain at every step.

Commentary: The third line states, "the serpent strikes only at the destined moment." Thus Cāṇakya Paṇḍita uses his analogy to also impart the Vedic concept of destiny seen by the word *kāla* in this verse. The Vedic understanding of *kāla,* "time" is a key factor in understanding the concept of *karma* (activity). What is generally called destiny is understood as *karma-phala* in Vedic understanding. *Phala* means the "fruit" or results of past *karmas* or activities. This blossoming of either good or bad results based on past deeds or misdeeds encapsulates the Vedic concept of destiny as *karma-phala.*

The Supreme Lord Kṛṣṇa asserts:

kālo 'smi loka-kṣaya-kṛt pravṛddho
lokān samāhartum iha pravṛttaḥ

Time I am, the destroyer of the worlds, and I have come here to destroy all people. (Bg 11.32)

Even the English word "calendar" comes from the Sanskrit *kāla,* while the word "month" comes from "moon" indicating the Vedic method of time measurement according to lunar cycles. "Solar" as in "solar year" is derived from Latin "solaris" which is derived from

Sanskrit "*sūrya.*" Syllables from the Sanskrit for day (*aho*) and night (*rātri*) form the word *horā,* from which the English "hour" is derived. Thus even modern measurements in time trace their roots to Vedic culture because the measurement of time is a gift to the world from ancient Vedic seers.

Vedic culture has so intricately comprehended natural measurements of time based upon the steady movements of the sun and moon that by comparison the methods of all other cultures on earth appear primitive. *Śrīmad-Bhāgavatam* has projected the life of the universe, accurately measuring that which no other culture on earth has ever dared to estimate. At the time of *pralaya* (universal destruction)—when Sūrya the sun god increases his scorching heat twelve-fold—one hundred years of Lord Brahmā will have passed and this very universe that maintains us will succumb to *kāla.* Vedic math can accurately calculate the lifespan of the universe because, like all other materially created things, even the vast universe has a fixed duration of existence based upon *kāla* the time factor.

In the various *Purāṇas,* especially the *Bhāgavata, Viṣṇu, Padma* and *Brahmāṇḍa,* the material universe is described as the *brahmāṇḍa* or "egg of Brahmā." This "egg" in which we live is formed of successive layers of the eight elements of material energy in order of density, and each layer is ten times thicker than the last. These eightfold elements include earth, water, fire, air, mind, ether, intelligence and false ego. There is a vast and unknowable number of universes—each predominated by a Brahmā—within this material world but, like us, each of them are subject to *kāla.* To help our understanding, it is roughly calculated that the sum of all material universes, that is all the unlimited number of material worlds, occupies about a quarter of Kṛṣṇa's domain. The spiritual sky, or the three-fourths energy, is inhabited by eternally unfettered entities who are all devotees of Lord Kṛṣṇa. In that anti-material world time is not a factor as it is here since the denizens of Vaikuṇṭha are liberated devotees living in *sat-cit-ānanda:* eternity, knowledge and bliss.

As Śrīla Prabhupāda describes:

> All the living entities are part and parcel of the Supreme Personality of Godhead and are as good as the Lord qualitatively, but quantitatively there is a great difference between them, for the Lord is unlimited whereas the living entities are limited. Thus the Lord possesses unlimited potency for pleasure, and the living entities have limited pleasure potency. *Ānanda-mayo 'bhyāsāt.* (*Vedānta-sūtra* 1.1.12) Both the Lord and the living entity, being qualitatively spirit soul, have the tendency for peaceful enjoyment, but when the part of the Supreme Personality of Godhead unfortunately wants to enjoy independently, without Kṛṣṇa, he is put into the material world, where he begins his life as Brahmā and is gradually degraded to the status of an ant or a worm in stool. (SB 9.24.58, purport)

Thus, having entered the material world due to his desire to enjoy a temporary situation, the living entity falls under the influence of *kāla* or the time factor.

From the insignificant worm to the great demigods, each *brahmāṇḍa* contains an uncountable number of souls trapped by the shackles of their own karma, each one suffering his timed destiny according to *kāla.* Living entities elevated by piety may rise up to the exalted posts of temporary *devatās.* These *devatās* (demigods) are just like supervisors in a large factory, but just as a supervisor is subject to the rules enforced by the factory owner, so the *devatās* remain under the laws of nature. As Śrīla Prabhupāda explains above, when even a demigod's stock of piety is exhausted, he is recycled through the lower planetary systems.

Once in Brooklyn, Śrīla Prabhupāda pointed to a clump of grass growing from the cracks of the sidewalk:

> "Just see," he began, pointing with his cane. "No one has come here to plant this grass. Then how did it get here?" Looking around at the large group of devotees following him, he answered his own question, "It is because demigods have fallen down here. They have come through the rain."

When Lord Viṣṇu inhales, each universe reenters into His body with the time factor bringing about the *pralaya* (destruction) of each *brahmāṇḍa.* And then on schedule Viṣṇu exhales and the cycle is repeated once again. In the *Bhagavad-gītā,* Kṛṣṇa—the original Viṣṇu—tells Arjuna:

sahasra-yuga-paryantam ahar yad brahmaṇo viduḥ
rātriṁ yuga-sahasrāntāṁ te 'ho-rātra-vido janāḥ

By human calculation, a thousand ages (*yugas*) taken together form the duration of a single day of Brahmā. And such is also the duration of Brahmā's night. (Bg 8.17)

See Śrīla Prabhupāda's purport on the above verse for a more detailed description of universal time measurement.

In this verse, Cāṇakya Paṇḍita points out that because the serpent strikes only when ordained by *kāla* according to one's own *karma-phala,* it is neither as culpable nor as venomous as an envious rascal who strikes *pade pade,* at every step. *Nīti-śāstra* wisely teaches the performance of good deeds to ensure fulfillment and relative happiness not only in this life, but in successive lives as well. The highest *nīti* is Kṛṣṇa consciousness, which teaches us to engage in devotional service for the satisfaction of Lord Kṛṣṇa, thus bringing our round of endless *karma-phala* within the *kāla-cakra* to a welcome close. See Kṛṣṇa's promise from Bg 8.5:

anta-kāle ca mām eva smaran muktvā kalevaram
yaḥ prayāti sa mad-bhāvaṁ yāti nāsty atra saṁśayaḥ

And whoever, at the time of death (*anta-kāle*), quits his body, remembering Me alone, at once attains My nature. Of this there is no doubt.

ŚLOKA 3.5

एतदर्थं कुलीनानां नृपाः कुर्वन्ति सङ्ग्रहम्।
आदिमध्यावसानेषु न त्यजन्ति च ते नृपम् ॥५॥

etad-arthaṁ kulīnānāṁ
nṛpāḥ kurvanti saṅgraham
ādi-madhyāvasāneṣu
na tyajanti ca te nṛpam

Therefore kings gather around themselves men of good families, for such men never forsake them in the beginning, the middle or the end.

Commentary: Even kings are ruined by low company, just as King Edward VII of England gave up his throne in 1936 to marry an American society woman. Cāṇakya Paṇḍita mentions "the beginning, middle and end" which constitutes the three facets of timeless time, *tri-kāla,* as seen in this material world. Although Cāṇakya Paṇḍita was the prime minister under King Candragupta Maurya, he accepted no salary and lived in a small hut. When the king called his services in question, Cāṇakya Paṇḍita resigned at once.

ŚLOKA 3.6

प्रलये भिन्नमर्यादा भवन्ति किल सागराः ।
सागरा भेदमिच्छन्ति प्रलयेऽपि न साधवः ॥६॥

pralaye bhinna-maryādā
bhavanti kila sāgarāḥ
sāgarā bhedam icchanti
pralaye 'pi na sādhavaḥ

At the time of pralaya the oceans exceed their limits and seek to change. Yet saintly men, even at the time of pralaya, do not change.

Commentary: *Pralaya* means "universal destruction" or "death." Cāṇakya Paṇḍita expects a proper gentleman, or *sādhu,* to remain composed and controlled even at *pralaya.* Cāṇakya's instruction may be compared to the lesson sage Jamadagni taught his son Lord Paraśurāma:

> O great hero, my dear son Paraśurāma, you have unnecessarily killed the king, who is supposed to be the embodiment of all the demigods. Thus you have committed a sin. We are all *brāhmaṇas* and have become worshipable for the people in general due to our quality of forgiveness. It is because of this quality that Lord Brahmā, the supreme spiritual master of this universe, has achieved his post. (SB 9.15.38–39)

As explained by Nārada Muni to King Prācīnabarhi, a man loses control when he becomes a slave of his senses, like a chariot pulled by many horses out of control (SB 4.29.18–20). The six senses—including the tongue, ears, eyes, nose, touch and mind—are controlled by the process of *yoga* as described in the *Bhagavad-gītā* (2.58):

> One who is able to withdraw his senses from the objects of the senses as a tortoise withdraws his limbs is firmly fixed in perfect consciousness.

Still, Arjuna counters with the objection (Bg 6.33):

> The system of *yoga* that You have summarized appears impractical and unendurable to me, for the mind is restless and unsteady.

Arjuna was the son of Indra—he was a powerful warrior and a personal friend of Lord Kṛṣṇa. If mighty Arjuna (the incarnation of Nara Ṛṣi) considered the system of *aṣṭāṅga-yoga,* the "eightfold path," as impractical due to the unsteady nature of the mind, then what to speak of us who are born 5100 years into the Age of Kali? For the devotee of the Lord, like Arjuna, these six senses (*ṣaḍ-indriya*) are automatically controlled by engaging each one in the service of Lord Śrī Kṛṣṇa. How is this achieved?

In the Ninth Canto of *Śrīmad-Bhāgavatam* (9.4.18–20), Śrīla Prabhupāda describes devotional service, *bhakti-yoga:*

> Mahārāja Ambarīṣa always engaged his mind in meditating upon the lotus feet of Kṛṣṇa, his words in describing the glories of the Lord, his hands in cleansing the Lord's temple, and his ears in hearing the words spoken by Kṛṣṇa or about Kṛṣṇa. He engaged his eyes in seeing the Deity of Kṛṣṇa, Kṛṣṇa's temples, and Kṛṣṇa's places like Mathurā and Vṛndāvana, he engaged his sense of touch in touching the bodies of the Lord's devotees, he engaged his sense of smell in smelling the fragrance of *tulasī* offered to the Lord, and he engaged his tongue in tasting the Lord's *prasāda.* He engaged his legs in walking to the holy places and temples of the Lord, his head in bowing down before the Lord, and all his desires in serving the Lord, twenty-four hours a day. Indeed Mahārāja Ambarīṣa never desired anything for his own sense gratification. He engaged all his senses in devotional service in various engagements related to the Lord. This is the way to increase attachment for the Lord and be completely free from all material desires.

In Kali-yuga, steadiness of heart and mind in *yoga* is perfected through singing the holy names of God. He who wishes to become a *sādhu*—or "more steady than the ocean," as described in this verse—must engage in chanting:

Hare Kṛṣṇa Hare Kṛṣṇa Kṛṣṇa Kṛṣṇa Hare Hare
Hare Rāma Hare Rāma Rāma Rāma Hare Hare

ŚLOKA 3.7

मूर्खस्तु परिहर्तव्यः प्रत्यक्षो द्विपदः पशुः ।
भिद्यते वाक्यशल्येन अदृश्यं कण्टकं यथा ॥७॥

mūrkhas tu parihartavyaḥ
pratyakṣo dvipadaḥ paśuḥ
bhidyate vākya-śalyena
adṛśyaṁ kaṇṭakaṁ yathā

Do not associate with a nincompoop, for as we can see he is nothing but a two-legged beast. Like an unseen thorn he pierces one with the spears of his words.

Commentary: A moron's *vāk* (speech) is equal to a *śalya* (spear). Choose your friends wisely and avoid the *mūrkha* (fool). This theme is echoed throughout all *nīti-śāstras*. Bṛhaspati observes that there are five types of fools, whom he refers to as *caṇḍālas* (eaters of dogs)—implying the lowest of the low:

> These five are *caṇḍālas:* he who is without gratitude, he in whom there are no redeeming qualities, he who continuously nurses a grudge, the crooked-natured and he who is actually born as a dog-eater. (GP 1.114.71)

ŚLOKA 3.8

रूपयौवनसम्पन्ना विशालकुलसम्भवाः ।
विद्याहीना न शोभन्ते निर्गन्धाः किंशुका यथा ॥८॥

rūpa-yauvana-sampannā
viśāla-kula-sambhavāḥ
vidyā-hīnā na śobhante
nirgandhāḥ kiṁśukā yathā

Although endowed with beauty, youth and noble birth, they who lack learning are like kiṁśuka flowers, which [though beautiful] are devoid of fragrance.

Commentary: Cāṇakya Paṇḍita uses the word *vidyā-hīna* (lacking knowledge) indicating an absolute absence of wisdom. On the other hand, Kṛṣṇa Himself describes the mature fruit of knowledge with the words:

rāja-vidyā rāja-guhyaṁ pavitram idam uttamam

> This knowledge is the king of education, the most secret of all secrets, pure and transcendent. (Bg 9.2)

Truly the difference between real knowledge (Kṛṣṇa consciousness) and imagined knowledge, which is "the cultivation of nescience," must be pondered by the thoughtful. Real education is the key to elevation to the spiritual world of eternal bliss. Materialistic learning can only assure us of continued miserable entanglements in the sea of birth and death where we remain like fish caught in a net.

Reason and self-realization separate mankind from animals. A lapdog seated on a king's throne will leap to the floor for a scrap of rotten meat as quickly as any mutt in the alley. It is ironic that the differences between man and beast are becoming less obvious rapidly as the modern world "progresses" in the regimented march of science and technology. Human advancement has become a great march towards bestiality. Character and wisdom should separate the two-leggeds from the four-leggeds, not technology which has turned men into virtual reality versions of their canine "friends."

In Sunol, California in 1981 the citizens thought it would be great fun to elect a Labrador retriever named Bosco as mayor. Not long thereafter, a great fire devoured much of the town. The subtle forces that magnetically vibrate from the leaders influence all those who are under them. Some leaders are called lucky—those who invisibly bring prosperity—while others cause only sorrow and want. The great march of progress has also brought about the political system of democracy by which insignificant mutts select with their votes a more powerful dog to lead them.

To quote Sir Winston Churchill on the subject of democracy, "It has been said that democracy is the worst form of government, except for all the others that have been tried." For most politicians, once they are elected their campaign promises are swiftly forgotten, though they never forget their obligations to the rich and influential who put them there. Only Kṛṣṇa consciousness can separate society from a pack of mongrels. Undoubtedly, most of today's scientists, scholars, clergymen and politicians reflect Cāṇakya Paṇḍita's description in this verse of "flowers without fragrance."

ŚLOKA 3.9

कोकिलानां स्वरो रूपं स्त्रीणां रूपं पतिव्रतम् ।
विद्या रूपं कुरूपाणां क्षमा रूपं तपस्विनाम् ॥९॥

kokilānāṁ svaro rūpaṁ
strīṇāṁ rūpaṁ pati-vratam
vidyā rūpaṁ kurūpāṇāṁ
kṣamā rūpaṁ tapasvinām

The beauty of a cuckoo is in its notes; a woman's beauty is her faithfulness to her husband; an ugly man's beauty is his learning; and an ascetic's beauty is his forgiveness.

Commentary: The *kokila* bird (cuckoo), though quite plain, is celebrated for its song.[8] Of the four qualities mentioned above, only the sweet warble of the cuckoo is a born trait. The other three must be purposely and deliberately cultivated. Indeed, beauty is more than skin deep.

ŚLOKA 3.10

त्यजेदेकं कुलस्यार्थे ग्रामस्यार्थे कुलं त्यजेत् ।
ग्रामं जनपदस्यार्थे आत्मार्थे पृथिवीं त्यजेत् ॥१०॥

tyajed ekaṁ kulasyārthe
grāmasyārthe kulaṁ tyajet
grāmaṁ janapadasyārthe
ātmārthe pṛthivīṁ tyajet

Give up a member to save a family, forego the family to save the village, forfeit the village to save the country, but renounce the world for your own spiritual benefit.

8. The *kokila* is a member of the cuckoo order of birds and thus commonly translated as a cuckoo. Its more precise name is the Asian koel.

Commentary: The conclusion is given in the fourth line. Cāṇakya Paṇḍita offers similar advice in 1.6. Lord Kṛṣṇa defines the key word of this verse, *tyāga* (renunciation), in the *Bhagavad-gītā* (18.2):

sarva-karma-phala-tyāgaṁ prāhus tyāgaṁ vicakṣaṇāḥ

> Giving up the results of activities (*karma-phala*) is called renunciation by the wise.

The concept of the *ātmā* (spirit soul) is fundamental to Vedic culture—unlike body-conscious societies all over the world which feed upon temporary religion, birth, race, nationality, status, patriotism, fads and fashions. We have earlier discussed the example of the two birds in the tree from *Śvetāśvatara* (4.7) and *Muṇḍaka Upaniṣads* (3.12) which describes the spiritual entity and the Lord in his heart. While one of the birds engages in eating the fruits of the tree, the other bird is a well-wishing onlooker. The bird absorbed in the temporary enjoyment of eating the fruits of the tree of life represents the individual soul, the *ātmā.* The watching bird symbolizes the Supreme Lord, the Paramātmā (Supersoul), who dwells in the heart of each living entity. Birth after birth, the Lord awaits the individual soul to turn to Him and surrender his temporary enjoyment and misery in exchange for blissful, eternal life. This is the significance of the fourth line (lit.) "For the 'wealth of the soul' renounce (the false enjoyments of) the earth."

The eternal *ātmā* (soul) is infinitesimal, so tiny that it is described in the *śāstras* as being one ten thousandth the tip of a hair in size. Kṛṣṇa advises *ātmany evātmanā tuṣṭaḥ,* "Be satisfied in the soul." (Bg 2.55) To learn this art of inner tranquility and satisfaction, as advised by Kṛṣṇa, we must turn our eyes inwards and away from the glare of *māyā's* world. Whether we achieve this in the next second—or in millions of births to follow—is our own choice. It is a fact that this human form of life offers the opportunity for spiritual benefit which if lost may not be regained for millions of births. We do not know when we will achieve this human form of life again. As stated in the

Vedānta-sūtra, athāto brahma-jijñāsā: "Now is the time for spiritual inquiry."

ŚLOKA 3.11

उद्योगे नास्ति दारिद्र्यं जपतो नास्ति पातकम् ।
मौनेन कलहो नास्ति नास्ति जागरिते भयम् ॥११॥

udyoge nāsti dāridryaṁ
japato nāsti pātakam
maunena kalaho nāsti
nāsti jāgarite bhayam

There is no poverty for the industrious. Sin does not attach to him who performs japa. There can be no quarrel with someone who is silent. He who is vigilant cannot be overcome by fear.

Commentary: In the second line is found Cāṇakya Paṇḍita's most valuable advice. *Japa* means the chanting of God's holy names on a *mālā* of 108 *tulasī* beads. Our spiritual master prescribed this chanting of sixteen rounds of beads daily, 108 times 16 recitations of the great chant for deliverance, the *mahā-mantra:*

Hare Kṛṣṇa Hare Kṛṣṇa Kṛṣṇa Kṛṣṇa Hare Hare
Hare Rāma Hare Rāma Rāma Rāma Hare Hare

Śrī Caitanya Mahāprabhu often quoted the *Bṛhan-Nāradīya Purāṇa* (38.126, quoted in Cc 1.17.21):

harer nāma harer nāma harer nāmaiva kevalam
kalau nāsty eva nāsty eva nāsty eva gatir anyathā

The holy name! The holy name! The holy name! In the Age of Kali there is no other way, no other way, no other way, to reach the goal.

Repeating *harer nāma* ("the holy name") and *nāsty eva* ("no other way") thrice each, the venerable *Purāṇa* puts to rest any argument in favor of *karma-yoga, jñāna-yoga,* or *aṣṭāṅga-yoga* as paths to enlightenment in the present age.

Cāṇakya's advice "there is no poverty for the industrious" is true for the devotee or *karmī* alike. Since *nīti-śāstras* are aimed at the general masses, *karma* is sometimes treated almost as supreme. For those who have not surrendered to the all-powerful Supreme Lord and are yet to achieve transcendence, *karma-phala*—the ongoing effect of past activities—is certainly insurmountable. For those who attain transcendence by the grace of *guru* and the holy name of the Lord, the effects of *karma* are softened in proportion to the devotee's surrender to the Lord. The *bhakta* who chants Hare Kṛṣṇa daily need not fear the reactions of past misdeeds (*vikarma*) because he lives under the shelter of the Supreme Personality of Godhead. As Lord Kṛṣṇa promises Arjuna:

ahaṁ tvāṁ sarva-pāpebhyo mokṣayiṣyāmi mā śucaḥ

I shall deliver you from all sinful reaction. Do not fear. (Bg 18.66)

ŚLOKA 3.12

अतिरूपेण वै सीता अतिगर्वेण रावणः ।
अतिदानाद्बलिर्बद्धो ह्यति सर्वत्र वर्जयेत् ॥१२॥

ati-rūpeṇa vai sītā
ati-garveṇa rāvaṇaḥ
ati-dānād balir baddho
hy ati sarvatra varjayet

The goddess of fortune Sītā was kidnapped by Rāvaṇa for her extreme beauty. Rāvaṇa himself was destroyed for his extreme vanity. Through his excessive charity Bali Mahārāja was tied up. Therefore, by all means avoid excesses.

Commentary: It is a point well-taken that excesses must be avoided, as seen by the excesses of the demon King Rāvaṇa. Even so, assuming that this verse and others like it were not added at a later date, Cāṇakya's example appears a bit excessive because his description of Queen Sītā, whose beauty is of an entirely transcendental nature, is unwarranted. Further, Bali was bound up by the Supreme Lord in His Vāmana incarnation who became satisfied with His devotee's complete surrender and awarded him his own planet called Sutala. Verses like this one indicate why Cāṇakya is not celebrated as a pure devotee but as a politician. Indeed, a *śuddha-bhakta,* as our own Guru Mahārāja, is very rare.

The name Rāvaṇa means "who causes distress to others." For his excessive greed, he won only the wrath of the Personality of Godhead who admonished him with the well-deserved words:

> You are the most abominable of the man-eaters. Indeed, you are like their stool. You resemble a dog, for as a dog steals food from the kitchen in the absence of the householder, in My absence you kidnapped My wife, Sītādevī. Therefore as Yamarāja punishes sinful men, I shall also punish you. You are most abominable, sinful and shameless. Today therefore I, whose attempt never fails, shall punish you. (SB 9.10.22)

ŚLOKA 3.13

को हि भारः समर्थानां किं दूरं व्यवसायिनाम् ।
को विदेशः सुविद्यानां कः परः प्रियवादिनाम् ॥१३॥

ko hi bhāraḥ samarthānāṁ
kiṁ dūraṁ vyavasāyinām
ko videśaḥ su-vidyānāṁ
kaḥ paraḥ priya-vādinām

What is too heavy for the strong? What place is too distant for those who put forth effort? What country is foreign to one of true learning? Who can be inimical to one who speaks pleasingly?

Commentary: A devotee can preach in any country of the world because he understands that all men are brothers. We all have the same father. Kṛṣṇa says in the *Bhagavad-gītā* (9.17): *pitāham asya jagataḥ,* "I am the father of this universe." Fixed in this realization, the sage finds the entire world is his home and sees no stranger anywhere. From this verse we ascertain that a wanderer's true assets are liberation from the confines of bodily misidentification and freedom from ignorance which would prejudice his vision of the spiritual brotherhood of man. Cāṇakya Paṇḍita uses the word *su-vidyā* (highest learning) rather than mere *vidyā* (education) to make this point.

ŚLOKA 3.14

एकेनापि सुवृक्षेण पुष्पितेन सुगन्धिना ।
वासितं तद्वनं सर्वं सुपुत्रेण कुलं यथा ॥१४॥

ekenāpi su-vṛkṣeṇa
puṣpitena su-gandhinā
vāsitaṁ tad vanaṁ sarvaṁ
su-putreṇa kulaṁ yathā

Just as an entire forest becomes fragrant by the presence of a single flowering tree, so a bright son glorifies an entire family line.

Commentary: This oft-quoted verse originally appears in the *Garuḍa Purāṇa* (1.114.57). It is stated that the mere presence of a devotee in a family insures liberation for the seven generations that both follow and precede his birth. When Kārttikeya Dāsa recounted to Śrīla Prabhupāda that he inspired his mother to chant Hare Kṛṣṇa on her deathbed, Śrīla Prabhupāda shed tears as he said, "You have saved your mother."

ŚLOKA 3.15

एकेन शुष्कवृक्षेण दह्यमानेन वह्निना ।
दह्यते तद्वनं सर्वं कुपुत्रेण कुलं यथा ॥१५॥

ekena śuṣka-vṛkṣeṇa
dahyamānena vahninā
dahyate tad vanaṁ sarvaṁ
ku-putreṇa kulaṁ yathā

As a single withered tree, if set ablaze, burns the entire forest, so a bad son can destroy the entire family.

Commentary: As it is said "to the crow its child is golden." Parental partiality generally prevents an objective look at one's own offspring. In America doting parents are often hauled into court, sued and fined for the transgressions of their spoiled brats, as in the case of the Columbine massacre in Colorado. Better to live an ascetic's life than to be dragged to hell by useless family members. This verse describes a situation that is exactly opposite to the one seen in the previous verse.

In his purport to *Śrīmad-Bhāgavatam* (6.11.4) Śrīla Prabhupāda discusses the curse of having a useless son:

> Both stool and a cowardly son come from the abdomen of the mother, and … there is no difference between them. A similar comparison was given by Tulasī Dāsa, who commented that both a son and urine come from the same channel. In other words, semen and urine both come from the genitals, but semen produces a child whereas urine produces nothing. Therefore if a child is neither a hero nor a devotee, he is not a son but urine. Similarly, Cāṇakya Paṇḍita also says:
>
> *ko 'rthaḥ putreṇa jātena yo na vidvān na dhārmikaḥ*
> *kāṇena cakṣuṣā kiṁ vā cakṣuḥ pīḍaiva kevalam*

What is the use of a son who is neither glorious nor devoted to the Lord? Such a son is like a blind eye, which simply gives pain but cannot see.[9]

ŚLOKA 3.16

एकेनापि सुपुत्रेण विद्यायुक्तेन साधुना ।
आह्लादितं कुलं सर्वं यथा चन्द्रेण शर्वरी ॥१६॥

ekenāpi su-putreṇa
vidyā-yuktena sādhunā
āhlāditaṁ kulaṁ sarvaṁ
yathā candreṇa śarvarī

Just as night is brightened by the moon, so the son who is a knowledgeable devotee of the Lord illuminates the entire family.

Commentary: Cāṇakya Paṇḍita makes the same point two verses back, in 3.14. The origin of this famous verse is the *Garuḍa Purāṇa* (1.114.56). As it is said, "Of what use are all the stars when the moon is full?" Similarly, one pure devotee in a family is worth a thousand ordinary members, as seen in the next verse.

Śrīla Prabhupāda emphasized this point from the very beginning of his founding of ISKCON in New York City. Prophetically he lectured on a similar verse (see CN 4.6) on 26 November 1966 while speaking on *Śrī Caitanya-caritāmṛta:*

> Of course, it is not expected that each and every man will become like that. At least ten percent of the population (should) become Kṛṣṇa conscious—there is guarantee, peace in the world. Because *ekaś candra*... We do not require many moons in the sky. Only

9. The source of this verse is a Bengali version of *Cāṇakya-nīti* called *Cāṇakya-śloka.* See Appendix I for more on *Cāṇakya-śloka.* The last two lines of CN 4.9 are almost identical to the first two lines of the verse under discussion.

one moon is sufficient to drive away the darkness. *Varam eko guṇī putro na ca mūrkha-śatair api.* Cāṇakya Paṇḍita says, "It is better to have a qualified son than to have hundreds of fools." So the modern civilization is going on in that way, godless civilization. If some percentage of the civilized human beings become Kṛṣṇa conscious, that will bring forth peace. Otherwise it is not possible. It is therefore a necessity.

ŚLOKA 3.17

किं जातैर्बहुभिः पुत्रैः शोकसन्तापकारकैः ।
वरमेकः कुलालम्बी यत्र विश्राम्यते कुलम् ॥१७॥

kiṁ jātair bahubhiḥ putraiḥ
śoka-santāpa-kārakaiḥ
varam ekaḥ kulālambī
yatra viśrāmyate kulam

Of what use are many sons who only cause grief and vexation? A single son adorned with the qualities of a pure devotee is the support and shelter of his entire family.

Commentary: Cāṇakya Paṇḍita devotes many *ślokas* to the subject of offspring. As Prabhupāda used to admonish, having children means rearing them in Kṛṣṇa consciousness, rather than producing two-legged cats and dogs. Sound *nīti* infers that since sex and procreation are concomitant factors of life, intercourse between a religiously married husband and wife should be used for elevation of the family rather than personal degradation. It is simply a question of how an act is applied. Illicit sex life is the cause of not only personal bondage and destruction, but social ruination as well. Vedic householders through *saṁskāras* and timing can become parents of wanted progeny who carry on their family's traditions.

Cupid is known in the Vedic literatures as Kāmadeva and his wife is called Rati. The Vedic science told in *Rati-śāstra,* a conversation between Lord Śiva and goddess Pārvatī, teaches householders how to calculate the time of union for the production of auspicious progeny. This process, based upon the menstrual cycle of the wife *vis-à-vis* the moon's movements and *prahara* of the day, should be learned by responsible *gṛhasthas* in order to stack the odds in favor of begetting good offspring. Indeed, Lord Kṛṣṇa says, "I am that sex life which does not violate religious principles." (Bg 7.11)

Despite all this, *nīti-śāstra* warns that the appearance of the son marks the beginning of the end of dalliance with the young sweet wife:

> There is no enemy equal to one's own son. First, he steals the attention of the wife. While growing up he plunders his father's wealth. Should he die, then the father's life comes to an end as well. (GP 1.114.60)

ŚLOKA 3.18

लालयेत् पञ्चवर्षाणि दशवर्षाणि ताडयेत् ।
प्राप्ते तु षोडशे वर्षे पुत्रे मित्रवदाचरेत् ॥१८॥

lālayet pañca-varṣāṇi
daśa-varṣāṇi tāḍayet
prāpte tu ṣoḍaśe varṣe
putre mitravad ācaret

Indulge your son up to his fifth year, and strictly discipline him for the next ten years. But when he reaches the age of sixteen, treat him as a friend.

Commentary: Disciplining a very young child is fruitless. When a son passes his teen years, he considers himself too old and wise to take advice. Discipline is meant for the ages of five through sixteen. Even though having children is the duty of a *gṛhastha,* parenthood is a huge responsibility that entails serious risks. This famous instruction, often quoted by Śrīla Prabhupāda, is repeated from the *Garuḍa Purāṇa* (1.114.59). For more on this verse, refer also to CN 2.12.

ŚLOKA 3.19

उपसर्गेऽन्यचक्रे च दुर्भिक्षे च भयावहे ।
असाधुजनसम्पर्के यः पलायेत्स जीवति ॥१९।

upasarge 'nya-cakre ca
durbhikṣe ca bhayāvahe
asādhu-jana-samparke
yaḥ palāyet sa jīvati

He who flees a fearful disaster, a foreign invasion, a terrible famine and the association of nondevotees alone protects his life.

Commentary: The origin of the word "disaster" is very telling. The Latin root *astrum* means "aster" or "star," which comes from the much older Sanskrit *nakṣatra.* Hence "dis-aster" means "under a bad *nakṣatra* or star." The word "influenza" likewise has its origin in astrology since plagues and widespread diseases were understood in ancient Europe to have been caused by the "influence" of the stars. Thus one who can read the foretellings of the stars is able to protect his life before untoward events strike. Line three warns against the association of the *asādhu* (nondevotee) as a danger equaling a great disaster.

ŚLOKA 3.20

धर्मार्थकाममोक्षाणां यस्यैकोऽपि न विद्यते ।
जन्मजन्मनि मर्त्येषु मरणं तस्य केवलम् ॥२०॥

dharmārtha-kāma-mokṣāṇāṁ
yasyaiko 'pi na vidyate

janma-janmani martyeṣu
maraṇaṁ tasya kevalam

He who has not acquired even one of the following: dharma [religious merit], artha [wealth], kāma [satisfaction of sense desires] and mokṣa [liberation] takes birth among other mortals repeatedly and thus is born only to die.

Commentary: Śrīla Prabhupāda often instructed his householder disciples that limited sense gratification (*kāma*) can add pleasure to life, as a pinch of salt adds flavor to the dish. But as too much salt ruins the meal, so overindulgence in the senses utterly spoils the human form of life. An honest devotee in *gṛhastha-āśrama* is better than a false renunciant who dons saffron to live at the expense of others. *Nīti-śāstras* speak in favor of only limited enjoyment during life's second stage or *gṛhastha-āśrama.* The other three orders of life are intended for *tapasya.*

As Cāṇakya Paṇḍita points out in many of his famous *ślokas,* lust is never satisfied. Just as a fire is never pacified with any amount of fuel so there is no end to sense desire. Material pleasures must be controlled, just as a poisonous serpent is defanged by engaging the senses in Kṛṣṇa's service.

Although most people never consider that their death is a possibility, this verse explains that the *karmīs* to the contrary only serve their purpose of existence when it ends with their death. By presenting a false show of happiness and enjoyment during a few short years, unfortunate *karmīs* incinerate in this very life their stock of accumulated *karma-phala.* Once having exhausted their assets (*pūrva-puṇya*), they are recycled back again into lower species of life for millions of years. The fourfold aspects of material existence discussed in this verse—*dharma, artha, kāma, mokṣa*—are considered by many to be the essence of life. However the devotee understands that ultimately each of them must be rejected in favor of Kṛṣṇa consciousness as explained in the *Gītā* (18.66).

ŚLOKA 3.21

मूर्खा यत्र न पूज्यन्ते धान्यं यत्र सुसञ्चितम् ।
दाम्पत्ये कलहो नास्ति तत्र श्रीः स्वयमागता ॥२१॥

mūrkhā yatra na pūjyante
dhānyaṁ yatra su-sañcitam
dāmpatye kalaho nāsti
tatra śrīḥ svayam āgatā

Where fools are never respected, grain is well stored and where the husband and wife do not quarrel—there of her own volition resides Lakṣmī the goddess of fortune.

Commentary: Śrīla Prabhupāda quotes this verse in his commentary on *Śrīmad-Bhāgavatam* (7.11.25). Therein Śrī Nārada instructs King Yudhiṣṭhira:

> To render service to the husband, to be always favorably disposed toward the husband, to be equally well disposed toward the husband's relatives and friends, and to follow thc vows of the husband—these are the four principles to be followed by women described as chaste.

In other words, if women are trained along the principles explained by Nārada in his instruction to Yudhiṣṭhira, then the family will never be sullied by quarrel.

Śrīla Prabhupāda also quotes this verse in his commentary to SB 4.1.6, wherein he adds:

> Where there is no disagreement between husband and wife, all material opulence is present, and good children are born. Generally, according to Vedic civilization, the wife is trained to be satisfied in all conditions, and the husband, according to Vedic instruction, is required to please the wife with sufficient food, ornaments and clothing. Then, if they are satisfied with their mutual dealings, good children are born. In this way the entire world can become peaceful,

> but unfortunately in this age of Kali there are no ideal husbands or wives; therefore unwanted children are produced, and there is no peace and prosperity in the present-day world.

Again, while giving a lecture on *Bhagavad-gītā* 16.10 in Hawaii on February 6, 1975, Śrīla Prabhupāda stated:

> And it is said by Cāṇakya Paṇḍita that if you want worldly happiness, then these things are required, "Don't worship rascals and fools." *Mūrkhā yatra na pūjyante dhānyaṁ yatra su-sañcitam.* "And food grains are properly stocked." That is the Vedic civilization; that you work for three months, not very hard, simply till the ground and sow some food grain seed, and within three months it will grow, and you will have ample food grains, and you'll keep it in stock. And keep some cows."

We may add to the three items listed in this verse a fourth one: "Where Lord Nārāyaṇa or Viṣṇu is worshipped by a pious family…" for goddess Lakṣmījī can never remain without the company of her husband.

Thus Ends Chapter Three

CHAPTER FOUR

ŚLOKA 4.1

आयुः कर्म च वित्तं च विद्या निधनमेव च ।
पञ्चैतानि हि सृज्यन्ते गर्भस्थस्यैव देहिनः ॥१॥

āyuḥ karma ca vittaṁ ca
vidyā nidhanam eva ca
pañcaitāni hi sṛjyante
garbha-sthasyaiva dehinaḥ

These five: life span, type of work, wealth, education, and the time of death are certainly inscribed on the forehead while one is still in the womb.

Commentary: With these words Cāṇakya Paṇḍita re-ignites the age-old debate of fate versus free will. Bṛhaspati looks at it this way:

> One gets that which he is destined to receive and even the *devatās* are unable to stop it. The line of fate cannot be erased. (GP 1.113.31)

Śukrācārya, the exalted son of Bhṛgu and presiding deity of Venus, offers another angle in his *Śukra-nīti:*

> Men who are wise and whose characters deserve praise, greatly respect *pauruṣa* or energetic endeavor. Only weaklings unable to exert themselves worship *daiva* or fate. All that which is achieved

> here in this world is founded upon both fate and work (that is, self-exertion). The latter is divided into two, work of the past lives and this one. (SN 1.48–49)

The concept of a preordained destiny is found throughout *nīti-śāstra.* Bṛhaspati concurs (GP 1.115.23) substituting character for wealth. The *Hitopadeśa* likewise echoes this verse. *Śukra-nīti* states:

> Of course everything in this world is founded upon both fate and self-exertion. The latter of them has two categories: work done in a previous life, and this one. When fate is favorable, even small exertions achieve good results. But when it is unfavorable, even great efforts may prove fruitless. Thus Bali Mahārāja was bound by Varuṇa's weapon despite all his charity, and King Hariścandra experienced a similar fate. (SN 1.57–58)

Śukrācārya continues:

> Benefits accrue out of pious activities. Suffering is a result of sinful activities. So one should know from *śāstra* what is pious and what is sinful and, leaving the sinful, perform only pious deeds. (SN 1.59)

It is interesting to note that Śukrācārya was the spiritual master of the demon Bali, who disobeyed the *guru's* order and became glorious by offering everything to Lord Vāmana.

Paṇḍitas may argue the issue of fate versus free will, but Śrī Kṛṣṇa Himself gives the final instruction:

> Abandon all varieties of religion and just surrender unto Me. I shall deliver you from all sinful reaction. Do not fear. (Bg 18.66)

By taking recourse of the words of Śrīla Prabhupāda we can get a clearer picture of this age-old debate. In *A Transcendental Diary* by Hari Śauri Dāsa (vol. 2, p. 248), Śrīla Prabhupāda dilates upon this debate. A life member from Lusaka, Zambia wrote to Śrīla Prabhupāda whether at the time of a heart transplant the individual soul is replaced with the soul from the donor's heart. Śrīla Prabhupāda replied:

> Life cannot be prolonged by heart transplant. You cannot increase the duration of life. One can perhaps give some relief to the disease, that is another thing, but the duration of life is destined. From the dead body one cannot bring life. Similarly, it may appear that one is prolonging the duration of life by medicines or heart transplant, but that is not the case. If one lives four years after having had a heart transplant, then by nature's law he was destined to live four years with or without having had a heart transplant. So what is the value of a heart transplant? Only by the yogic process can one prolong the life. By stopping the breathing process, keeping in *samādhi,* the breath period is not being misused and he increases the life span. Therefore, destiny can only be changed by devotional service or *yoga.* Otherwise, what you must suffer, you must suffer, and what you must enjoy, you must enjoy. For a devotee, however it may be, he takes the opportunity to chant Hare Kṛṣṇa, and if by Kṛṣṇa's grace destiny is changed, it is all right.

His Bhaktivedanta purport to the *Bhagavad-gītā* 7.9 carries the same theme:

> The duration of man's life is also due to Kṛṣṇa. Therefore by the grace of Kṛṣṇa, man can prolong his life or diminish it. So Kṛṣṇa consciousness is active in every sphere.

Śrīla Prabhupāda spoke on the fragility of this *āyur* (life) in a lecture on *Śrīmad-Bhāgavatam* (7.6.4) delivered in Vṛndāvana on 5 December 1975:

> *Āyur-vyayaḥ param. Āyur-vyayaḥ.* This duration of life, human life—Prahlāda Mahārāja has begun with the words *durlabhaṁ mānuṣaṁ janma*—this life is very, very important, and after many, many births you have got it. So you should always remember that every moment of this life is so important as explained by Cāṇakya Paṇḍita. Anyone can understand. He is not a Kṛṣṇa conscious person, but a moralist. He was the prime minister. He says, *āyuṣaḥ kṣaṇa eko 'pi na labhyaḥ svarṇa-koṭibhiḥ.*[10] Your duration of life… You have got a certain years' duration of life. You cannot live more

10. For more on this verse, see Appendix I.

than that. If you have got your duration of life for fifty years, you can live up to fifty years, not hundred years. These are all destined.

The wise duck flew away when he heard the hunter's rustle in the bushes, while the others of his flock became "sitting ducks." And whatever fate may dictate, the individual must exert personal effort to improve his lot. This is why in Vedic civilization and culture, astrology is used in the timing and planning of events, thereby helping to assure a beneficial outcome. Certainly there is a destiny that each one of us must contend with, as written in our natal stars, and engraved upon the forehead and palms of our hands. Nonetheless, Śukrācārya speaks highly of those "whose characters deserve praise, for honorable are they who create for themselves, for their families and for the world a better life through their own deeds." One's own destiny is a powerful factor in the individual soul's quest for liberation from matter. Still, we are given by God the ability to choose right over wrong, wakefulness over sloth, piety over sin and devotion over atheism. It is for each man to improve his life through using his own intelligence in Kṛṣṇa consciousness and thus spread the benefit of his enlightened association throughout the world. Only a fool sits idly and expects the goddess of fortune to come at his beck and call.

Lord Kṛṣṇa's verdict is final. He instructs Arjuna (Bg 4.20–23) that although work is necessary, attachment to the fruits of one's activities is not. By remaining satisfied with one's lot, all sense of proprietorship is abandoned. Even while engaged in work, the devotee must rise above all dualities, and remain steady in both success and failure. By fixing the mind in transcendence even while endeavoring here on earth, the spiritual platform can be achieved even in this lifetime. Then, in the next life the devotee achieves the kingdom of God.

yasya sarve samārambhāḥ kāma-saṅkalpa-varjitāḥ
jñānāgni-dagdha-karmāṇaṁ tam āhuḥ paṇḍitaṁ budhāḥ

One is understood to be in full knowledge whose every endeavor is devoid of desire for sense gratification. He is said by sages to be a worker for whom the reactions of work have been burned up by the fire of perfect knowledge. (Bg 4.19)

ŚLOKA 4.2

साधुभ्यस्ते निवर्तन्ते पुत्रमित्राणि बान्धवाः ।
ये च तैः सह गन्तारस्तद्धर्मात्सुकृतं कुलम् ॥२॥

sādhubhyas te nivartante
putra-mitrāṇi bāndhavāḥ
ye ca taiḥ saha gantāras
tad-dharmāt sukṛtaṁ kulam

Offspring, friends and relatives usually flee from the sādhu. But his piety benefits the entire family of those who follow him.

Commentary: A true *sādhu* is one whose mind is sharpened through *bhakti-yoga,* constant meditation upon the Supreme Lord Śrī Kṛṣṇa. Yet dull materialists consider *sādhus* to be madmen and therefore they shun them. Since *sādhus* are very rare, even members of their own families cannot understand them at all, leaving the *sādhu* no choice but to renounce them. Apparently things were no different 2500 years ago when Cāṇakya Paṇḍita wrote this verse, as they are now when many members of ISKCON have found no other choice but to bid adieu to unsympathetic relatives. Now, as then, those family members who tag along are glorified. In truth, nothing of value is lost to the family while that which is most precious is gained when a member becomes a devotee.

ŚLOKA 4.3

दर्शनध्यानसंस्पर्शैर्मत्सी कूर्मी च पक्षिणी ।
शिशुं पालयते नित्यं तथा सज्जनसङ्गतिः ॥३॥

darśana-dhyāna-saṁsparśair
matsī kūrmī ca pakṣiṇī
śiśuṁ pālayate nityaṁ
tathā saj-jana-saṅgatiḥ

Through sight, meditation and touch; the fish, tortoise and bird, respectively, bring up their young. In the same way, saintly devotees of the Lord protect their associates.

Commentary: The following example demonstrates the rarity of meeting a pure devotee of the Lord: somewhere in the ocean there is a plank of lumber with a knothole in it. Somewhere swimming beneath the surface of that ocean is a tortoise who surfaces for air once a year. What are the odds of the tortoise's head poking through the knothole? Answer: the same as one has of meeting a pure devotee of the Supreme Lord. Lord Śrī Caitanya Mahāprabhu explained to Rūpa Gosvāmī:

brahmāṇḍa bhramite kona bhāgyavān jīva
guru-kṛṣṇa-prasāde pāya bhakti-latā-bīja

> One wanders in all directions of the universe until by the grace of Lord Kṛṣṇa he meets his *guru,* who plants the seed of devotional service. (Cc 2.19.151)

Since the pure devotee offers loving support and shelter to his disciples in a myriad of ways, the sincere disciple must reciprocate through rendering constant loving service for the satisfaction of the *guru.* This is the only means by which transcendental knowledge is transmitted. As Śrī Kṛṣṇa instructs Arjuna:

> Just try to learn the truth by approaching a spiritual master. Inquire from him submissively and render service unto him. The self-realized soul can impart knowledge unto you because he has seen the truth. (Bg 4.34)

Jñāninas tattva-darśinaḥ: "Seers of the Absolute Truth alone are wise." The exalted platform of Kṛṣṇa consciousness rests solely upon attaining the shelter of the Lord's pure devotee. For the disciple who is serious about going back to home back to Godhead, there is no other alternative but service at the feet of Lord Kṛṣṇa's representative.

ŚLOKA 4.4

यावत्स्वस्थो ह्ययं देहो यावन्मृत्युश्च दूरतः ।
तावदात्महितं कुर्यात्प्राणान्ते किं करिष्यति ॥४॥

yāvat svastho hy ayaṁ deho
yāvan mṛtyuś ca dūrataḥ
tāvad ātma-hitaṁ kuryāt
prāṇānte kiṁ kariṣyati

As long as your body is healthy and under control—and death is distant—try to save your eternal soul through Kṛṣṇa consciousness. What can be done at your final moment of life?

Commentary: The inevitable moment of death—or rather, that time when the soul exits the physical frame—is most unpleasant. Who looks forward to death, except with a sense of fear and dread? We have heard many travelers brag about their upcoming foreign vacation, but who boasts about his unavoidable journey at the time of death—and his transfer to the next womb?

Cāṇakya Paṇḍita's advice is essentially the same instruction that the pilgrim Vidura offered King Dhṛtarāṣṭra:

> You have been blind from your very birth, and recently you have become hard of hearing. Your memory is shortened, and your intelligence is disturbed. Your teeth are loose, your liver is defective and you are coughing up mucus. Alas, how powerful are the hopes of a living being to continue his life. Verily, you are living just like a household dog and are eating the remnants of food given by Bhīma. There is no need to live a degraded life and subsist on the charity of those whom you tried to kill … (SB 1.13.22–24)

Though certainly lacking etiquette, Vidura's words were meant for the elevation of King Dhṛtarāṣṭra. Vidura sought to awaken the king from his situation as an envious family man—a *gṛhamedhī*—even as death was knocking at his door.

If the mind is trained through meditation upon the holy name of God, then final transition to the spiritual world can be achieved upon exiting this body. The holy name of God can save even the greatest sinner, as it did the vile Ajāmila who called out for his son Nārāyaṇa and was thereby "accidentally" liberated, as described in *Śrīmad-Bhāgavatam* (6.1). Ajāmila was lucky but as far as we are concerned, we should not take chances. Through daily practice of *japa,* as recommended by Cāṇakya Paṇḍita in verse 3.11, the mind becomes gradually trained and prepared for that inevitable final moment during which our fate will be either sealed or dissolved. Kṛṣṇa says *yajñānāṁ japa-yajño 'smi,* "Of sacrifices I am chanting the holy names." (Bg 10.25) All that we do in this life is meant to prepare us for our final breath. By the grace of the spiritual master that breath will be offered to Kṛṣṇa.

The afterlife of the envious *gṛhamedhī* who dies in ignorance is also described in *Śrīmad-Bhāgavatam.* Therein Lord Kapila tells His mother Devahūti:

> In a diseased condition one's eyes bulge due to the presence of air from within, and his glands become congested with mucus. He has difficulty breathing, and upon exhaling and inhaling he produces a sound like '*ghura-ghura,*' a rattling within the throat. In this way he comes under the clutches of death and lies down, surrounded by lamenting friends and relatives, and although he wants to speak to them, he no longer can because he is under the control of time. Thus the man, who engages with uncontrolled senses in maintaining a family, dies in great grief, seeing his relatives crying. He dies most pathetically, in great pain and without consciousness. At death he sees the Yamadūtas come before him, their eyes full of wrath, and in great fear he passes stool and urine. As a criminal is arrested for punishment by the constables of the state, a person engaged in

> criminal sense gratification is similarly arrested by the Yamadūtas, who bind him by the neck with a strong rope and cover his subtle body so that he may undergo severe punishment. While carried by the constables of Lord Yamarāja, he is overwhelmed and trembles in their hands. While passing on the road he is bitten by dogs, and he can remember the sinful activities of his life. He is thus terribly distressed. (SB 3.30.16–23)

Subsequently the sinful *gṛhamedhī* is tortured in a series of hells, some of which are described in the Fifth Canto of the *Bhāgavatam,* for a long period of time. Afterwards, he is born in some lower species of life wherein the opportunity to become Kṛṣṇa conscious is not an option. Thus Cāṇakya Paṇḍita, like Śrīla Prabhupāda, herewith advises us to carefully consider our own options, for eternal destiny is being decided through our choices here and now.

ŚLOKA 4.5

कामधेनुगुणा विद्या ह्यकाले फलदायिनी ।
प्रवासे मातृसदृशी विद्या गुप्तं धनं स्मृतम् ॥५॥

kāmadhenu-guṇā vidyā
hy akāle phala-dāyinī
pravāse mātṛ-sadṛśī
vidyā guptaṁ dhanaṁ smṛtam

Learning is like the sacred kāmadhenu, the wish-fulfilling cow; for, like her, it yields in all seasons. When away from home it nourishes like a mother. Therefore, learning is a hidden treasure.

Commentary: The Vedic scriptures are the reservoirs of true knowledge and are our only life boat across this terrible ocean of Kali-yuga. Śukrācārya states:

> He who lives according to the precepts of the *śāstras* speaks with the voice of God. (SN 4.5.27)

As per the instructions of this verse, the wanderer who knows the *śāstras* will never be alone for he has a ready store of what Cāṇakya Paṇḍita calls *guptaṁ dhanam,* secret wealth, which can never be taken away.

ŚLOKA 4.6

एकोऽपि गुणवान्पुत्रो निर्गुणेन शतेन किम् ।
एकश्चन्द्रस्तमो हन्ति न च तारा: सहस्रश: ॥६॥

eko 'pi guṇavān putro
nirguṇena śatena kim
ekaś candras tamo hanti
na ca tārāḥ sahasraśaḥ

A single son endowed with good qualities is far better than a hundred devoid of them. Candra [the moon] though one, dispels the darkness, which the stars, though numerous, cannot.

Commentary: This verse echoes the instruction of CN 3.17. As recorded in *A Transcendental Diary* (vol. 2, p. 69), this was one of Śrīla Prabhupāda's favoritc *ślokas.* Hc addcd, "Wc should bc quality devotee, not quantity devotee."

Śrīla Prabhupāda spoke on this point in Hyderabad on 12 April 1975. In a conversation with guests he quoted a different version of this verse, but with an identical meaning:

> So we are trying to preach this philosophy in that way. Maybe, (we are) very small (in) number, but ... if there is one moon, that is sufficient. What is the use of millions of stars twinkling? So that is our propaganda. If one man can understand what Kṛṣṇa philosophy is, then my preaching is successful, that's all. We don't want many millions of stars with no light. What is the use of millions of stars with no light? That is Cāṇakya Paṇḍita's advice, *varam eko guṇī putro na ca mūrkha-śatair api.* One son, if he is learned, that is sufficient. What is the use of hundreds of sons, all fools and rascals? *Ekaś*

> *candras tamo hanti na ca tārāḥ sahasraśaḥ.* One moon is sufficient to illuminate. There is no need of millions of stars. Similarly, we are not after many millions of disciples. I want to see that one disciple has understood Kṛṣṇa's philosophy. That is success. That's all.

Regarding the rare gift of a worthy son, there is an episode narrated in *Śrīmad-Bhāgavatam* (Canto Twelve, chapters 8–10), about the sage Mṛkaṇḍu. Mṛkaṇḍu Ṛṣi performed rigorous penance to obtain a boon from Lord Śiva. Eventually the all-auspicious Śiva appeared before Mṛkaṇḍu, and offered him an unusual choice. Would the sage prefer a long-lived son of average qualities or a short-lived son of exceptional merit? Mṛkaṇḍu chose the latter, and his wife soon gave birth to the famous Mārkaṇḍeya Ṛṣi, destined to live a mere sixteen years.

Mārkaṇḍeya, the "son of Mṛkaṇḍu," grew to become a celebrated master of *yoga.* He was a constant source of joy to his parents. On his sixteenth birthday, while the young ascetic was worshipping Lord Śiva, Lord Yamarāja appeared before him, intent on transferring him to the next world. Suddenly, an angry Lord Śiva appeared from the *śiva-liṅga* and gave Yamarāja a very hard kick to his chest. Śiva blessed Mārkaṇḍeya with a long life, adding that he would retain his youthful comeliness throughout his life. Mārkaṇḍeya is still famous as the sage whose devotion defeated death. A true credit to his parents, his deeds are also sung in the *Mahābhārata* wherein he instructs the Pāṇḍavas in the *Mārkaṇḍeya-samasyā-parva.*

ŚLOKA 4.7

मूर्खश्चिरायुर्जातोऽपि तस्माज्जातमृतो वरः ।
मृतः स चाल्पदुःखाय यावज्जीवं जडो दहेत् ॥७॥

mūrkhaś cirāyur jāto 'pi
tasmāj jāta-mṛto varaḥ
mṛtaḥ sa cālpa-duḥkhāya
yāvaj jīvaṁ jaḍo dahet

A still-born son is superior to a foolish son endowed with a long life. The first causes grief for but a moment, while the latter like a blazing fire consumes his parents for life.

Commentary: Harsh terms sometimes used in the *śāstras* such as *mūrkha* (fool) are meant to guide us, and we should not be offended by such strong language. Kṛṣṇa Himself frankly discusses foolish persons in the *Bhagavad-gītā:*

na māṁ duṣkṛtino mūḍhāḥ prapadyante narādhamāḥ
māyayāpahṛta-jñānā āsuraṁ bhāvam āśritāḥ

Those foolish miscreants (*duṣkṛtī*) who are of the nature of asses (*mūḍha*), who are the lowest of mankind (*narādhama*), whose knowledge is stolen by illusion (*māyayāpahṛta-jñāna*), and who partake in the atheistic nature of demons (*āsuraṁ bhāvam āśritāḥ*) do not surrender unto Me. (Bg 7.15)

Just as the strong language of the parent is for the guidance of the child, so the *śāstras* are meant for our correction and upliftment. They were not written to flatter the reader and thereby clear their way to hell.

ŚLOKA 4.8

कुग्रामवासः कुलहीनसेवा
कुभोजनं क्रोधमुखी च भार्या ।
पुत्रश्च मूर्खो विधवा च कन्या
विनाग्निना षट् प्रदहन्ति कायम् ॥८॥

kugrāma-vāsaḥ kula-hīna-sevā
kubhojanaṁ krodha-mukhī ca bhāryā
putraś ca mūrkho vidhavā ca kanyā
vināgninā ṣaṭ pradahanti kāyam

Residence in a village of low-class people, service to the lowborn, unwholesome food, a frowning wife, a fool for a son and a widowed daughter: these six burn without fire.

Commentary: Bṛhaspati adds to the list:

kāntā-viyogaḥ svajanāpamānam
ṛṇasya śeṣaḥ kujanasya sevā
dāridrya-bhāvād vimukhaṁ ca mitraṁ
vināgninā pañca dahanti tīvrāḥ

> These five burn without fire: separation from one's wife, a kinsman's insult, unpaid debts, service to a crude boss, and desertion of friends in poverty. (GP 1.115.18)

For that husband whose wife is obliging and cooperative, separation from her burns like fire. For the man whose wife is argumentative and always expresses her dissatisfaction by contorting her features, her association burns like fire. Cāṇakya Paṇḍita calls the latter type here with the words *krodha-mukhī ca bhāryā,* "angry-faced wife." In verse 2.14 Cāṇakya repeats the last line almost verbatim: *vināgninā te pradahanti kāyam.*

In this world the man with a devotee wife is truly lucky because he has Vaikuṇṭha in his own home. The unfortunate householder condemned to live with a shrew should consider entering the next *āśrama,* or *vānaprastha,* and the opportunity to associate with devotees.

ŚLOKA 4.9

किं तया क्रियते धेन्वा या न दोग्ध्री न गर्भिणी ।
कोऽर्थः पुत्रेण जातेन यो न विद्वान्न भक्तिमान् ॥९॥

kiṁ tayā kriyate dhenvā
yā na dogdhrī na garbhiṇī

ko 'rthaḥ putreṇa jātena
yo na vidvān na bhaktimān

What good is a cow that neither gives milk nor conceives? What is the use of a son who neither becomes a vidvān [scholar] nor a bhakta [devotee]?[11]

Commentary: A cow is far better company than an unlettered fool or an atheist. If the son is a fool, then life is truly painful. Note that here Cāṇakya Paṇḍita draws a distinction between a scholar and a devotee. The *bhakta* is mentioned last (as the final word). Naturally, parents are proud of a learned son or daughter. But only a devotee child can return the gifts of the parents with eternal liberation, as Śrī Prahlāda did for countless family members including Hiraṇyakaśipu.

ŚLOKA 4.10

संसारतापदग्धानां त्रयो विश्रान्तिहेतवः ।
अपत्यं च कलत्रं च सतां सङ्गतिरेव च ॥१०॥

saṁsāra-tāpa-dagdhānāṁ
trayo viśrānti-hetavaḥ
apatyaṁ ca kalatraṁ ca
satāṁ saṅgatir eva ca

He who is scorched by the miseries of material life attains peaceful shelter in the company of these three: his offspring, his wife and the transcendental company of the devotees of the Lord.

Commentary: The household of a devotee should be centered around the service and worship of Śrī Śrī Rādhā-Kṛṣṇa as the transcendental shelter from the turbulent ocean of the *karmī* world swirling just beyond his doorstep. Śrīla Prabhupāda created the International Society for Kṛṣṇa Consciousness specifically to fulfill the purport of

11. See Appendix I (Purport: *Śrīmad-Bhāgavatam* 6.11.4) for a similar verse.

this verse's last line: to provide a place for *sat-saṅga.* Just as small sparks combined create a great fire so when many devotees gather the fire of devotion burns away all material ignorance. All *śāstras* are clear on this point of *sādhu-saṅga.*

ŚLOKA 4.11

सकृज्जल्पन्ति राजानः सकृज्जल्पन्ति पण्डिताः ।
सकृत्कन्याः प्रदीयन्ते त्रीण्येतानि सकृत्सकृत् ॥११॥

sakṛj jalpanti rājānaḥ
sakṛj jalpanti paṇḍitāḥ
sakṛt kanyāḥ pradīyante
trīṇy etāni sakṛt sakṛt

Kings speak their demands once, paṇḍitas offer their opinions once and the daughter is given in marriage once. These three occur once and once only.

Commentary: The situation of marriage in Western society reflects a diametrically opposite point of view than the one described in this verse. So frustrated are modern men and women that many seek out hundreds if not thousands of sexual partners, inviting fell diseases, in a hopeless search for happiness. Frustration only increases after each affair because real happiness remains elusive while the goal of life is never comprehended. Many mistakenly think that promiscuity will eventually land them with the right partner. Rather than leading to peace and satisfaction, illicit sex invariably causes misery, mental derangement, physical debility, unwanted population, crime and deadly epidemics.

Regarding a *paṇḍita's* prerogative of offering his opinion once, if Śrīla Prabhupāda was excessively questioned on a certain point, he would often declare, "I have told you my instruction, now you do as you like."

ŚLOKA 4.12

एकाकिना तपो द्वाभ्यां पठनं गायनं त्रिभिः ।
चतुर्भिर्गमनं क्षेत्रं पञ्चभिर्बहुभी रणः ॥१२॥

ekākinā tapo dvābhyāṁ
paṭhanaṁ gāyanaṁ tribhiḥ
caturbhir gamanaṁ kṣetraṁ
pañcabhir bahubhī raṇaḥ

Penance should be practiced alone, study by two, singing by three, travel by four, agriculture by five, but battle by as many as possible.

ŚLOKA 4.13

सा भार्या या शुचिर्दक्षा सा भार्या या पतिव्रता ।
सा भार्या या पतिप्रीता सा भार्या सत्यवादिनी ॥१३॥

sā bhāryā yā śucir dakṣā
sā bhāryā yā pati-vratā
sā bhāryā yā pati-prītā
sā bhāryā satya-vādinī

She is the true wife who is clean and expert, she is a wife who is devoted to her husband, she is a wife who lives to please her husband, and she is a wife who speaks the truth.

Commentary: *Śukra-nīti* (4.4.6–30) and *Manu-saṁhitā* (5.147–166) describe the qualities and duties of the chaste wife. Each one of us must serve according to our own particular duty. Homemaking duties may appear outdated and old-fashioned to women displaying their bodies at swimming pools, or fighting in divorce court for control of their husbands' assets. Yet if śāstric codes are obsolete in modern society, why then are families not happier today? We leave it to the pensive amongst us to decide whether independence and anarchy, with evenings spent huddled around a radioactive television, are superior to dutiful service and devotion.

Bṛhaspati says:

> That man who has a wife endowed with the following qualities is no ordinary man, indeed he is no less than Indra, the king of heaven and husband of Śacī: His wife bathes daily, applies sweet scents to her body, speaks sweetly, is satisfied with a moderate meal, is not garrulous, has always auspicious things around her, is scrupulous in virtuous activities, exhibits her love and devotion to her husband in every action and is pleased to surrender herself to him after her period. Such an auspicious and chaste wife enhances the good luck all around her. She is truly beloved of her husband. (GP 1.108.19–21)

Again, Bṛhaspati states:

> If your wife desires your heart, if she is attractive, well dressed and delightful and if you live in your own house—then you have achieved heaven which is obtained only through pious deeds performed in the previous birth. (GP 1.109.44)

> These five uproot miseries: an obedient son, putting learning to use, freedom from sickness, association with saintly people, and the companionship of a good wife surrendering herself. (GP 1.115.20)

Manu, the lawgiver of society, agrees:

> Not by observing fasts or vows does a woman become exalted. If she obeys her husband alone, she becomes exalted in heaven. (MS 5.155)

Further:

> A wife will naturally feel disgusted with a husband who is cruel, barbarous, severe, always away, impoverished, in ill-health, attached to other women or always in the company of his friends. Men should avoid these defects and treat their wives properly. (SN 3.22–23)

Scriptures often give various points of view, as we see from the following instructions of Lord Kapiladeva:

> A living entity, who as a result of attachment to a woman in the previous life, has been endowed with the form of a woman, foolishly looks upon *māyā* in the form of a man, her husband, as the bestower of wealth, progeny, house and other material assets. A woman, therefore, should consider her husband, her house and her children to be the arrangement of the external energy of the Lord for her death, just as the sweet singing of the hunter is death for the deer. (SB 3.31.41–42)

Cāṇakya Paṇḍita discusses the opposite type of wife—the Xanthippe or shrew—in 16.2.

ŚLOKA 4.14

अपुत्रस्य गृहं शून्यं दिशः शून्यास्त्वबान्धवाः ।
मूर्खस्य हृदयं शून्यं सर्वशून्या दरिद्रता ॥१४॥

aputrasya gṛhaṁ śūnyaṁ
diśaḥ śūnyās tv abāndhavāḥ
mūrkhasya hṛdayaṁ śūnyaṁ
sarva-śūnyā daridratā

Without a son the household is void; all directions are void to him who is without relatives; the heart of a fool is also void. But all is void to a poor man.

Commentary: Śrīla Prabhupāda quotes this verse while explaining the *Śrīmad-Bhāgavatam* verse (4.13.31):

> The purpose of marrying is to beget a son, because a son is necessary to deliver his father and forefathers from any hellish condition of life in which they may be. Cāṇakya Paṇḍita therefore says, *putra-hīnaṁ gṛhaṁ śūnyam:* without a son, married life is simply abominable … It is concluded that if a person does not get a son it is due to his past sinful life.

Notice that Śrīla Prabhupāda has quoted another slightly different Sanskrit version, although the meaning is identical.

The concept of void (*śūnya*) is discussed although there is actually no such thing as a void anywhere in the creation. Since everything everywhere is God's energy, wherever one ventures, something must be there. Thus the concept of void is herewith given figuratively and not in the atheistic or Buddhistic sense of merging oneself into some imagined nothingness. Family, society and a means of generating wealth are essential for almost all who live in this material world, the exception being the *paramahaṁsa,* or fully self-realized devotee who relies on the Lord alone. As it is said, there are two happy classes in this material world: pigs and *paramahaṁsas.*

Indeed only a very few rare souls are bold enough to throw fate to the wind and renounce material affection. *Sannyāsa-āśrama* is for those who are committed to depend entirely upon God's will. It is impossible to totally renounce desires; our feelings must be dovetailed in Kṛṣṇa consciousness. Searching after that which does not exist is fruitless. Achieving the object of desire without thankfulness to God is no solution. One can live comfortably here while aspiring to attain the hereafter, providing he remembers the divine benefactor at every step. One need neither feign renunciation nor hanker after limitless wealth, but he should always be satisfied with his lot. It is better to be grateful to the Lord for whatever gifts He has been kind enough to bless us with. Life here is fragile and tenuous. Whatever we consider ours will be lost when the body is lost. True happiness, or freedom from the analogous void of forgetfulness of our original position, will only be found by the surrendered devotee.

As far as the last line is concerned, *nīti-śāstra* emphasizes the necessity of sufficient wealth because without means one will be shunned in all circles. Money is required for the married devotee not for the sake of becoming materially attached but as a means to run a dignified and spiritually-oriented household.

ŚLOKA 4.15

अनभ्यासे विषं शास्त्रमजीर्णे भोजनं विषम् ।
दरिद्रस्य विषं गोष्ठी वृद्धस्य तरुणी विषम् ॥१५॥

anabhyāse viṣaṁ śāstram
ajīrṇe bhojanaṁ viṣam
daridrasya viṣaṁ goṣṭhī
vṛddhasya taruṇī viṣam

Scriptural lessons not put into practice are poison. For someone who suffers from indigestion, food is poison. To a poor man, a social function is poison. But for an old man, a young woman is poison.

Commentary: Which aspect of material life is not poison? The only means of counteracting this poison is applied Kṛṣṇa consciousness, serving the Supreme Lord in our daily lives under the guidance of Śrī Guru. That will put every scriptural instruction into practical application. That which is studied must be practiced or it is no learning at all.

ŚLOKA 4.16

त्यजेद्धर्मं दयाहीनं विद्याहीनं गुरुं त्यजेत् ।
त्यजेत्क्रोधमुखीं भार्यां निःस्नेहान् बान्धवांस्त्यजेत् ॥१६॥

tyajed dharmaṁ dayā-hīnaṁ
vidyā-hīnaṁ guruṁ tyajet
tyajet krodha-mukhīṁ bhāryāṁ
niḥsnehān bāndhavāṁs tyajet

Abandon that religion in which no mercy is found. That guru who is lacking in learning must be forsaken. Reject also the frowning wife and relatives who have no affection.

Commentary: Cāṇakya Paṇḍita advises that the so-called religion described here as *dayā-hīnam* or "void of mercy," must be rejected wholesale. Undoubtedly, this description includes all of the many "beliefs" or "faiths" that sanction devouring innocent animals.

There are many poseur *gurus* who charm the public with wise-sounding truisms, "magical" sleight of hand, offers of becoming God or simply by giving free hugs. But can such *vidyā-hīna gurus* lead the aspirant to Kṛṣṇa consciousness? That Māyāvādī who has no understanding of the Supreme Personality of Godhead must be rejected as a *guru* even if he appears to be learned in many *śāstras.*

As in 4.8, Cāṇakya again brings up the subject of the *krodha-mukhī bhāryā* (the sneering wife). Śrīla Prabhupāda quotes the following verse from *Cāṇakya-śloka* in several places (SB 4.26.15, 6.14.40, 9.4.29):

> *mātā yasya gṛhe nāsti   bhāryā cāpriya-vādinī*
> *araṇyaṁ tena gantavyaṁ   yathāraṇyaṁ tathā gṛham*

> A person who has no mother at home and whose wife is not agreeable with him should immediately renounce his family life and go away to the forest. For such a person, living at home and living in the forest are equal.[12]

This rare gift of the human form of life is meant for spiritual advancement only, and one's wife must be helpful in the endeavor of serving the Lord as a family unit. Without cooperation from one's wife there is no need of household life and one may make plans to become a *vānaprastha* or *sannyāsī.* This example was also set by Śrīla Prabhupāda who before renouncing the world asked his former wife, "Would you prefer tea or me?" She replied that she preferred tea, and with that her husband soon set out for Vṛndāvana never to return.

He writes in his purport to *Śrīmad-Bhāgavatam* 9.14.36:

12. See Appendix I, Lecture: *Śrīmad-Bhāgavatam* 1.16.21.

> Kṛṣṇa conscious *gṛhasthas* must be very careful of the sly fox woman. If the wife at home is obedient and follows her husband in Kṛṣṇa consciousness, the home is welcome. Otherwise one should give up one's home and go to the forest.

However, the great *ācārya* adds this caveat:

> When one is elevated to the platform of Kṛṣṇa consciousness, whether one is a man, woman or whatever, everyone is equal.

He also points out that if a husband does not care for his wife properly, treating her like a maidservant, she, too, is better off vacating her home in favor of the forest. (SB 6.14.40, purport)

Ultimately a devotee must reject all that is unfavorable for spiritual life and embrace whatever enhances transcendence. Śrīla Prabhupāda summarizes this with two rules: (1) always remember Kṛṣṇa, and (2) never forget Him.

ŚLOKA 4.17

अध्वा जरा देहवतां पर्वतानां जलं जरा।
असंभोगो जरा स्त्रीणां वाक्शल्यं मनसो जरा ॥१७॥

adhvā jarā dehavatāṁ
parvatānāṁ jalaṁ jarā
asaṁbhogo jarā strīṇāṁ
vāk-śalyaṁ manaso jarā

Constant traveling invites old age for the body, a hill is worn away by running water, lack of intimacy makes a young wife prematurely old and one's mind becomes weary after hearing scathing words.

Commentary: In another version of *Cāṇakya-nīti,* line three reads *amaithunaṁ jarā strīnām,* but the meaning is the same. That householder who imagines himself to be a *brahmacārī* and thereby neglects his family is guilty of failing to execute the duties of his *āśrama*. Artificial renunciation brings no success. *Śukra-nīti* advises:

> Just as the child becomes docile through feeding and caressing, so also does the wife. (SN 3.263)

The other version of this verse also mentions that a horse that is tied too much and garments left out in the sun become prematurely old (*vājināṁ bandhanaṁ jarā, vastrāṇām ātapaṁ jarā*). Regarding conversation, devotees naturally delight in endless Kṛṣṇa-*kathā* but they cannot tolerate a moment of mundane chit chat.

ŚLOKA 4.18

कः कालः कानि मित्राणि को देशः कौ व्ययागमौ ।
कस्याहं का च मे शक्तिरिति चिन्त्यं मुहुर्मुहुः ॥१८॥

kaḥ kālaḥ kāni mitrāṇi
ko deśaḥ kau vyayāgamau
kasyāhaṁ kā ca me śaktir
iti cintyaṁ muhur muhuḥ

What is my situation in time? What of my friends—who are they? And this country—what of it? What is my means of earning money? Under whose superior power must I serve? What power do I possess? Think hard over these time and again.

Commentary: A small practical advice: Cāṇakya Paṇḍita advises that no man should consider himself so high and mighty that a little solitary self-assessment (which should also include appraising his spiritual assets) is not called for.

ŚLOKA 4.19

अग्निर्देवो द्विजातीनां मुनीनां हृदि दैवतम् ।
प्रतिमा स्वल्पबुद्धीनां सर्वत्र समदर्शिनाम् ॥१९॥

agnir devo dvijātīnāṁ
munīnāṁ hṛdi daivatam
pratimā svalpa-buddhīnāṁ
sarvatra sama-darśinām

Twice-born brāhmaṇas see Agni, the fire god, as the representative of God. The thoughtful munis see the Personality of Godhead as residing in their own hearts (and in the hearts of all creatures). People of average intelligence see God only in temples, but those of equal vision see Him everywhere.

Commentary: Fire can never be contaminated because it is a representative of God. As stated in *Śrīmad-Bhāgavatam* (3.14.9), *iṣṭvāgni-jihvaṁ payasā puruṣaṁ yajuṣāṁ patim.* Yajñapati, the Supreme Lord, is worshipped through the fire god Agni who represents His tongue (*jihvā*). Śrīla Prabhupāda comments on this verse:

> Fire is considered to be the tongue of the Personality of Godhead Viṣṇu, and oblations of grains and clarified butter offered to the fire are thus accepted by Him. That is the principle of all sacrifices, of which Lord Viṣṇu is the master. In other words, the satisfaction of Lord Viṣṇu includes the satisfaction of all demigods and other living beings.

Men of average intelligence, described by Cāṇakya Paṇḍita here as *alpa-buddhi,* believe that God resides only in His temples. As stated in the *Bhagavad-gītā, paṇḍitāḥ sama-darśinaḥ:* the true *paṇḍita* sees all with equal vision. (Bg 5.18) Śrīla Prabhupāda used to quote his own Guru Mahārāja:

Rather than trying to see Kṛṣṇa, act in a way that He will want to see you.

Thus Ends Chapter Four

CHAPTER FIVE

ŚLOKA 5.1

गुरुरग्निर्द्विजातीनां वर्णानां ब्राह्मणो गुरुः ।
पतिरेव गुरुः स्त्रीणां सर्वस्याभ्यागतो गुरुः ॥१॥

gurur agnir dvijātīnāṁ
varṇānāṁ brāhmaṇo guruḥ
patir eva guruḥ strīṇāṁ
sarvasyābhyāgato guruḥ

Agni is the guru of the twice-born. The brāhmaṇa is the guru of the other castes. The husband is the guru of his wife. Yet the guest is the guru of all.

Commentary: For millennia India has celebrated a tradition of *atithi devo bhava,* "the guest is God." Ancient Christians felt likewise: "Be hospitable to the stranger for many have served angels thereby." (*Bible, Hebrews* 13.2) Of the *dvija,* literally "twice-born," Jesus Christ also taught this concept when he preached, "You must be born again." The first birth is the material one, and the second birth is initiation by the bona fide spiritual master. Upon acceptance by the spiritual master, the student is awarded the sacred thread as a mark of his rebirth in spirit by the grace of Śrī Guru. Regarding a husband becoming the *guru* of his wife, Śrīla Prabhupāda noted that marriage is not a *carte* *blanche* for having a free servant. Unless a man can responsibly offer his wife and offspring the knowledge that leads to liberation, or Kṛṣṇa consciousness, he becomes their enemy, not *guru.*

That advanced devotees of ISKCON must become responsible *gurus* has been the subject of much heated debate, just as when Śrīla Prabhupāda created the first *brāhmaṇas* and *sannyāsīs* in the West. In his purport to *Caitanya-caritāmṛta* 2.8.128 Śrīla Prabhupāda writes:

> Actually the *brāhmaṇa* is supposed to be the spiritual master of all other *varṇas,* or classes, but as far as Kṛṣṇa consciousness is concerned, everyone is capable of becoming a spiritual master because knowledge in Kṛṣṇa consciousness is on the platform of the spirit soul. To spread Kṛṣṇa consciousness, one need only be cognizant of the science of the spirit soul. It does not matter whether one is a *brāhmaṇa, kṣatriya, vaiśya, śūdra, sannyāsī, gṛhastha* or whatever. If one simply understands this science, he can become a spiritual master.
>
> It is stated in the *Hari-bhakti-vilāsa* that one should not accept initiation from a person who is not in the brahminical order if there is a fit person in the brahminical order present. This instruction is meant for those who are overly dependent on the mundane social order and is suitable for those who want to remain in mundane life. If one understands the truth of Kṛṣṇa consciousness and seriously desires to attain transcendental knowledge for the perfection of life, he can accept a spiritual master from any social status, provided the spiritual master is fully conversant with the science of Kṛṣṇa. Śrīla Bhaktisiddhānta Sārasvatī Ṭhākura also states that although one is situated as a *brāhmaṇa, kṣatriya, vaiśya, śūdra, brahmacārī, vānaprastha, gṛhastha* or *sannyāsī,* if he is conversant in the science of Kṛṣṇa he can become a spiritual master as *vartma-pradarśaka-guru, dīkṣā-guru* or *śikṣā-guru.* The spiritual master who first gives information about spiritual life is called the *vartma-pradarśaka-guru,* the spiritual master who initiates according to the regulations of the *śāstras* is called the *dīkṣā-guru,* and the spiritual master who gives instructions for elevation is called the *śikṣā-guru.* Factually the qualifications of a spiritual master depend on his knowledge of

the science of Kṛṣṇa. It does not matter whether he is a *brāhmaṇa, kṣatriya, sannyāsī* or *śūdra.* This injunction given by Śrī Caitanya Mahāprabhu is not at all against the injunctions of the *śāstras.* In the *Padma Purāṇa* it is said:

na śūdrāḥ bhagavad-bhaktās te 'pi bhāgavatottamāḥ
sarva-varṇeṣu te śūdrā ye na bhaktā janārdane

One who is actually advanced in spiritual knowledge of Kṛṣṇa is never a *śūdra,* even though he may have been born in a *śūdra* family. However, even if a *vipra,* or *brāhmaṇa,* is very expert in the six brahminical activities (*paṭhana, pāṭhana, yajana, yājana, dāna, pratigraha*) and is also well versed in the Vedic hymns, he cannot become a spiritual master unless he is a Vaiṣṇava. But if one is born in the family of *caṇḍālas* yet is well-versed in Kṛṣṇa consciousness, he can become a *guru.* These are the śāstric injunctions, and strictly following these injunctions, Śrī Caitanya Mahāprabhu, as a *gṛhastha* named Śrī Viśvambhara, was initiated by a *sannyāsī-guru* named Īśvara Purī. Similarly, Śrī Nityānanda Prabhu was initiated by Mādhavendra Purī, a *sannyāsī.* According to others, however, He was initiated by Lakṣmīpati Tīrtha. Advaita Ācārya, although a *gṛhastha,* was initiated by Mādhavendra Purī, and many devotees born in caste *brāhmaṇa* familes were initiated by Śrī Rasikānanda (a disciple of Śrī Śyāmānanda Prabhu), although Rasikānanda was not born in a *brāhmaṇa* family. There are many instances in which a born *brāhmaṇa* took initiation from a person who was not born in a *brāhmaṇa* family. The brahminical symptoms are explained in *Śrīmad-Bhāgavatam* (7.11.35), wherein it is stated:

yasya yal-lakṣaṇaṁ proktaṁ puṁso varṇābhivyañjakam
yad anyatrāpi dṛśyeta tat tenaiva vinirdiśet

If a person is born in a *śūdra* family but has all the qualities of a spiritual master, he should be accepted not only as a *brāhmaṇa* but as a qualified spiritual master also. This is also the instruction of Śrī Caitanya Mahāprabhu. Śrīla Bhaktisiddhānta Sārasvatī Ṭhākura therefore introduced the sacred thread ceremony for all Vaiṣṇavas according to the rules and regulations.

Sometimes a Vaiṣṇava who is a *bhajanānandī* does not take the *sāvitra-saṁskāra* (sacred thread initiation), but this does not mean that this system should be used for preaching work. There are two kinds of Vaiṣṇavas—*bhajanānandī* and *goṣṭhy-ānandī.* A *bhajanānandī* is not interested in preaching work, but a *goṣṭhy-ānandī* is interested in spreading Kṛṣṇa consciousness to benefit the people and increase the number of Vaiṣṇavas. A Vaiṣṇava is understood to be above the position of a *brāhmaṇa.* As a preacher, he should be recognized as a *brāhmaṇa;* otherwise there may be a misunderstanding of his position as a Vaiṣṇava. However, a Vaiṣṇava *brāhmaṇa* is not selected on the basis of his birth but according to his qualities. Unfortunately, those who are unintelligent do not know the difference between a *brāhmaṇa* and a Vaiṣṇava. They are under the impression that unless one is a *brāhmaṇa* he cannot be a spiritual master. For this reason only, Śrī Caitanya Mahāprabhu makes the statement in this verse (Cc 2.8.128):

kibā vipra, kibā nyāsī, śūdra kene naya
yei kṛṣṇa-tattva-vettā, sei 'guru' haya

If one becomes a *guru,* he is automatically a *brāhmaṇa.* Sometimes a caste *guru* says that *ye kṛṣṇa-tattva-vettā, sei guru haya* means that one who is not a *brāhmaṇa* may become a *śikṣā-guru* or a *vartma-pradarśaka-guru* but not an initiator *guru.* According to such caste *gurus,* birth and family ties are considered foremost. However, the hereditary consideration is not acceptable to Vaiṣṇavas. The word *guru* is equally applicable to the *vartma-pradarśaka-guru, śikṣā-guru* and *dīkṣā-guru.* Unless we accept the principle enunciated by Śrī Caitanya Mahāprabhu, this Kṛṣṇa consciousness movement cannot spread all over the world. According to Śrī Caitanya Mahāprabhu's intentions:

pṛthivīte āche yata nagarādi-grāma
sarvatra pracāra haibe mora nāma

The cult of Śrī Caitanya Mahāprabhu must be preached all over the world. This does not mean that people should take to His teachings and remain *śūdras* or *caṇḍālas.* As soon as one is trained as a pure Vaiṣṇava, he must be accepted as a bona fide *brāhmaṇa.* This is the essence of Śrī Caitanya Mahāprabhu's instructions in this verse. (end of Śrīla Prabhupāda's purport to Cc 2.8.128)

ŚLOKA 5.2

यथा चतुर्भिः कनकं परीक्ष्यते
निघर्षणच्छेदनतापताडनैः ।
तथा चतुर्भिः पुरुषः परीक्ष्यते
त्यागेन शीलेन गुणेन कर्मणा ॥२॥

yathā caturbhiḥ kanakaṁ parīkṣyate
nigharṣaṇa-cchedana-tāpa-tāḍanaiḥ
tathā caturbhiḥ puruṣaḥ parīkṣyate
tyāgena śīlena guṇena karmaṇā

There are four ways of testing gold: rubbing, cutting, heating and hammering. Similarly, the four ways of testing a man are through his renunciation, his character, his qualities and his actions.

Commentary: Poet Vidyāpati said, "Just as gold is tested on the black stone, so is a man tested by his nature." Just as a casual observation is not considered a test, so must a person's character over time be tested in different ways.

ŚLOKA 5.3

तावद्भयेषु भेतव्यं यावद्भयमनागतम् ।
आगतं तु भयं वीक्ष्य प्रहर्तव्यमशङ्कया ॥३॥

tāvad bhayeṣu bhetavyaṁ
yāvad bhayam anāgatam
āgataṁ tu bhayaṁ vīkṣya
prahartavyam aśaṅkayā

That which is dreadful may be feared as long as it remains distant. But once it befalls you, immediately try to get rid of it.

Commentary: Referring to the *Gītā* (2.40), Śrīla Prabhupāda commented that the greatest *bhaya* (fear) is demotion into an animal species due to neglecting spiritual values. This great fear can only be countered through becoming Kṛṣṇa conscious here and now.

Procrastination is a serious obstacle to success in any activity. As it is said, "there is no time like the present." Now is the only time to become Kṛṣṇa conscious and thereby free ourselves of the fear of losing the opportunity of human birth. Common sense means doing the right thing at the right time, and this theme of timeliness is echoed throughout all *nīti-śāstras.*

Timing is everything. A woman once asked Prabhupāda why he did not come to the USA earlier, and he replied, "Because you were not ready." Lord Śrī Caitanya Mahāprabhu prophesized, "My holy name will be chanted in every town and village of the world." We once stumbled upon an old volume from the early twentieth century written by a British missionary who had visited Nabadwip around the lifetime of Bhaktivinoda Ṭhākura. *Bābājīs* along the banks of the Ganges had told this missionary that rather than their converting to Christianity, instead their religion Gauḍīya Vaiṣṇavism would be spread throughout the world within a few years. The author was dumbfounded by their audacity. Five or six decades after the missionary published his book, "Hare Kṛṣṇa" became a household expression all over the world due to the timing of one pure devotee.

Before Śrīla Prabhupāda departed for America, he invited any number of his friends and fellow devotees from the Gauḍīya Maṭha to join him in this glorious mission. Our Godsister, the late Mūlaprakṛti Dāsī, interviewed many of Śrīla Prabhupāda's old friends who knew him before he departed Calcutta for Boston aboard the steamship *Jaladuta.* Śrīmatī Mūlaprakṛti compiled these interviews in her wonderful book *Our Śrīla Prabhupāda: A Friend to All.* What is most remarkable about these conversations is the large number of people who Prabhupāda invited to join him in his mission of world enlightenment. Yet each one of them preferred to procrastinate, citing reasons like health, ongoing education, family and job obligations, etc.

Fortunately for us, Lord Śrī Caitanya Mahāprabhu's prophecy regarding the worldwide Hare Kṛṣṇa movement was not left up to procrastinators who could not read the handwriting on the wall. If that had been the case, then to this day there would be no all-auspicious *saṅkīrtana-yajña* (chanting of the holy names of Kṛṣṇa) throughout the world. Śrīla Prabhupāda's ability to judge time and circumstance alone was responsible for fulfilling a prophecy of the Supreme Lord, saving millions from a dreadful fate. Truly, the ability to interpret time and circumstance by judging what is to be done and what is not to be done is a rare gift.

ŚLOKA 5.4

एकोदरसमुद्भूता एकनक्षत्रजातकाः ।
न भवन्ति समाः शीले यथा बदरकण्टकाः ॥४॥

ekodara-samudbhūtā
eka-nakṣatra-jātakāḥ
na bhavanti samāḥ śīle
yathā badara-kaṇṭakāḥ

Though born from the same womb and under the same stars people do not develop the same qualities, as the badarī tree produces both thorns and berries.

Commentary: With the words *eka-nakṣatra-jātakāḥ* (born under the same constellation), Cāṇakya Paṇḍita once again ignites the debate of nature versus nurture. Subtle changes of planetary influence, especially in the case of the rising sign and moon, are in constant flux. Hence, astrology, which relies upon time and place of birth, does not consider that two different individuals can be born under exactly the same circumstances.

As seen in this verse, the reading of a chart is not based only on the twelve signs (*rāśis*), as it is in the West, but upon the more subtle forces of the *nakṣatras*. These twenty-seven *nakṣatras,* though long ago dropped from the invented, non-sampradāyic system of Western astrology, are important for both the judgment of character and prediction of events. These *nakṣatras* are divided into three types: (1) nine *deva-nakṣatras* or "godly" constellations, (2) nine *mānuṣa-nakṣatras* or those "belonging to the world of man," and (3) nine *rākṣasa-nakṣatras* denoting a more materialistic nature.

Modern social science lays a huge stress upon upbringing. However, until today's universities research the science of the *nakṣatras* vis-à-vis lunar transits and the psychological influence that *jyotiṣa-śāstra* brings to bear, pseudo-scientific conclusions regarding nature versus nurture will be merely an incomplete guesswork that is top-heavy and one-sided.

ŚLOKA 5.5

निःस्पृहो नाधिकारी स्यान्नाकामो मण्डनप्रियः ।
नाविदग्धः प्रियं ब्रूयात्स्पष्टवक्ता न वञ्चकः ॥५॥

niḥspṛho nādhikārī syān
nākāmo maṇḍana-priyaḥ
nāvidagdhaḥ priyaṁ brūyāt
spaṣṭa-vaktā na vañcakaḥ

He who is desireless does not like to hold a post. He who is not sensuous does not enjoy bodily ornamentation. Endearing speech

does not emit from the lips of foolish men. And he who speaks the blunt truth can never deceive.

Commentary: This *śloka* puts to question men who seek political posts as being "selfless human beings who only wish to serve their fellow man." Regarding the last line, it is an irony that the straightforward and outspoken speaker of truth is the individual most often accused of lying just because he speaks what others fear to hear. Nothing causes consternation more than honest words plainly spoken. Society elects many silver-tongued villains and honors them as men of sterling character simply because they gratify the public with hollow promises and lies. For the straightforward person, finding the narrow path that runs between abrasive veracity and tactful candor can be a real exercise.

ŚLOKA 5.6

मूर्खाणां पण्डिता द्वेष्या अधनानां महाधनाः ।
पराङ्गना कुलस्त्रीणां सुभगानां च दुर्भगाः ॥६॥

mūrkhāṇāṁ paṇḍitā dveṣyā
adhanānāṁ mahā-dhanāḥ
parāṅganā kula-strīṇāṁ
subhagānāṁ ca durbhagāḥ

Fools envy paṇḍitas, the poor envy the rich, prostitutes envy chaste women and widows envy women with husbands.

Commentary: Only the short-sighted allow themselves to fall victim to envy. One should take a moment to consider how quickly people are born only to die after a few short breaths and heartbeats. Here, in this *mṛtyu-loka* or "planet of death" we are forced to leave behind our social position, wealth and family when the date with destiny appears like a red flag popping up on an expired parking meter. The bottom line is that our time should not be wasted envying other souls who are just as helplessly conditioned as our poor selves.

ŚLOKA 5.7

आलस्योपगता विद्या परहस्तगतं धनम् ।
अल्पबीजं हतं क्षेत्रं हतं सैन्यमनायकम् ॥७॥

ālasyopagatā vidyā
para-hasta-gataṁ dhanam
alpa-bījaṁ hataṁ kṣetraṁ
hataṁ sainyam anāyakam

One's learning is ruined by failure to apply it; savings are ruined by lending; agricultural crops are ruined by sparse sowing of seeds; and an army is ruined without a leader.

Commentary: And one's life is utterly wasted without a bona fide spiritual master.

Regarding an army being ruined without a general, there is an example from Sikh history of the great warrior Śrī Hari Singh Nalwa, a general in the army of the "Lion of Punjab" King Ranjit Singh. Killed in a battle during an 1837 offensive into Afghanistan, General Hari Singh's dead body was visibly propped up on the roof of the fort. The mere sight of the deceased general's mortal coil was enough to send the Afghans into retreat.

ŚLOKA 5.8

अभ्यासाद्धार्यते विद्या कुलं शीलेन धार्यते ।
गुणेन ज्ञायते त्वार्यः कोपो नेत्रेण गम्यते ॥८॥

abhyāsād dhāryate vidyā
kulaṁ śīlena dhāryate

guṇena jñāyate tv āryaḥ
kopo netreṇa gamyate

Learning is retained through practice and a family's prestige through proper behavior. A gentleman is judged by his qualities and anger is seen in the eyes.

Commentary: Regarding practical application of learning, the spiritual master instructs, but it is the disciple's duty to follow. This includes chanting the prescribed number of *japa* daily, following the regulative principles and remaining constantly engaged in Kṛṣṇa consciousness. The bond between *guru* and *śiṣya* is a contract, and it is up to the initiate to honor that agreement. The entire spiritual family of ISKCON will be judged by the behavior of each individual devotee as described herein.

The state of mind is reflected through the eyes. The eyes are sometimes called "the windows to the soul." Many doctors have admitted to witnessing a certain glow that vanishes from patients' eyes at the time of death, as the pure spirit soul departs.

ŚLOKA 5.9

वित्तेन रक्ष्यते धर्मो विद्या योगेन रक्ष्यते ।
मृदुना रक्ष्यते भूपः सत्स्त्रिया रक्ष्यते गृहम् ॥९॥

vittena rakṣyate dharmo
vidyā yogena rakṣyate
mṛdunā rakṣyate bhūpaḥ
sat-striyā rakṣyate gṛham

Wealth preserves religion, practice preserves learning, words of conciliation preserve a king and a faithful wife preserves a household.

Commentary: Money used for spiritual purposes represents goddess Lakṣmī. Therefore, money is not in and of itself "the root of all evil," as many believe.[13] The value of a thing can be judged by its use. For the devotee in Kṛṣṇa consciousness, whatever can be used to serve the Lord has value, while all other things are worthless. For example, Śrīla Prabhupāda knew that Bombay—the greatest city of the world's most spiritual country—had no grand temple wherein all members of society could worship the Lord. Therefore, as a *sannyāsī* he personally went along with his disciples to the homes of well-to-do industrialists to beg for alms. After a tremendous struggle, he built India's greatest spiritual resort, Hare Kṛṣṇa Land at Juhu Beach, where all pious souls regardless of social position are welcome. Thus in Bombay, and throughout the globe, he has fulfilled the purport of "wealth preserving religion."

Śrīla Prabhupāda writes:

> The great learned scholar Cāṇakya Paṇḍita says, therefore, whatever one has in his possession had better be spent for the cause of *sat* or the Supreme Personality of Godhead, because one cannot take possessions with him. These remain here and will be lost. Either we leave the money or the money leaves us, but we will be separated. The best use of money as long as it is within our possession is to spend it to acquire Kṛṣṇa consciousness. (SB 3.30.31, purport)

Today, thirty-five years after the opening ceremony, Hare Kṛṣṇa Land at Juhu Beach, Mumbai, is one of the most popular religious centers in all of India, attracting millions yearly to the lotus feet of Śrī Śrī Rādhā-Rāsabihārī, Gaura-Nitāi and Sītā-Rāma. Money collected by members of the Hare Kṛṣṇa movement from willing donors has subsequently been used to build colossal ISKCON centers in Śrīdhāma Māyāpur, Vṛndāvana, New Delhi, Baroda, Ahmedabad, Tirupati and in major cities throughout the world.

---

13. For instance, Jesus said, "Love of money is the root of all evil." (1 *Timothy* 6.10)

Since all things, both material and spiritual, have their origin in Kṛṣṇa, the energies of this world are also meant for His glorification. Those who can serve God here and now with His energies, including money, will soon be privileged to serve Him in the hereafter. This is the lesson and legacy of Śrīla Prabhupāda.

Regarding "words of conciliation to preserve a king," *asura-guru* Śukrācārya advises:

> Approach a king as you would a burning fire, as though he is the lord and master of your life or a furious cobra. Serve him with care, never considering your own status. Speak clearly and sweetly in his presence… Sitting with pleasure at that place where the king so orders, give up all vanity. (condensed from SN 2.215-222)

Why does the king deserve this kind of behavior from us?

> The king is the lord of this earth because of the good deeds performed in previous births as well as by his penance. (SN 1.20)

The last line credits the faithful wife with the preservation of the household. Vedic civilization and culture respects the position of the woman like no other culture on earth. Loving protection of the mother, daughter or wife does not mean enslavement. In fact, the yin and yang of the home is meant to reflect Lord Śiva and his *śakti* of this material universe. In the false quest for gender equality, women are leaving their position as the *gṛha-lakṣmī* (goddess of the household) and are accepting menial employment to compete with men on a presumed level playing field. With the increased household income of another paycheck, the shrewd landlords respond by raising rents while greedy governments levy additional taxes. Thus the wife's hard earned money is taken away while the home fires turn cold. When a woman is forced out of her home and sent off to work, the children are neglected and grow up lacking in moral and spiritual guidance. A wife who competes with her husband creates the ludicrous situation of two husbands in the family. Women and men can never be equal because both have abilities that the other does not. In fact, none ever born have ever been equal to any other. The universe is made up of infinite manifestations of individuality because that is the way that Śrī Kṛṣṇa, the Supreme Individual, has so ordained it.

ŚLOKA 5.10

अन्यथा वेदपाण्डित्यं शास्त्रमाचारमन्यथा ।
अन्यथा यद्वदन् शान्तं लोकः क्लिश्यति चान्यथा ॥१०॥

anyathā veda-pāṇḍityaṁ
śāstram ācāram anyathā
anyathā yad vadan śāntaṁ
lokaḥ kliśyati cānyathā

Those who blaspheme Vedic scholarship, the revealed scriptures and the lifestyle recommended in them, and who deride men of peaceful temperament, come to grief unnecessarily.

Commentary: Lord Śrī Caitanya Mahāprabhu instructs Śrīla Rūpa Gosvāmī:

> If the devotee commits an offense at the feet of a Vaiṣṇava while cultivating the creeper of devotional service in the material world, his offense is compared to a mad elephant that uproots the creeper and breaks it. In this way the leaves of the creeper are dried up. (Cc 2.19.156)

Needless faultfinding and baseless criticism are the banes of spiritual progress.

As an infuriated elephant tramples everything in its path, so the "mad elephant offense" of disparaging sacred texts and devotees of the Lord leads to quick ruination. The delicate creeper struggling to grow by the efforts of past devotion must be carefully nourished through the waters of the holy name and pure devotional service, *bhakti-yoga.*

Like an expert gardener, the devotee tends to his grove of devotion by uprooting the analogous weeds of illusion that grow due to neglecting the orders of the spiritual master. The wise devotee must erect a strong fence constructed of the regulative principles to keep out wild animals that invade his garden in the form of illicit desires. Finally, as Lord Caitanya instructs, the creeper of devotion must wrap itself around the tree of Lord Kṛṣṇa.

ŚLOKA 5.11

दारिद्र्यनाशनं दानं शीलं दुर्गतिनाशनम् ।
अज्ञाननाशिनी प्रज्ञा भावना भयनाशिनी ॥११॥

dāridrya-nāśanaṁ dānaṁ
śīlaṁ durgati-nāśanam
ajñāna-nāśinī prajñā
bhāvanā bhaya-nāśinī

Acts of charity put an end to poverty; righteous conduct destroys misfortune; knowledge destroys ignorance; and circumspection destroys fear.

Commentary: Miserliness leads to penury; impropriety leads to despair; foolishness leads to darkness; and callousness leads to danger.

ŚLOKA 5.12

नास्ति कामसमो व्याधिर्नास्ति मोहसमो रिपुः ।
नास्ति कोपसमो वह्निर्नास्ति ज्ञानात्परं सुखम् ॥१२॥

nāsti kāma-samo vyādhir
nāsti moha-samo ripuḥ
nāsti kopa-samo vahnir
nāsti jñānāt paraṁ sukham

There is no disease equal to lust; there is no enemy equal to infatuation; and there is no fire like wrath. But there is no happiness higher than spiritual knowledge.

Commentary: Bhartṛhari, the author of the *Nīti-śataka,* says that "touching fire burns even the performer of a fire sacrifice." Bhartṛhari knew well the results of uncontrollable lust (*kāma*). It is said that a *brāhmaṇa* presented Bhartṛhari with an apple that could bless whoever ate it with immortality. Now, Bhartṛhari harbored a secret weakness for his paramour. Thinking that it would be impossible to live forever without her, he gave her the fruit of eternal life. But Bhartṛhari's paramour had a lover, an officer in the court, and she presented him with the apple. This officer dearly loved another woman who cleaned his stables, so he offered it to her. Each day the stable maid carried out the horse dung in a basket balanced upon her head. As the story goes, Bhartṛhari looked out his window and saw his apple in her basket with the horse dung as she walked by. Then and there he vowed to become a renunciant, and he was inspired to write his *Vairāgya-śataka* or "one hundred verses on the subject of renunciation."

Bhartṛhari describes this conundrum of material life:

> Lust is a river, which has the objects of desire for its waters. It is agitated by waves in the form of hankering, and has sharks for its passions. Its constant flow destroys the tree of fortitude. It is difficult to cross due to its whirlpools in the form of infatuation. It is very deep and has anxiety for its steep banks. Only the self-controlled renunciant who has crossed this river of lust (with the boat of knowledge) experiences the joy of transcendental bliss. (VS 11)

Cāṇakya Paṇḍita offers the solution to unregulated senses in the last line with the words *nāsti jñānāt paraṁ sukham.* Kṛṣṇa advises Arjuna:

> In this world, there is nothing as sublime and pure as transcendental knowledge. Such knowledge is the mature fruit of all mysticism.

> And one who has achieved this enjoys the self within himself in due course of time. (Bg 4.38)

ŚLOKA 5.13

जन्ममृत्यू हि यात्येको भुनक्त्येकः शुभाशुभम् ।
नरकेषु पतत्येक एको याति परां गतिम् ॥१३॥

janma-mṛtyū hi yāty eko
bhunakty ekaḥ śubhāśubham
narakeṣu pataty eka
eko yāti parāṁ gatim

One is born alone and dies alone. Alone he experiences the good and bad consequences of his past deeds. Alone he is either sent to hell or to the supreme destination.

Commentary: A student pilot learns to fly an airplane in the company of his teacher, but once he takes off solo he is on his own. In the same way, the disciple receives many instructions from his spiritual master, but it is up to him to execute his *guru's* orders with diligence. All that we learn in life should be spent in preparation for our final breath and solitary departure. Neither doting family nor caring friends can accompany us to the next birth. Therefore, at the final curtain call, we should take shelter of Kṛṣṇa's name and exit here accompanied by our supreme friend, Lord Kṛṣṇa, the indwelling guide within the heart of each spirit soul.

We are individual souls, each endowed with the gift of free will. We must consider the laws of *karma* and exercise the ability to choose right over wrong. Bhartṛhari says:

> Before undertaking any action whether good or bad, a wise man must carefully ponder its consequences. That activity which is performed in haste pierces the heart like an arrow even after death. (NS 100)

Assets gained at birth are little more than an empty field. The field of this rare human form of birth must be deliberately tilled with the plow of righteous, God-conscious deeds and watered with the holy names of the Lord to produce the desired results.

During a visit to the British Museum in the early 1970's, we met the famous Egyptologist Dr. Delsham-Denshaw. We listened as he translated the pictorial hieroglyphs that depict the sinful *jīva* in the hands of a Yamadūta. It was surprising to learn how close the Egyptian concept of the afterlife was to the description of *Śrīmad-Bhāgavatam's* Fifth Canto. Similarly, devotees who visit the Christian Orthodox Rila Monastery in Bulgaria will be surprised at the extensive murals depicting specific hells complete with eager Yamadūtas dispensing various forms of punishment fitting specific sins.

Indeed, the teachings of Islam, Jainism and Buddhism likewise share similar concepts, although the most precise descriptions of Naraka are found only in the *Purāṇas.* The excruciating detail with which the *Bhāgavatam* deals with the unsavory subject of hell is meant as a wake-up call for those of us who heedlessly violate nature's laws in denial of karmic reactions. Verily the manifestations of hell, heaven and even the spiritual world can be seen right here on earth. Since our next life's happiness or suffering hinge upon deeds performed in this lifetime, how we choose to spend our lives here and now is crucial for the hereafter. The ticket for riding the Back to Godhead Express is not cheap. That journey requires full surrender.

Regarding the last line, Vidura the pilgrim instructs:

> He is called undisturbed who goes to an unknown, remote place and, freed from all obligations, quits his material body when it has become useless. (SB 1.13.26)

With the words *yāti parāṁ gatim* Cāṇakya Paṇḍita also hints at the supreme destination attained by saintly devotees. Beyond the various hells and heavens of this world lies the devotee's destination in the spiritual sky.

ŚLOKA 5.14

तृणं ब्रह्मविदः स्वर्गस्तृणं शूरस्य जीवितम् ।
जिताक्षस्य तृणं नारी निःस्पृहस्य तृणं जगत् ॥१४॥

tṛṇaṁ brahma-vidaḥ svargas
tṛṇaṁ śūrasya jīvitam
jitākṣasya tṛṇaṁ nārī
niḥspṛhasya tṛṇaṁ jagat

Svarga is but a straw to the man of spiritual knowledge. Life itself is but a straw for the man of courage. For the man of controlled senses, the beautiful female is a mere straw. And for someone who is detached, the entire universe is but a straw.

Commentary: Cāṇakya Paṇḍita herewith discusses the *brahma-vit* or "knower of spirit." He who sees the universe as a mere straw must fix his mind not upon some imagined void, but upon the transcendental destination. Kṛṣṇa tells Arjuna:

> I am the basis of the impersonal Brahman, which is the constitutional position of ultimate happiness, and which is immortal, imperishable and eternal. (Bg 14.27)

As read in the pages of *Śrīmad-Bhāgavatam* (1.2.11), Śrī Śukadeva Gosvāmī kindly explains to Mahārāja Parīkṣit the three stages of higher understanding:

vadanti tat tattva-vidas tattvaṁ yaj jñānam advayam
brahmeti paramātmeti bhagavān iti śabdyate

> Learned transcendentalists who know the Absolute Truth call this nondual substance Brahman, Paramātmā or Bhagavān.

At the first platform or Brahman realization, the aspirant achieves the transcendental plane and becomes fixed in the knowledge that he is born of spirit. At level two he realizes that within the heart sits Paramātmā, the Supreme Soul. At the third and final stage known as Bhagavān realization he achieves *bhakti-yoga* where the devotee wholeheartedly surrenders at the lotus feet of the all-encompassing Supreme Personality of Godhead Śrī Kṛṣṇa. This process of approaching the Supreme Lord (as described in the following verse from *Śrī Īśopaniṣad, mantra* 15) may take millions of births or only as long as it takes to read these few words. Each makes his own choice.

hiraṇmayena pātreṇa satyasyāpihitaṁ mukham
tat tvaṁ pūṣann apāvṛṇu satya-dharmāya dṛṣṭaye

O my Lord, sustainer of all that lives, Your real face is covered by Your dazzling effulgence. Kindly remove that covering and exhibit Yourself to Your pure devotee.

ŚLOKA 5.15

विद्या मित्रं प्रवासेषु भार्या मित्रं गृहेषु च ।
व्याधितस्यौषधं मित्रं धर्मो मित्रं मृतस्य च ॥१५॥

vidyā mitraṁ pravāseṣu
bhāryā mitraṁ gṛheṣu ca
vyādhitasyauṣadhaṁ mitraṁ
dharmo mitraṁ mṛtasya ca

Knowledge is a friend while on a journey; the wife is a friend at home; when ill, medicine is your friend. Yet at the time of death the only friend is dharma.

Commentary: *Vidyā,* described here, means "learning" or "gathered knowledge" whereas *jñāna* (described in 6.1, 8.8, 17.17 and others) indicates "realized learning." That is the generally accepted difference between *vidyā* and *jñāna.* Material so-called conceptions of *dharma* or bodily conceptions of religion will help the soul neither in acquiring knowledge nor when he passes from this world. Therefore, Cāṇakya Paṇḍita implies that once the time arrives for exhaling our final breath, *sanātana-dharma* or Kṛṣṇa consciousness is the only salvation.

So forgiving is the Almighty Lord that even he who has wasted his life and has accrued no religious merit can save himself even at the last moment through *dharma* as described in 12.12. The *Bhāgavata's* Sixth Canto, chapters one and two, narrates the episode of the miserable sinner Ajāmila. At the point of death, Ajāmila summoned his son Nārāyaṇa. The Yamadūtas were standing ready to drag Ajāmila to the hellish regions of the universe where he was to suffer prolonged torture for his sins.

Suddenly, a group of four-armed Viṣṇudūtas chased away the servants of Yamarāja with bows and arrows. The Yamadūtas were perplexed; after all Ajāmila was a great sinner who had abandoned his young and beautiful *brāhmaṇa* wife and had lived with a prostitute for many years. Still the Viṣṇudūtas persisted:

> If one chants the holy name of Hari and then dies because of an accidental misfortune, such as falling from the top of a house, slipping and suffering broken bones while traveling on the road, being bitten by a serpent, being afflicted by pain and high fever, or being injured by a weapon, one is immediately absolved from having to enter hellish life, even though he is sinful. (SB 6.2.16)

Although Ajāmila had chanted the name of Nārāyaṇa accidentally, simply by calling for his son, the potency of the holy name saved him from a terrible fate in hell. By the potency of the name of God, Ajāmila became liberated and went back to home, back to Godhead.

As far as Cāṇakya Paṇḍita's comment *bhāryā mitraṁ gṛheṣu,* the *Śatapatha Brāhmaṇa* states:

> The wife is indeed the half of one's own self. So long as a man is not married he remains without emotional integration.

For her part, if the wife keeps her husband peaceful then her home will be heaven. But an angry, domineering banshee abruptly sends the household on the fast track to the nether regions.

There is a story about a man who approached a *guru* in order to take *sannyāsa.* "Tell me why you are leaving household life," asked the *guru.* "Well," the candidate replied, "my wife is a goddess." "Then, if your wife is a goddess why do you wish to become a renunciant?" queried the *guru.* The man replied, "Because she is the goddess of hell!"

ŚLOKA 5.16

वृथा वृष्टिः समुद्रेषु वृथा तृप्तेषु भोजनम् ।
वृथा दानं धनाढ्येषु वृथा दीपो दिवापि च ॥१६॥

vṛthā vṛṣṭiḥ samudreṣu
vṛthā tṛpteṣu bhojanam
vṛthā dānaṁ dhanāḍhyeṣu
vṛthā dīpo divāpi ca

Useless is rain upon the sea; useless is food for one who is satiated; useless is charity to the rich; and useless is a lamp in daylight.

Commentary: But there is nothing as useless as trying to enlighten a dolt.

ŚLOKA 5.17

नास्ति मेघसमं तोयं नास्ति चात्मसमं बलम् ।
नास्ति चक्षुःसमं तेजो नास्ति धान्यसमं प्रियम् ॥१७॥

nāsti megha-samaṁ toyaṁ
nāsti cātma-samaṁ balam
nāsti cakṣuḥ-samaṁ tejo
nāsti dhānya-samaṁ priyam

There is no water like that which falls from the cloud, and no strength like one's own. No radiance shines like that from the eyes, and no wealth is dearer than stored food grains.

Commentary: Just across the way from the Viśvanātha Mandira in Kāśī, as well as at Viśrāma-ghāṭa in Mathurā, are temples to the goddess of food grains, Annapūrṇā-devī. Standing not with weapons, but rather holding a bowl and a large spoon, she epitomizes maternal love and nourishment. Indeed stored grains are real protection against lean times. As our Guru Mahārāja sometimes said when proud factory owners came for his *darśana,* "You can't eat nuts and bolts." Lord Kṛṣṇa appeared amongst the society of cowherdsmen and agriculturists. Indeed a return to the earth is the need of the age.

There is no place on earth where rain is more revered than India. At the first sign of the *varṣā* season, the monsoon rains, India's village folk run outside to enjoy the heavenly drops as though they were Gaṅgā water thrown by a *pūjārī.*

In some places in the scriptures, rainfall is described as the semen of the Supreme Personality of Godhead because it is only by the agency of rain that the seeds of all species of life are born and thrive on the earth. In *Śrīmad-Bhāgavatam* Brahmā turns to the Supreme Lord with this instructive prayer:

ambhas tu yad-reta udāra-vīryaṁ sidhyanti jīvanty uta vardhamānāḥ
lokā yato 'thākhila-loka-pālāḥ prasīdatāṁ naḥ sa mahā-vibhūtiḥ

> The entire cosmic manifestation has emerged from water, and it is because of water that all living entities endure, live and develop. This water is nothing but the semen of the Supreme Personality of Godhead. Therefore, may the Supreme Personality of Godhead, who has such great potency, be pleased with us. (SB 8.5.33)

Our Guru Mahārāja comments:

> Despite the theories of so-called scientists, the vast quantities of water on this planet and on other planets are not created by a mixture of hydrogen and oxygen. Rather, the water is sometimes explained to be the perspiration and sometimes the semen of the Supreme Personality of Godhead. It is from water that all living entities emerge, and because of water they live and grow. If there

> were no water, all life would cease. Water is the source of life for everyone. Therefore, by the grace of the Supreme Personality of Godhead, we have so much water all over the world.

Though essential for life, rain is no longer regular because there is a lack of *brāhmaṇas* to perform sacrifices. If intelligent persons around the globe can seriously take to this *saṅkīrtana-yajña* that Prabhupāda introduced to the world, then Lord Kṛṣṇa will be pleased and the result will be sufficient rainfall, peacefulness and prosperity worldwide.

ŚLOKA 5.18

अधना धनमिच्छन्ति वाचं चैव चतुष्पदाः ।
मानवाः स्वर्गमिच्छन्ति मोक्षमिच्छन्ति देवताः ॥१८॥

adhanā dhanam icchanti
vācaṁ caiva catuṣpadāḥ
mānavāḥ svargam icchanti
mokṣam icchanti devatāḥ

The poor crave riches, while four-legged beasts long for the ability to speak. Men desire heaven, while demigods pray for eternal life.

Commentary: This material world runs on desire: dogs desire attributes of humans, humans desire greater wealth, wealthy men long for extended life spans in heaven, and the *devas* desire freedom from birth and death. As Prabhupāda says:

> You will not achieve what you desire even when you desire desirelessness. You must desire to become Kṛṣṇa conscious. That is all.

In Śrīla Prabhupāda's *Kṛṣṇa, The Supreme Personality of Godhead,* we find that the demigods themselves gathered as Kṛṣṇa appeared on earth. The *devas* prayed:

Our dear Lord, You are appearing as the best of the Yadu dynasty, and we are offering our respectful, humble obeisances unto Your lotus feet. Before this appearance, You also appeared as Matsya, Hayagrīva, Kūrma, Nṛsiṁha, Varāha, Haṁsāvatāra, Śrī Rāma, Śrī Paraśurāma and many other incarnations as well. You appeared just to protect Your devotees. We submit to You in this present incarnation as the Supreme Lord Himself to protect us throughout the three worlds. Please remove all obstacles in our service to You so that we may obtain Your unalloyed devotional service.

Since even demigods pray to Kṛṣṇa for the liberation of pure devotional service, wise men should follow their example rather than hankering after becoming temporary denizens of heaven.

The greatest blunder of the impersonalist *yogīs*—those who deny the form and personality of the Supreme Godhead—is to imagine that the incarnations of God manifest through material energy. The mistaken conception of such Māyāvādīs is that the limitless spiritual expanse called Brahman accepts various forms of material energy. In fact, the form of Kṛṣṇa or Nārāyaṇa, even while upon this earth, is always transcendental to the three modes of material nature namely, goodness, passion and ignorance. Śaṅkarācārya himself has stated:

nārāyaṇaḥ paro 'vyaktāt

Lord Nārāyaṇa is not a creation of this material world. Nārāyaṇa is above the material creation. (*Gītā-bhāṣya,* invocation)

ŚLOKA 5.19

सत्येन धार्यते पृथ्वी सत्येन तपते रविः ।
सत्येन वाति वायुश्च सर्वं सत्ये प्रतिष्ठितम् ॥१९॥

satyena dhāryate pṛthvī
satyena tapate raviḥ
satyena vāti vāyuś ca
sarvaṁ satye pratiṣṭhitam

By truth the earth is sustained. By truth the sun shines, and truth causes Vāyu the wind god to blow. Verily all things rest upon truth.

Commentary: One's ability to perceive the Supreme Absolute Truth is obscured by his contact with material nature. The three *guṇas* (modes of material nature) are *sattva* (goodness), *rajas* (passion) and *tamas* (ignorance). One meaning of *guṇa* is "rope," and all created living beings are tied up by the ropes of material nature. Just as the three strands of a rope intertwine, so the three modes of nature influence a man's activities differently at different times. Sometimes he is in the mood for charity, sometimes working hard and sometimes chasing after intoxication and wanton sex. Lord Śiva the destroyer predominates over *tamo-guṇa.* Lord Brahmā the creator predominates over *rajo-guṇa.* Lord Viṣṇu the maintainer predominates over *sattva-guṇa.* It is said that the world is created in passion, maintained in goodness and destroyed in ignorance.

Creation and destruction are temporary duties, but only maintenance is eternal—for truth and goodness are everlasting. Hence Lord Viṣṇu who maintains the world in truth has been accepted by wise sages as supreme. As identified throughout the Vedic literature, the Supreme Absolute Truth is none other than Śrī Kṛṣṇa. In *Śrīmad-Bhāgavatam* (3.29.40) Lord Kapila, the incarnation of Kṛṣṇa, expresses a similar conception:

> Out of fear of the Supreme Personality of Godhead the wind blows, out of fear of Him the sun shines, out of fear of Him the rain pours forth showers, and out of fear of Him the host of heavenly bodies shed their luster.

ŚLOKA 5.20

चला लक्ष्मीश्चला: प्राणाश्चले जीवितमन्दिरे ।
चलाचले च संसारे धर्म एको हि निश्चल: ॥२०॥

calā lakṣmīś calāḥ prāṇāś
cale jīvita-mandire
calācale ca saṁsāre
dharma eko hi niścalaḥ

Unsteady is Lakṣmījī, the goddess of wealth. The duration of life and the house where we live are also uncertain. This very world with its continuous cycle of saṁsāra is unpredictable. Religious merit alone is steady.

Commentary: In the previous verse, Cāṇakya Paṇḍita establishes that truth is the basis and shelter for creation, and here he shows that *dharma,* or the pursuance of that eternal truth, is man's ultimate duty. In this world there are material *dharmas* which include all the temporary religious beliefs. Such material *dharmas* can be switched back and forth; a Hindu may convert to Christianity or Islam, or a Jew may transform into a Buddhist. Such back and forth *dharma*-swapping in the dressing rooms of material religion can do nothing to extricate the soul rooted in material moorings. Cāṇakya Paṇḍita calls true *dharma* "the one certainty." The religion of the soul is eternal and is therefore called *sanātana-dharma.* Only when *sanātana-dharma* is properly executed under the guidance of the bona fide spiritual master will there be any effect. Thus Kṛṣṇa instructs Arjuna:

sarva-dharmān parityajya mām ekaṁ śaraṇaṁ vraja
ahaṁ tvāṁ sarva-pāpebhyo mokṣayiṣyāmi mā śucaḥ

Abandon all varieties of religion and just surrender unto Me. I shall deliver you from all sinful reaction. Do not fear. (Bg 18.66)

It is our duty to cultivate *sanātana-dharma* before we find ourselves next in line as unwilling holders of a ticket that was purchased with uncertain *karma.* Each of us must come to *dharma* someday, but the nondevotee will meet *dharma* as Dharmarāja, the king of death.

Regarding the fickle nature of worldly wealth, as discussed in lines one to three, Cāṇakya Paṇḍita has dealt with this subject earlier in 1.7.

The money we hoard, the house in which we dwell, even this very body we inhabit can all be lost in the blink of an eyelid. We witness thousands of examples every year, yet we stubbornly presume that such tragedies only befall others. Śrīla Prabhupāda spoke on the unsteadiness of wealth in this world:

> In this material world, Lakṣmī, the goddess of fortune, is called Cañcalā. She does not remain at one place. We have got experience. Today one man is very rich; but (his family's) next generation is no longer rich. That is also nation-wise applicable. Just like we have seen in the case of the British Empire. While I was in London I was thinking that 'These Britishers brought money from all parts of the world, by business or all other means.' I saw in front of St. James Park, Lord Clive's statue. Very, very nice buildings, but it is now difficult for them to repair. That opulence has gone. They have lost their empire. No more income, sufficient income. This is the nature of material world. So many empires were there. There was the Roman Empire, there was Carthaginian Empire, there was Mogul Empire, there was British Empire, and so many empires. They are no longer existing. Sometimes when I pass by the side of the Red Fort, we see the apartments of the great Mogul emperors in Red Fort are now vacant. So this is the material nature. (Lecture, SB 1.2.8, Bombay, 26 Dec 1972)

ŚLOKA 5.21

नराणां नापितो धूर्तः पक्षिणां चैव वायसः ।
चतुष्पदां शृगालस्तु स्त्रीणां धूर्ता च मालिनी ॥२१॥

narāṇāṁ nāpito dhūrtaḥ
pakṣiṇāṁ caiva vāyasaḥ
catuṣ-padāṁ śṛgālas tu
strīṇāṁ dhūrtā ca mālinī

Among men, the barber is cunning, among birds the crow, among four-leggeds the jackal, and among women, the mālinī (flower girl).

Commentary: Merchants are notoriously clever, but one who sells flowers must do so before they wilt, hence many cunning sales tactics are devised. The barber hears the gossip of the entire community, but can never take sides lest he offend his next customer. He listens but is cunning enough to keep his opinion to himself. Crows are said to be among the longest lived of birds, clever at staying alive. Jackals may be cunning, but according to the *Pañca-tantra,* even the other animals despise them. Cunning and craft may be useful in this material world, but we do not find them on the list of a devotee's qualifications, given in the commentary on 6.22.

ŚLOKA 5.22

जनिता चोपनेता च यस्तु विद्यां प्रयच्छति ।
अन्नदाता भयत्राता पञ्चैते पितरः स्मृताः ॥२२॥

janitā copanetā ca
yas tu vidyāṁ prayacchati
anna-dātā bhaya-trātā
pañcaite pitaraḥ smṛtāḥ

These five should be considered as your fathers: your father at birth, the spiritual master who initiated you with the sacred thread, your teacher, he who has fed you and he who protects you from a fearful situation.

Commentary: Of these five "fathers," the spiritual master stands supreme. Although there is no way he can ever be repaid, the disciple must try by rendering him service in a humble mood of utter selflessness. In Vedic civilization and culture the bona fide *guru* is respected as on the same platform of God Almighty, because only by his grace can the door to God's kingdom be opened. The spiritual master never claims to be anything more than a humble servant of God; he never says that he has become God, yet through him alone are the blessings of God realized. Devotees pray at the feet of the spiritual master:

om ajñāna-timirāndhasya jñānāñjana-śalākayā
cakṣur unmīlitaṁ yena tasmai śrī-gurave namaḥ

I was born in the darkest ignorance, and my spiritual master opened my eyes with the torch of knowledge. I offer my respectful obeisances unto him.

ŚLOKA 5.23

राजपत्नी गुरोः पत्नी मित्रपत्नी तथैव च ।
पत्नीमाता स्वमाता च पञ्चैता मातरः स्मृताः ॥२३॥

rāja-patnī guroḥ patnī
mitra-patnī tathaiva ca
patnī-mātā sva-mātā ca
pañcaitā mātaraḥ smṛtāḥ

These five should be considered as mothers: the wife of the king, the wife of a guru, the wife of your friend, your wife's mother and your natural mother.

Commentary: *Sādhus* respectfully look upon all women as their mothers, not as objects of potential sense gratification. Exploitation of women who should be revered as equal to one's own mother is the greatest cause of hopeless material entanglement. By the illusory glare of *māyā* (material nature), that which is abominable and leads only to misery, appears as enjoyable. While ordinary men leer at the delicate curves of beautiful women, *sādhus* look respectfully to their feet (and thereby escape the blinding glare of material nature).

To the above list three additional mothers may be added: the holy Vedic *śāstras,* mother earth who maintains us, and the cow who nourishes us with her milk.[14] Just as a mother never misguides her children, so the *Vedas* and the ancillary *śāstras* written in pursuance of the Vedic version promise to never mislead us. By respecting the qualities of *śāstras,* the earth, women and the cow, one's life will become sinless, the starting point of spiritual life. There is no way the debt to our mothers can be repaid. Indeed, the *Manu-saṁhitā* teaches:

> One's mother is worth a thousand fathers. (MS 2.145)

Cāṇakya Paṇḍita further dilates upon this point in 12.14.

Thus Ends Chapter Five

14. According to scriptures, there are seven mothers: (1) the real mother, (2) the wife of the spiritual master, (3) the wife of a *brāhmaṇa,* (4) the wife of the king, (5) the cow, (6) the nurse, and (7) the earth. (SB 1.11.28)

CHAPTER SIX

ŚLOKA 6.1

श्रुत्वा धर्मं विजानाति श्रुत्वा त्यजति दुर्मतिम् ।
श्रुत्वा ज्ञानमवाप्नोति श्रुत्वा मोक्षमवाप्नुयात् ॥१॥

śrutvā dharmaṁ vijānāti
śrutvā tyajati durmatim
śrutvā jñānam avāpnoti
śrutvā mokṣam avāpnuyāt

Through hearing, spiritual principles are realized; through hearing malevolence vanishes; through hearing one becomes knowledgeable. Indeed, only through hearing is liberation attained.

Commentary: In this verse Cāṇakya Paṇḍita emphasizes the importance of hearing from the proper authority in spiritual life. The spiritual master-to-disciple system of transmitting knowledge, called the *guru-paramparā* (disciplic succession) is based upon submissive aural reception. Śrīla Prabhupāda describes the importance of disciplic succession in the introduction to his *Bhagavad-gītā As It Is.*

There are four bona fide *sampradāyas* (disciplic chains). Śrīla Prabhupāda appeared as the *ācārya* of the Brahma-Madhva-Gauḍīya-

sampradāya. This disciplic succession has its origin in Lord Kṛṣṇa, who personally transmitted this knowledge into the heart of Lord Brahmā at the time of the creation of the universe. From Brahmā, this knowledge was passed on to his son Śrī Nārada Muni, who taught it to Vyāsadeva, who in turn instructed Madhvācārya. Through a succession of spiritual masters this knowledge was imparted to Mādhavendra Purī who initiated Īśvara Purī, who initiated Śrī Caitanya Mahāprabhu in Gayā around 1510.

Lord Śrī Caitanya Mahāprabhu taught the six Gosvāmīs, whose message was passed down to Kṛṣṇadāsa Kavirāja, Narottama Dāsa Ṭhākura, Viśvanātha Cakravartī and Baladeva Vidyābhūṣaṇa. The disciplic chain continued, and in the nineteenth century Śrī Jagannātha Dāsa Bābājī accepted the great Bhaktivinoda Ṭhākura, who passed this crucial knowledge to his son Śrīla Bhaktisiddhānta Sarasvatī (who was formally initiated by Śrīla Gaurakiśora Dāsa Bābājī Mahārāja). Our spiritual master Śrīla Prabhupāda became the leading disciple of his Guru Mahārāja and continued the work of personally spreading the *saṅkīrtana* movement all over the world until he entered *mahā-samādhi* on *caturthī, śukla-pakṣa* of Kārttika-*māsa* in 1977 in Vṛndāvana. Śrīla Prabhupāda taught that the post of *ācārya* must not be an official appointment; rather an *ācārya* rises by his qualities. It could be said that the next *ācārya* will be he who has listened most carefully, carrying out those instructions without any change and with full faith in what he has heard from his spiritual master.

Lord Kṛṣṇa stresses the importance of this system of *sampradāya* in *Bhagavad-gītā.* He tells Arjuna:

> This supreme science was thus received through the chain of disciplic succession, and the saintly kings understood it in that way. But in course of time the succession was broken, and therefore the science as it is appears to be lost. That very ancient science of the relationship with the Supreme is today told by Me to you because you are My devotee as well as My friend; therefore you can understand the transcendental mystery of this science. (Bg 4.2–3)

ŚLOKA 6.2

पक्षिणः काकश्चाण्डालः पशूनां चैव कुक्कुरः ।
मुनीनां पापश्चाण्डालः सर्वचाण्डालनिन्दकः ॥२॥

pakṣiṇaḥ kākaś cāṇḍālaḥ
paśūnāṁ caiva kukkuraḥ
munīnāṁ pāpaś cāṇḍālaḥ
sarva-cāṇḍāla-nindakaḥ

Among birds the crow is a cāṇḍāla, and the dog amongst creatures. Amongst munis the sage who revels in sin is a cāṇḍāla, but he who enjoys blasphemy is the greatest cāṇḍāla of all.

Commentary: A *cāṇḍāla* is "one who eats dogs." To quote George Bernard Shaw, "you are what you eat." The dog eater is considered the lowest among humans. Dog cattle farms were spotlighted in the peculiar 1960's documentary *Mondo Cane.* After the Vietnam War, when many South Asians were settled in America, pet dogs went missing from California neighborhoods. Local governments opted for re-education rather than punishment. The eating of dogs continues in certain parts of the world to this day. America's national food, the "hot dog" is sometimes made of leftover meat and gristle ground up and neatly stuffed into pig intestines, but it is sanitized by being sold in a neat package with a smiling pig on the wrapper. Such are the *cāṇḍālas* in sophisticated dress.

Crows, like fans at modern sporting events, are famous for their ability to turn anything into a meal. Yet lower than the *kāka* (crow), indeed the lowest of all *cāṇḍālas,* is the *nindaka* who enjoys deriding others. A born aversion to fault-finding is the mark of a devotee. "Point one finger at another and you point three at yourself." As we can see from this verse, dressing as a *sādhu* does not make one a sage; activities alone determine one's status.

ŚLOKA 6.3

भस्मना शुद्धयते कांस्यं ताम्रमम्लेन शुद्धयति ।
रजसा शुद्धयते नारी नदी वेगेन शुद्धयति ॥३॥

bhasmanā śuddhyate kāṁsyaṁ
tāmram amlena śuddhyati
rajasā śuddhyate nārī
nadī vegena śuddhyati

Brass is polished by ashes; copper is burnished with tamarind; a woman is cleansed by her monthly cycle; and a river is purified by its flow.

Commentary: *Manu-saṁhitā* (5.108) adds to this list that "a *brāhmaṇa* becomes pure when he becomes a renunciant." When a river flows, filth is forced to the bottom, a process that naturally cleans flowing water. The śāstric version of the cause of the woman's cycle is related in the *Bhāgavata Purāṇa* (6.9.9).

While all the above forms of cleansing are material, a devotee is most interested in cleaning his heart through Kṛṣṇa consciousness. As Lord Śrī Caitanya Mahāprabhu sings in His *Śikṣāṣṭaka* (1):

> Glory to the Śrī Kṛṣṇa *saṅkīrtana,* which cleanses the heart of all the dust accumulated for years and extinguishes the fire of conditional life, of repeated birth and death. This *saṅkīrtana* movement is the prime benediction for humanity at large because it spreads the rays of the benediction moon. It is the life of all transcendental knowledge. It increases the ocean of transcendental bliss, and it enables us to fully taste the nectar for which we are always anxious.

ŚLOKA 6.4

भ्रमन्सम्पूज्यते राजा भ्रमन्सम्पूज्यते द्विजः ।
भ्रमन्सम्पूज्यते योगी स्त्री भ्रमन्ती विनश्यति ॥४॥

bhraman sampūjyate rājā
bhraman sampūjyate dvijaḥ
bhraman sampūjyate yogī
strī bhramantī vinaśyati

The king, the brāhmaṇa, and the yogī who travel are respected, but a woman who wanders is utterly destroyed.

Commentary: That which is duty for one is death to another. This concept of *sva-dharma,* or the performance of one's own duty, is described by Śrī Kṛṣṇa in the *Bhagavad-gītā* with the words:

> It is better to engage in one's own occupation, even though one may perform it imperfectly, than to accept another's occupation and perform it perfectly. Prescribed duties according to one's nature are never affected by sinful reactions. (Bg 18.47)

ŚLOKA 6.5

यस्यार्थास्तस्य मित्राणि यस्यार्थास्तस्य बान्धवाः ।
यस्यार्थाः स पुमाँल्लोके यस्यार्थाः स च पण्डितः ॥५॥

yasyārthās tasya mitrāṇi
yasyārthās tasya bāndhavāḥ
yasyārthāḥ sa pumāl̐ loke
yasyārthāḥ sa ca paṇḍitaḥ

He who has money has friends and relatives. The man of means is respected all over the world. Indeed, a rich man is even hailed as a learned paṇḍita.

Commentary: Many a college or university bears the name of a rich criminal who has paid for the buildings in hope that his crimes will be overlooked and forgotten. In his day, industrialist Leeland Stanford was known as the "robber baron" by the farmers whose land he took for his railroad. Today, however, a diploma from California's Stanford University carries exclusive weight and prestige. Hence, at least in this degraded age, only the rich are respected as learned.

Money makes friends through spending and enemies through hoarding. The great boxer Mohammed Ali had a constant entourage of over a dozen friends, all of whom abandoned him when his funds dried up. Packing our checkbook for the journey to the next life is not an option, but even if we could take it with us, would our paltry funds impress Yamarāja? Money that is acquired through transgressing the laws of nature or violating the rights of others cannot buy our way out of bad *karma.* The rich man who can buy his way out of hell is yet to be born.

Śrīla Prabhupāda was instructed by his Guru Mahārāja, "If you ever get money, print books." In pursuance of that order, Śrīla Prabhupāda printed millions of books in dozens of languages all in glorification of the Supreme Lord. When he heard that ISKCON's funds were discussed in India's parliament, Prabhupāda noted, "We have fabulous resources, but we do not obtain them through magic tricks. Our secret is Hare Kṛṣṇa." There will always be flaws in the acquisition and spending of wealth, therefore money must be purified by being engaged in Kṛṣṇa's service. This movement will continue to grow and spread world-wide as long as the members of ISKCON do not neglect their *japa* and congregational *saṅkīrtana* and the all-important four regulative principles that each initiate is avowed to follow.

See CN 7.15 for an almost identical *śloka.*

ŚLOKA 6.6

तादृशी जायते बुद्धिर्व्यवसायोऽपि तादृशः ।
सहायास्तादृशा एव यादृशी भवितव्यता ॥६॥

tādṛśī jāyate buddhir
vyavasāyo 'pi tādṛśaḥ

sahāyās tādṛśā eva
yādṛśī bhavitavyatā

The intellect functions by the desire of Providence, and activities are controlled by Providence. Those who come forward with assistance gather around us solely by the divine will of Providence.

Commentary: One of our first impressions of Hindu hospitality came from a host who invited us to dine with the words, "Every grain of rice on your plate has your name on it." Since we come together and then are drawn apart by the will of the Supreme Lord, we should remember Him who controls us at all times. "Not a blade of grass moves but by the will of Providence."

ŚLOKA 6.7

कालः पचति भूतानि कालः संहरते प्रजाः ।
कालः सुप्तेषु जागर्ति कालो हि दुरतिक्रमः ॥७॥

kālaḥ pacati bhūtāni
kālaḥ saṁharate prajāḥ
kālaḥ supteṣu jāgarti
kālo hi duratikramaḥ

Time perfects all living beings as well as kills them. Time alone is vigilant while others sleep. Truly time is insurmountable.

Commentary: Lord Kṛṣṇa says, "Among subduers I am time." (Bg 10.30), and "I am inexhaustible time." (Bg 10.33) But the most stunning verse on the subject was quoted by Oppenheimer, the inventor of the atom bomb, when he saw the A-bomb's destructive power on the Nevada desert: "Time I am the destroyer of the worlds, and I have come to engage all men." (Bg 11.32)

Bṛhaspati observes:

> Even Rāvaṇa perished at the hands of time; Rāvaṇa—whose fortress was Mount Trikūṭa; whose moat was the very ocean; whose soldiers were fierce Rākṣasas; and whose teacher was Uśanā (Śukrācārya) himself. Certainly everything happens in the age, time, day, night, hour or moment when it is ordained, not otherwise. (GP 1.113.21–22)

Though time is timeless our days, like grains of sand running through the hour glass, are numbered. Neither do we receive a phone call nor a polite e-mail reminding us in advance which breath will be our last. *Māre kṛṣṇa rākhe ke, rākhe kṛṣṇa māre ke.* "Whomsoever Kṛṣṇa wants to save cannot be killed, and who Kṛṣṇa wants to die cannot be saved." We must be prepared for the rider of the pale horse through constant engagement in Kṛṣṇa consciousness.

ŚLOKA 6.8

न पश्यति च जन्मान्धः कामान्धो नैव पश्यति ।
मदोन्मत्ता न पश्यन्ति अर्थी दोषं न पश्यति ॥८॥

na paśyati ca janmāndhaḥ
kāmāndho naiva paśyati
madonmattā na paśyanti
arthī doṣaṁ na paśyati

He who is born blind will never see. One gripped by lust is likewise blind. A proud man is blind to the evil of his ways. And he who is bent upon gathering riches is blind to his sins.

Commentary: Ambrose Bierce jests at the miser's fate in his *Devil's Dictionary:* "*Mausoleum, n.,* the final and funniest folly of the rich."

ŚLOKA 6.9

स्वयं कर्म करोत्यात्मा स्वयं तत्फलमश्नुते ।
स्वयं भ्रमति संसारे स्वयं तस्माद्विमुच्यते ॥९॥

svayaṁ karma karoty ātmā
svayaṁ tat-phalam aśnute
svayaṁ bhramati saṁsāre
svayaṁ tasmād vimucyate

Alone the spirit soul creates his own karma, and he suffers alone the good or bad results thereby accrued. Alone the soul revolves through saṁsāra and by his own efforts alone can he be extricated.

Commentary: Spiritual life means accepting responsibility for our own deeds. Lack of self-responsibility binds uncountable souls to the modes of material nature. Even so, the person who takes responsibility for his own actions is rare indeed.

ŚLOKA 6.10

राजा राष्ट्रकृतं पापं राज्ञः पापं पुरोहितः ।
भर्ता च स्त्रीकृतं पापं शिष्यपापं गुरुस्तथा ॥१०॥

rājā rāṣṭra-kṛtaṁ pāpaṁ
rājñaḥ pāpaṁ purohitaḥ
bhartā ca strī-kṛtaṁ pāpaṁ
śiṣya-pāpaṁ gurus tathā

The king is obliged to accept the sins of his subjects; the purohita suffers for the sins of the king; the husband suffers for the sins of his wife; and the guru suffers for the sins of his initiates.

Commentary: Spiritual initiation is the most solemn of all contracts. A disciple must make every effort to remain faithful to his vows. The *guru* must likewise be a genuine *sādhu,* thoroughly dependent upon the will of God alone. The neophyte devotee who accepts disciples indiscriminately crushes himself beneath the weight of their misdeeds, as described in line four. The mark of an unqualified disciple who needlessly causes his *guru* to suffer is ingratitude. Manu declares of such *guru-drohīs* (ungrateful disciples):

By detraction of his *guru* he is reborn as an ass, through blaming his *guru* he becomes a dog in his next life, through stealing from his *guru* he will become a worm next time around and through envying his *guru* he becomes an insect. (MS 2.201)

ŚLOKA 6.11

ऋणकर्ता पिता शत्रुर्माता च व्यभिचारिणी ।
भार्या रूपवती शत्रुः पुत्रः शत्रुरपण्डितः ॥११॥

ṛṇa-kartā pitā śatrur
mātā ca vyabhicāriṇī
bhāryā rūpavatī śatruḥ
putraḥ śatrur apaṇḍitaḥ

The father who is a chronic debtor, the mother who commits adultery, the extremely beautiful wife and the unlearned son: these four are enemies in the home.

Commentary: A popular 1950s rock and roll song advised, "If you want to be happy for the rest of your life, never make a pretty woman your wife. So from my personal point of view. Get an ugly woman to marry you." Ordinary family life is described as difficult as rolling a huge boulder up hill, while having a *śatru* (enemy) in the household makes the situation even worse.

Śrīla Prabhupāda referred to this verse in his commentary on *Śrīmad-Bhāgavatam* (3.23.2) and quoted it in his lecture on 27 September 1976 in Vṛndāvana:

> Cāṇakya Paṇḍita has analyzed how in the family we can become enemies of one another. Cāṇakya Paṇḍita says, *ṛṇa-kartā pitā śatruḥ:* "A father in debts to others is enemy." Because according to *Manu-saṁhitā,* the son inherits the property of the father. That is everywhere. So *Manu-saṁhitā* also makes responsible the son for the father's debt. Nowadays, if my father is a debtor, I am not

responsible. But according to the Vedic laws, the son is responsible for the father's debt. Because he inherits the property, why he shall not inherit the debts of the father? According to *Manu-saṁhitā's* law he is obliged to pay the debts of the father.

We have seen one very practical example. Even fifty years ago, in Calcutta there was a very big barrister. He was a political leader. He was Mr. C.R. (Chittaranjan) Das … His father was also very respectable man, but later on he became so much debtor that he died insolvent … This Mr. C.R. Das, he did not get any property from the father, but by his practice as a barrister he became very rich man. In those days his monthly income was fifty thousand rupees. So he called all the creditors of his father and paid paisa to paisa: "My father died in debt. Now I have got money, you can take." So this is the duty of the son.

But if one is poor man, he cannot pay. So he becomes a subject matter of criticism. Under the circumstances the father becomes the enemy … And *mātā ca vyabhicāriṇī.* And if the mother, either she becomes prostitute or marries for the second time in the presence of elderly children, she is enemy … And Cāṇakya Paṇḍita had very bad experience with his wife. So he says, *rūpavatī bhāryā śatruḥ:* "If the wife is very beautiful, she is enemy." And "If the son is a rascal, no education, he is enemy." So these are the family enemies.

This *śloka* is also repeated in the *Hitopadeśa* of Nārāyaṇa.

ŚLOKA 6.12

लुब्धमर्थेन गृह्णीयात्स्तब्धमञ्जलिकर्मणा ।
मूर्खं छन्दानुवृत्त्या च यथार्थत्वेन पण्डितम् ॥१२॥

lubdham arthena gṛhṇīyāt
stabdham añjali-karmaṇā
mūrkhaṁ chandānuvṛttyā ca
yathārthatvena paṇḍitam

Appease a greedy man with a gift, an obstinate man with hands folded in salutation, a fool by humoring him and a paṇḍita with words of truth.

Commentary: As is it said, "Different *ślokas* for different folks."

ŚLOKA 6.13

वरं न राज्यं न कुराजराज्यं
वरं न मित्रं न कुमित्रमित्रम् ।
वरं न शिष्यो न कुशिष्यशिष्यो
वरं न दारा न कुदारदाराः ॥१३॥

varaṁ na rājyaṁ na kurāja-rājyaṁ
varaṁ na mitraṁ na kumitra-mitram
varaṁ na śiṣyo na kuśiṣya-śiṣyo
varaṁ na dārā na kudāra-dārāḥ

Better to have no kingdom than a worthless one; better to have no friend than to befriend a rascal; better to be without a disciple than have a stupid one; better to have no wife than a wicked one.

Commentary: Better no *guru* than to be misled by some charlatan who claims to be an incarnation of God. Commenting broadly on the subject of friendship, Śrīla Prabhupāda states in his small book *Perfection of Yoga:*

> A person is said to have attained to *yoga* when, having renounced all material desires, he neither acts for sense gratification nor engages in fruitive activities. A man must elevate himself by his own mind, not degrade himself. The mind is the friend of the conditioned soul, and his enemy as well. (Bg 6.4–5)

We have to raise ourselves to the spiritual standard by ourselves. In this sense I am my own friend and I am my own enemy. The opportunity is ours. There is a very nice verse by Cāṇakya Paṇḍita:

No one is anyone's friend, no one is anyone's enemy. It is only by behavior that one can understand who is his friend and who is his enemy.[15]

ŚLOKA 6.14

कुराजराज्येन कुतः प्रजासुखं
कुमित्रमित्रेण कुतोऽभिनिर्वृतिः ।
कुदारदारैश्च कुतो गृहे रतिः
कुशिष्यमध्यापयतः कुतो यशः ॥१४॥

kurāja-rājyena kutaḥ prajā-sukhaṁ
kumitra-mitreṇa kuto 'bhinirvṛtiḥ
kudāra-dāraiś ca kuto gṛhe ratiḥ
kuśiṣya-madhyāpayataḥ kuto yaśaḥ

How can citizens be happy in the kingdom of a wicked king? Can satisfaction be found in the company of a bad friend? If one is married to a shrew, will the home yield contentment? What sort of fame can be achieved by initiating rascals?

Commentary: And when the *guru* is an unqualified imposter, can the student expect liberation? Verse 6.14 is Cāṇakya Paṇḍita's commentary on verse 6.13.

ŚLOKA 6.15

सिंहादेकं बकादेकं शिक्षेच्चत्वारि कुक्कुटात् ।
वायसात्पञ्च शिक्षेच्च षट् शुनस्त्रीणि गर्दभात् ॥१५॥

siṁhād ekaṁ bakād ekaṁ
śikṣec catvāri kukkuṭāt

15. See Appendix I: Lecture: *Bhagavad-gītā As It Is,* 6.4–12—New York City, 4 September 1966.

vāyasāt pañca śikṣec ca
ṣaṭ śunas trīṇi gardabhāt

Learn one lesson from a lion, one from a crane, four from a cock, five from a crow, six from a dog and three from a donkey.

ŚLOKA 6.16

प्रभूतं कार्यमल्पं वा यन्नरः कर्तुमिच्छति ।
सर्वारम्भेण तत्कार्यं सिंहादेकं प्रचक्षते ॥१६॥

prabhūtaṁ kāryam alpaṁ vā
yan naraḥ kartum icchati
sarvārambheṇa tat kāryaṁ
siṁhād ekaṁ pracakṣate

The one excellent lesson that should be learned from a lion is that whatever a man is set upon doing should be achieved with great vitality and vigorous effort.

ŚLOKA 6.17

इन्द्रियाणि च संयम्य रागद्वेषविवर्जितः ।
समदुःखसुखः शान्तः तत्त्वज्ञः साधुरुच्यते ॥१७॥

indriyāṇi ca saṁyamya
rāga-dveṣa-vivarjitaḥ
sama-duḥkha-sukhaḥ śāntaḥ
tattva-jñaḥ sādhur ucyate

The excellent lesson the wise learn from a crane is through controlling your senses become indifferent to aversion and attraction, remaining peaceful and equipoised in misery and happiness.

Commentary: Another edition of *Cāṇakya-nīti* reads thusly:

indriyāṇi ca saṁyamya bakavat paṇḍito naraḥ
deśa-kāla-balaṁ jñātvā sarva-kāryāṇi sādhayet

The one excellent lesson the wise should learn from a crane is to restrain the senses and achieve one's goal with due knowledge of time, place and one's own ability.

ŚLOKA 6.18

प्रत्युत्थानं च युद्धं च संविभागं च बन्धुषु ।
स्वयमाक्रम्य भुक्तं च शिक्षेच्चत्वारि कुक्कुटात् ॥१८॥

pratyutthānaṁ ca yuddhaṁ ca
saṁvibhāgaṁ ca bandhuṣu
svayam ākramya bhuktaṁ ca
śikṣec catvāri kukkuṭāt

Awakening at the correct hour, taking a bold stand and fighting with courage, fair division (of property) among the family and earning by one's own efforts: these four excellent qualities should be learned from a cock.

ŚLOKA 6.19

गूढमैथुनं धार्ष्टर्यं च काले काले च सङ्ग्रहम् ।
अप्रमत्तमविश्वासं पञ्च शिक्षेच्च वायसात् ॥१९॥

gūḍha-maithunaṁ dhārṣṭyaṁ ca
kāle kāle ca saṅgraham
apramattam aviśvāsaṁ
pañca śikṣec ca vāyasāt

Union in privacy with one's wife, boldness, storing useful items, constant alertness, and caution in trusting others: these five things should be learned from a crow.

ŚLOKA 6.20

बह्वाशी स्वल्पसन्तुष्टः सनिद्रो लघुचेतनः ।
स्वामिभक्तश्च शूरश्च षडेते श्वानतो गुणाः ॥२०॥

bahvāśī svalpa-santuṣṭaḥ
sa-nidro laghu-cetanaḥ
svāmi-bhaktaś ca śūraś ca
ṣaḍ ete śvānato guṇāḥ

Being satisfied with little or nothing to eat despite having a strong appetite; sleeping deeply with the ability to awaken at once; unflinching devotion to the master; and bravery: these six qualities should be learned from a dog.

ŚLOKA 6.21

सुश्रान्तोऽपि वहेद्भारं शीतोष्णं न च पश्यति ।
सन्तुष्टश्चरते नित्यं त्रीणि शिक्षेच्च गर्दभात् ॥२१॥

suśrānto 'pi vahed bhāraṁ
śītoṣṇaṁ na ca paśyati
santuṣṭaś carate nityaṁ
trīṇi śikṣec ca gardabhāt

Ability to carry the burden despite fatigue; indifference to heat and cold; and contentment: these three qualities should be learned from a donkey.

ŚLOKA 6.22

य एतान्विंशतिगुणानाचरिष्यति मानवः ।
कार्यावस्थासु सर्वासु अजेयः स भविष्यति ॥२२॥

ya etān viṁśati-guṇān
ācariṣyati mānavaḥ
kāryāvasthāsu sarvāsu
ajeyaḥ sa bhaviṣyati

He who practices these twenty virtues will become invincible in all he does.

Commentary: Devotees of the Lord are decorated with the following twenty-six virtues which are described by Śrī Caitanya Mahāprabhu in the *Caitanya-caritāmṛta* (2.22.78–80). Śrīla Prabhupāda listed them for his disciples when he established his League of Devotees in Jhansi in 1956, and again in 1966 at his first ISKCON center in New York:

1. *Kṛpālu:* kind to everyone
2. *Akṛta-droha:* never creates enmity with others
3. *Satya-sāra:* truthful
4. *Sama:* equal to everyone
5. *Nidoṣa:* faultless
6. *Vadānya:* charitable
7. *Mṛdu:* mild
8. *Śuci:* clean
9. *Akiñcana:* without possessions and lives simply
10. *Sarvopakāraka:* benevolent, works for the benefit of others
11. *Śānta:* peaceful
12. *Kṛṣṇaika-śaraṇa:* always surrendered to Lord Kṛṣṇa

13. *Akāma:* has no material desires
14. *Anīha:* meek
15. *Sthira:* steady, always fixed in the Absolute Truth
16. *Vijita-ṣaḍ-guṇa:* self-controlled
17. *Mita-bhuk:* does not eat more than required
18. *Apramatta:* sane, does not fall under the spell of *māyā*
19. *Mānada:* respectful to others
20. *Amānī:* does not hanker for respect
21. *Gambhīra:* very grave
22. *Karuṇa:* merciful and compassionate
23. *Maitra:* friendly
24. *Kavi:* poetic
25. *Dakṣa:* expert
26. *Maunī:* silent, speaks only that which is necessary

Thus Ends Chapter Six

CHAPTER SEVEN

ŚLOKA 7.1

अर्थनाशं मनस्तापं गृहे दुश्चरितानि च ।
नीचं वाक्यं चापमानं मतिमान्न प्रकाशयेत् ॥१॥

artha-nāśaṁ manas-tāpaṁ
gṛhe duścaritāni ca
nīcaṁ vākyaṁ cāpamānaṁ
matimān na prakāśayet

A wise man does not reveal his own loss of money, the vexation of his mind, the misconduct of his own family members, base words spoken by others and personal disgrace.

Commentary: As it is said, do not hang out dirty laundry. Bṛhaspati offers the same advice in the *Garuḍa Purāṇa* (1.109.15).

ŚLOKA 7.2

धनधान्यप्रयोगेषु विद्यासङ्ग्रहणेषु च ।
आहारे व्यवहारे च त्यक्तलज्जः सुखी भवेत् ॥२॥

dhana-dhānya-prayogeṣu
vidyā-saṅgrahaṇeṣu ca
āhāre vyavahāre ca
tyakta-lajjaḥ sukhī bhavet

He who renounces shyness in monetary transactions, in giving and receiving food grains, in acquiring knowledge, in eating and in social dealings becomes happy.

Commentary: *Lajjā* (shyness) may be the adornment of a woman (see CN 1.17), but it is the downfall of a businessman. The purpose of *nīti-śāstra* is to teach us to become adept at judging what is to be done under each moment and circumstance. The material advice of lines one, three and four are meant to emphasize line two, which is especially useful for a devotee.

ŚLOKA 7.3

सन्तोषामृततृप्तानां यत्सुखं शान्तिरेव च ।
न च तद्धनलुब्धानामितश्चेतश्च धावताम् ॥३॥

santoṣāmṛta-tṛptānāṁ
yat sukhaṁ śāntir eva ca
na ca tad dhana-lubdhānām
itaś cetaś ca dhāvatām

That happiness and peace attained by those satisfied with the nectar of spiritual tranquility is never found by those who roam about impelled by greed.

Commentary: Cāṇakya Paṇḍita's description of happiness is *santoṣāmṛta,* literally "deathless contentment" or "satisfaction that exists on the eternal plane." The demigods are said to drink an elixir that imparts deathlessness, hence *amṛta* (lit. "no death") is often translated as "nectar." *Santa,* means "a man of peace," and has found its way into English as "saint." This is ironic since for centuries Western religionists were reluctant to admit to the godly qualities of saints of India, from where the very concept of *santa* originated. Instead, these "religionists" have denigrated austere and pious *yogīs* as heathens, and have awarded official "sainthood" to cow eaters.

A genuine saint lives only to serve the Supreme Lord. Kṛṣṇa defines the qualities of a true saint in the *Bhagavad-gītā:*

> One who is equal to friends and enemies, who is equiposed in honor and dishonor, heat and cold, happiness and distress, fame and infamy, who is always free from contamination, always silent and satisfied with anything, who does not care for any residence, who is fixed in knowledge and engaged in devotional service, is very dear to Me. (Bg 12.18–19)

ŚLOKA 7.4

सन्तोषस्त्रिषु कर्तव्यः स्वदारे भोजने धने ।
त्रिषु चैव न कर्तव्योऽध्ययने जपदानयोः ॥४॥

santoṣas triṣu kartavyaḥ
sva-dāre bhojane dhane
triṣu caiva na kartavyo
'dhyayane japa-dānayoḥ

A man should feel satisfied with the following three: his wife, food given by Providence, and wealth acquired by honest effort. He should never be satisfied with these three: study, chanting and offering of charity.

Commentary: Nowadays many men are dissatisfied with their live-in "wives," so they bundle them off to the scalpels of plastic surgeons to become silicon-stuffed mutants. As far as wealth is concerned, many who are dissatisfied with their lot fall victim to talkative, self-styled "motivational *gurus*." They claim their new *karma*-altering techniques will turn paupers into millionaires. Although the "*gurus*" become rich by selling books, no one's fate has ever improved through such empty promises. Vedic intelligence understands that our income and the food we eat have been fixed at conception. No one has the ability to change the stars under which he was born except Kṛṣṇa's bona fide representative. But rather than change our *karma,* he unburdens us of it.

Cāṇakya Paṇḍita advises that we do not become too satisfied with our moral and spiritual duties. He specifically mentions *japa,* chanting of the holy names of the Supreme Lord. Our spiritual master chanted the holy names twenty-four hours a day, even in his sleep. He chanted continually despite writing five dozen large volumes, scribing ten thousand instructive letters, establishing dozens of Rādhā-Kṛṣṇa temples, initiating thousands of disciples and thereby reestablishing a true conception of religious thought for the entire world. Not surprisingly, his work became known by the *mantra* itself, and today the "Hare Krishna Movement" is recognized as a bona fide worldwide religion, though hardly a handful of Westerners had heard the name of Kṛṣṇa before Śrīla Prabhupāda arrived in the USA in 1965.

Regarding *japa* mentioned in line four above, in his biography of Śrīla Bhaktisiddhānta Sārasvatī Ṭhākura entitled *Ray of Viṣṇu,* Śrīmān Rūpa Vilāsa Dāsa explains our *parama-gurudeva's* vow of chanting one billion names of God:

> In 1905, at the age of 31, he began his great vow, following the footsteps of Nāmācārya Haridāsa Ṭhākura, of chanting three *lakhs* names (192 rounds) per day. He determined that at the rate of 300,000 names daily, it would take about nine years to complete one billion names. ... He would take rest on the ground, never using any pillows, and constantly chant and study the scriptures. ... When the roof of his *kuṭīra* became broken, rather than take time away from his chanting, he would simply use an umbrella when it rained and go on chanting.

ŚLOKA 7.5

विप्रयोर्विप्रवह्न्योश्च दम्पत्योः स्वामिभृत्ययोः ।
अन्तरेण न गन्तव्यं हलस्य वृषभस्य च ॥५॥

viprayor vipra-vahnyoś ca
dampatyoḥ svāmi-bhṛtyayoḥ
antareṇa na gantavyaṁ
halasya vṛṣabhasya ca

Do not pass between two brāhmaṇas, between a brāhmaṇa and his sacrificial fire, between a wife and her husband, a master and his servant, a bull and his plow.

Commentary: Bṛhaspati counsels likewise in the *Garuḍa Purāṇa* (1.114.45). Vedic etiquette emphasizes avoiding offenses, especially to cows, *brāhmaṇas* and holy persons. Once caused, offenses can be difficult to remove, even with great *prāyaścitta* (atonement). Offenses committed in holy places are even more difficult to shed, hence one should not stay so long in a holy place like Vṛndāvana that he becomes too lax towards the saints who live there.

ŚLOKA 7.6

पादाभ्यां न स्पृशेदग्निं गुरुं ब्राह्मणमेव च ।
नैव गां न कुमारीं च न वृद्धं न शिशुं तथा ॥६॥

pādābhyāṁ na spṛśed agniṁ
guruṁ brāhmaṇam eva ca
naiva gāṁ na kumārīṁ ca
na vṛddhaṁ na śiśuṁ tathā

Do not let your foot touch fire, the guru or a brāhmaṇa. It must never touch a cow, a virgin, an old person or a child.

Commentary: Since the foot touches the ground, it is considered a great insult in Vedic society to touch another with one's foot, even by accident. To this day in India kicking another is an invitation for one's own swift death. In order to be excused, such an accident must be followed by a genuine apology to the person who was offended.

ŚLOKA 7.7

शकटं पञ्चहस्तेन दशहस्तेन वाजिनम् ।
हस्तिनं शतहस्तेन देशत्यागेन दुर्जनम् ॥७॥

śakaṭaṁ pañca-hastena
daśa-hastena vājinam
hastinaṁ śata-hastena
deśa-tyāgena durjanam

Keep five cubits away from a cart, ten cubits from a horse, one hundred cubits from an elephant, but keep away from rogues by leaving the country.

Commentary: In this verse, Cāṇakya Paṇḍita describes the old Vedic system of measurement called *hasta* (hand). This system of measuring by hands is still used by horsemen today, an unknowing appreciation of the *kṣatriya* horsemen of old Bhārata. The archaic English "cubit" equals the length of an arm up to the elbow, and is therefore derived from the concept of "hand" since *hasta* means either the hand itself, or the hand-plus-forearm. A cubit measures about eighteen inches, and doubled, it equals a yard or three feet. The measurement of *caraṇa* (foot) is also known in Vedic society and is used in measuring astrological distances of four *caraṇas* per *nakṣatra.* There is an unseen abundance of Vedic-Sanskrit influence in modern language, science, tradition and religion. Therefore the conclusion must be that modern vernacular and religion must have their origin in Vedic culture. Indeed, an unbiased study easily reveals ancient India to be the birthplace of civilization.

Cāṇakya Paṇḍita advises "keep one hundred hands away from an elephant," but "entirely renounce that place inhabited by a crooked man." In other words, the association of nondevotees addicted to sense gratification is more dangerous than a wild elephant. If necessary, bad association must be avoided to the extent of abandoning one's own country. Lord Kṛṣṇa defines the activities of the nondevotee as he who "performs action in illusion, disregards scriptural injunctions, has no concern for future bondage, and whose cruelty causes distress for others." (Bg 18.25) The company of such blind materialists who revel in the mode of *tamo-guṇa* (ignorance) is a death knell for spiritual life.

Another slight variation of this verse substitutes *śakaṭa* (cart) in the first line for this: *śṛṅgiṇāṁ daśa-hastena,* or "keep ten cubits from beasts with horns."

ŚLOKA 7.8

हस्ती ह्यङ्कुशमात्रेण वाजी हस्तेन ताड्यते ।
शृङ्गी लगुडहस्तेन खड्गहस्तेन दुर्जनः ॥८॥

hastī hy aṅkuśa-mātreṇa
vājī hastena tāḍyate
śṛṅgī laguḍa-hastena
khaḍga-hastena durjanaḥ

Control an elephant with an aṅkuśa, a horse with the slap of your hand, a horned animal by showing a stick and a rascal with a sword.

Commentary: Cāṇakya Paṇḍita continues the thought of the previous verse: if you are not able to forsake the country inhabited by a rascal, then show him a *khaḍga* (sword)! Bhartṛhari notes:

> It may be possible to forcibly retrieve a gem from the fanged jaws of a crocodile; swim the turbulent waves of the ocean; or even

adorn one's head with an angry cobra instead of a flower; but it is impossible to please a perverse and conceited fool. (NS 3)

ŚLOKA 7.9

तुष्यन्ति भोजने विप्रा मयूरा घनगर्जिते ।
साधवः परसम्पत्तौ खलाः परविपत्तिषु ॥९॥

tuṣyanti bhojane viprā
mayūrā ghana-garjite
sādhavaḥ para-sampattau
khalāḥ para-vipattiṣu

Brāhmaṇas are satisfied with a fine meal, peacocks by the clap of thunder, sādhus by seeing the prosperity of others and the wicked by the miseries of others.

Commentary: And so it is that various types of entities are born upon this earthly stage. Good people shine before the glow of another's success, while the envious wilt. In India, the peacocks dancing together at the start of the monsoon season are a wondrous sight. It is said that the call of the peacocks is *megh-ho* ("come cloud").

ŚLOKA 7.10

अनुलोमेन बलिनं प्रतिलोमेन दुर्जनम् ।
आत्मतुल्यबलं शत्रुं विनयेन बलेन वा ॥१०॥

anulomena balinaṁ
pratilomena durjanam
ātma-tulya-balaṁ śatruṁ
vinayena balena vā

Conciliate a strong man through submission, a wicked man by opposition and an enemy who is your equal in strength by either politeness or force.

Commentary: Any attempt at a friendly relationship with a *durjana* (crooked man) results only in misery. Therefore Cāṇakya Paṇḍita advises us that such persons should be opposed. Treat those who are equal with politeness, but show your resolve if the situation calls for it. The English word "politics" shares the same root with words like "polite" or "policy;" and has its origin from the Latin *politicus.* Therefore politics doesn't always mean "dirty politics." From the life of the political whiz Cāṇakya Paṇḍita, we learn that an intelligent man makes his judgment according to time and circumstances. Then he draws up a plan accordingly that is aimed at achieving his ends with as little resistance as possible. How he goes about that depends upon the nature of those who he must deal with.

ŚLOKA 7.11

बाहुवीर्यं बलं राज्ञो ब्राह्मणो ब्रह्मविद्बली ।
रूपयौवनमाधुर्यं स्त्रीणां बलमनुत्तमम् ॥११॥

bāhu-vīryaṁ balaṁ rājño
brāhmaṇo brahma-vid balī
rūpa-yauvana-mādhuryaṁ
strīṇāṁ balam anuttamam

A king's might is in the strength of his arms; the brāhmaṇa's power is in his spiritual knowledge; and a woman's power is her comeliness, youth and sweetness.

Commentary: Here the qualities of the king, *brāhmaṇa* and woman are mentioned, but of those mentioned only the *brāhmaṇa's* are everlasting. In this material world nothing stands forever. Relics washed up from the sands of time leave archaeologists guessing, while new kingdoms that arise atop the old ones only tempt fate with another losing battle. That which begins will end, including the greatest civilizations of earth. History will record this to be so, even for our modern oil-based society in which we have misplaced so much faith. When a guest noted that America's wealth would continue forever, Prabhupāda chuckled wryly, "There is no guarantee." The poet Percy Bysshe Shelley wrote of this in his *Ozymandias:*

I met a traveler from an antique land
Who said: Two vast and trunkless legs of stone
Stand in the desert... Near them, on the sand,
Half sunk, a shattered visage lies, whose frown,
And wrinkled lip, and sneer of cold command,
Tell that its sculptor well those passions read,
Which yet survive, stamped on those lifeless things,
The hand that mocked them, and the heart that fed:
And on the pedestal these words appear:
"My name is Ozymandias, king of kings:
Look on my works, ye Mighty, and despair!"
Nothing beside remains. Round the decay
Of that colossal wreck, boundless and bare
The lone and level sands stretch far away.

The lone ray of hope in this verse is the *brahma-vidyā,* or spiritual knowledge (the *bala* or strength of the *brāhmaṇa*). Only he who knows the all-encompassing spiritual energy Brahman—which includes the source of Brahman who is Śrī Kṛṣṇa—can be called a *brāhmaṇa.* Cultivation of Kṛṣṇa consciousness alone can save the fettered conditioned soul who is wandering and lost in the three worlds. By the grace of the spiritual master, our transcendental realizations of *bhakti* are the only assets we can hope to transport from this life unto the eternal service of the Lord in His own abode.

ŚLOKA 7.12

नात्यन्तं सरलैर्भाव्यं गत्वा पश्य वनस्थलीम् ।
छिद्यन्ते सरलास्तत्र कुब्जास्तिष्ठन्ति पादपाः ॥१२॥

nātyantaṁ saralair bhāvyaṁ
gatvā paśya vana-sthalīm
chidyante saralās tatra
kubjās tiṣṭhanti pādapāḥ

Do not be very upright in your dealings for you can see by going to the forest that the straight trees are cut down while the crooked ones are left to stand.

Commentary: This is an essential point of *nīti-śāstra.* It is one of Cāṇakya Paṇḍita's most famous verses though it has been repeated from the *Garuḍa Purāṇa* 1.114.50. Absolutely straight-forward persons are condemned as villains by those who feign honesty. Therefore, don't be perfectly truthful in the marketplace unless you don't mind being called a cheat. The wise tutored in political wisdom know how to bend without breaking. This was a lesson Śrī Kṛṣṇa taught Arjuna when he explained how to defeat Droṇācārya at Kurukṣetra (as told in the *Droṇa-parva* of the *Mahābhārata*).

ŚLOKA 7.13

यत्रोदकं तत्र वसन्ति हंसा-
स्तथैव शुष्कं परिवर्जयन्ति ।
न हंसतुल्येन नरेण भाव्यं
पुनस्त्यजन्ते पुनराश्रयन्ते ॥१३॥

yatrodakaṁ tatra vasanti haṁsās
tathaiva śuṣkaṁ parivarjayanti

na haṁsa-tulyena nareṇa bhāvyaṁ
punas tyajante punar āśrayante

Swans live wherever water is found and leave when it dries up. Let not a man act so, coming and going as he pleases.

Commentary: One of the most poignant lessons of *nīti-śāstra* is devotion to one's duty. As poet Wordsworth has said: "Duty—stern daughter of the voice of God." A devotee demonstrates his mettle through his steadiness of character and fidelity in his service to Śrī Guru. Whether in material or spiritual life, steadfast dedication is the key to success. Even today there are some who believe that Śrīla Prabhupāda whimsically altered the teachings of the *sampradāya* during his last days in order to institute a so-called *ṛtvik* system. Such speculation is an incorrect assumption on the part of disciples who have understood imperfectly. A genuine *ācārya's* teachings can only echo the system of *guru-paramparā* that has been in effect since time immemorial.

ŚLOKA 7.14

उपार्जितानां वित्तानां त्याग एव हि रक्षणम् ।
तडागोदरसंस्थानां परीवाह इवाम्भसाम् ॥१४॥

upārjitānāṁ vittānāṁ
tyāga eva hi rakṣaṇam
taḍāgodara-saṁsthānāṁ
parīvāha ivāmbhasām

Accumulated wealth is preserved by spending just as incoming fresh water is saved by letting out the stagnant water.

Commentary: Cāṇakya Paṇḍita does not advise hoarding wealth because stored funds can be taken away in one fell swoop, as happened to the honey bee (CN 11.18). As seen in that verse, the recommended means of preserving wealth is spiritual charity. The resultant good *karma* created by altruistic spending creates the materially favorable reaction of continued income. Wealth is only achieved via past piety, but miserly attachment to such wealth results in continued rebirth and misery. *Nīti-śāstra* ordains that wealth can be accumulated honestly and it should be managed and expended properly. Even so, a wise person never becomes attached to wealth thinking he will enjoy it forever.

While charity never goes unrewarded, simple altruism alone is not sufficient to gain eternal life in the kingdom of God. The fate of one who does not achieve liberation due to some lingering material desire is described by Lord Kṛṣṇa:

> The unsuccessful *yogī* after many, many years of enjoyment on the planets of the pious living entities, is born into a family of righteous people, or into a family of rich aristocracy. (Bg 6.41)

Kṛṣṇa describes those who have fallen from *yoga* practice as *yoga-bhraṣṭa. Yoga* means "to link" with God and *bhraṣṭa* means "broken." Thus, those who do not achieve the goal, whose *yoga* becomes *bhraṣṭa,* are given another chance. *Śucīnāṁ śrīmatāṁ gehe:* the *yoga-bhraṣṭa* is either born into a well-to-do household or into a family of *brāhmaṇas.* Real charity means that one must become a devotee of Lord Śrī Kṛṣṇa and offer everything at His lotus feet as a qualification for going back to Godhead.

ŚLOKA 7.15

यस्यार्थस्तस्य मित्राणि यस्यार्थस्तस्य बान्धवाः ।
यस्यार्थः स पुमाँल्लोके यस्यार्थः स च जीवति ॥१५॥

yasyārthas tasya mitrāṇi
yasyārthas tasya bāndhavāḥ

yasyārthaḥ sa pumāl̐ loke
yasyārthaḥ sa ca jīvati

He alone who has money has friends and relatives. Only one who is wealthy survives and is respected as a man.

Commentary: Although Cāṇakya Paṇḍita chose to live as a poor *brāhmaṇa,* as the author of the *Artha-śāstra* written under the name Kauṭilya, he was a past master on the subject of *artha* or "the science of economic development."

Bṛhaspati notes:

> Riches dwindle when fortune dwindles and not by enjoyment. If sufficient merit had been acquired earlier, riches would never perish. (GP 1.113.12)

> Friends, sons, the wife and relatives abandon a man who becomes devoid of wealth. When he regains his lost wealth, they return to him. Hence wealth alone is a man's kith and kin, none other. (GP 1.111.18)

With tongue in cheek, Bhartṛhari agrees:

> Only he who is wealthy is regarded as having a line of noble descent; he alone is a *paṇḍita,* a scholar of the scriptures, a connoisseur, an orator and good looking as well. All virtues are sheltered in gold. (NS 40)

ŚLOKA 7.16

स्वर्गस्थितानामिह जीवलोके
चत्वारि चिह्नानि वसन्ति देहे ।
दानप्रसङ्गो मधुरा च वाणी
देवार्चनं ब्राह्मणतर्पणं च ॥१६॥

svarga-sthitānām iha jīva-loke
catvāri cihnāni vasanti dehe

dāna-prasaṅgo madhurā ca vāṇī
devārcanaṁ brāhmaṇa-tarpaṇaṁ ca

These four qualities of the denizens of Svargaloka may be observed even here on earth: charity, sweet words, worship of the Supreme Lord and satisfying the needs of brāhmaṇas.

Commentary: At times "*deva*" may refer to the demigods, but in this case it refers to the Supreme Lord Himself (who is worshipped by all the *devas*).

ŚLOKA 7.17

अत्यन्तकोपः कटुका च वाणी
दरिद्रता च स्वजनेषु वैरम् ।
नीचप्रसङ्गः कुलहीनसेवा
चिह्नानि देहे नरकस्थितानाम् ॥१७॥

atyanta-kopaḥ kaṭukā ca vāṇī
daridratā ca svajaneṣu vairam
nīca-prasaṅgaḥ kula-hīna-sevā
cihnāni dehe naraka-sthitānām

The following qualities of the residents of the hellish planets may characterize men of this earth: extreme wrath, harsh speech, poverty, enmity with one's relations, the company of the base and service to men of low extraction.

Commentary: Though life here on earth is a mere flash in the pan, it is still nothing more than what we have created by our past activities. It is either a launching pad to the higher regions of the universe, a swift chute to hell or the last stop on the road back to Godhead. The earthly planetary system is a crossroads of the universe and many types of persons can be found here: godly, demonic and those of mixed qualities. A man is judged by his speech, and two types of speech are described in verses 7.16 and 7.17.

ŚLOKA 7.18

गम्यते यदि मृगेन्द्रमन्दिरं
लभ्यते करिकपालमौक्तिकम् ।
जम्बुकालयगते च प्राप्यते
वत्सपुच्छखरचर्मखण्डनम् ॥१८॥

gamyate yadi mṛgendra-mandiraṁ
labhyate kari-kapāla-mauktikam
jambukālaya-gate ca prāpyate
vatsa-puccha-khara-carma-khaṇḍanam

By entering the den of a lion, one may obtain pearls from the heads of elephants, but by entering into the cave of a jackal one may find nothing but the tail of a calf or a bit of the hide of an ass.

Commentary: Regarding those with whom we choose to associate, Bhartṛhari observes:

> Water when splashed upon a hot iron evaporates without a trace. A drop of water resting upon a lotus leaf glistens in the sun. The same droplet, when entering an oyster while the moon is conjoined with the Svātī star, becomes a pearl. In the same way, a man's qualities become base, middling or exalted through his association. (NS 66)

ŚLOKA 7.19

शुनः पुच्छमिव व्यर्थं जीवितं विद्यया विना ।
न गुह्यगोपने शक्तं न च दंशनिवारणे ॥१९॥

śunaḥ puccham iva vyarthaṁ
jīvitaṁ vidyayā vinā

na guhya-gopane śaktaṁ
na ca daṁśa-nivāraṇe

He who is without learning passes life as uselessly as the tail of a dog—it neither covers the rear nor offers protection from biting insects.

Commentary: Cāṇakya Paṇḍita thus makes his feelings for the illiterate well understood. That which is considered as learning, as taught in today's colleges and universities, is mostly the cultivation of nescience. The system of piling illusion upon ignorance grows worse each year as preposterous theories are taught as scientific facts. In his *Devil's Dictionary,* Ambrose Bierce wryly notes that education is "the kind of ignorance distinguishing the studious." There is a great need for the introduction of the Absolute Truth as revealed in the Vedic scriptures as it was taught in the *gurukulas* of ancient Bhārata. Only when genuine Vedic knowledge and transcendental realization are added to the college regimen of mundane arts and speculative sciences can material education be judged as useful.

Bṛhaspati concurs:

> That son who has not earned a reputation for valor, austerity, charity, the acquisition of wealth or learning, is but the excrement of his mother. (GP 1.115.32)

Bhartṛhari likewise condemns the unlettered:

> Those who are devoid of literature, music and art are but animals without horns and tail. It is the great luck of other animals that such people survive without eating grass! (NS 11)

ŚLOKA 7.20

वाचां शौचं च मनसः शौचमिन्द्रियनिग्रहः ।
सर्वभूतदया शौचमेतच्छौचं परार्थिनाम् ॥२०॥

vācāṁ śaucaṁ ca manasaḥ
śaucam indriya-nigrahaḥ
sarva-bhūta-dayā śaucam
etac chaucaṁ parārthinām

Purity of speech, of mind, of the senses and purity of a compassionate heart are needed by one who desires to rise to the divine platform.

Commentary: How to avoid "living as uselessly as the tail of a dog," as described in the previous verse, is revealed in this *śloka.* The awakening of these qualities through engaging in Kṛṣṇa consciousness is the platform from which true and genuine learning can begin.

ŚLOKA 7.21

पुष्पे गन्धं तिले तैलं काष्ठेऽग्निं पयसि घृतम् ।
इक्षौ गुडं तथा देहे पश्यात्मानं विवेकतः ॥२१॥

puṣpe gandhaṁ tile tailaṁ
kāṣṭhe 'gniṁ payasi ghṛtam
ikṣau guḍaṁ tathā dehe
paśyātmānaṁ vivekataḥ

There is fragrance in a flower, oil in sesame, fire in wood, ghee in milk, and brown sugar in sugarcane. In the same way the discriminating perceive the spirit soul residing within the body.

Commentary: Cāṇakya Paṇḍita closes chapter seven by continuing to develop the train of thought of the previous several verses (which discuss either learning or the absence of it). The great *paṇḍita* now discusses higher, spiritual knowledge. Self-realized knowledge lies dormant in the hearts of all living entities. It is said that the musk deer runs in every direction searching for the scent that originates from his own body. In exactly the same way, we wander the universe seeking exotic pleasures, all the while never realizing that true happiness lies within. Kṛṣṇa tells Arjuna:

brahma-bhūtaḥ prasannātmā   na śocati na kāṅkṣati
samaḥ sarveṣu bhūteṣu   mad-bhaktiṁ labhate parām

> One who is transcendentally situated becomes joyous in his realization of the Supreme Brahman. He never laments nor desires to have anything; he is equally disposed to every living entity. In that state he obtains pure devotional service unto Me. (Bg 18.54)

Thus Ends Chapter Seven

CHAPTER EIGHT

ŚLOKA 8.1

अधमा धनमिच्छन्ति धनमानौ च मध्यमाः ।
उत्तमा मानमिच्छन्ति मानो हि महतां धनम् ॥१॥

adhamā dhanam icchanti
dhana-mānau ca madhyamāḥ
uttamā mānam icchanti
māno hi mahatāṁ dhanam

Low class men desire wealth; middle class men covet both wealth and respect; but the noble value honor alone. Hence honor is the true wealth for a noble man.

Commentary: Bhartṛhari observes:

> Let men versed in *nīti-śāstra* praise or condemn me. Let Lakṣmījī enter my house or leave it as she desires. Let death visit me today or after several *yugas*. But sober men do not swerve from the path of justice. (NS 80)

ŚLOKA 8.2

इक्षुरापः पयो मूलं ताम्बूलं फलमौषधम् ।
भक्षयित्वापि कर्तव्याः स्नानदानादिकाः क्रियाः ॥२॥

ikṣur āpaḥ payo mūlaṁ
tāmbūlaṁ phalam auṣadham
bhakṣayitvāpi kartavyāḥ
snāna-dānādikāḥ kriyāḥ

There is no harm to the ritual incurred by him who—after partaking sugarcane, water, milk, roots, betel nut, fruit or medicines—engages in his daily religious duties of bathing, giving alms and other religious rites.

Commentary: Chewing *pān* (betel nut) is very popular in the Indian states of Uttar Pradesh and Bihar. Śrīla Bhaktisiddhānta Sārasvatī Gosvāmī would not allow his disciples to chew *pān,* and thus bringing new members into the Gauḍīya Maṭha from these areas proved daunting. In Uttar Pradesh and Bihar chewers of *pān* often discharge their reddish saliva all over walls, on doorways, temples and sidewalks, leaving an offensive red stain. Nowadays owners of buildings have begun putting up pictures from every religion in their hallways to prevent *pān* chewers from leaving their permanent marks all over their walls. Like the members of the Gauḍīya Maṭha, members of ISKCON are proscribed from chewing *pān.*

ŚLOKA 8.3

दीपो भक्षयते ध्वान्तं कज्जलं च प्रसूयते ।
यदन्नं भक्ष्यते नित्यं जायते तादृशी प्रजा ॥३॥

dīpo bhakṣayate dhvāntaṁ
kajjalaṁ ca prasūyate
yad annaṁ bhakṣyate nityaṁ
jāyate tādṛśī prajā

The oil lamp eats the darkness and then spits out lamp black. In the same way, according to the nature of our diet we produce offspring of similar qualities.

Commentary: Here Cāṇakya Paṇḍita points out the importance of diet. The types of food we eat not only affect our *karma,* our consciousness and our health, but also are determining factors in the children we produce. The poet reasons that since a lamp eats only darkness, what else can it produce but soot?

As explained by Śrī Kṛṣṇa in the *Bhagavad-gītā* (17.8–10) foodstuffs fall into three basic categories: *sattva-guṇa* (the mode of goodness), *rajo-guṇa* (the mode of passion) and *tamo-guṇa* (the mode of ignorance). The *Rati-śāstra,* a Purāṇic conversation between Lord Śiva and Pārvatī about the proper means of procreation, warns against sexual intercourse "while one's belly is filled with food cooked by a *śūdra.*" "You are what you eat" is a well-known adage. Here we learn that "what you eat is what you procreate" as well.

The sins of the parents are vested on the children, including the very diet of the parents, which can cause the birth of children imbued with undesirable qualities, or even physical defects. Kṛṣṇa says *dvau bhūta-sargau loke 'smin daiva āsura eva ca.* "In this world there are two types of created beings, the divine and the demonic." (Bg 16.6) Kṛṣṇa observes that the latter type of persons "engage in unbeneficial, horrible works meant to destroy the world." (Bg 16.9) Those words are just as true today as when Kṛṣṇa spoke them to Arjuna. With its polluting vehicles, factories, slaughterhouses, and foolish dependency upon oil—all of which in turn create horrible wars—this sick and demonic society can only be cured through Kṛṣṇa consciousness and *saṅkīrtana-yajña.*

The recommended process for expanding spiritual growth from one generation to the next is to eat only fresh *sattva-guṇa* foods such as milk, grains, nuts, fruits and vegetables that have been properly prepared and offered to the Lord. Such foodstuffs are accepted as *prasāda* (mercy) of God and protect the devotee in every way—including the quality of souls that will take birth in his family.

ŚLOKA 8.4

वित्तं देहि गुणान्वितेषु मतिमन्नान्यत्र देहि क्वचित्
प्राप्तं वारिनिधेर्जलं घनमुखे माधुर्ययुक्तं सदा ।
जीवान्स्थावरजङ्गमांश्च सकलान्सञ्जीव्य भूमण्डलं
भूयः पश्य तदेव कोटिगुणितं गच्छन्तमम्भोनिधिम् ॥४॥

vittaṁ dehi guṇānviteṣu matiman nānyatra dehi kvacit
prāptaṁ vāri-nidher jalaṁ ghana-mukhe mādhurya-yuktaṁ sadā
jīvān sthāvara-jaṅgamāṁś ca sakalān sañjīvya bhū-maṇḍalaṁ
bhūyaḥ paśya tad eva koṭi-guṇitaṁ gacchantam ambho-nidhim

O wise one! Offer your wealth only to the worthy—never to others. That water which the cloud receives from the sea is always sweet. When it returns again as rain water, it enlivens all living beings of the earth: both movable and unmovable. It then returns to the ocean with its value multiplied a millionfold.

Commentary: Varuṇa, the ocean god, is as noble as he is deep and vast. Thus he freely gives his waters to the cloud. Sea water, though saline, becomes sweet when offered up in this way. The cloud shares these waters as a blessing to all creatures of the land, mother Bhūmi. As water becomes streams, it cleanses and nourishes all living things. It then joins with the rivers and returns to the ocean after blessing the earth. This may be compared with charity in the mode of goodness which, rather than becoming a source of loss, is the means to increase one's own wealth and prosperity. Cāṇakya Paṇḍita stresses charity in many places, but in this verse he indicates which acts of charity are beneficial. In Vedic society, *brāhmaṇas* (like the cloud in this verse), are authorized to accept offerings because of their vow to offer everything to the Supreme Brahman, Śrī Kṛṣṇa. Offering money to a devotee therefore not only augments public good, but also increases one's own wealth through transcendental piety.

ŚLOKA 8.5

चाण्डालानां सहस्रैश्च सूरिभिस्तत्त्वदर्शिभिः ।
एको हि यवनः प्रोक्तो न नीचो यवनात्परः ॥५॥

cāṇḍālānāṁ sahasraiś ca
sūribhis tattva-darśibhiḥ
eko hi yavanaḥ prokto
na nīco yavanāt paraḥ

The wise who discern the substance of things have stated that one yavana equals a thousand cāṇḍālas. Hence the yavana is the basest of mankind—there is none lower.

Commentary: Here the word *yavana* meaning "meat-eater" refers to the Greeks. Cāṇakya Paṇḍita thrived at a time when India was under attack by Alexander the Great and his army. Many myths have arisen around why Alexander left India. In fact, according to India's version of history, it was Cāṇakya Paṇḍita's protégé King Candragupta Maurya who defeated Alexander and forced the Greeks to turn back. India's history has suffered from misrepresentation for centuries because it was written by invading enemies, especially the Mughals and the British. One thousand years of scholastic prejudice has kept the real glory of India hidden.

In his encyclopedic volume *The Wonder That Was India,* indological scholar A.L. Basham begins with a quote from the Syrian monk-astronomer Sererus Sebokht (seventh century AD):

> I shall now speak of the knowledge of the Hindus… of their subtle discoveries of astronomy—discoveries even more ingenious than those of the Greeks and Babylonians… of their rational system of mathematics, or of their method of calculation which no words can praise strongly enough—I mean the system using nine symbols. If these things were known by the people who think that they alone have mastered the sciences because they speak Greek, they would be perhaps convinced, though a little late in the day, that other folk, not only Greeks, but men of a different tongue, know something as well as they.

ŚLOKA 8.6

तैलाभ्यङ्गे चिताधूमे मैथुने क्षौरकर्मणि ।
तावद्भवति चाण्डालो यावत्स्नानं न चाचरेत् ॥६॥

tailābhyaṅge citā-dhūme
maithune kṣaura-karmaṇi
tāvad bhavati cāṇḍālo
yāvat snānaṁ na cācaret

After having oil rubbed on his body, after passing through the smoke of a funeral pyre, after sexual intercourse and after being shaved, one remains a cāṇḍāla until he bathes.

Commentary: No society in the world places as much emphasis upon the ritual of the daily bath as does Vedic civilization and culture. Water, the representative of the *brāhmaṇa* class, is the purifier of the world. Common sense tells us that cleanliness is conducive to health and longevity. Indeed, many *brāhmaṇas* regularly bathe thrice in a day.

ŚLOKA 8.7

अजीर्णे भेषजं वारि जीर्णे वारि बलप्रदम् ।
भोजने चामृतं वारि भोजनान्ते विषप्रदम् ॥७॥

ajīrṇe bheṣajaṁ vāri
jīrṇe vāri bala-pradam
bhojane cāmṛtaṁ vāri
bhojanānte viṣa-pradam

Water is a medicine for indigestion, it is invigorating when the food that is eaten is well digested. In the middle of a dinner it is like nectar, but at the end of a meal it is poison.

Commentary: Lord Kṛṣṇa tells Arjuna, *raso 'ham apsu kaunteya:* "O son of Queen Kuntī, I am the taste of water." (Bg 7.8) Śrīla Prabhupāda advised devotees how to accept *prasāda* according to the science of *Āyur-veda-śāstra:* fill half the stomach with food, one quarter with water and leave air in the remaining one quarter for optimum digestion. There is a sort of fire in the belly called *vaiśvānara* which helps digest food; thus *Āyur-veda* advises that drinking too much water immediately after meals can lead to indigestion.

ŚLOKA 8.8

हतं ज्ञानं क्रियाहीनं हतश्चाज्ञानतो नरः ।
हतं निर्णायकं सैन्यं स्त्रियो नष्टा ह्यभर्तृकाः ॥८॥

hataṁ jñānaṁ kriyā-hīnaṁ
hataś cājñānato naraḥ
hataṁ nirṇāyakaṁ sainyaṁ
striyo naṣṭā hy abhartṛkāḥ

Knowledge is lost without practical application; a man is lost due to ignorance; an army is lost without a commander; and a woman is lost without a husband.

Commentary: The great conundrum with modern education is that the bulk of what is taught is so nebulous and impractical that it can never be utilized. Since that which is learned, but not used, is wasted along with the time spent studying it, modern education is a lesson in futility. It is sad but true that to many a CEO the degree on the applicant's resume is rather a yardstick for the job seeker's tenacity than a true measure of what he knows. "Hire the college graduate, because if he could muster the determination to sit through years of college babble, he will be just the man to spend decades pushing papers around the same desk." Truly those with the heaviest load of cultivation of ignorance are rewarded with the most degrees, though much of what is assimilated is landfill.

For more on the subject of husbands and wives from the Vedic perspective, we turn to *Śrīmad-Bhāgavatam* (3.23.2):

viśrambheṇātma-śaucena gauraveṇa damena ca
śuśrūṣayā sauhṛdena vācā madhurayā ca bhoḥ

O Vidura, Devahūti served her husband with intimacy and great respect, with control of the senses, with love and with sweet words.

Bhaktivedanta purport: Here two words are very significant. Devahūti served her husband in two ways, *viśrambheṇa* and *gauraveṇa.* These are two important processes in serving the husband or the Supreme Personality of Godhead. *Viśrambheṇa* means "with intimacy," and *gauraveṇa* means "with great reverence." The husband is a very intimate friend; therefore, the wife must render service just like an intimate friend, and at the same time she must understand that the husband is superior in position, and thus she must offer him all respect. A man's psychology and woman's psychology are different. As constituted by bodily frame, a man always wants to be superior to his wife, and a woman, as bodily constituted, is naturally inferior to her husband. Thus the natural instinct is that the husband wants to post himself as superior to the wife, and this must be observed. Even if there is some wrong on the part of the husband, the wife must tolerate it, and thus there will be no misunderstanding between husband and wife. *Viśrambheṇa* means "with intimacy," but it must not be familiarity that breeds contempt. According to the Vedic civilization, a wife cannot call her husband by name. In the present civilization the wife calls her husband by name, but in Hindu civilization she does not. Thus the inferiority and superiority complexes are recognized. *Damena ca:* a wife has to learn to control herself even if there is a misunderstanding. *Sauhṛdena vācā madhurayā* means always desiring good for the husband and speaking to him with sweet words. A person becomes agitated by so many material contacts in the outside world; therefore, in his home life he must be treated by his wife with sweet words.

Regarding the husband's position, Śukrācārya says:

That house prospers which has many members, lamps, cows, children and only one head—not many. (SN 3.241)

ŚLOKA 8.9

वृद्धकाले मृता भार्या बन्धुहस्तगतं धनम् ।
भोजनं च पराधीनं तिस्रः पुंसां विडम्बनाः ॥९॥

vṛddha-kāle mṛtā bhāryā
bandhu-hasta-gataṁ dhanam
bhojanaṁ ca parādhīnaṁ
tisraḥ puṁsāṁ viḍambanāḥ

He who must suffer the following three is unfortunate: the death of his wife in old age; entrusting his money into the hands of his relatives; and depending upon others for food.

Commentary: These four: *janma-mṛtyu-jarā-vyādhi* (birth, death, disease and old age as mentioned in Bg 8.9) are life's four miserable conditions. Common sense dictates that one should plan in such a way that in his later years his basic needs will be met. In Vedic society, therefore, a man is enjoined to disappear into the woods or hills at around the age of fifty, leaving his wife and other family members under the care of a grown-up son, never to have any contact with his wife again. Such a renunciant departs this world gloriously in full self-realization with his mind fixed upon the names of God, headed for the supreme abode. On the other hand, that unfortunate and worn-out old fool who exhausts his final breath in the service of an ungrateful family is described as follows:

> Thus he remains at home just like a pet dog and eats whatever is negligently placed before him. Afflicted with many illnesses, such as dyspepsia and loss of appetite, he eats only very small morsels of food, and he becomes an invalid who can no longer work. (SB 3.30.15)

ŚLOKA 8.10

नाग्निहोत्रं विना वेदा न च दानं विना क्रिया ।
न भावेन विना सिद्धिस्तस्माद्भावो हि कारणम् ॥१०॥

nāgni-hotraṁ vinā vedā
na ca dānaṁ vinā kriyā
na bhāvena vinā siddhis
tasmād bhāvo hi kāraṇam

Chanting of the Vedas without making ritualistic sacrifices to the Supreme Lord through the medium of Agni the fire god, and sacrifices not followed by bountiful gifts are futile. Perfection can be achieved only through devotion to the Supreme Lord, for devotional service is the basis of all success.

Commentary: Whatever one does should be done as an offering to the worshipable Supreme Lord. Indeed, all perfections automatically follow the *bhakta* (pure devotee of the Supreme Lord). Thus Kṛṣṇa advises Arjuna:

man-manā bhava mad-bhakto mad-yājī māṁ namaskuru
mām evaiṣyasi satyaṁ te pratijāne priyo 'si me

Always think of Me, become My devotee, worship Me and offer your homage unto Me. Thus you will come to Me without fail. I promise you this because you are My very dear friend. (Bg 18.65)

ŚLOKAS 8.11–12

न देवो विद्यते काष्ठे न पाषाणे न मृन्मये।
भावे हि विद्यते देवस्तस्माद्भावो हि कारणम् ॥११॥
काष्ठपाषाणधातूनां कृत्वा भावेन सेवनम्।
श्रद्धया च तथा सिद्धिस्तस्य विष्णुप्रसादतः ॥१२॥

na devo vidyate kāṣṭhe
na pāṣāṇe na mṛn-maye
bhāve hi vidyate devas
tasmād bhāvo hi kāraṇam

kāṣṭha-pāṣāṇa-dhātūnāṁ
kṛtvā bhāvena sevanam
śraddhayā ca tathā siddhis
tasya viṣṇu-prasādataḥ

The Lord in wooden, stone, or earthen Deity forms does not reveal Himself if He is not worshipped with devotion. He who with faith and devotion serves the Lord's Deity [formed of wood, stone, or metal] attains perfection by the mercy of the all-pervasive Supreme Lord Viṣṇu.

Commentary: The installation in the home and daily worship of the *śrī-mūrti,* the Deity form of Lakṣmī-Nārāyaṇa, Sītā-Rāma or Rādhā-Kṛṣṇa, is necessary for spiritual advancement. In Vaiṣṇava families wherein the Deity form of the Lord is the center, there happiness and freedom from anxiety are prevalent (as opposed to homes wherein the pet dog, gossip, sports, TV shows or computer games take center stage).

Vedic civilization has documented many historical instances of the all-spiritual Supreme Lord manifesting Himself through His Deity form. In Vṛndāvana when Śrī Gopāla Bhaṭṭa Gosvāmī desired to worship the Deity of Kṛṣṇa, his *śālagrāma-śilā* actually grew into the resplendent Deity of Rādhā-Ramaṇa. Lord Rādhā-Ramaṇa is worshipped to this day in His temple just off Loi Bazaar. On another occasion when a poor *brāhmaṇa* needed a witness, the Deity of Lord Kṛṣṇa walked behind him from Vṛndāvana to Odisha, where He is still worshipped today as Sākṣī-gopāla, "Gopāla the witness."

In another such incident, Śrī Baladeva Vidyābhūṣaṇa prayed to Kṛṣṇa's Deity to help him write a *bhāṣya* (commentary) on the *Vedānta-sūtra.* The Deity of Govindajī, today worshipped in Jaipur, agreed and spoke the commentary to him. The great eighteenth-century *ācārya* wrote down whatever the Deity spoke to him, and his commentary on the *Vedānta-sūtras,* called *Govinda-bhāṣya,* is read to this day as an authoritative scripture of the Gauḍīya Vaiṣṇavas.

It is common for some religionists to condemn our worship of the *arcā-vigraha* form of the Lord as idolatry even though they mostly worship their own idols. Yet, since God is everywhere—as any religious person will agree—He is certainly manifest to the faithful devotee in His form as the *arcā-vigraha.*

ŚLOKA 8.13

शान्तितुल्यं तपो नास्ति न सन्तोषात्परं सुखम् ।
न तृष्णायाः परा व्याधिर्न च धर्मो दयापरः ॥१३॥

śānti-tulyaṁ tapo nāsti
na santoṣāt paraṁ sukham
na tṛṣṇāyāḥ parā vyādhir
na ca dharmo dayā-paraḥ

There is no austerity equal to a peaceful balanced mind, and no happiness higher than contentment. There is no disease like covetousness, and no virtue like mercy.

ŚLOKA 8.14

क्रोधो वैवस्वतो राजा तृष्णा वैतरणी नदी ।
विद्या कामदुघा धेनुः सन्तोषो नन्दनं वनम् ॥१४॥

krodho vaivasvato rājā
tṛṣṇā vaitaraṇī nadī
vidyā kāmadughā dhenuḥ
santoṣo nandanaṁ vanam

Anger is the personification of the god of death; thirst is like the river Vaitaraṇī; knowledge is like the wish-fulfilling cow and contentment is like Nandana, the garden of Lord Indra.

Commentary: There is a certain thread to this verse. Yamarāja, king of death, sends his servants the Yamadūtas to forcibly remove sinful souls to Naraka, the hellish regions. There they are hurled into the terrible torrents of the river Vaitaraṇī which surrounds hell. The wish-fulfilling cow of heaven is called the *kāmadhenu.* Those who have supported *gośālās* where cows are protected from slaughter, are said to be ferried across the treacherous Vaitaraṇī on the back of a waiting cow, which is why Hindu pilgrims often feed cows when visiting temples. The pleasures of Nandana, the garden of Indra, await the pious in their next lives. As far as the allegorical *kāmadhenu* of *vidyā* is concerned, Śrīla Prabhupāda states:

> And because the living entity is partially cognizant, he is therefore sometimes forgetful of his own identity. This forgetfulness is specifically manifested in the field of the *ekapād-vibhūti* (¼ energy) of the Lord, or in the material world, but in the *tripād-vibhūti* (¾ energy) field of actions, or in the spiritual world, there is no forgetfulness by the living entities, who are free from all kinds of contaminations resulting from the forgetful state of existence. The material body is the symbol of the gross and subtle form of forgetfulness; therefore the whole atmosphere of the material world is called *avidyā,* or nescience, whereas the whole atmosphere of the

spiritual world is called *vidyā,* or full of knowledge. (SB 2.6.21, purport)

ŚLOKA 8.15

गुणो भूषयते रूपं शीलं भूषयते कुलम् ।
सिद्धिर्भूषयते विद्यां भोगो भूषयते धनम् ॥१५॥

guṇo bhūṣayate rūpaṁ
śīlaṁ bhūṣayate kulam
siddhir bhūṣayate vidyāṁ
bhogo bhūṣayate dhanam

Good qualities are an ornament for personal beauty, righteous conduct for high birth, success for learning and proper spending for wealth.

ŚLOKA 8.16

निर्गुणस्य हतं रूपं दुःशीलस्य हतं कुलम् ।
असिद्धस्य हता विद्या ह्यभोगेन हतं धनम् ॥१६॥

nirguṇasya hataṁ rūpaṁ
duḥśīlasya hataṁ kulam
asiddhasya hatā vidyā
hy abhogena hataṁ dhanam

Beauty is spoiled by immorality, noble birth by bad conduct, lack of perfection is the destruction of learning, wealth is destroyed when not used.

Commentary: In the above two verses Cāṇakya Paṇḍita offers formulas for making the ugly beautiful and vice versa.

ŚLOKA 8.17

शुद्धं भूमिगतं तोयं शुद्धा नारी पतिव्रता ।
शुचिः क्षेमकरो राजा सन्तोषी ब्राह्मणः शुचिः ॥१७॥

śuddhaṁ bhūmi-gataṁ toyaṁ
śuddhā nārī pati-vratā
śuciḥ kṣema-karo rājā
santoṣī brāhmaṇaḥ śuciḥ

Water seeping into the earth is pure; pure is the wife whose sole vow is the pleasure of her husband; the king who is the benefactor of his subjects is pure; and pure is the contented brāhmaṇa.

Commentary: The Vedic concept of a chaste woman is a *pati-vratā,* literally, "she whose vow is her husband." Bṛhaspati observes:

> A wife's faithfulness is recognized when her husband's fortune dwindles. (GP 1.109.32)

Kings of the Vedic age were devoted to the welfare of their subjects, unlike today's "kings." Modern so-called "leaders" are devoted only to fabricating promises in exchange for votes, then fleecing the pockets of those who voted them in.

A proper king is passionate about the welfare of his subjects. On the other hand, a *brāhmaṇa's* duties are centered in *sattva-guṇa* (goodness). What is duty for one is destruction for the other. The ambitious and materialistic descendants of *brāhmaṇas* today found working in the modes of passion and ignorance cannot be accepted as true representatives of the order of the twice born. Neither can today's greedy *śūdras* posing as political leaders be accepted as genuine *kṣatriyas.*

ŚLOKA 8.18

असन्तुष्टा द्विजा नष्टाः सन्तुष्टाश्च महीभृतः ।
सलज्जा गणिका नष्टा निर्लज्जाश्च कुलाङ्गनाः ॥१८॥

asantuṣṭā dvijā naṣṭāḥ
santuṣṭāś ca mahī-bhṛtaḥ
salajjā gaṇikā naṣṭā
nirlajjāś ca kulāṅganāḥ

Discontented brāhmaṇas, contented kings, shy prostitutes and immodest housewives are all ruined.

Commentary: This verse comments on the previous one. Fancied equality among people is a modern imagination; therefore the duties and temperaments of different persons must likewise vary. Since each one is a unique and individual part and parcel of the Supreme Lord, no two souls can ever equal each other. Equality under the law is not meant to artificially endow two disparate entities with the same propensities.

ŚLOKA 8.19

किं कुलेन विशालेन विद्याहीनेन देहिनाम् ।
दुष्कुलं चापि विदुषो देवैरपि स पूज्यते ॥१९॥

kiṁ kulena viśālena
vidyā-hīnena dehinām
duṣkulaṁ cāpi viduṣo
devair api sa pūjyate

Of what value is high birth for him who is destitute of scholarship? Even the family of a lowborn scholar is honored by the demigods.

Commentary: Lord Brahmā or Deva-śreṣṭha, "leader of the demigods," took birth as a Muslim just to imbibe the supreme teachings offered by Śrī Kṛṣṇa in His advent as Śrī Caitanya Mahāprabhu. Born as Śrī Haridāsa Ṭhākura, he was honored with the title of *nāmācārya* by Mahāprabhu Himself. Thus even Lord Brahmā, unto whom the essence of Vedic learning was revealed by Lord Kṛṣṇa at the beginning of creation, perfected his knowledge through chanting the *mahā-mantra:*

Hare Kṛṣṇa Hare Kṛṣṇa Kṛṣṇa Kṛṣṇa Hare Hare
Hare Rāma Hare Rāma Rāma Rāma Hare Hare

ŚLOKA 8.20

विद्वान्प्रशस्यते लोके विद्वान्सर्वत्र गौरवम् ।
विद्यया लभते सर्वं विद्या सर्वत्र पूज्यते ॥२०॥

vidvān praśasyate loke
vidvān sarvatra gauravam
vidyayā labhate sarvaṁ
vidyā sarvatra pūjyate

A learned person is honored all over the world. The learned command respect everywhere. By knowledge anything can be gained. Indeed, learning is universally honored.

Commentary: A *vidvān* is he who possesses *vidyā,* or knowledge of the *Vedas. Vidyā* at its highest level means realized learning, which settles the difference between materialistic education and spiritual realization. The need of the hour is the creation of colleges and universities that adhere to the divine principles of the *Vedas.* Thus *vidvāns,* or persons of true understanding, can go forth to share the highest realization or Kṛṣṇa consciousness.

Śrīla Prabhupāda frequently quoted a different version of this verse, and even cited it in a letter to Prime Minister of India Jawaharlal

Nehru written on 20 January 1952. Our Guru Mahārāja advised the nation's leader:

> Pandit Jawaharlal Nehru,
> President—All-India National Congress Working Committee.
> New Delhi.
>
> Dear Panditji,
>
> "... In the old days even a politician Brahmin like Chanakya would say that:
>
> Vidwatamcha Nrpatamcha Naiva Tulaya Kadachana
>
> Swadesa Pujyate Raja Vidvan Sarbatra Pujyato.[16]
>
> "A really cultured learned fellow is far above a politician. Because a politician is honoured by the votes of his countrymen while a cultured and learned fellow is honoured everywhere all over the world. So we say that Ravindra Natha and Gandhi were never dependant for the votes of their countrymen but they were honoured all over the world for their cultural contribution. The same Chanakya Pandit defined the standard of learning. The standard of learning had to be testified by its result and not by the manner of University degrees. He said that one who looks upon all women—except one's married wife—as mothers; all other's wealth as the pebbles on the street; and all livings beings as one's own self is a really learned fellow.[17] He never stressed on the point of standard of how many grammars, rhetorics or other books of knowledge one might have gone through, or how many Doctorates of different Universities one might be decorated with.
>
> "At the present moment we know very well that a few men look upon other women, besides one's married wife as mothers; very few men will look upon other's wealth as pebbles on the street and very few men will try to behave with other living beings as one wants to be treated oneself.

16. A diacritized version of the verse:

vidvatāṁ ca nṛpatyāṁ ca naiva tulyaṁ kadācana
sva-deśe pūjyate rājā vidvān sarvatra pūjyate

17. CN 12.14.

"The sages of old age discovered that by spiritual culture man's energy should be utilized only for spiritual realization. Not to speak of Lord Sri Krishna who spoke the philosophy of Bhagavad-gita near about 5000 years ago, we know that within 2000 years of human history no sages including Jesus Christ, Prophet Mohammed, Lord Buddha, Shankaracharya, Madhvacharya, Ramanuja or even Lord Sri Chaitanya Mahaprabhu gave any importance to materialistic way of living. Material necessities were always subordinate to the spiritual realization. They saw that the bread problem, clothing problem and shelter problem are never solved by material activities because by the law of Nature the elephant is given the whole jungle to eat, and the little ant is given a grain of sugar to solve their respective bread problems…

Yours sincerely,
Abhaya Charan De"

ŚLOKA 8.21

मांसभक्ष्यैः सुरापानैर्मूर्खैश्चाक्षरवर्जितैः ।
पशुभिः पुरुषाकारैर्भाराक्रान्ता हि मेदिनी ॥२१॥

māṁsa-bhakṣyaiḥ surā-pānair
mūrkhaiś cākṣara-varjitaiḥ
paśubhiḥ puruṣākārair
bhārākrāntā hi medinī

The earth is encumbered by the heavy load of animals in the form of men: meat-eaters, wine-bibblers, fools and the illiterate.

Commentary: Śukrācārya advises:

> Hunting, gambling, womanizing and drinking spirituous liquor: one should give up these four and be rational. (SN 3.156)

Here in verse 8.21 Cāṇakya Paṇḍita identifies meat as *māṁsa,* a term still in vogue in India today. The etymology of *māṁsa,* as given in the *Manu-smṛti* (5.55) is:

māṁ sa bhakṣayitāmutra yasya māṁsam ihādmy aham
etan māṁsasya māṁsatvaṁ pravadanti manīṣiṇaḥ

> "That creature whose flesh I am eating here and now will consume me in the next life." Thus meat is called *māṁsa,* as described by learned authorities.

So, *mām* (me) and *sa* (he), or "He will eat me." *Māṁsa* or "me he" means that he who eats animal flesh will become somebody's meat dinner in a future life. The terrible truth is that the eater of flesh must return as a helpless creature in the same species of animal life he has feasted upon, and undergo slaughter over and over again for each mouthful of meat he enjoyed. Śrīla Prabhupāda commented that the owner of a chain of chicken restaurants would be re-born as a chicken for each and every chicken that is sold in every one of his thousands of restaurants.

Cāṇakya Paṇḍita recommends a vegetarian diet, as do all genuine sages, for it is nearly impossible for the meat-eater to extricate himself from the cycle of *saṁsāra.* The meat industry is so vile and sinful that everyone involved in the death of each creature becomes liable, like members of a crime ring who have conspired a murder. A restaurateur may himself be repeatedly served as a steak or chicken dinner perhaps even until *pralaya,* the destruction of the universe. Manu gives the following judgment:

> All these are implicated as slayers in the death of an animal: he who permits the slaughter, the butcher, his helper, the seller, the buyer, the cook, the server and the one who eats the meat of the animal. (MS 5.51)

Likewise, doctors who murder unborn babies by performing abortions will themselves return as aborted fetuses along with their nurses and secretaries for many births. In our sojourn through this world, we must tread softly for the laws of nature are indeed stringent.

Lord Kṛṣṇa, the Supreme Personality of Godhead, tells King Mucukunda (SB 10.51.62–63): "Because you followed the principles of a *kṣatriya,* you killed living beings while hunting and performing other duties. You must vanquish the sins thus incurred by carefully executing penances while remaining surrendered to Me. O King, in your very next life you will become an excellent *brāhmaṇa,* the greatest well-wisher of all creatures, and certainly come to Me alone." Śrīla Prabhupāda comments in *Kṛṣṇa, the Supreme Personality of Godhead* (ch. 50): "In this statement it appears that although the *kṣatriyas* are allowed to kill animals in the hunting process, they are not freed from the contamination of other sinful reactions. Therefore it does not matter whether one is a *kṣatriya, vaiśya,* or *brāhmaṇa;* everyone is recommended to take *sannyāsa* at the end of life, to engage himself completely in the service of the Lord and thus become freed from all sinful reactions of his past life."

It appears that even though King Mucukunda obtained the *darśana* of Kṛṣṇa and even directly offered prayers at His lotus feet, still the Lord guided him to perform further penance now and in his next life to rid himself of the sin of killing animals. However, due to the dispensation of Lord Caitanya's mercy in this Kali-yuga, the holy names of the Lord are sufficient to grant liberation to the devotee in this very lifetime, even those who have taken their births in the families of *mlecchas* and *yavanas.*

ŚLOKA 8.22

अन्नहीनो दहेद्राष्ट्रं मन्त्रहीनश्च ऋत्विजः ।
यजमानं दानहीनो नास्ति यज्ञसमो रिपुः ॥२२॥

anna-hīno dahed rāṣṭraṁ
mantra-hīnaś ca ṛtvijaḥ
yajamānaṁ dāna-hīno
nāsti yajña-samo ripuḥ

No enemy consumes the kingdom like a yajña which is performed without feeding on a large scale; it consumes the priests when

chanting is not properly done; and consumes the yajamāna when gifts are not made.

Commentary: The scriptures cite several instances of mishaps caused by mispronounced *mantras.* When Aṣṭāvakra Muni was in the womb of his mother, he flinched repeatedly at his father's improper pronunciation of Vedic hymns, and thus was born with eight bends in his body. Hence his name became *aṣṭa* (eightfold) *vakra* (crooked points). As described in Śrīla Prabhupāda's *Kṛṣṇa, the Supreme Personality of Godhead,* the king of Kāśī performed a grand *yajña* to produce a fiery demon that would kill Lord Kṛṣṇa. Unfortunately for the demonic king, the malevolent spirit that emerged from his fire was naturally unable to harm the Supreme Lord. Since the *mantras* could not go in vain, the demon marched back to the *yajña-śālā* and killed the priests and the king before returning into the fire. Thus, he who sponsors a *yajña,* the *yajamāna,* must bear responsibility if something goes awry.

Śrīla Prabhupāda never allowed any *yajña* to be performed without feeding on a large scale. Not only did he offer free of charge grand multi-course feasts each Sunday and on Vedic holidays, but a feast always accompanied each rite of initiation or marriage. To this day at ISKCON centers around the world, food served is always prepared from scratch in the highest standard of cleanliness and austerity. Śrīla Prabhupāda's concept for mass distribution of *prasāda* is that the Lord's mercy is meant for all, rich and poor alike. Consequently Guru Mahārāja fed the masses indiscriminately, and to this day the *prasāda* "Love Feast" program he began in 1966 continues all over the world.

The Vedic scriptures are replete with purpose-specific *mantras* for all occasions. Due to the overwhelming influence of Kali-yuga, Śrīla Prabhupāda taught that it is best that we settle all affairs with one "great *mantra*" the *mahā-mantra:*

Hare Kṛṣṇa Hare Kṛṣṇa Kṛṣṇa Kṛṣṇa Hare Hare
Hare Rāma Hare Rāma Rāma Rāma Hare Hare

CHAPTER NINE

ŚLOKA 9.1

मुक्तिमिच्छसि चेत्तात विषयान्विषवत्त्यज ।
क्षमार्जवदयाशौचं सत्यं पीयूषवत्पिब ॥१॥

muktim icchasi cet tāta
viṣayān viṣavat tyaja
kṣamārjava-dayā-śaucaṁ
satyaṁ pīyūṣavat piba

My dear child, if you desire freedom from the cycle of birth and death, then abandon the objects of sense desire as poison. Drink instead the nectar of forbearance, upright conduct, mercy, cleanliness and truth.

Commentary: Cāṇakya Paṇḍita's words are imbued with potency because he taught first by his example and then by precept. His name and fame have survived millennia because he practiced what he preached. Although the great *paṇḍita* is renowned for his stand on moral ethics, herewith he shows that the highest *nīti* is: *muktiṁ icchasi,* "to desire to free oneself from the cycle of birth and death." *Mukti* (liberation) does not mean to get oneself bathed in some imaginary divine light as taught by pretenders in fashionable storefront *yoga* parlors. *Mukti* means to actually transcend this material plane and at the end of this life to permanently enter into the anti-material worlds in service to the Supreme Lord. There is no way to *mukti* other than qualifying oneself through *bhakti-yoga,* or heartfelt surrender in love and humility before God. Śrī Kṛṣṇa, who awards liberation to His own elects, tells Arjuna:

kāma-krodha-vimuktānāṁ yatīnāṁ yata-cetasām
abhito brahma-nirvāṇaṁ vartate viditātmanām

They who are free from anger and all material desires, who are self-realized, self-disciplined and who constantly endeavor for perfection, are assured of liberation in the Supreme in the very near future. (Bg 5.26)

ŚLOKA 9.2

परस्परस्य मर्माणि ये भाषन्ते नराधमाः ।
त एव विलयं यान्ति वल्मीकोदरसर्पवत् ॥२॥

parasparasya marmāṇi
ye bhāṣante narādhamāḥ
ta eva vilayaṁ yānti
valmīkodara-sarpavat

Those base men who gossip about the secrets of others destroy themselves like a serpent who enters an anthill.

Commentary: Twenty-five hundred years prior to the life and times of Cāṇakya Paṇḍita, Śrī Kṛṣṇa also used the same derogatory term *narādhamāḥ* in His conversation with Arjuna:

na māṁ duṣkṛtino mūḍhāḥ prapadyante narādhamāḥ
māyayāpahṛta-jñānā āsuraṁ bhāvam āśritāḥ

Those miscreants who are grossly foolish, lowest among mankind, whose knowledge is stolen by illusion, and who partake of the atheistic nature of demons, do not surrender unto Me. (Bg 7.15)

Cāṇakya Paṇḍita says that a symptom of the *narādhama* ("lowest among mankind") is his propensity to gossip. Due to being oblivious to the pastimes of the Lord and His devotees, such *narādhamas* simply pass their days involved in idle prattle about one another. Śrīla Prabhupāda called this propensity to gossip "a disease of Kali-yuga." Nowadays idle rumors saturate the air like a cloud of toxic gas. Newsprint scandalmongers and TV talebearers all run on this insidious hearsay, which conveniently provides a smokescreen behind which the powers that be can hide their real interests of megalomania. While the family huddles around the tube to watch celebrity trash talk, one-sided warfare is waged upon helpless foreign lands with nary a word from the corporate-controlled media.

Gossip may appear to be little more than harmless conversation as a single ant poses no threat to a mighty serpent. But the cumulative effect of a constant bombardment of chatter is the death knell to spiritual aspirations or even the acquisition of mundane knowledge. Taken together, many tiny sins create a crushing load, like the attack from an entire colony of red ants that devours the flesh of the serpent within an hour.

ŚLOKA 9.3

गन्धः सुवर्णे फलमिक्षुदण्डे
नाकारि पुष्पं खलु चन्दनस्य ।
विद्वान्धनाढ्यश्च नृपश्चिरायुः
धातुः पुरा कोऽपि न बुद्धिदोऽभूत् ॥३॥

gandhaḥ suvarṇe phalam ikṣu-daṇḍe
nākāri puṣpaṁ khalu candanasya
vidvān dhanāḍhyaś ca nṛpaś cirāyuḥ
dhātuḥ purā ko 'pi na buddhi-do 'bhūt

Perhaps no one has advised Lord Brahmā to impart perfume to gold, fruit to the sugarcane, flowers to the sandalwood tree, wealth to the learned and long life to the king.

Commentary: Even without fragrance, gold is beautiful, at least here in a relative sense. Likewise, things must be appreciated for the qualities that they do possess. Cāṇakya Paṇḍita is of course exercising a *paṇḍita's* right to be tongue-in-cheek, and for his sake hopefully Lord Brahmā has not taken offense to the *paṇḍita's* sense of humor. Brahmā, born from the lotus of the navel of Lord Viṣṇu, creates the universe under Viṣṇu's direction. The Lord Brahmā of our particular universe is a pure devotee of the Supreme Lord Kṛṣṇa. He stands at the head of our disciplic succession, the great Brahma-Madhva-Gauḍīya *sampradāya.*

There are few temples of Lord Brahmā in India, the only major one being alongside the blue waters of Puṣkara Lake in Rajasthan. Therefore, the position of Lord Brahmā is not widely understood. However, he is intimately connected to the *līlā* of Lord Kṛṣṇa in the form of a "four-faced hill" at Varṣāṇā, ancient Vṛṣabhānupura in Mathurā Vraja. This hill is said to be a manifestation of Lord Brahmā here on earth. Varṣāṇā is where Rādhārāṇī, the pleasure potency of the Supreme Lord Kṛṣṇa, grew to girlhood. Hence Lord Brahmā in the form of a hill has been blessed by the footprints of the Lord's greatest devotees, the *gopīs* of Vṛndāvana. It is one of three such hills in the area. Nearby are the hilly manifestations of Lord Viṣṇu (Giri Govardhana) and Lord Śiva (Nandagrāma).

Another wit, Bhartṛhari has written:

> Brahmā can deprive the swan of the luxury of residing in a bed of lotuses; but he cannot take away his celebrated ability of separating milk from water. (NS 17)

The swan's celebrated ability to separate milk from water, achieved through releasing a chemical from its mouth, is analogous to the devotee's ability to savor the essence of life, leaving the undesirable behind. In other words a saintly man, who is transcendental to this material world created by Brahmā, retains his qualities even in an inhospitable atmosphere. Thus Śrīla Prabhupāda and all previous *ācāryas* are also worshipped as *paramahaṁsas,* or "supreme swans."

ŚLOKA 9.4

सर्वौषधीनाममृता प्रधाना
सर्वेषु सौख्येष्वशनं प्रधानम् ।
सर्वेन्द्रियाणां नयनं प्रधानं
सर्वेषु गात्रेषु शिरः प्रधानम् ॥४॥

sarvauṣadhīnām amṛtā pradhānā
sarveṣu saukhyeṣv aśanaṁ pradhānam
sarvendriyāṇāṁ nayanaṁ pradhānaṁ
sarveṣu gātreṣu śiraḥ pradhānam

The best medicine of all is amṛtā; the highest material pleasure is a good meal; the eye is the chief of all organs; and the head is the chief of all parts of the body.

Commentary: *Amṛtā* (derived from *amṛta* which means nectar) is the name of several medicinal plants. Devotees consider the best medicine and the best nectar to be the holy names of the Lord. Just as the head is the best part of the body, etc., similarly chanting the holy names of the Lord, Hare Kṛṣṇa, is the best means for overcoming all evils on the path back to home back to Godhead. The *amṛta* or nectar of the Lord's holy name is the medicine for every material disorder. In this regard, the great nineteenth-century *ācārya* in this Brahma-Madhva-Gauḍīya disciplic line, Śrīla Bhaktivinoda Ṭhākura, sings in his Bengali song "Aruṇodaya (sunrise) Kīrtana":

enechi auṣadhi māyā nāśibāra lāgi'
hari-nāma mahā-mantra lao tumi māgi'

> I have brought the medicine to eradicate your *māyā,* the disease of illusion. Please pray for the holy name of Kṛṣṇa, the *mahā-mantra,* and take it at once.

That this chanting of the glories of the holy name of God is the path of exalted devotees is confirmed by Śrī Kṛṣṇa Himself:

satataṁ kīrtayanto māṁ yatantaś ca dṛḍha-vratāḥ
namasyantaś ca māṁ bhaktyā nitya-yuktā upāsate

> Always chanting My glories, endeavoring with great determination, bowing down before Me, these great souls perpetually worship Me with devotion. (Bg 9.14)

ŚLOKA 9.5

दूतो न सञ्चरति खे न चलेच्च वार्ता
पूर्वं न जल्पितमिदं न च सङ्गमोऽस्ति ।
व्योम्नि स्थितं रविशशिग्रहणं प्रशस्तं
जानाति यो द्विजवरः स कथं न विद्वान् ॥५॥

dūto na sañcarati khe na calec ca vārtā
pūrvaṁ na jalpitam idaṁ na ca saṅgamo 'sti
vyomni sthitaṁ ravi-śaśi-grahaṇaṁ praśastaṁ
jānāti yo dvija-varaḥ sa kathaṁ na vidvān

No messenger can travel about in the sky and no tidings come from there. The voice of its inhabitants is never heard, nor can any contact be established with them. Therefore the brāhmaṇa who predicts the eclipses of the sun and moon, which occur in the sky, must be considered a vidvān.

Commentary: The meaning of the word *vidvān,* "a man of great learning," is discussed in CN 8.20. It is said *kalau śūdra-sambhavaḥ,* "in Kali-yuga everyone is born a *śūdra.*" Since an overwhelming *śūdra* influence has overtaken the planet, there is a great need for *brāhmaṇas* and *vidvāns* to once again re-introduce the social system of organization under which India prospered for millennia. Progress today is measured in terms of the construction of oil wells, factories, jails, hospitals, shopping malls and military bases. In truth tearing down these blights would be a better measure of progress. Punishing criminals, treatment of disease and awful earth-destroying mini-hells called factories that create products for an artificial lifestyle are by no means a determination of progress. Elimination of war, crime and sickness by living in accordance with nature's laws would be a better measurement of social advancement. To accomplish this, the world requires the guidance of intelligent *vidvāns* or *brāhmaṇas,* devotees fixed in Kṛṣṇa consciousness. Progress towards a civilization based upon simple living and high thinking will not take place on its own.

By Vedic standards, a *brāhmaṇa* is one who lives according to the principles of mercy, cleanliness, austerity and truthfulness. Therefore, only that person who follows these principles can be a *brāhmaṇa.* Śukrācārya observes:

> There is no syllable which is not a part of a Vedic *mantra.* There is no plant the root of which possesses no medicinal properties. So also there is no man who is utterly unfit. The rarity is a person who can usefully connect all of them. (SN 2.127)

By connecting to Śrīla Prabhupāda and through that connection serving the disciplic succession sincerely, all things in proper perspective are revealed from the heart and then manifest in the world in due course of time.

ŚLOKA 9.6

विद्यार्थी सेवकः पान्थः क्षुधार्तो भयकातरः ।
भाण्डारी प्रतिहारी च सप्त सुप्तान्प्रबोधयेत् ॥६॥

vidyārthī sevakaḥ pānthaḥ
kṣudhārto bhaya-kātaraḥ
bhāṇḍārī pratihārī ca
sapta suptān prabodhayet

The student, the servant, the traveler, the hungry person, the frightened man, the treasury guard and the gate keeper: these seven must be awakened should they fall asleep.

ŚLOKA 9.7

अहिं नृपं च शार्दूलं वरटिं बालकं तथा ।
परश्वानं च मूर्खं च सप्त सुप्तान्न बोधयेत् ॥७॥

ahiṁ nṛpaṁ ca śārdūlaṁ
varaṭiṁ bālakaṁ tathā
para-śvānaṁ ca mūrkhaṁ ca
sapta suptān na bodhayet

The serpent, the king, the tiger, the stinging wasp, the small child, the dog owned by someone else and the fool: these seven should not be awakened from sleep.

Commentary: With his undying wit, Cāṇakya Paṇḍita's serpentine examples undulate through the following verses.

ŚLOKA 9.8

अर्थाधीताश्च यैर्वेदास्तथा शूद्रान्नभोजिनः ।
ते द्विजाः किं करिष्यन्ति निर्विषा इव पन्नगाः ॥८॥

arthādhītāś ca yair vedās
tathā śūdrānna-bhojinaḥ
te dvijāḥ kiṁ kariṣyanti
nirviṣā iva pannagāḥ

Of those dvijas who have studied the Vedas for material rewards and who have accepted food offered by śūdras, what potency have they? They are like serpents without poison.

Commentary: In many verses, such as 9.5, Cāṇakya Paṇḍita shows us what a true *brāhmaṇa* is made of. Here he reveals the downward path by which a *brāhmaṇa* loses his qualifications: sloth and easy living. When a *dvija* has such an eye out for a free lunch that he will dine with *śūdras,* his potency naturally becomes lost. Indeed, this verse fits like a glove many useless caste *brāhmaṇas* in today's India. We were once attacked and robbed by a mob in India, and it was no surprise when several culprits were later arrested that they had high caste *brāhmaṇa* surnames. Just as austerities elevate the power of true *brāhmaṇas,* so neglecting the scriptures transforms *brāhmaṇas* into showmen only, like vipers without venom.

ŚLOKA 9.9

यस्मिन्रुष्टे भयं नास्ति तुष्टे नैव धनागमः ।
निग्रहोऽनुग्रहो नास्ति स रुष्टः किं करिष्यति ॥९॥

yasmin ruṣṭe bhayaṁ nāsti
tuṣṭe naiva dhanagamaḥ
nigraho 'nugraho nāsti
sa ruṣṭaḥ kiṁ kariṣyati

He who neither rouses fear by his anger nor confers a favor when he is pleased can neither control nor protect. What can he do?

Commentary: Cāṇakya Paṇḍita asks, *kiṁ kariṣyati:* "what can he do." As noted in the previous verse, he is a serpent without fangs. Now see the next.

ŚLOKA 9.10

निर्विषेणापि सर्पेण कर्तव्या महती फणा ।
विषमस्तु न चाप्यस्तु घटाटोपो भयङ्करः ॥१०॥

nirviṣeṇāpi sarpeṇa
kartavyā mahatī phaṇā
viṣam astu na cāpy astu
ghaṭāṭopo bhayaṅkaraḥ

Even the non-poisonous variety of serpent must raise high his head and expand his hood. The show of terror is sufficient to scare people off, poisonous or not.

Commentary: Ordinary *śūdras* dressed as *sādhus* may receive the adoration of the ignorant masses. A *brāhmaṇa* who sings for food may never go hungry, but neither will his followers become enlightened!

Our Guru Mahārāja once told the story of a snake who, upon becoming a disciple of Nārada Muni, turned to nonviolence. No longer afraid of the snake, people began abusing him. When the snake asked his spiritual master what should be done, he suggested, "Simply raise your hood and scare them away." In Kali-yuga, people in general are impressed by a show of renunciation or pretension of divinity, they lack the perspicacity to understand the genuine *sādhu.*

ŚLOKA 9.11

प्रातर्द्यूतप्रसङ्गेन मध्याह्ने स्त्रीप्रसङ्गतः ।
रात्रौ चौरप्रसङ्गेन कालो गच्छति धीमताम् ॥११॥

prātar dyūta-prasaṅgena
madhyāhne strī-prasaṅgataḥ
rātrau caura-prasaṅgena
kālo gacchati dhīmatām

They who are wise spend their mornings in the discussion of gambling; they pass their afternoons discoursing on the pastimes of women; and absorb their evening hours sermonizing on acts of theft.

Commentary: Is Cāṇakya Paṇḍita suggesting we poison ourselves with materialistic conversation? Which "venom" destroys spiritual life, and what activity has the power to poison our roots to this material world?

Spend your mornings discussing the adventures of King Yudhiṣṭhira who gambled away his throne, as seen in the pages of the *Mahābhārata.* In the afternoon, discuss the devotion of Queen Sītā who, as we learn from the *Rāmāyaṇa,* followed her Lord Rāma into exile. In the evening, glorify Him who steals butter from His mother, the garments from the *gopīs* and the hearts of His devotees. Cāṇakya Paṇḍita recommends the hours following sunset for discoursing upon *Śrīmad-Bhāgavatam* and ruminating upon the glories of Mākhana-cora, the butter thief of Vṛndāvana.

Pure devotees invariably recommend spending the entire day discussing the *līlā* of the Lord and the activities of His confidential associates. Any doctor can tell you about poisons that become effective medicines when taken in the prescribed dosage. Spiritual talks are like a beneficial poison. When the medicine of Śrī Kṛṣṇa-*kathā* is poured upon the roots of material desire, our sojourn through *saṁsāra* dries up and attachments wilt. By awakening a higher taste, the devotee soon loses all attachment for artificial pleasures of the senses.

The world was created through sound vibrations, and the vibrations that we create—even through casual speech—have the power to liberate or enslave. Mundane conversation as overheard in pubs and restaurants appears like the nectar of joyous friendship at first, but such useless prattle offers no solution to our ever-present problems of birth and death. Mankind has created complex systems of relaying gossip through the internet, radio, television, newspapers and magazines. Discussions of worldly affairs are compared in the *Bhāgavata* to the babble of ocean waves. So gentlemen, name your poison. Choose transcendental discussions of the pastimes of the Lord, the antidote for worldly fellowship, and thereby achieve your release from all anxiety through Kṛṣṇa consciousness. Or settle for the poison of worldly blather and continue this eternal confinement in the whirlpool of *saṁsāra* in which we are presently drowning.

ŚLOKA 9.12

स्वहस्तग्रथिता माला स्वहस्तघृष्टचन्दनम् ।
स्वहस्तलिखितं स्तोत्रं शक्रस्यापि श्रियं हरेत् ॥१२॥

sva-hasta-grathitā mālā
sva-hasta-ghṛṣṭa-candanam
sva-hasta-likhitaṁ stotraṁ
śakrasyāpi śriyaṁ haret

By preparing a garland for the Deity with one's own hand, by grinding sandalwood paste for the Lord with one's own hand, and by penning sacred verses with one's own hand, one becomes blessed with opulence equal to that of Indra.

Commentary: Activities performed for the glorification of the Lord, as seen in the previous verse, result in all auspiciousness. The goddesses of (1) learning (Sarasvatī), (2) liberation (Mokṣā) and (3) fortune (Lakṣmī) wait with folded hands upon the pure devotee of the Lord.

Paṇḍita Śrī V. Badarayana Murthy's understanding of the verse appears above. K. Raghunathji, a nineteenth-century translator of the version of *Cāṇakya-nīti* called *Vriddha-Chanakya,* translated this verse as: "Indra himself may lose his greatness if he should attempt to wear garlands made by him with his own hands, or daub his body with sandalwood powder ground by himself, or study a book composed by himself." Activities performed for the service of Kṛṣṇa, the Supreme Personality of Godhead, are always enlightening and liberating. By looking at this verse from the opposite point of view, we can conclude that the same activities performed for self-gratification can produce the opposite of transcendental effects and result in ignorance, anxiety and loss.

ŚLOKA 9.13

इक्षुदण्डास्तिलाः शूद्राः कान्ता हेम च मेदिनी ।
चन्दनं दधि ताम्बूलं मर्दनं गुणवर्धनम् ॥१३॥

ikṣu-daṇḍās tilāḥ śūdrāḥ
kāntā hema ca medinī
candanaṁ dadhi tāmbūlaṁ
mardanaṁ guṇa-vardhanam

The hidden qualities or usefulness of the following nine are brought out only through exertion and effort: sugarcane, sesame seed, śūdras, women, gold, clay, sandalwood, yogurt and betel nut.

Commentary: Each of the items listed above yields its benefit only after receiving much attention. One edition of Cāṇakya Paṇḍita's work translates *mardanaṁ guṇa-vardhanam* as "pounding makes them sweeter." A later edition translates this phrase as "pressing and squeezing makes them beneficial." Did Cāṇakya Paṇḍita advise us to pound our wives and squeeze our employees? *Mardanam* implies domination, which can take on different aspects according to its usage, like conquering with love or force of character.

ŚLOKA 9.14

दरिद्रता धीरतया विराजते
कुवस्त्रता शुभ्रतया विराजते ।
कदन्नता चोष्णतया विराजते
कुरूपता शीलतया विराजते ॥१४॥

daridratā dhīratayā virājate
kuvastratā śubhratayā virājate
kadannatā coṣṇatayā virājate
kurūpatā śīlatayā virājate

Poverty is offset by courage and fortitude; tattered garments by cleanliness; food that has cooled by reheating it and ugliness by good behavior.

Commentary: *Nīti-śāstra's* bottom line is this: use your intelligence to make the best use of a bad bargain. In the ultimate analysis, we have negotiated a very bad deal to have come to the material world in the first place. On the plus side, we now have this rare human form of life, our precious platform for extraction from birth and death. Neither do we know for sure what the next life will bring. Only by immediately seeking out the lotus feet of Kṛṣṇa's representative can we hope to make this life successful and bring to an end this cruel sojourn through the material world. Had Cāṇakya Paṇḍita been fortunate enough to meet Śrīla Prabhupāda, he might have added another line: "The defects of this material birth are offset by chanting:

Hare Kṛṣṇa Hare Kṛṣṇa Kṛṣṇa Kṛṣṇa Hare Hare
Hare Rāma Hare Rāma Rāma Rāma Hare Hare!"

Thus Ends Chapter Nine

CHAPTER TEN

ŚLOKA 10.1

धनहीनो न हीनश्च धनिकः स सुनिश्चयः ।
विद्यारत्नेन हीनो यः स हीनः सर्ववस्तुषु ॥१॥

dhana-hīno na hīnaś ca
dhanikaḥ sa su-niścayaḥ
vidyā-ratnena hīno yaḥ
sa hīnaḥ sarva-vastuṣu

He who is devoid of wealth is not destitute, he is indeed rich [if he is learned]. Yet the man of means who has not acquired the jewel of learning is destitute in every way.

Commentary: The essence of real education lies in understanding one's total dependency upon the Lord with every breath. By the grace of God, each elephant daily receives his hundred pounds of hay, and the ant is given his single grain to eat. Therefore, why is a graduate degree required to learn how to fill the stomach? After removing their caps and gowns, college graduates must go from door to door with their resumes begging for jobs like stray dogs looking for scraps of food.

The *vidyā-ratna* or "jewel of learning" is never taught in the great colleges and universities which year after year churn our far-fetched opinions as though they were facts. True gems of wisdom are ignored by the demonic elements that run society because they have found no way to turn transcendental knowledge into paper currency. Although there are hundreds of thousands of institutes of higher learning all over the globe, not one of them even teaches the difference between a dead body and a living body. When discrimination is so blunt that the ability to explain the difference between a corpse and a living person is lacking, then what is the use of such an education? Modern education is centered around enjoying a dead body and is therefore doomed to failure. Higher education will become successful only when Kṛṣṇa's message to Arjuna—*Bhagavad-gītā As It Is*—is introduced into the college curriculum.

A poor man who has obtained this eternal *vidyā-ratna* is far better than a wealthy ignoramus who spends his time in vain guarding a temporary treasure he mistakes to be his. Regarding the spiritually destitute misers mentioned in this verse, King Pṛthu tells the four Kumāras:

> Even though full of opulence and material prosperity, any householder's home where the devotees of the Lord are never allowed to enter, and where there is no water for washing their feet, is to be considered a tree in which all venomous serpents live. (SB 4.22.11)

The Bhaktivedanta purport to this verse explains:

> It is said that around a sandalwood tree, which is a very valuable tree, there are venomous serpents. Sandalwood is very cold, and venomous serpents, because of their poisonous teeth, are always very warm and they take shelter of the sandalwood trees to cool themselves. Similarly, there are many rich men who keep watchdogs or doormen and put up signs that say, 'Do Not Enter,' 'Trespassers Not Allowed', 'Beware of the Dog', etc. Sometimes in Western countries a trespasser is shot, and there is no crime for such shooting. This is the position of demoniac householders, and such houses are

considered to be the residential quarters of venomous snakes. The members of such families are no better than snakes because snakes are very envious, and when that envy is directed to saintly persons, their position becomes more dangerous.

ŚLOKA 10.2

दृष्टिपूतं न्यसेत्पादं वस्त्रपूतं पिबेज्जलम् ।
शास्त्रपूतं वदेद्वाक्यं मनःपूतं समाचरेत् ॥२॥

dṛṣṭi-pūtaṁ nyaset pādaṁ
vastra-pūtaṁ pibej jalam
śāstra-pūtaṁ vaded vākyaṁ
manaḥ-pūtaṁ samācaret

Carefully examine the spot where you place your foot, drink only filtered water, speak only that which is sanctioned by śāstra, and perform only those deeds which are carefully considered.

Commentary: He who studies the *śāstras* under the guidance of the bona fide spiritual master and carefully bases his words upon scriptural injunctions properly applied can never mislead. Indeed, whatever such a *śāstrī* says may be considered as the very utterances of Śrīla Vyāsadeva himself. That is why the exalted seat (*āsana*) of the spiritual master is called the *vyāsāsana,* and his holy appearance day is celebrated as Vyāsa-pūjā. The genuine *dīkṣā-guru* speaks only that which is sanctioned by the *guru-paramparā.* No bona fide spiritual master ever engages in fanciful word jugglery that he has "become God."

Dale Carnegie in his modern day book of common sense advice entitled *How to Win Friends and Influence People* gives an example of "performing only those deeds which have been carefully considered." In the German army, complaints against fellow soldiers were accepted only the day following an offense, to give the complainant sufficient time to reconsider the situation.

Cāṇakya Paṇḍita's counsel regarding filtered water is as true today as it was twenty-five centuries ago. Over the past few decades, it has become a fashion to drink only expensive bottled water. Fearful of pollutants, people are commonly seen today smartly toting plastic water bottles as they stroll about, a phenomenon that was never seen before 1980. Factories, oil refineries, nuclear plants, huge farming conglomerates and other mammoths of the modern age appear bent upon poisoning every drop of water on the earth. Carcinogenic insecticides and chemical fertilizers used in farming, as well as nuclear waste and sewage, pose serious threats to the waters that cover 60% of our planet's surface.

Vedic culture offers wise direction for all activities and counsels all stages of life, even seemingly minor details. See this:

> He who urinates upon fire, in the direction of the sun and the moon, into water, towards a *brāhmaṇa* or a cow or into the wind will lose his intelligence. One should not blow upon fire, gaze upon a naked woman, place unclean items into fire or even warm the feet against fire. (MS 4.52–53)

ŚLOKA 10.3

सुखार्थी चेत्त्यजेद्विद्यां विद्यार्थी चेत्त्यजेत्सुखम् ।
सुखार्थिनः कुतो विद्या सुखं विद्यार्थिनः कुतः ॥३॥

sukhārthī cet tyajed vidyāṁ
vidyārthī cet tyajet sukham
sukhārthinaḥ kuto vidyā
sukhaṁ vidyārthinaḥ kutaḥ

He whose "wealth" is enjoyment must abandon any quest for knowledge. He who values knowledge must not desire sense gratification. How can the seeker of pleasure acquire knowledge, and how can the seeker of wisdom enjoy base pleasures?

Commentary: Here Cāṇakya Paṇḍita describes both the *sukhārthī* and the *vidyārthī.* A *sukhārthī* is "he who considers pleasures to be his wealth." Though found in exotic resorts, exclusive country clubs and in fine restaurants all over the world, the polished *sukhārthī's* basis for happiness is suspiciously similar to that of pigs and dogs. Since base physical pleasures are fleeting and can produce no permanent satisfaction, Cāṇakya Paṇḍita's advice is that the wise man should restrict sense enjoyment. He counsels, become a *vidyārthī* by placing your values in the everlasting wealth of realized knowledge.

Any attempt at gathering knowledge while wallowing in the muck of sensuality is like trying to light a fire while pouring water on it. The overwhelming flaw of modern schooling is its focus on facilitating sense gratification rather than controlling it. Today a college degree is more a measure of success in the cultivation of ignorance than learning anything remotely useful.

ŚLOKA 10.4

कवयः किं न पश्यन्ति किं न खादन्ति वायसाः ।
मद्यपाः किं न जल्पन्ति किं न कुर्वन्ति योषितः ॥४॥

kavayaḥ kiṁ na paśyanti
kiṁ na khādanti vāyasāḥ
madyapāḥ kiṁ na jalpanti
kiṁ na kurvanti yoṣitaḥ

What slips past the observation of a poet? What will a crow not eat? What will a drunkard not rant? What is that act of which women are incapable?

Commentary: With the words *kavayaḥ kiṁ na paśyanti,* Cāṇakya Paṇḍita praises the intellect and wit of the *kavis,* the poets of Vedic culture and civilization. The words of a *kavi* flow like poetry and while his knowledge covers diverse subjects he is able to understand the essence of learning. *Kavi* is also used respectfully to indicate an Āyurvedic physician; hence *kavi* means "doctor" as well as "learned poet." Here linguistic evidence shows that the ancient Vedic system of schooling has set the precedent for Western education. Today's highest degree of Western study is referred to as the "doctorate," or PhD, as derived from the more ancient understanding of the *kavi.* In the Vedic educational system called *gurukula,* a period of *brahmacarya* (celibate study) is required. In the same way, in Western education, the prerequisite for post-graduate study is the BA or BS, the bachelor degree. Bachelor means "unmarried man" and draws its source from the *brahmacārī* (celibate student).

The qualities of a true *kavi* were seen in the person of Śrīla Prabhupāda, who was capable of discussing any subject from any point of view without ever repeating himself. He was at home chatting on all topics with any ruffian or uptown gentleman, always bringing the conversation to the level of Kṛṣṇa consciousness. A learned *kavi* can take both sides of an issue. For example, as seen here (and in 6.2) the crow is a *cāṇḍāla* amongst birds due to its repulsive eating habits. Yet we are also advised (CN 6.9) that there are many things we can learn from a crow. A *kavi* (scholar) like Cāṇakya Paṇḍita knows the art of learning from any situation and sees all sides of a picture. Even the mighty King Yudhiṣṭhira valued the example of a mere dog's loyalty as told in the *Mahābhārata's Svargārohaṇa-parva.*

Line three discusses the effects of intoxicants that bloat the ego and dull discrimination. An intoxicated man is convinced that any *prajalpa* that spills from his mouth carries profound wit. Liquors and other intoxicants that are especially prized by boastful *asuras* are shunned by *suras* (devotees). Concerning the fourth line, it is well known that "hell hath no fury like a woman scorned." Conversely, if a husband maintains his wife and family in a loving and affectionate atmosphere, then there is no sacrifice a devoted lady is unwilling to accept for the maintenance of her family. Therefore, one message of this verse is to see both sides of an issue.

ŚLOKA 10.5

रङ्कं करोति राजानं राजानं रङ्कमेव च ।
धनिनं निर्धनं चैव निर्धनं धनिनं विधिः ॥५॥

raṅkaṁ karoti rājānaṁ
rājānaṁ raṅkam eva ca
dhaninaṁ nirdhanaṁ caiva
nirdhanaṁ dhaninaṁ vidhiḥ

Fate makes a beggar a king and a king a beggar, it makes a rich man poor and a poor man rich.

Commentary: Destiny or fate, the creation of past *karma,* is a favorite subject of *nīti-śāstra.* Bṛhaspati waxes eloquently:

> Man enjoys only the fruits of his previous actions. Whatever he has done in his previous life has its reactions now. (GP 1.113.18)
>
> Whether one ascends into the sky or enters deeply into the nether world, whether he travels in every quarter of the universe, he will not receive that which is not specified by *karma.* (GP 1.113.23)
>
> In the physical body born as a result of *karma,* different kinds of illusions—physical and mental—fall in quick succession like shafts discharged by a skillful archer. Hence man should see things in the light of the *śāstras* only. (GP 1.113.28)
>
> Actions alone are consequential. Queen Sītā, who was married while the planets were exalted and the *lagna* or ascendant was decided by Ṛṣi Vasiṣṭha himself, had to undergo many miseries. Indeed auspicious effects and omens are of no effect at the time of karmic reactions. (GP 1.113.25–26)

Regarding Bṛhaspati's verse quoted just above from the *Garuḍa Purāṇa,* Queen Sītā is none other than Lakṣmī herself who appeared with her husband Lord Nārāyaṇa or Rāma in Tretā-yuga. Such verses are for our instruction; yet those who believe that the Lord's *līlā* falls under the sway of material nature and *karma* can themselves never become free from the modes of nature. The Personality of Godhead and His expansions can never be subject to the same laws of nature that vex us. Rather, as the master of both the spiritual kingdom and the material universe, He is adored as Patita-pāvana, the deliverer of fallen souls. Hence Sītā-Rāma are still worshipped today millions of years after Their advent.

Although *Rāmāyaṇa* is the story of the Lord's transcendental *līlā* upon this earth, there are many lessons of *nīti-śāstra* and the effects of *karma* within its divine pages. Lord Rāma's father King Daśaratha, grief-stricken after the exile of his son to the forest, confided in Rāma's mother Queen Kauśalyā the karmic causes and reactions that lead to their fateful loss. As a young prince Daśaratha was so expert at archery that he could hit a target simply by sound. Mistaking the sounds of a *ṛṣi* filling his water pot for an elephant drinking water along the Sarayū River, he released his arrow into the night only to pierce a young gentle ascetic in the heart. As Śravaṇa-kumāra Ṛṣi lay dying, he told Daśaratha that his single arrow had killed three innocent people because he was the support of his old and blind parents. In the *Ayodhyā-kāṇḍa,* chapter 63, Vālmīki describes King Daśaratha's deathbed conversation with Kauśalyā wherein the monarch admits that his accidental sin in youth is responsible for the loss of their son now.

Sorely grieving for his son, King Daśaratha recalled a sin from his past and spoke the following words to Kauśalyā who was also suffering:

> O auspicious and gentle lady, the doer of any action, whether good or bad, certainly reaps its consequences. One who at the commencement of any endeavor does not consider the degree of its good or bad karmic results, is certainly a fool. (*Rāmāyaṇa, Ayodhyā-kāṇḍa,* chapter 63, verses 5–7)

There is no end to karmic entanglement for the conditioned soul. The Lord appears in His original form as Śrī Kṛṣṇa or as His own devotee as Śrī Caitanya Mahāprabhu to free us from the bondage of our past sinful reactions. Unless one understands *nīti-śāstras* in the light of the messages of higher scriptures like the *Bhagavad-gītā As It Is* or *Śrīmad-Bhāgavatam* he may become misled. In this world fate is all-powerful until one surrenders himself before the transcendental Lord and becomes His devotee.

ŚLOKA 10.6

लुब्धानां याचकः शत्रुर्मूर्खानां बोधको रिपुः ।
जारस्त्रीणां पतिः शत्रुश्चौराणां चन्द्रमा रिपुः ॥६॥

lubdhānāṁ yācakaḥ śatrur
mūrkhānāṁ bodhako ripuḥ
jāra-strīṇāṁ patiḥ śatruś
caurāṇāṁ candramā ripuḥ

The beggar is a miser's enemy; the wise counselor is the fool's enemy; the husband is the adulterous wife's enemy; and the moon is the enemy of a thief.

Commentary: In the *Vidura-nīti* of the *Mahābhārata* Vidura advises King Dhṛtarāṣṭra:

> Burning brands emit only smoke when separated, but blaze forth when brought together. And relatives are no different. (VN 4.58)

Vidura's example was intended to awaken the blind king to the fact that divisiveness between his sons led by Duryodhana on one side and his nephews, the Pāṇḍavas on the other side, would lead to destruction of the entire family. By working together, the Pāṇḍavas and the sons of Dhṛtarāṣṭra could light the world. The king proved to be not only blind to reason, but deaf to good counsel. He considered Vidura as an enemy, just as it is described in this verse. As a consequence of failing to heed the good *nīti* of Vidura, an avoidable war ensued that wiped out many vast armies, including all the king's sons! Vidura, seen as an enemy by the blind king, left the palace in disgust.

ŚLOKA 10.7

येषां न विद्या न तपो न दानं
ज्ञानं न शीलं न गुणो न धर्मः ।
ते मर्त्यलोके भुवि भारभूता
मनुष्यरूपेण मृगाश्चरन्ति ॥७॥

yeṣāṁ na vidyā na tapo na dānaṁ
jñānaṁ na śīlaṁ na guṇo na dharmaḥ
te martya-loke bhuvi bhāra-bhūtā
manuṣya-rūpeṇa mṛgāś caranti

Those who are destitute of learning, penance, charity, realized knowledge, character, good qualities, and religion are burdens of the earth. They are indeed beasts in the form of men.

Commentary: The six qualities listed here by Cāṇakya Paṇḍita that separate man from animal are *vidyā* (learning), *tapasya* (voluntary sense restraint), *dāna* (charity), *jñāna* (realized knowledge), *śīla* (character), *guṇa* (good qualities) and *dharma* (service to God).

Most presume that the mere act of walking on two legs rather than four distinguishes man from an animal. But here Cāṇakya Paṇḍita explains *manuṣya-rūpeṇa mṛgāḥ:* they are animals in the form of men, while in 3.7 he calls them "two-legged beasts." Animals have but four interests or propensities, which are: mating, eating, sleeping and defending. Since time immemorial most of the activities of mankind can be grouped under these four headings.

Packs of semi-wild dogs loitering on the outskirts of villages behave with remarkable similarity to today's political and religious leaders who guide modern society. For mutual protection stray dogs take a stand together when they feel themselves threatened by outsiders. Yet when there is no danger from outside their pack, they scrap amongst themselves for the choicest spots in the dirt. In the same way today's corporations, governments, banks and religious institutions conduct their business and rule the world!

Śrīla Prabhupāda explained this point in a Vṛndāvana lecture on *Śrīmad-Bhāgavatam* 1.7.8 delivered on September 7, 1976:

> There are four-legged beasts and two-legged beasts. Four-legged beasts are the animals—cats, dogs, tigers, cows, asses, etc. They are four-legged beasts. And there are two-legged beasts, *dvi-pāda-paśu.*[18] It is not manufactured; it is there in the *śāstra. Dvi-pāda-paśu. Dvi* means two, and *pāda* means legged. So any human being who is attached to this *pravṛtti-mārga*—sex, meat-eating, intoxication, gambling—he is *dvi-pāda-paśu,* a two-legged animal.

The great glitch of modern society with its advancement in politics, education, science, technology and medicine is the promotion of body consciousness and sense gratification rather than advocating the wisdom of restraint and spiritual realization. Physical enjoyment is widely available to the dogs and hogs. Control of the five senses is the only means by which the unlimited joy of the spiritual entity can be awakened. Since over-indulgence in the fourfold propensities of eating, sleeping, mating and defending only increases misery, this sophisticated modern society has simply become an express lane to hell.

Bṛhaspati puts it this way:

> They who have not secured success in their studies (Kṛṣṇa consciousness), a decent wife and sufficient wealth during youth are to be forever pitied. They are beasts in human form. (GP 1.109.48)

18. See CN 3.7.

ŚLOKA 10.8

अन्त:सारविहीनानामुपदेशो न जायते ।
मलयाचलसंसर्गान्न वेणुश्चन्दनायते ॥८॥

antaḥ-sāra-vihīnānām
upadeśo na jāyate
malayācala-saṁsargān
na veṇuś candanāyate

The empty-headed are never benefited by instruction any more than bamboo will become sandalwood by growing upon the slopes of the Malaya Mountain.

Commentary: The *nīti-śāstras* give many similar examples: A crane does not become a swan by occupying the same lake, nor does a donkey become a horse after a hundred baths. Coal does not become clean if scrubbed repeatedly. Here Cāṇakya Paṇḍita discusses the effect of *upadeśa* (instruction) upon nondevotees.

For the highest instructions we turn to the *Nectar of Instruction* (*Upadeśāmṛta* 2) by Śrīla Rūpa Gosvāmī. There he instructs us how to preserve progress in devotional service:

> *Bhakti* will be destroyed by the six following activities: *atyāhāra* (overeating), *prayāsa* (over endeavor for things that are ultimately unnecessary), *prajalpa* (idle chit-chat), *niyamāgraha* (either blindly following rules simply for the sake of following them, or neglecting the scriptural regulations altogether), *jana-saṅga* (association with the worldly) and *laulyam* (hankering after mundane achievements).

ŚLOKA 10.9

यस्य नास्ति स्वयं प्रज्ञा शास्त्रं तस्य करोति किम् ।
लोचनाभ्यां विहीनस्य दर्पण: किं करिष्यति ॥९॥

yasya nāsti svayaṁ prajñā
śāstraṁ tasya karoti kim
locanābhyāṁ vihīnasya
darpaṇaḥ kiṁ kariṣyati

Of what value are the scriptures to him who has no intelligence of his own? Of what value is a mirror to a blind man?

Commentary: Carrying the theme of the previous verse, Cāṇakya Paṇḍita describes those without sufficient brainpower as *yasya nāsti svayaṁ prajñā* (lit. "lacking self-intelligence"). Fire immediately ignites straw. Green grass takes longer to burn. Wet grass is nearly impossible to set ablaze. In the same way, those who are of bright intelligence and situated in the mode of goodness will more easily gravitate to the teachings of the *śāstras.* Far greater effort is required to impart wisdom to those persons who are in the mode of passion. And, as described here, it is nearly impossible to impart wisdom unto those who are in the mode of ignorance.

ŚLOKA 10.10

दुर्जनं सज्जनं कर्तुमुपायो न हि भूतले ।
अपानं शतधा धौतं न श्रेष्ठमिन्द्रियं भवेत् ॥१०॥

durjanaṁ sajjanaṁ kartum
upāyo na hi bhū-tale
apānaṁ śatadhā dhautaṁ
na śreṣṭham indriyaṁ bhavet

There is no way to reform an evil man just as the rear end does not become the face though washed a hundred times.

Commentary: This example mirrors the message of 10.8. For the deliverance of such *durjanas* as are described herein, the Lord Himself is sometimes forced to take extreme measures as seen below.

The *Bhāgavata Purāṇa* (12.2.18–24) predicts the wondrous advent of Lord Kalki 427,000 years from now:

> Lord Kalki will appear in the home of the most eminent *brāhmaṇa* of Śambhala village, the great soul Viṣṇuyaśā. Lord Kalki, the Lord of the universe, will mount His swift horse Devadatta and, sword in hand, He will travel over the earth exhibiting His eight mystic opulences and eight special qualities of Godhead. Displaying His unequaled effulgence and riding with great speed, He will kill by the millions those thieves who have dared dress as kings. After all the impostor kings have been killed, the residents of the cities and towns will feel the breezes carrying the most sacred fragrance of the sandalwood paste and other decorations of Lord Vāsudeva, and their minds will thereby become transcendentally pure. When Lord Vāsudeva, the Supreme Personality of Godhead, appears in their hearts in His transcendental form of goodness, the remaining citizens will abundantly repopulate the earth. When the Supreme Lord has appeared on earth as Kalki, the maintainer of religion, Satya-yuga will begin, and human society will bring forth progeny in the mode of goodness. When the moon, the sun and Bṛhaspati (Jupiter) are together in the constellation Karkaṭa (Cancer the crab), and all three enter simultaneously into the lunar mansion (*nakṣatra*) Puṣyā—at that exact moment the age of Satya, or Kṛta, will begin.

ŚLOKA 10.11

आप्तद्वेषाद्भवेन्मृत्युः परद्वेषाद्धनक्षयः ।
राजद्वेषाद्भवेन्नाशो ब्रह्मद्वेषात्कुलक्षयः ॥११॥

āpta-dveṣād bhaven mṛtyuḥ
para-dveṣād dhana-kṣayaḥ
rāja-dveṣād bhaven nāśo
brahma-dveṣāt kula-kṣayaḥ

Offending a superior brings death; by offending others wealth is lost; by offending the king everything is lost; and by offending a brāhmaṇa one's entire family is ruined.

Commentary: He who knows *nīti-śāstra* lives peacefully without unnecessarily causing pain to others, including one's own family, the representatives of the government or holy personages. The *Bhāgavata Purāṇa,* Canto Ten, narrates the life of King Nṛga who, though innocent of purposeful offense, took birth as a lizard in a deep well by angering two *brāhmaṇas* when a cow he gave one wandered back and was inadvertently given to the other *brāhmaṇa.*

The king would later explain to Kṛṣṇa:

> O Lord of lords, O master of the universe, the agents of Yamarāja, taking advantage of the opportunity thus created, later carried me to his abode. There Yamarāja himself questioned me. (The demigod of death said:) "My dear King, do you wish to experience the results of your sins first, or those of your piety? Indeed, I see no end to the dutiful charity you have performed, or to your consequent enjoyment in the radiant heavenly planets." I replied, "First, my lord, let me suffer my sinful reactions," and Yamarāja said, "Then fall!" "At once I fell, and while falling I saw myself becoming a lizard, O master. O Keśava, as Your servant I was devoted to the *brāhmaṇas* and generous to them, and I always hankered for Your audience. Therefore even till now I have never forgotten (my past life)." (SB 10.64.22–25)

King Nṛga's past piety saved him, however, and ultimately he was rescued by the hand of Lord Kṛṣṇa.

Śrī Caitanya-caritāmṛta (3.3.190–215) narrates the episode of Gopāla Cakravartī, a high-born *brāhmaṇa* who blasphemed Nāmācārya Haridāsa Ṭhākura. In a public assembly, Cakravartī pointed his long and delicate finger at Haridāsa, ridiculing the Nāmācārya's understanding of devotional philosophy. Soon leprosy paid a visit to the *brāhmaṇa's* fingers and nose. Cāṇakya Paṇḍita's words are *brahma-dveṣāt kula-kṣayaḥ,* literally meaning that "an offense to a *brāhmaṇa* causes one's family (*kula*) to waste away (*kṣaya*)." Offenses to anyone, what to speak of exalted Vaiṣṇavas, must be avoided at all costs.

ŚLOKA 10.12

वरं वनं व्याघ्रगजेन्द्रसेवितं
द्रुमालयं पत्रफलाम्बुसेवनम् ।
तृणेषु शय्या शतजीर्णवल्कलं
न बन्धुमध्ये धनहीनजीवनम् ॥१२॥

varaṁ vanaṁ vyāghra-gajendra-sevitaṁ
drumālayaṁ patra-phalāmbu-sevanam
tṛṇeṣu śayyā śata-jīrṇa-valkalaṁ
na bandhu-madhye dhana-hīna-jīvanam

It is better to dwell under a tree in the jungle inhabited by tigers and elephants, to live on wild fruits and spring water, to lie down on the grass and wear the ragged barks of trees, than to live amongst relations when reduced to poverty.

Commentary: Once our Guru Mahārāja shared the story of a boss who (while upbraiding his employee) challenged, "Aren't you smart?" The employee began rubbing his pants pocket, and the boss demanded to know what he was doing. The employee responded, "Sir, I'm seeing if I have money in my pocket. If I have money, then I am smart!" For the householder it is a rule of *nīti* that money is essential. A life of poverty—*dhana-hīna-jīvana*—is no life at all.

ŚLOKA 10.13

विप्रो वृक्षस्तस्य मूलं च सन्ध्या
वेदः शाखा धर्मकर्माणि पत्रम् ।
तस्मान्मूलं यत्नतो रक्षणीयं
छिन्ने मूले नैव शाखा न पत्रम् ॥१३॥

vipro vṛkṣas tasya mūlaṁ ca sandhyā
vedaḥ śākhā dharma-karmāṇi patram

tasmān mūlaṁ yatnato rakṣaṇīyaṁ
chinne mūle naiva śākhā na patram

The brāhmaṇa is like a tree: his sandhyā-vandana prayers are the roots, his chanting of the Vedas is the branches, and his religious acts are the leaves. Consequently, efforts should be made to preserve his roots for should the roots be destroyed there can be no branches or leaves.

Commentary: Cāṇakya Paṇḍita advises that society must protect the *brāhmaṇas* or *vipras* since the blessings of their prayers nourish, sustain and uplift the entire social order. Śrīla Sanātana Gosvāmī says:

> As bell metal, when mixed with mercury, is transformed to gold, a person, even though not golden pure, can be transformed into a *brāhmaṇa,* or *dvija,* simply by the initiation process. (*Hari-bhakti-vilāsa* 2.12)

A *brāhmaṇa* lives by blessing others. The benefits that saintly devotees shower upon the world cannot be overestimated. Hence in the Vedic age, the power of kings was invariably employed in protecting the *brāhmaṇas.* Satisfied *brāhmaṇas* in turn caused prosperity to rain upon society through their religious sacrifices to the Supreme Lord. Likewise, the governments of the world must support and facilitate ISKCON's brahminical *saṅkīrtana* devotees since the all-auspicious sound of the holy name of God benefits all classes of society. Indeed the peace, plenty and prosperity pledged by politicians actually comes not by hollow campaign promises, but will be seen only as a result of the highest work, *saṅkīrtana-yajña.*

Similarly, Śrī Nārada instructs the Pracetās:

> As pouring water on the root of a tree energizes the trunk, branches, twigs and everything else, and as supplying food to the stomach enlivens the senses and limbs of the body, simply worshipping the Supreme Personality of Godhead through devotional service automatically satisfies the demigods, who are parts of that personality. (SB 4.31.14)

ŚLOKA 10.14

माता च कमला देवी पिता देवो जनार्दनः ।
बान्धवा विष्णुभक्ताश्च स्वदेशो भुवनत्रयम् ॥१४॥

mātā ca kamalā devī
pitā devo janārdanaḥ
bāndhavā viṣṇu-bhaktāś ca
sva-deśo bhuvana-trayam

He who understands his mother to be Lakṣmī-devī, his father to be Lord Viṣṇu Himself, and whose relatives and friends are all devotees of Viṣṇu, is at home in all the three worlds.

Commentary: Śrīla Prabhupāda praised Cāṇakya Paṇḍita as the "world's greatest politician," but the *paṇḍita* must also have had at least some inclination towards Kṛṣṇa consciousness as seen from this verse. A devotee is sometimes called upon to serve the Lord in different ways, even in the ocean of sharks that is the political arena.

Because goddess Lakṣmī sits upon a lotus flower, therefore she is called Kamalā-devī in this verse. Her husband Lord Viṣṇu is Janārdana, the shelter of all mankind. Cāṇakya Paṇḍita's highest instructions are given herewith: Surrender to the Supreme Lord Lakṣmī-Nārāyaṇa, always associate with the Viṣṇu-*bhaktas* and live at peace anywhere throughout the universe. Viṣṇu means "the all-pervasive Lord." Thus, since His devotee sees Him everywhere, he is certainly at home in any part of the universe.

ŚLOKA 10.15

एकवृक्षसमारूढा नानावर्णा विहङ्गमाः ।
प्रातर्दश दिशो यान्ति का तत्र परिदेवना ॥१५॥

eka-vṛkṣa-samārūḍhā
nānā-varṇā vihaṅgamāḥ
prātar daśa diśo yānti
kā tatra paridevanā

[Through the night] many different kinds of birds perch upon the different branches of the same tree. In the morning they fly off in all ten directions. Why should we lament for that?

Commentary: Death, the agent of the Supreme Lord in this world, is awake while others sleep. Separation from our near and dear is not a mere possibility, it is inevitable. In the *Gītā,* Kṛṣṇa urges Arjuna:

> All the great warriors—Droṇa, Bhīṣma, Jayadratha, Karṇa—are already destroyed. Simply fight, and you will vanquish your enemies. (Bg 11.34)

Although Arjuna was grief-stricken on the Battlefield of Kurukṣetra, the Supreme Lord Śrī Kṛṣṇa spoke to him while smiling.

We have all been born into ignorance in this world of temporary names and labels, which are simply shrouds of the soul. We come together like weeds floating on a stream and, when fate so ordains, we are helplessly torn apart by the currents of time. We may be born in this race or that, in this or that species, on earth or in heaven. We are forced to continue on our way according to the fate written by our stars at birth. Nonetheless, we foolishly try to create a permanent position out of whatever name and address we are born with. This life of names, labels and other fallible soldiers is but a temporary halt on the long road to liberation. The real value of this human form of life is that it can be our springboard to Kṛṣṇa consciousness. For he who arrives at the shelter of the lotus feet of the Lord, all miseries vanish in the bliss of spirit, even while living in this world of names.

Cāṇakya Paṇḍita has taken this verse from the *Bṛhaspati-nīti-sāra* (GP 1.113.45). The ten directions mentioned in line three are the eight points of the compass, plus up and down.

ŚLOKA 10.16

बुद्धिर्यस्य बलं तस्य निर्बुद्धेश्च कुतो बलम् ।
वने हस्ती मदोन्मत्तः शशकेन निपातितः ॥१६॥

buddhir yasya balaṁ tasya
nirbuddheś ca kuto balam
vane hastī madonmattaḥ
śaśakena nipātitaḥ

He who possesses intelligence is strong: how can the unintelligent be powerful? Through pride, the elephant lost his senses in the forest and was killed by a hare.

Commentary: By citing this example Cāṇakya Paṇḍita points us to another *nīti-śāstra,* the *Pañca-tantra* of Viṣṇuśarmā. In some versions of the fable the example of a proud elephant is given, while at other times the foolish victim is a *siṁha* (lion). The story as told in Tantra One goes like this: A family of hares was facing extinction due to the activities of a lion named Bhāsuraka. A clever hare well-versed in *nīti-śāstra* convinced the lion that a second lion had now occupied his territory. "Where is this intruder?" demanded Bhāsuraka. "He's hiding out of fear of your royal majesty down there," replied the hare, showing Bhāsuraka a well. The arrogant lion peered into the well and saw his own reflection. The echo of his fearful roar only increased his rage. Proud Bhāsuraka dived in to make quick work of the "intruder" but by the intelligence of the hare he quickly drowned.

In the other version of this verse, quoted from Tantra Three of *Pañca-tantra,* a hare convinced a dull elephant king to abandon a pond because it was the property of Candra, the moon god. The elephant bowed to the reflection of the moon, and departed leaving the hares to enjoy the lake. Whichever version is accepted, the moral point is the same: authority does not come from mere physical strength alone. Influence sits with those who are not afraid to use their intelligence. Even a small boy seated atop an elephant can control the beast by means of an *aṅkuśa.*

ŚLOKA 10.17

का चिन्ता मम जीवने यदि हरिर्विश्वम्भरो गीयते
नो चेदर्भकजीवनाय जननीस्तन्यं कथं निर्मयेत् ।
इत्यालोच्य मुहुर्मुहुर्यदुपते लक्ष्मीपते केवलं
त्वत्पादाम्बुजसेवनेन सततं कालो मया नीयते ॥१७॥

kā cintā mama jīvane yadi harir viśvambharo gīyate
no ced arbhaka-jīvanāya jananī-stanyaṁ kathaṁ nirmayet
ity ālocya muhur muhur yadupate lakṣmīpate kevalaṁ
tvat-pādāmbuja-sevanena satataṁ kālo mayā nīyate

Why should I be concerned for my maintenance while absorbed in praising the glories of Lord Viśvambhara, the supporter of all? Without the grace of Lord Hari, how could milk flow from a mother's breast for the nourishment of her child? Repeatedly thinking only in this way, O Yadupati, O Lakṣmīpati, all my time is spent in the service of Your lotus feet.

Commentary: In this devotion-charged stanza, Cāṇakya Paṇḍita identifies Śrī Kṛṣṇa as the Godhead through His name Yadupati. Kṛṣṇa appeared as the *pati* (lord) of the dynasty headed by King Yadu. In 3.14 Cāṇakya Paṇḍita observes that a worthy son glorifies a family as a fragrant tree enhances a forest. Similarly, the entire dynasty of King Yadu became famous by the appearance of Lord Kṛṣṇa, Yadupati. Cāṇakya Paṇḍita also identifies Śrī Kṛṣṇa as Viśvambhara, the sustainer of the universe (*viśva*).

Cāṇakya Paṇḍita also glorifies Śrī Kṛṣṇa as Lakṣmīpati, the Lord of the goddess of fortune. Since Śrī Kṛṣṇa is the owner of all opulence, all gifts of Lakṣmī should be directly used in the service of her *pati.* In the last line and with the words *tvat-pādāmbuja-sevanena satatam* Cāṇakya sets the example of "eternally serving the lotus feet of the Lord." In a lecture delivered in London on 22 August 1973, Śrīla Prabhupāda noted:

> Although Cāṇakya Paṇḍita was the prime minister, he was living in a cottage. That is the distinction between Vedic or Indian civilization and the modern civilization. The Indian civilization means they are interested in *sat,* and others are interested in *asat. Asat* means "that which will not exist." Five thousand years ago, of course India was also very opulent. But why five thousand years ago? Even only five or four hundred years ago, India was so opulent that Europeans were attracted to India. During the time of the Mogul Empire it was so opulent. Those of you who go to India, you'll find at Delhi's Red Fort there are jeweled inlays of birds and trees on the wall. Today only a hole remains where the eyes of the birds were. This means that the eye of each bird was ornamented with a precious jewel and the walls were inlaid with precious stones. Not only the eyes and other parts of the bird, but the trees and flowers decorating the wall—all were inlaid with different types of jewels. All these jewels were taken away while the British government was ruling India and, so far I have heard, they are now protected in the British Museum. But the jewels were taken away. That's a fact that anyone can see.
>
> Of course, in India the standard of wealth was not considered owning a big tin car or some plastic plates. Material opulence means jewels, gold, silk, butter; that is the meaning of material opulence. Not plastic pots or a plastic bucket or plastic cloth. These things have no value. So, anyway, India's standard of material opulence was whatever is obtained from nature and not by engaging oneself in industry. Therefore, India … that is, India's leaders … are now finding that on account of our neglecting the material side of life we have become poor.
>
> So the purport is that the difference between East and West is that the Eastern people, the Indian people, stressed on this *sat* portion, the

permanent portion, the spiritual civilization. Their aim was how to make this life perfect so that I can become immortal. As I explained the other day, *aihiṣṭaṁ yad punar-janma-jayāya.* The whole effort was how to conquer over birth and death. So modern people they do not understand that birth and death can be conquered. They can imagine it. Sometimes they say, "By scientific advancement, someday we shall become immortal."

ŚLOKA 10.18

गीर्वाणवाणीषु विशिष्टबुद्धि-
स्तथापि भाषान्तरलोलुपोऽहम् ।
यथा सुधायाममरेषु सत्यां
स्वर्गाङ्गनानामधरासवे रुचिः ॥१८॥

gīr-vāṇa-vāṇīṣu viśiṣṭa-buddhis
tathāpi bhāṣāntara-lolupo 'ham
yathā sudhāyām amareṣu satyāṁ
svargāṅganānām adharāsave ruciḥ

Definitely I regard Sanskrit as the best of all languages, yet I still enjoy other tongues; just as the devas, though they quaff nectar, enjoy kissing the lips of heavenly damsels.

Commentary: Sanskrit script is called the *devanāgarī* because it is spoken in the towns (*nagaras*) of the demigods (*devas*). In a letter dated 7 October 1968, Śrīla Prabhupāda wrote:

> Besides that, we understand from reliable sources that Sanskrit is spoken by the higher planetary denizens. It is therefore called Devanagari. Devanagari means the cities of the demigods. This language is spoken there.

Sanskrit is the eternal spiritual tongue, the first speech, the perfect vernacular as well as the literary tongue that is the origin and source of all other forms of language. When Kṛṣṇa spoke the *Bhagavad-gītā,*

He spoke to Arjuna in Sanskrit. Indeed, tracing modern language back through time to Sanskrit reveals a hidden root of Vedic civilization and culture exerting its influence even today.

Cāṇakya Paṇḍita, who was a strict *brahmacārī,* obliquely hints at the weakness that even the *devatās* harbor for temporary pleasures of the senses. Indeed, even the denizens of Svarga are not exempt from the impulses of nature. In the celestial regions headed by Indra, liberation does not come easily due to the abundance of sensual enjoyment there. After millions of years of enjoyment in the upper strata of the universe, the demigods are forced by the modes of nature and their material desires to return to earth once again. No *jīva* born in this material world transcends the laws of *karma,* no matter how materially powerful he may become, except through pure devotional service. Entwined by the three *guṇas,* all souls must travel roundabout through all levels of this material world until each finds the shelter of the lotus feet of Śrī Kṛṣṇa through the pure devotee's divine grace.

ŚLOKA 10.19

अन्नाद्दशगुणं पिष्टं पिष्टाद्दशगुणं पयः ।
पयसोऽष्टगुणं मांसं मांसाद्दशगुणं घृतम् ॥१९॥

annād daśa-guṇaṁ piṣṭaṁ
piṣṭād daśa-guṇaṁ payaḥ
payaso 'ṣṭa-guṇaṁ māṁsaṁ
māṁsād daśa-guṇaṁ ghṛtam

Flour is ten times more nutritious than grain, milk is ten times more nutritious than flour, meat has ten times the nutrition of milk, and ten times better still is ghee.

Commentary: In this verse, which we purposely omitted from the verse-only first edition, Cāṇakya Paṇḍita discusses the nourishment, rather than the morality (or lack of it) of animal flesh. Cāṇakya Paṇḍita himself states that the eater of animal flesh will never be merciful, a quality of *brāhmaṇas* (CN 11.5). Even in the Vedic society, lower grades of men, the *śūdras* and outcaste hunters, ate flesh because they did not have the intelligence to understand the karmic reactions thereby created. Nowadays there is unlimited slaughter of innocent creatures in modern slaughterhouses. As a result of this violation of nature's unseen karmic laws, nations turn on nations to create wars every few years, men slaughtering one another. This understanding was conveyed by the renowned writer and vegetarian George Bernard Shaw (1856–1950) in his poem "Living Graves." Shaw became a vegetarian at the age of twenty-five for spiritual and moral reasons.

We are the living graves of murdered beasts,
Slaughtered to satisfy our appetites.
We never pause to wonder at our feasts,
If animals, like men, can possibly have rights.
We pray on Sundays that we may have light,
To guide our footsteps on the path we tread.
We're sick of war, we do not want to fight –
The thought of it now fills our hearts with dread,
And yet – we gorge ourselves upon the dead.

Like carrion crows we live and feed on meat,
Regardless of the suffering and the pain
we cause by doing so, if thus we treat
defenceless animals for sport or gain,
how can we hope in this world to attain,
the PEACE we say we are so anxious for.
We pray for it o'er hecatombs of slain,
to God, while outraging the moral law,
thus cruelty begets its offspring — WAR.

For members of ISKCON meat-eating is absolutely forbidden. Sometimes nondevotees who must eat meat at any cost are allowed to eat a chicken, goat or sheep if they slaughter it themselves. This may reduce but not save the meat-eater from the karmic reaction and it will save the earth from the terrible blight of sinful slaughterhouses which any decent government would immediately shut down. However, the slaughter of a cow or bull is never sanctioned.

Diet is an important consideration of *nīti* or common sense. Just as the stomach must nourish the entire body, so the Vedic civilization and culture is based around the *vaiśya* class, who practice agriculture and cow protection. *Brāhmaṇas* are compared to the head, *kṣatriyas* to the arms, *vaiśyas* to the belly and *śūdras* (the working class) to the feet. All parts of the body are important, but the stomach provides nourishment for every other part. For this and other reasons Lord Kṛṣṇa appeared in Vṛndāvana as the son of the *vaiśya* king, Nanda Mahārāja.

Śrīla Prabhupāda always insisted that offerings in his temples should be cooked in pure ghee, not oil. Before our spiritual master introduced his "love feasts" to America and Europe in the mid-sixties, hardly any member of Western society had even heard of ghee (purified butter), which is now sold in many places of the Western world. Ghee is used in all *yajñas,* hence the cow who produces ghee is considered sacred.

The bull is important for plowing the land in the cultivation of food grains and vegetables. Agriculture that is artificially propped up by crops sprayed with poisonous insecticides, treated with chemical fertilizers and harvested with gasoline-powered machines can only implode upon itself. Once the forests are destroyed, vast regions are turned into desert, the waters of lakes and rivers are rendered poisonous and the ocean of oil beneath the earth's surface has been drained and burned by billions of automobiles it will be the end of the line for this self-destructive so-called civilization.

Our present so-called modern civilization has chalked out a steep path to hell in the name of scientific advancement, and no leader has arisen to raise a whimper of protest. No Nobel Prize laureate has addressed the current crises. Even many so-called *sannyāsīs* today mislead the public by advocating the eating of chicken, fish and animals. Therefore, the only hope for the world is the *saṅkīrtana* movement inaugurated by Śrī Caitanya Mahāprabhu.

ŚLOKA 10.20

शोकेन रोगा वर्धन्ते पयसा वर्धते तनुः ।
घृतेन वर्धते वीर्यं मांसान्मांसं प्रवर्धते ॥२०॥

śokena rogā vardhante
payasā vardhate tanuḥ
ghṛtena vardhate vīryaṁ
māṁsān māṁsaṁ pravardhate

Diseases are nourished by sorrow, the body by milk, semen by ghee and flesh by meat.

Commentary: Like 10.19, this is another verse we purposely omitted in the first edition. During a walk on Juhu Beach, on 18 December 1975, our Guru Mahārāja commented:

> Just like Cāṇakya Paṇḍita, he was not a spiritual man, but he was a prime minister.

Prabhupāda even called him "the greatest politician in history," but never as a "devotee." Another instruction (from Indore, 13 December 1970) is given below:

> **Prabhupāda:** Cāṇakya Paṇḍita, a great politician and *brāhmaṇa*...
>
> **Yamunā:** Was he in Lord Caitanya's time?
>
> **Prabhupāda:** No, no. He was five thousand years..., not. Three thousand years.
>
> **Haṁsadūta:** He was a great devotee...?

Prabhupāda: He was very learned scholar, *brāhmaṇa,* rigid *brāhmaṇa*. That's all....

Yamunā: He was a great devotee?

Prabhupāda: No.

Yamunā: So he's not authority.

Prabhupāda: No, no, he was not authority in the spiritual sense. He was a politician, a moralist. Politician. That's all. Worldly man.

Thus Ends Chapter Ten

CHAPTER ELEVEN

ŚLOKA 11.1

दातृत्वं प्रियवक्तृत्वं धीरत्वमुचितज्ञता ।
अभ्यासेन न लभ्यन्ते चत्वारः सहजा गुणाः ॥१॥

dātṛtvaṁ priya-vaktṛtvaṁ
dhīratvam ucita-jñatā
abhyāsena na labhyante
catvāraḥ sahajā guṇāḥ

Generosity, pleasing address, courage and discriminative intelligence are not acquired but are inbred qualities.

Commentary: According to the scientific system of *jyotiṣa-śāstra,* the innate qualities of anyone who has taken birth can be read through the horoscope. Those who bring extraordinary qualities to the present lifetime do so only as a result of previous lifetimes of development. Those who are born in miserable circumstances or with unfavorable qualities are suffering due to past *vikarmas* (misdeeds).

ŚLOKA 11.2

आत्मवर्गं परित्यज्य परवर्गं समाश्रयेत् ।
स्वयमेव लयं याति यथा राजान्यधर्मतः ॥२॥

ātma-vargaṁ parityajya
para-vargaṁ samāśrayet
svayam eva layaṁ yāti
yathā rājānya-dharmataḥ

One who whimsically abandons his own community and joins another dooms himself like the king who embraces duties other than those prescribed for the royal class.

Commentary: Vedic culture and civilization are based upon the genuine qualities of *dharma,* and never upon capricious and speculative inventions. This verse warns against whimsical changes and concocted processes that disturb social order. Kṛṣṇa warns Arjuna:

> *śreyān sva-dharmo viguṇaḥ para-dharmāt sv-anuṣṭhitāt*
>
> It is far better to discharge one's prescribed duties, even though they may be faulty, than another's duties. Destruction in the course of performing one's own duty is better than engaging in another's duties, for to follow another's path is dangerous. (Bg 3.35)

However, the emphasis in this verse is on "whimsically adopting the path of another." Kali-yuga's organized society, religion and education have conspired to mislead us with their comfortable reliance upon tired and false dogmas. We are expected to stoically follow these false masters to hell. A higher path must be accepted and the path of Kṛṣṇa consciousness is the only solution for the social emergency at hand. Like the *gopīs* of Vṛndāvana who renounced their material situations to meet Kṛṣṇa, ISKCON devotees have obtained complete shelter in the teachings of Śrīla Prabhupāda. We have obtained what our religion at birth could not give. Neither empty sermons from the pulpit about the world's problems, nor ingenious yet godless fixes by science provide real solutions to myriad social crises. World salvation will be found in a single solution: the *saṅkīrtana-yajña* (public chanting of the holy names of God).

ŚLOKA 11.3

हस्ती स्थूलतनुः स चाङ्कुशवशः किं हस्तिमात्रोऽङ्कुशो
दीपे प्रज्वलिते प्रणश्यति तमः किं दीपमात्रं तमः ।
वज्रेणापि हताः पतन्ति गिरयः किं वज्रमात्रं नगा-
स्तेजो यस्य विराजते स बलवान्स्थूलेषु कः प्रत्ययः ॥३॥

hastī sthūla-tanuḥ sa cāṅkuśa-vaśaḥ kiṁ hasti-mātro 'ṅkuśo
dīpe prajvalite praṇaśyati tamaḥ kiṁ dīpa-mātraṁ tamaḥ
vajreṇāpi hatāḥ patanti girayaḥ kiṁ vajra-mātraṁ nagās
tejo yasya virājate sa balavān sthūleṣu kaḥ pratyayaḥ

The elephant, though huge, is controlled by an aṅkuśa. Is the aṅkuśa as great as the elephant? A single candle banishes darkness. Is the candle as vast as the darkness? A bolt of lightning can break a mountain peak. Is the lightning as large as the mountain? No, he whose power prevails is truly mighty, what is there in bulk?

Commentary: And the *mahā-mantra,* though only sixteen words, can obliterate all the ignorance of Kali-yuga:

Hare Kṛṣṇa Hare Kṛṣṇa Kṛṣṇa Kṛṣṇa Hare Hare
Hare Rāma Hare Rāma Rāma Rāma Hare Hare

ŚLOKA 11.4

कलौ दशसहस्राणि हरिस्त्यजति मेदिनीम् ।
तदर्धं जाह्नवीतोयं तदर्धं ग्रामदेवताः ॥४॥

kalau daśa-sahasrāṇi
haris tyajati medinīm
tad-ardhaṁ jāhnavī-toyaṁ
tad-ardhaṁ grāma-devatāḥ

After ten thousand years of Kali-yuga, Lord Hari abandons the earth. After five thousand years, the Gaṅgā abandons the earth, and after twenty-five hundred years the predominating deities of the villages abandon the earth.

Commentary: Looking back in time, an unbiased historical analysis reveals that Vedic culture was once spread throughout Europe and Asia. In the Dvāpara-yuga, the center of civilization was India's Yamunā-Gangetic plain and, like rays of the sun, Vedic civilization spread far and wide. Remnants of old shrines of Vedic worship like the Agni Temple at Baku, Azerbaijan, have been uncovered all over Asia. To the impartial historian, it is obvious that Vedic culture and civilization in general emanated from India, that is Bhārata, and spread throughout Europe, Northern Africa, Southeast Asia, China, etc. Vedic civilization and the Sanskrit language were not imported into India as per some ridiculous, British Raj-concocted Aryan invasion theory. When the evidence is viewed with impartiality, understanding history from a Vedic point of view is a fascinating study that leads to enlightenment. Not only does historical linguistics prove a world Vedic past, but there is an abundance of archaeological evidence in Europe and much of Asia that cannot be ignored. Therefore it is true that in many villages all over the world, as described in line four of this verse, the local deities have long since been forgotten.

However we are into fifty-one hundred years of Kali-yuga and the goddess of the Gaṅgā still rides her *makara-vāhana* (alligator carrier) from Gaṅgotri in the Himālayas to Gaṅgā-sāgara at the Bay of Bengal. Her waters are two miles wide at Patna. To this day the Gaṅgā is one of the world's mightiest rivers. Cāṇakya Paṇḍita's information therefore does not appear to be infallible. We do not know the origin of this *śloka*—yet because it is written here it may come to pass eventually with the advancement of Kali-yuga.

Today the *saṅkīrtana* movement of Lord Śrī Caitanya Mahāprabhu has reestablished the worship of Lord Hari, or Kṛṣṇa, all over the world. Hari is a name of God that literally means, "He who takes away all that is inauspicious." Prabhupāda describes that material attachment is like a fever, which rises in proportion to worldly attachment. When Lord Hari favors His devotee, He takes away his analogous material disease, thus lowering the material fever. This is the meaning of "Hari."

Śrīla Prabhupāda is the prophet of a coming "mini-Satya-yuga" lasting ten thousand years and arising out of the darkness of Kali-yuga. When His Divine Grace established the first center of ISKCON at 26 2nd Avenue, New York City, in 1966, there was not even one Hindu temple in North and South America, whereas today there are hundreds if not thousands. The Hindus, emboldened by Śrīla Prabhupāda's pioneer example of creating Rādhā-Kṛṣṇa temples in America, have themselves been inspired by the example of one pure devotee. Thus, as a single grain creates a field of grains, the *jagad-guru* of the world *saṅkīrtana* movement also became the inspiration for the reestablishment of other Vedic deities in all corners of the earth.

Lord Kṛṣṇa is called Tri-yuga that is, He appears in three *yugas,* viz. Satya-yuga (the golden age), Tretā-yuga (the silver age) and the Dvāpara-yuga (the bronze age). When Lord Kṛṣṇa appears in the Kali-yuga (the iron age), He does so as a "covered" or "hidden" incarnation. To the great fortune of our fallen selves, Lord Kṛṣṇa came Himself during this particular Kali-yuga, and did not send a partial incarnation or expansion. Consequently, this Kali-yuga is particularly special.

Since we are at the dawn of a mini-Satya-yuga, and it is prophesized to last ten thousand years, then Cāṇakya Paṇḍita's prediction may be fulfilled after 15,000 years of Kali-yuga have passed, not 10,000. Scriptural foretellings regarding the advent of Kṛṣṇa or Hari as Śrī Caitanya Mahāprabhu must have been hard nuts to crack, though with 20/20 hindsight they are open books. Here are a few researched and published by our late, beloved Godbrother Śrīmān Kuśakratha Dāsa Brahmacārī:

Because in Kali-yuga You appear as a "covered incarnation," You are known as Tri-yuga or He who appears in three *yugas.* (*Śrīmad-Bhāgavatam* 7.9.38)

With My true identity always concealed, I will assume the form of a *brāhmaṇa* devotee of the Lord and in this form I shall deliver the worlds. (*Ādi Purāṇa* and *Nārada Purāṇa*)

To deliver the conditioned souls burning in Kali-yuga, in the first *sandhyā* of the age, the Lord will take birth in the home of a *brāhmaṇa.* (*Kūrma Purāṇa,* and repeated with slight variation in the *Garuḍa Purāṇa*)

In the first *sandhyā* of Kali-yuga, the Lord will assume a golden form. First He will be the husband of Lakṣmī and then He will be a *sannyāsī* at Jagannātha Purī. (*Garuḍa Purāṇa*)

In Kali-yuga intelligent persons will perform the congregational chanting of the holy names of the Lord. Although His complexion is not blackish, He is nonetheless Śrī Kṛṣṇa Himself. He will be accompanied by His confidential associates and weapons. (*Śrīmad-Bhāgavatam* 11.5.32)

The Supreme Lord said, "When between four and five thousand years of Kali-yuga have passed, I shall descend upon the earth at a place that is near the shore of the Gaṅgā. I will be a tall, saintly *brāhmaṇa* devotee, and will have a golden complexion. I will be free from all desire and will accept the order of renunciation—*sannyāsa.* I will be advanced in *bhakti-yoga,* and I will chant continuously the holy names of the Lord. Only the devotees will understand Me." (*Atharva Veda*)

The Supreme Lord said, "To deliver the people devoured by the sins of Kali-yuga, I will descend accompanied by My associates to a place along the shore of the Gaṅgā. I will be a *brāhmaṇa sannyāsī,* an *avadhūta* or mystic. Again and again will I chant the holy names of the Lord." (*Sāma Veda*)

In Kali-yuga Lord Kṛṣṇa will appear in the family of *brāhmaṇas.* He will teach the message of the *Upaniṣads* and the *dharma-śāstras.*

He will defeat atheists and offenders and He will establish the truth about Vaiṣṇava *dharma*. (*Kṛṣṇa Upaniṣad*)

The Lord will again appear in this world. His name will be Śrī Kṛṣṇa Caitanya and He will spread the chanting of the Lord's holy names. (*Devī Purāṇa*)

The Supreme Lord who enjoyed pastimes with the *gopīs,* who day and night filled the people of Vṛndāvana with happiness, who killed the demon Kaṁsa, and who in the war with the Kauravas befriended the Pāṇḍavas, will once again appear on the earth. Of this there is no doubt. His arm will be decorated with a bamboo *daṇḍa* or staff. He will be a *sannyāsī* and His name will be Caitanya. (*Garuḍa Purāṇa*)

In the first *sandhyā* of Kali-yuga I shall appear on the earth at a beautiful place beside Gaṅgā's shore. I will appear as the son of Śacī-devī and My complexion will be golden. (*Padma Purāṇa*)

O *brāhmaṇa,* in Kali-yuga I will appear disguised as a devotee of the Lord and I will deliver the worlds. (*Nārada Purāṇa*)

O sage whose wealth is austerity, in Kali-yuga everyone will see Me as a *sannyāsī,* whose form is filled with bliss with hairs standing on end in ecstasy. (*Bhaviṣya Purāṇa*)

Outwardly of golden complexion, but blackish on the inside, I will take My birth in the womb of Śacī-devī. Accompanied by My confidential associates and weapons, I shall assume the form of a human being. (*Skanda Purāṇa*)

Those who are illusioned by My bewildering potency will not understand the great secret of My appearance in this world in My personal form, in My form as the incarnation as a devotee, with the name of a devotee and the giver of devotional service. This secret is not to be revealed to them. Only the saintly, pure renounced devotees, diligently engaged in My devotional service, will be able to understand Me in these forms. (*Ananta-saṁhitā*)

In a foreword to one of the Bengali editions of the *Cāṇakya-śloka* we read that Cāṇakya Paṇḍita once prophesized in the royal assembly of the Mauryas that the Supreme Lord would appear in Kali-yuga as a *dvija* to uplift the people. The *śloka* he uttered was:

bhaviṣyati kalau kāle bhagavān bhūta-bhāvanaḥ
dvijātīnāṁ kule janma- grāhakaḥ puruṣottamaḥ

In the Age of Kali the Supreme Lord, the origin of everything, will appear in the family of *brāhmaṇas*.

ŚLOKA 11.5

गृहासक्तस्य नो विद्या नो दया मांसभोजिनः ।
द्रव्यलुब्धस्य नो सत्यं स्त्रैणस्य न पवित्रता ॥५॥

gṛhāsaktasya no vidyā
no dayā māṁsa-bhojinaḥ
dravya-lubdhasya no satyaṁ
straiṇasya na pavitratā

He who is engrossed in family affairs can never acquire knowledge. He who eats animal flesh can never be merciful. He who is greedy cannot be truthful. He who hunts women can never be pure.

Commentary: Sin is defined as "those activities which violate the laws of nature." Herewith Cāṇakya condemns meat eating and illicit sex, two of the four sins shunned by the members of ISKCON. Along with gambling and intoxication, these four transgressions represent the four great teeth in the mouth of Kali, lord of the *yuga.* Although sin has been promoted to the level of glamour, sin nonetheless remains sin and judgement is not far afield. The four great pillars of religion, analogously seen as legs of the bull of *dharma,* are being razed by Kali. Austerity is dismantled through intoxication; mercy is destroyed through meat eating; cleanliness is ruined through illicit sex; and truthfulness is decimated through gambling. However, the rising sunlight of the *saṅkīrtana* movement is destined to flood the world with Kṛṣṇa consciousness before the darkness of immorality destroys it.

ŚLOKA 11.6

न दुर्जनः साधुदशामुपैति
बहुप्रकारैरपि शिक्ष्यमाणः ।
आमूलसिक्तः पयसा घृतेन
न निम्बवृक्षो मधुरत्वमेति ॥६॥

na durjanaḥ sādhu-daśām upaiti
bahu-prakārair api śikṣyamāṇaḥ
ā-mūla-siktaḥ payasā ghṛtena
na nimba-vṛkṣo madhuratvam eti

A wicked man will not attain sanctity even if he is instructed in different ways, just as the neem tree does not become sweet even if sprinkled from top to root with milk and ghee.

Commentary: The same idea is expressed by Śrī Kṛṣṇa who tells Arjuna:

> This confidential knowledge may not be explained to those who are not austere, or devoted, or engaged in devotional service, nor to one who is envious of Me. (Bg 18.67)

ŚLOKA 11.7

अन्तर्गतमलो दुष्टस्तीर्थस्नानशतैरपि ।
न शुध्यति यथा भाण्डं सुराया दाहितं च तत् ॥७॥

antargata-malo duṣṭas
tīrtha-snāna-śatair api
na śudhyati yathā bhāṇḍaṁ
surāyā dāhitaṁ ca tat

Impurities of the mind and heart cannot be washed away even by one hundred baths in sacred waters, just as a wine pot cannot be purified through evaporating all the wine by fire.

Commentary: In verses 11.6–7 Cāṇakya Paṇḍita warns against associating with the *durjanas* (crooked men) whose hearts are contaminated with lust, even if they make a show of purification. This verse also hints at the opinion Vedic society has for intoxicating wine. Vedic culture and civilization takes very seriously the quest for purity, and *sādhus* undergo harsh self-imposed penances and austerities to transcend their desires until they are able to move in perfect harmony with the will of the Lord. Contrarily, in the West, nearly all priests eat meat, drink wine and are paid a salary with retirement and health benefits, as well as a free yearly vacation. The unusual idea of being paid to serve God is foreign to genuine *sādhus* and *yogīs* of India who abnegate the pleasures of the senses to depend upon the will of God alone. The *sādhu* is content to accept his "payment" in terms of inner satisfaction and in whatever way the Lord by His sweet will sustains him. When the elephant and the ant are both maintained by the Supreme Lord, will not the Lord also care for His devotees?

It is very common for an exposed culprit to make a show of religious conversion, like the "purified" wine flask mentioned in line four. A typical example is the notorious American cannibal Jeffrey Dahmer, who claimed to become a born again Christian as soon as he was arrested and imprisoned. It takes more than a beatific smile or priestly robes to make one holy. Real religion involves purification of the consciousness through absolute faith in Śrī Kṛṣṇa and His devotees.

ŚLOKA 11.8

न वेत्ति यो यस्य गुणप्रकर्षं
स तं सदा निन्दति नात्र चित्रम् ।
यथा किराती करिकुम्भलब्धां
मुक्तां परित्यज्य बिभर्ति गुञ्जाम् ॥८॥

na vetti yo yasya guṇa-prakarṣaṁ
sa taṁ sadā nindati nātra citram
yathā kirātī kari-kumbha-labdhāṁ
muktāṁ parityajya bibharti guñjām

It is not strange if a man reviles a thing of which he has no knowledge, just as a lady of the Kirāta tribe throws away an elephant pearl to decorate herself with a guñjā berry.

Commentary: The Kirātas (fem. *kirātī*) are members of a wild tribe of forest dwellers from the Santhal Pargana section of Bihar down to Chhota Nagpur (in the modern state of Jharkhand). They are mentioned in *Śrīmad-Bhāgavatam* (2.4.18). Like uncivilized hunters who do not know the value of gemstones, similarly our modern materialistic scientists generally criticize the *Purāṇas* simply because they cannot fathom the superior intelligence and depth of the Sanskrit literature.

Even basic truths like the very existence of the eternal soul have yet to be accepted by dull-witted "scholars" who prefer concocted theories over genuine facts. Lettered hypocrites will lend their research to continuing "humane" slaughter houses or medical abortions while refusing to acknowledge the very laws of *karma* which ensnare them forever. Although a cavalier ignoramus may be labeled as a "scientist" and feel authorized to denigrate a thing of value, it does not affect the value of that thing. Rather than have any bearing upon scriptural veracity, a fool's criticism of śāstric truths only illustrates the latter's inability to reason. For example, the scientists' disbelief in the authoritative statements of the *śāstras* regarding life on the moon has not kept them from spending billions of tax-payers' dollars in trying to reach planets they claim to be uninhabited deserts.

As explained in the *Purāṇas,* the other planets are made of the same elements as ours, although the eight elements are arranged in different proportions on each one. Just as a fish is at home within water, but not on land, so the living entities on the other planets have different body types suited for variegated environments. The denizens of Varuṇa-loka, predominated over by the demigod of water, have bodies in which water is the principal element. One who wishes to live on the fiery sun planet requires a fire body. The demigod of air Vāyu lives with his subordinates on a planet that is principally made of air. Therefore, our gross rocket ships will not find a welcome mat on the other planets, because our earth bodies cannot survive in such places just as a human cannot live underwater. Due to the different mixes of material elements on various *lokas,* the human form of life created by Kṛṣṇa for living comfortably here on earth will be unsuitable for other planets.

"Man has gone to the moon!" is a common boast among those who have been misled by America's hoax, but more accurately the collective intelligence of the scientists has taken a vacation to the moon. Our top guns at NASA should take some clues from the *śāstras* and cease wasting taxpayers' hard-earned money on ridiculous promises to build coffee shops and shopping malls in space. Better that they put their efforts here on war-torn earth where attention is needed. In the Bhaktivedanta purport to the *Bhāgavata* verse mentioned above, Śrīla Prabhupāda described the plan for creating social harmony, prosperity and plenty all over the earth:

> Even those who are constantly engaged in sinful acts are all corrigible to the standard of perfect human beings if they take shelter of the devotees of the Lord. Jesus Christ and Muhammad, two powerful devotees of the Lord, have done tremendous service on behalf of the Lord on the surface of the globe. And from the version of Śrīla Śukadeva Gosvāmī it appears that instead of running a godless civilization in the present context of the world situation, if the leadership of world affairs is entrusted to the devotees of the Lord, for which a worldwide organization under the name and style of the International Society for Kṛṣṇa Consciousness has already been started, then by the grace of the Almighty Lord there can be a thorough change of heart in human beings all over the world

because the devotees of the Lord are able authorities to effect such a change by purifying the dust-worn minds of the people in general.

The politicians of the world may remain in their respective positions because the pure devotees of the Lord are not interested in political leadership or diplomatic implications. The devotees are interested only in seeing that the people in general are not misguided by political propaganda and in seeing that the valuable life of a human being is not spoiled in following a type of civilization which is ultimately doomed. If the politicians, therefore, would be guided by the good counsel of the devotees, then certainly there would be a great change in the world situation by the purifying propaganda of the devotees, as shown by Lord Śrī Caitanya Mahāprabhu.

As Śukadeva Gosvāmī began his prayer by discussing the word *yat-kīrtanam,* so also Lord Śrī Caitanya Mahāprabhu recommended that simply by glorifying the Lord's holy name, a tremendous change of heart can take place by which the complete misunderstanding between the human nations created by politicians can at once be extinguished. And after the extinction of the fire of misunderstanding, other profits will follow. The destination is to go back home, back to Godhead, as we have several times discussed in these pages.

According to the cult of devotion, generally known as the Vaiṣṇava cult, there is no bar against anyone's advancing in the matter of God realization. A Vaiṣṇava is powerful enough to turn into a Vaiṣṇava even the Kirāta, etc., as above mentioned. In the *Bhagavad-gītā* (9.32) it is said by the Lord that there is no bar to becoming a devotee of the Lord even for those who are lowborn. (SB 2.4.18, purport)

The elephant pearl mentioned in this verse is a natural pearl which grows inside the elephant's forehead. It is extremely rare and precious.

ŚLOKA 11.9

ये तु संवत्सरं पूर्णं नित्यं मौनेन भुञ्जते ।
युगकोटिसहस्रं तैः स्वर्गलोके महीयते ॥९॥

ye tu saṁvatsaraṁ pūrṇaṁ
nityaṁ maunena bhuñjate
yuga-koṭi-sahasraṁ taiḥ
svarga-loke mahīyate

He who eats his meals for one year in silence will be honored in Svarga for one thousand crores of yugas.

Commentary: One crore equals ten million. So Cāṇakya Paṇḍita has outlined an austerity by which one may obtain a long life in heaven numbering 1,000 times 10,000,000 *yugas.* One year as measured in Svarga is far longer than one of our years. Nonetheless, a lifetime in Svarga still equals only one hundred years by the calculation of the celestials. Concluding his one hundred years of enjoyment when the results of his good *karma* are exhausted, the fettered ex-demigod returns to earth or some other planet in this or that species of life, and continues on his way in the near hopeless whirlpool of birth and death. Hence, austerities for material gain as described here are fruitless. This is the hidden meaning of this verse. Instead, one should dedicate his every activity unto the lotus feet of the Supreme Lord, honoring only Śrī Kṛṣṇa-*prasāda,* and be done with his pogo stick sojourn through this material world.

There are many "fashion *yogīs*" who, claiming to observe a vow of silence, communicate instead by either writing on a slate, blowing noises or making hand gestures. Showbottle *yogīs* who make stagecraft of the observances of *mauna* (silence) are as effective as bottles of colored water in the chemist's window. True silence means to avoid discoursing about material topics, and to discuss only those topics that pertain to transcendence. Just as the *gopīs* of Vṛndāvana spent their days sharing the pastimes of Lord Kṛṣṇa amongst themselves, so we should keep our conversation focused upon spiritual topics. This is true silence as recommended in CN 9.11.

Kṛṣṇa-*kathā* or conversations regarding the pastimes of the Supreme Lord are far better than a pretentious show of silence and false renunciation. There is a holy stream in Bihar State that runs through Gayā called the Phalgu River, known for its soft and sandy shore. Today's citified *yogīs* and other cozy renunciants are sardonically referred to as *phalgu-tyāgīs.* Of these, Śrīla Prabhupāda says:

> *Phalgu-vairāgya. Phalgu* means false. False. The *phalgu,* from river Phalgu is… Here, in India, there is a river Phalgu. You'll see that there is no water on the surface of the river. But if you push your hand within the sand, you'll get water. So *phalgu-vairāgya* means that I am giving up, renouncing everything, superficially, but within me there is a desire how to become God. I am giving up, but I cannot give up this desire. (Lecture, Bg 7.4, Vṛndāvana, 10 Aug 1974)

Regarding daily meals, devotees of the Lord dine upon the remnants of foodstuffs offered to Lord Kṛṣṇa called *prasāda,* meaning "mercy." Kṛṣṇa says in the *Bhagavad-gītā:*

> If one offers Me with love and devotion a fruit, a flower, or water, then I will accept that offering. (Bg 9.26)

To this He adds:

> Devotees are released from all sinful reactions because they eat food first offered in *yajña.* Others who eat only for pleasure devour only sin. (Bg 3.13)

A devotee's only goal is service to Kṛṣṇa in the transcendental realm called Vaikuṇṭha, therefore it would be a prison sentence for the *bhakta* to be sent to heaven for an extended vacation of sense gratification. Kṛṣṇa's devotees belong in Vṛndāvana, not Svarga.

ŚLOKA 11.10

कामक्रोधौ तथा लोभं स्वादुशृङ्गारकौतुके ।
अतिनिद्रातिसेवे च विद्यार्थी ह्यष्ट वर्जयेत् ॥१०॥

kāma-krodhau tathā lobhaṁ
svādu-śṛṅgāra-kautuke

ati-nidrāti-seve ca
vidyārthī hy aṣṭa varjayet

The student must completely renounce the eight following flaws: lust, anger, greed, desire for rich foods, bodily decoration, excessive curiosity for worldly affairs, excessive sleep and excessive endeavor for bodily maintenance.

Commentary: Spending a period of one's youth as a *brahmacārī* (celibate student) provides a sound platform for the entire life. It is said that a sapling whose liquid is drained never grows to bear fruits. In the same way young men who waste their strength in illicit sex find their intelligence, memory and overall health deteriorating in later life. A *brahmacārī* is always involved in spiritually-oriented works. Therefore *brahmacārī* means "he who executes activities of Brahman." The more time and effort spent in youth reflecting on transcendence, the easier it will be to remain Kṛṣṇa conscious in old age. The effects of a youth wasted in "sowing wild oats" can be seen in America's gloomy old age homes which are haunted by addle-pated relics wondering in vain what happened to their "golden years."

ŚLOKA 11.11

अकृष्टफलमूलानि वनवासरतिः सदा ।
कुरुतेऽहरहः श्राद्धमृषिर्विप्रः स उच्यते ॥११॥

akṛṣṭa-phala-mūlāni
vana-vāsa-ratiḥ sadā
kurute 'harahaḥ śrāddham
ṛṣir vipraḥ sa ucyate

A vipra who subsists on roots and fruits from an uncultivated land, lives happily in the forest, and daily performs the śrāddha offering is called a ṛṣi.

Commentary: The strict rules for offerings of *śrāddha* are given in *Śrīmad-Bhāgavatam* (7.14.19–23). *Śrāddha* means the offerings to ancestors, some of whom may be lingering in subtle bodies as ghosts. By making offerings of foodstuffs to one's ancestors, their lost souls become eligible to take birth once again. India's center for this sacrifice of *śrāddha* or *piṇḍa-dāna,* is the sacred temple of Śrī Viṣṇupāda at Gayā in Bihar State. When Śrī Caitanya Mahāprabhu (as Nimāi Paṇḍita) visited this temple for the purposes of *śrāddha,* He met His spiritual master Śrī Īśvara Purī, and said to him:

> By offering oblations to the forefathers, only those souls to whom the offerings are made receive benefit. But just by seeing you, many generations of My ancestors are liberated. (*Śrī Caitanya-bhāgavata,* 1.17.51–52)

Hence, the rituals of the *śrāddha* ceremony, as of all other *yajñas,* are naturally included in Kṛṣṇa consciousness.

Although the *tapasya* that Cāṇakya Paṇḍita describes in this verse is very austere, there is a type of *yoga* which is far more rigid called *jaḍa-yoga.* A *jaḍa-yogī* eats only those things that enter his mouth by the will of Providence. While traveling in the vicinity of the Kāverī River, the "Ganges of South India," Prahlāda Mahārāja met such a *jaḍa-yogī* lying on the ground as still and as satisfied as a python. The episode is described in the Seventh Canto, thirteenth chapter of *Śrīmad-Bhāgavatam,* where the *yogī* instructed Prahlāda Mahārāja:

> In the course of the evolutionary process, which is caused by fruitive activities (*karma*) due to undesirable material sense gratification, I have received this human form of life, which can lead to the heavenly planets (Svarga), to liberation (*mokṣa*), to the lower species or to rebirth among human beings. In this human form of life, a man and a woman unite for the sensual pleasure of sex, but by actual experience we have observed that none of them are happy. Therefore seeing the contrary results, I have stopped taking part in materialistic activities. The real purpose of life is spiritual happiness, which is genuine happiness. This can be achieved only

> after stopping all materialistic activities. Material sense enjoyment is simply an imagination. Therefore, considering this subject matter, I have ceased from all materialistic activities and am lying down here. (SB 7.13.25–27)

Prahlāda Mahārāja is a celebrated authority, one of the twelve *mahājanas,* and he accepted as genuine this *yogī's* version of austerity and renunciation as leading to inner bliss. In his short dialogue with Prahlāda, the *jaḍa-yogī* established that renunciation and spiritual awakening are the purpose of *yoga.* Actual *yoga* or "linking" with the Supreme Lord by the grace of the *guru-paramparā* is quite different than what is touted by today's storefront *yogīs.* Such upstarts teach that *yoga* is meant for improved sex life. Other charlatans have stooped so low nowadays that they teach a concocted "*yoga* for dogs."

ŚLOKA 11.12

एकाहारेण सन्तुष्टः षट्कर्मनिरतः सदा ।
ऋतुकालाभिगामी च स विप्रो द्विज उच्यते ॥१२॥

ekāhāreṇa santuṣṭaḥ
ṣaṭ-karma-nirataḥ sadā
ṛtu-kālābhigāmī ca
sa vipro dvija ucyate

A brāhmaṇa who is satisfied with one meal daily, who is always engaged in the six traditional duties of brāhmaṇas [paṭhana, pāṭhana, yajana, yājana, dāna and pratigraha] and who shares intimacy with his wife only once in a month on an auspicious day selected after her period is called a dvija.

Commentary: Bṛhaspati notes of the qualified twice-born:

> The best among men is the *brāhmaṇa,* the best among luminaries is the sun, the best among limbs is the head, and the best among religious vows is the truth. (GP 1.115.53)

Here in verses 9 to 12 of this chapter, Cāṇakya Paṇḍita describes the various activities and penances of pious *brāhmaṇas,* the *gurus* of the other classes. In CN 11.13–17 he will discuss how *brāhmaṇas* lose their qualities through degradation.

Regarding the subject of sex mentioned herein, in many circles of modern Western society sexual intercourse is almost as casual as a handshake. But in the Vedic civilization and culture, sex life was undertaken between a religiously married husband and wife only for the purpose of procreation. The science of obtaining good progeny, as described in the *Rati-śāstra,* takes into consideration: the health and mood of the husband and wife, the number of days since the wife's period, the constellation (*nakṣatra*) and lunar day (*tithi*), the position of the moon in relation to the natal moon of both husband and wife, the quarterly division (*prahara*) of the night and the position of the planets nine months hence. The husband should preserve his strength by avoiding too much sexual intercourse so that he will be properly equipped to produce strong offspring. Once children appear, they must be responsibly instructed in the science of transcendence, for the parents who do not teach their offspring Kṛṣṇa consciousness, the only means of liberation from birth and death, are their enemies. Śrīla Prabhupāda instructed many a *gṛhastha* couple for whom he personally performed the marriage rituals, "Do not produce children like cats and dogs."

ŚLOKA 11.13

लौकिके कर्मणि रतः पशूनां परिपालकः ।
वाणिज्यकृषिकर्मा यः स विप्रो वैश्य उच्यते ॥१३॥

laukike karmaṇi rataḥ
paśūnāṁ paripālakaḥ
vāṇijya-kṛṣi-karmā yaḥ
sa vipro vaiśya ucyate

The brāhmaṇa who is engrossed in worldly affairs, raises cattle and is engaged in trade is really called a vaiśya.

Commentary: Noticing the degradation of society due to the accruing momentum of Kali-yuga, Cāṇakya Paṇḍita, himself a perfect *brāhmaṇa,* herewith begins his five-verse tirade against pollution among members of the highest caste. *Brāhmaṇas* are meant to be the head of society and, without a head, society becomes like a headless body. A father's chastisement is meant for the betterment of the son or disciple. Cāṇakya is not a faultfinder, but is rather performing a teacher's duty of correcting.

ŚLOKA 11.14

लाक्षादितैलनीलीनां कौसुम्भमधुसर्पिषाम् ।
विक्रेता मद्यमांसानां स विप्रः शूद्र उच्यते ॥१४॥

lākṣādi-taila-nīlīnāṁ
kausumbha-madhu-sarpiṣām
vikretā madya-māṁsānāṁ
sa vipraḥ śūdra ucyate

The brāhmaṇa who deals in lac-die articles, oil, indigo, silk, honey, ghee, liquor or flesh is a śūdra.

ŚLOKA 11.15

परकार्यविहन्ता च दाम्भिकः स्वार्थसाधकः ।
छली द्वेषी मृदुः क्रूरो विप्रो मार्जार उच्यते ॥१५॥

para-kārya-vihantā ca
dāmbhikaḥ svārtha-sādhakaḥ
chalī dveṣī mṛduḥ krūro
vipro mārjāra ucyate

The brāhmaṇa who thwarts the doings of others, who is a hypocrite, selfish, a deceitful hater and who while speaking mildly cherishes cruelty in his heart—is called a cat.

Commentary: *Manu-saṁhitā* (4.195–7) states:

> He who while waving the flag of virtue is ever covetous, a hypocrite, a deceiver of the world, is known as a cat-like person; mischievous and a slanderer of all. The twice-born (*dvija*) with downcast eyes, malignant, intent on gaining his own ends, fraudulent and falsely humble, is like a crane. Such *brāhmaṇas* who act like cranes and those that have the character of cats fall by their sinful conduct into the hell called Andha-tāmisra.

The hell (*naraka*) called Andha-tāmisra is described in the *Bhāgavatam* (3.30.28) as a horrible place, very dark (*andha*) and where ignorance (*tamo-guṇa*) abounds. Śrīla Prabhupāda comments (SB 3.4.20, purport):

> The unauthorized dry speculators are offenders at the lotus feet of the Lord Śrī Kṛṣṇa because they distort the purports of *Bhagavad-gītā* and *Śrīmad-Bhāgavatam* to mislead the public and prepare a direct path to the hell known as Andha-tāmisra.

In verses 11 through 14 Cāṇakya Paṇḍita describes various *karmas* that determine status, but here he describes the *guṇas* (qualities) by which to discern true *brāhmaṇas* from posers. Hangers-on who are born into families of the first caste, but who have not qualified themselves, are called *brahma-bandhus,* "mere friends of *brāhmaṇas.*" Such is the situation of the first order of society today. Cāṇakya Paṇḍita calls *brāhmaṇas* who harbor ill intentions as *mārjāra-vipras,* "cat *brāhmaṇas.*"

ŚLOKA 11.16

वापीकूपतडागानामारामसुरवेश्मनाम् ।
उच्छेदने निराशङ्कः स विप्रो म्लेच्छ उच्यते ॥१६॥

vāpī-kūpa-taḍāgānām
ārāma-sura-veśmanām
ucchedane nirāśaṅkaḥ
sa vipro mleccha ucyate

The brāhmaṇa who unhesitatingly destroys a pond, a well, a tank, a garden or a temple is actually a mlecchа.

Commentary: Sometimes a hereditary *brāhmaṇa* will sell out a temple garden, meant to produce fruits and flowers for the deity under his care, to pay for his daughter's wedding. Thus in India's sacred *dhāmas* and *purīs,* it is not uncommon to see large commercial buildings towering inches from temples. Sometimes a *brāhmaṇa* in charge of several temples will sell off some of these temples and bring all the temple deities together on one altar. Cāṇakya Paṇḍita's verse may be taken as a future warning to *brāhmaṇas* not to violate the trust that has been placed in them by such unauthorized dealings. Even in Vedic times many *brāhmaṇas* abused their positions because kings were unwilling to punish even those *brāhmaṇas* who were caught red-handed due to a sort of diplomatic immunity. However, the laws of material nature are not so lenient, and *brāhmaṇas* are not exempt from karmic reactions in the next birth. *Brāhmaṇas* are meant for serving the spiritual needs of society and should never think of themselves as above the law.

ŚLOKA 11.17

देवद्रव्यं गुरुद्रव्यं परदाराभिमर्शनम् ।
निर्वाहः सर्वभूतेषु विप्रश्चाण्डाल उच्यते ॥१७॥

deva-dravyaṁ guru-dravyaṁ
para-dārābhimarśanam
nirvāhaḥ sarva-bhūteṣu
vipraś cāṇḍāla ucyate

The brāhmaṇa who steals the property of the deity and the guru, who cohabits with another's wife and who lives among all kinds of living beings is a cāṇḍāla.

Commentary: Those who eat dogs are called *cāṇḍālas*. Even today in certain parts of the world, dog farms raise canine cattle. An unqualified "birth *brāhmaṇa*" is actually nothing more than a *muci* (cobbler). A cobbler deals in hides of animals and the *brāhmaṇa* who claims to be a *brāhmaṇa* based upon his body or skin is no different. Hence Śrīla Prabhupāda often quoted this verse from a Bengali poem:

śuci hañā muci haya yadi kṛṣṇa tyaje
muci hañā śuci haya yadi kṛṣṇa bhaje

> The cobbler becomes *śuci* or brahminical if he knows the science of Kṛṣṇa consciousness. But if the *brāhmaṇa* renounces God consciousness, he becomes *muci* or like a cobbler.

Lord Kṛṣṇa says:

> I am the basis of Brahman. (Bg 14.27)

This Brahman is the unseen, transcendental, spiritual effulgence that permeates the universe. One cannot be a *brāhmaṇa* without knowing Brahman. Since Kṛṣṇa is the basis of spirituality, therefore the *brāhmaṇa* who renounces Kṛṣṇa consciousness becomes a "skin merchant," passing himself off on the basis of his skin or birth.

ŚLOKA 11.18

देयं भोज्यधनं धनं सुकृतिभिर्नो सञ्चयस्तस्य वै
श्रीकर्णस्य बलेश्च विक्रमपतेरद्यापि कीर्तिः स्थिता
अस्माकं मधु दानभोगरहितं नष्टं चिरात्सञ्चितं
निर्वाणादिति नैजपादयुगलं घर्षन्त्यहो मक्षिकाः ॥१८॥

deyaṁ bhojya-dhanaṁ dhanaṁ sukṛtibhir no sañcayas tasya vai
śrī-karṇasya baleś ca vikrama-pater adyāpi kīrtiḥ sthitā
asmākaṁ madhu dāna-bhoga-rahitaṁ naṣṭaṁ cirāt sañcitaṁ
nirvāṇād iti naija-pāda-yugalaṁ gharṣanty aho makṣikāḥ

Men of merit should give away in charity all that exceeds their needs. By charity alone the fame of Karṇa, Bali and Vikramāditya survives even today. Just see the plight of the honeybees rubbing their legs in despair. They are crying, "Alas! We neither enjoyed our stored-up honey nor gave it in charity, and now someone has plundered it in an instant!"

Commentary: Charitable personalities are often celebrated for generations. The incident concerning the great warrior Karṇa, who gave away the divine earrings and armor he was born with—even though they had to be cut off—is told in the *Mahābhārata.* The history of Mahārāja Bali, who offered everything to the Lord in His Vāmana (dwarf) incarnation, is narrated in the Eighth Canto of *Śrīmad-Bhāgavatam.* King Vikramāditya was the ruler of Avantikā, now Ujjain, in Madhya Pradesh. So magnanimously did he reign that even today the years of the Vedic calendar are measured from his ascent to the throne in 56 BC.

Though King Vikramāditya is well known for his charity, as stated herewith, he prospered some centuries after Cāṇakya Paṇḍita. Hence his name must have been added to this *śloka* at a later date. However Kiśora Dāsa adds that Vikrama-pati (lit. "lord of prowess") could refer to any one of many earlier Vedic kings. Vikrama-pati is a common honorific apellation for valiant *kṣatriyas.* The *Monier-Williams Sanskrit Dictionary* records that the title Vikrama-deva was similarly used for Candragupta Maurya, as evidenced from inscriptions of his time.

Bees are sometimes seen beating themselves upon the ground in a sort of dance that points the others of their hive in the direction of flowers rich in pollen. Here Cāṇakya Paṇḍita has made a wonderful analogy out of this activity. Lord Kṛṣṇa Himself discusses a miser's fate, the essential point of this *śloka,* in the *Śrīmad-Bhāgavatam* chapter entitled "The Song of the Avantī *Brāhmaṇa.*" Quoting the *brāhmaṇa,* Kṛṣṇa tells His dear friend Uddhava:

> The *brāhmaṇa* spoke as follows: "O what great misfortune! I have simply tormented myself uselessly, struggling so hard for money that was not even intended for religiosity or material enjoyment. Generally the wealth of misers never allows them any happiness. In this life it causes their self-torment, and when they die it sends them to hell." (SB 11.23.14)

Thus Ends Chapter Eleven

CHAPTER TWELVE

ŚLOKA 12.1

सानन्दं सदनं सुतास्तु सुधियः कान्ता प्रियालापिनी
इच्छापूर्तिधनं स्वयोषिति रतिः स्वाज्ञापराः सेवकाः ।
आतिथ्यं शिवपूजनं प्रतिदिनं मिष्टान्नपानं गृहे
साधोः सङ्गमुपासते च सततं धन्यो गृहस्थाश्रमः ॥१॥

sānandaṁ sadanaṁ sutās tu sudhiyaḥ kāntā priyālāpinī
icchā-pūrti-dhanaṁ sva-yoṣiti ratiḥ svājñā-parāḥ sevakāḥ
ātithyaṁ śiva-pūjanaṁ prati-dinaṁ miṣṭānna-pānaṁ gṛhe
sādhoḥ saṅgam upāsate ca satataṁ dhanyo gṛhasthāśramaḥ

That gṛhastha is blessed in whose home there is a blissful atmosphere, whose sons are talented, whose wife speaks sweetly, whose wealth is sufficient to satisfy his desires, who finds pleasure in the company of his wife, whose servants are obedient, in whose house hospitality is shown, the Supreme Lord is worshipped daily, delicious food and drink are partaken each day, and who finds joy in the company of sādhus.

Commentary: The word *śiva-pūjana* in this verse has been translated either as "worship of the demigod Lord Śiva" or as "auspicious (*śiva*) worship of the Supreme Lord." Generally materialists pray to Lord Śiva for the fulfillment of material benedictions, such as those mentioned here in this verse. Śrīla Prabhupāda describes the relationship of Lord Śiva to Lord Kṛṣṇa:

> Lord Śiva is not an ordinary living being. He is the plenary portion of the Lord, but because Lord Śiva is in direct touch with material nature, he is not exactly in the same transcendental position as Lord Viṣṇu. The difference is like that between milk and curd. Curd is nothing but milk, and yet it cannot be used in place of milk. (SB 1.3.5, purport)

Both yogurt and milk are in one sense the same, dairy. But milk is the source of yogurt. Milk can become yogurt, but yogurt cannot be returned to milk. For the devotee of Lord Viṣṇu, Śiva is one of the twelve *mahājanas* (great authorities). (SB 6.3.20) He is respected as the greatest Vaiṣṇava: *vaiṣṇavānāṁ yathā śambhuḥ.* (SB 12.13.16) The full verse reads:

> Just as the Gaṅgā is the greatest of all rivers, Lord Acyuta the supreme among deities and Lord Śambhu the greatest of Vaiṣṇavas, so *Śrīmad-Bhāgavatam* is the greatest of all *Purāṇas.*

Śiva is automatically worshipped in the household of a devotee because he worships Lord Nārāyaṇa or Lord Kṛṣṇa.

Lord Śiva explains his subordinance to Lord Nārāyaṇa in his conversation with his own expansion Durvāsā Muni (SB 9.4.56):

> My dear son, I, Lord Brahmā and the other demigods, who rotate within this universe under the misconception of our greatness, cannot exhibit any power to compete with the Supreme Personality of Godhead, for innumerable universes and their inhabitants come into existence and are annihilated by the simple direction of the Lord.

ŚLOKA 12.2

आर्तेषु विप्रेषु दयान्वितश्च
यच्छ्रद्धया स्वल्पमुपैति दानम् ।
अनन्तपारं समुपैति राजन्
यद्दीयते तन्न लभेद्द्विजेभ्यः ॥२॥

ārteṣu vipreṣu dayānvitaś ca
yac chraddhayā svalpam upaiti dānam
ananta-pāraṁ samupaiti rājan
yad dīyate tan na labhed dvijebhyaḥ

Even by making a small contribution to a distressed brāhmaṇa, one is rewarded abundantly. Therefore, O King, charity offered to a gentleman of the twice-born caste is not returned in an equal quantity, but in an infinitely higher degree.

Commentary: It is said that if charity is offered to a partially-educated *brāhmaṇa,* then whatever is given will be returned in an equal amount. But if the *brāhmaṇa* is highly educated, selfless and spiritually situated, then the charity is returned in great abundance. There are many spiritual quacks who take advantage of this Hindu sense of alms-giving, so one should ascertain very carefully to whom a gift is offered. Money creates spiritual rewards when offered to the pure devotees who invest every penny in spiritual activities.

ŚLOKA 12.3

दाक्षिण्यं स्वजने दया परजने शाठ्यं सदा दुर्जने
प्रीतिः साधुजने स्मयः खलजने विद्वज्जने चार्जवम् ।
शौर्यं शत्रुजने क्षमा गुरुजने नारीजने धूर्तता
इत्थं ये पुरुषा कलासु कुशलास्तेष्वेव लोकस्थितिः ॥३॥

dākṣiṇyaṁ svajane dayā para-jane śāṭhyaṁ sadā durjane
prītiḥ sādhu-jane smayaḥ khala-jane vidvaj-jane cārjavam
śauryaṁ śatru-jane kṣamā guru-jane nārī-jane dhūrtatā
itthaṁ ye puruṣā kalāsu kuśalās teṣv eva loka-sthitiḥ

They are happy in this world who are generous towards their relatives, kind to strangers, cunning with the wicked, loving to the good, shrewd in their dealings with the base, frank with the learned, valorous towards the enemy, patient with elders and who deal with women in a roundabout manner.

Commentary: This verse encapsulates *nīti-śāstra's* common sense teachings of self-reliance and personal responsibility. We have no one to blame but ourselves for our lot, because we alone are the creators of our own happiness or misery. Only a responsible man can know contentment, while the life of a disorganized man spins out of control in this life and into the never-ending vortex of *saṁsāra.* Regarding the advice to be "cunning with the wicked," there is this well-known proverb:

śaṭhe śāṭhyaṁ samācaret

> One should be cunning with those who are cunning. With a cheat behave like a cheat.

Śrīla Prabhupāda explains in *Śrī Caitanya-caritāmṛta* (2.1.218):

> If a Vaiṣṇava, by the mercy of the Lord, is empowered by Him to distribute the Lord's holy name all over the world, other Vaiṣṇavas become very joyful—that is, if they are truly Vaiṣṇavas. One who is envious of the success of a Vaiṣṇava is certainly not a Vaiṣṇava himself, but an ordinary mundane man. Envy and jealousy are manifested by mundane people, not by Vaiṣṇavas. Why should a Vaiṣṇava be envious of another Vaiṣṇava who is successful in spreading the holy name of the Lord? An actual Vaiṣṇava is very pleased to accept another Vaiṣṇava who is bestowing the Lord's mercy. A mundane person in the dress of a Vaiṣṇava should not be

respected but rejected. This is enjoined in the *śāstra* (*upekṣā*). The word *upekṣā* means neglect. One should neglect an envious person. A preacher's duty is to love the Supreme Personality of Godhead, make friendships with Vaiṣṇavas, show mercy to the innocent and reject or neglect those who are envious or jealous. There are many jealous people in the dress of Vaiṣṇavas in this Kṛṣṇa consciousness movement, and they should be completely neglected. There is no need to serve a jealous person who is in the dress of a Vaiṣṇava.

ŚLOKA 12.4

हस्तौ दानविवर्जितौ श्रुतिपुटौ सारस्वतद्रोहिणौ
नेत्रे साधुविलोकनेन रहिते पादौ न तीर्थं गतौ ।
अन्यायार्जितवित्तपूर्णमुदरं गर्वेण तुङ्गं शिरो
रे रे जम्बुक मुञ्च मुञ्च सहसा नीचं सुनिन्द्यं वपुः ॥४॥

hastau dāna-vivarjitau śruti-puṭau sārasvata-drohiṇau
netre sādhu-vilokanena rahite pādau na tīrthaṁ gatau
anyāyārjita-vitta-pūrṇam udaraṁ garveṇa tuṅgaṁ śiro
re re jambuka muñca muñca sahasā nīcaṁ sunindyaṁ vapuḥ

O jackal, immediately leave aside the degraded body of that man whose hands have never given in charity, whose ears have never heeded the voice of learning, whose eyes have not beheld a pure devotee of the Lord, whose feet have never walked to holy tīrthas, whose belly is fed by illegal earnings, and whose head is held high by vanity. Do not eat it, O jackal, lest you become polluted.

Commentary: Described herein is that sinner beside whom the loathsome jackal becomes pious by comparison. It is said in the *Pañca-tantra* that the jackal is even hated by its fellow jungle dwellers. To appreciate that, one must reside for a time near a jungle that is infested by jackals, such as those found in Bihar or Madhya Pradesh. He who has seen their vicious grins and has heard their blood-chilling chorus understands that among animals, the lowly jackal is the outcaste. Yet here Cāṇakya counsels the jackal.

Cāṇakya Paṇḍita observes here that the arrogant brute, a two-legged beast in human dress, is even lower than the jackal because he has spoiled his human form of life. Such unfortunate persons may have to wait millions of lifetimes to receive this invaluable benefit of human birth once again. According to *The Devil's Dictionary: "Hypocrite:* One who, professing virtues that he does not respect, secures the advantages of seeming to be what he despises." Thus Cāṇakya Paṇḍita ironically advises the jackal, "Do not eat such hypocrites if you value your purity."

ŚLOKA 12.5

येषां श्रीमद्यशोदासुतपदकमले नास्ति भक्तिर्नराणां
येषामाभीरकन्याप्रियगुणकथने नानुरक्ता रसज्ञा ।
येषां श्रीकृष्णलीलाललितरसकथासादरौ नैव कर्णौ
धिक्तान् धिक्तान् धिगेतान् कथयति सततं कीर्तनस्थो मृदङ्गः ॥५॥

yeṣāṁ śrīmad-yaśodā-suta-pada-kamale nāsti bhaktir narāṇāṁ
yeṣām ābhīra-kanyā-priya-guṇa-kathane nānuraktā rasajñā
yeṣāṁ śrī-kṛṣṇa-līlā-lalita-rasa-kathā-sādarau naiva karṇau
dhik tān dhik tān dhig etān kathayati satataṁ kīrtana-stho mṛdaṅgaḥ

"Shame upon those who are without devotion to the lotus feet of Śrī Kṛṣṇa, the darling son of mother Yaśodā; who are not attached to discussing the glories of Śrīmati Rādhārāṇī; and whose ears are not eager to listen to the pastimes of Śrī Kṛṣṇa." This is the exclamation of the mṛdaṅga's beat at kīrtana: dhik tān dhik tān dhig etān.

Commentary: As described in the Tenth Canto of the *Śrīmad-Bhāgavatam,* Lord Śrī Kṛṣṇa, the Supreme Personality of Godhead, displayed His Vṛndāvana-*līlā* or pastimes upon the earth just before the dawn of Kali-yuga. The Lord appeared over 5000 years ago as the son of King Nanda and mother Yaśodā in Vraja-*maṇḍala* or Mathurā. Cāṇakya Paṇḍita herewith identifies Lord Kṛṣṇa as Yaśodā-suta (the son of Yaśodā) and as the worshipable Lord whose praises are sung at *kīrtana* to the beat of the *mṛdaṅga* drum. His admonition to non-believers is just as true today now that beats of the "earth-bodied drum" are heard throughout the world thanks to Prabhupāda's vision for global *saṅkīrtana.*

Cāṇakya's pun should be noted: aside from being a *mṛdaṅga* beat *mantra,* the word *dhik* in Sanskrit means "fie, shame" and the words *tān* and *etān* mean "(fie) on these, (fie) on those."

Lord Kṛṣṇa Himself explains the essence of perfect spiritual knowledge to Śrī Uddhava:

> Firm faith in the blissful narrations of My pastimes, constant chanting of My glories, unwavering attachment to ceremonial worship of Me, praising Me through beautiful hymns, great respect for My devotional service, offering obeisances with the entire body, performing first-class worship of My devotees, consciousness of Me in all living entities, offering of ordinary bodily activities in My devotional service, use of words to describe My qualities, offering the mind to Me, rejection of all material desires, giving up wealth for My devotional service, renouncing material sense gratification and happiness, and performing all desirable activities such as charity, sacrifice, chanting, vows, and austerities with the purpose of achieving Me—these constitute actual religious principles, by which those human beings who have actually surrendered themselves to Me automatically develop love for Me. What other purpose or goal could remain for My devotee? (SB 11.19.20–24)

In the *Mahābhārata* (*Vana-parva,* ch. 12) Śrī Kṛṣṇa assures Draupadī:

> The heavenly planets may fall down, and Mount Himavat may move, the earth may be rent asunder and the ocean may go dry,

but—O Draupadī—know for certain that My words will never prove futile.

The *mṛdaṅga* was unknown to the West before Śrīla Prabhupāda introduced it. As a boy, Śrīla Prabhupāda was encouraged by his father Śrī Gour Mohan De to learn to play it, and Prabhupāda personally taught its beats to his disciples. Since the advent of the worldwide *saṅkīrtana* movement by ISKCON, the *mṛdaṅga* has become a common sight in towns and villages all over the world. Its beat accompanies those devotees who broadcast the message of *saṅkīrtana* of Śrī Caitanya Mahāprabhu (as given in His *Śikṣāṣṭaka,* quoted in Cc 3.20.12):

ceto-darpaṇa-mārjanaṁ bhava-mahā-dāvāgni-nirvāpaṇaṁ
śreyaḥ-kairava-candrikā-vitaraṇaṁ vidyā-vadhū-jīvanam
ānandāmbudhi-vardhanaṁ prati-padaṁ pūrṇāmṛtāsvādanaṁ
sarvātma-snapanaṁ paraṁ vijayate śrī-kṛṣṇa-saṅkīrtanam

Glory to the Śrī Kṛṣṇa *saṅkīrtana,* which cleanses the heart of all the dust accumulated for years and extinguishes the fire of conditional life, of repeated birth and death. This *saṅkīrtana* movement is the prime benediction for humanity at large because it spreads the rays of the benediction moon. It is the life of all transcendental knowledge. It increases the ocean of transcendental bliss, and it enables us to fully taste the nectar for which we are always anxious.

ŚLOKA 12.6

पत्रं नैव यदा करीलविटपे दोषो वसन्तस्य किं
नोलूकोऽप्यवलोकते यदि दिवा सूर्यस्य किं दूषणम् ।
वर्षा नैव पतन्ति चातकमुखे मेघस्य किं दूषणं
यत्पूर्वं विधिना ललाटलिखितं तन्मार्जितुं कः क्षमः ॥६॥

patraṁ naiva yadā karīla-viṭape doṣo vasantasya kiṁ
nolūko 'py avalokate yadi divā sūryasya kiṁ dūṣaṇam

varṣā naiva patanti cātaka-mukhe meghasya kiṁ dūṣaṇaṁ
yat pūrvaṁ vidhinā lalāṭa-likhitaṁ tan mārjituṁ kaḥ kṣamaḥ

Can it be the fault of spring that the bamboo shoot grows without leaves? Is the sun to blame for the owl's blindness in daytime? Should the clouds be faulted if no drops fall into the mouth of the waiting cātaka bird? Who can erase that which Lord Brahmā has written upon the brow at the time of conception?

Commentary: Lord Brahmā, the creator, has written the lines of fate on each of our foreheads, but is it his fault that we provided the ink? The *Hitopadeśa* explains:

> Just as out of a lump of clay a potter makes whatever he desires, so out of the deeds performed by him, a man creates his own destiny and reaps his own results. Undertakings succeed by effort and not by mere wishes. The deer did not enter the mouth of the sleeping lion on its own!

In the *Mahābhārata,* Lord Kṛṣṇa succinctly explains the laws of *karma* to the sorely lamenting King Dhṛtarāṣṭra. The blind and wicked king—usurper of the throne of Hastināpura—queried from Śrī Kṛṣṇa at the end of the Battle of Kurukṣetra:

> "I had one hundred sons and all of them were killed in the war. How could this happen to me?"
>
> Kṛṣṇa replied, "O king, fifty lifetimes ago, you were a hunter. While hunting, you attempted to shoot a male bird, but he flew away. In anger, you ruthlessly set fire to the tree of the male bird while his hundred baby birds cried out for him from their nest. As the father-bird looked on in helpless horror, his eyes became burnt by the fire you set. Therefore, because you were the cause of that bird's pain of seeing the death of his hundred sons and of his blindness, too, you were born sightless and had to bear the pain of seeing your hundred sons dying."
>
> Dhṛtarāṣṭra queried further, "O Kṛṣṇa, but why did I have to wait for fifty lifetimes?"

> Lord Kṛṣṇa replied, "You required fifty lifetimes of piety in order to win the merit for having one hundred sons. Thus it was only after many lifetimes that sufficient *puṇya* could be accrued so that you could now have one hundred sons only to suffer the reactions to your sins of killing the baby birds and blinding their father."

Indeed, Kṛṣṇa explains to Arjuna:

> "The intricacies of action are very hard to understand. Therefore one should know properly what action is, what forbidden action is, and what inaction is." (Bg 4.17)

Next Cāṇakya Paṇḍita will explain how one's individual fate can be improved.

ŚLOKA 12.7

सत्सङ्गाद्भवति हि साधुता खलानां
साधूनां न हि खलसङ्गतः खलत्वम् ।
आमोदं कुसुमभवं मृदेव धत्ते
मृद्गन्धं न हि कुसुमानि धारयन्ति ॥७॥

sat-saṅgād bhavati hi sādhutā khalānāṁ
sādhūnāṁ na hi khala-saṅgataḥ khalatvam
āmodaṁ kusuma-bhavaṁ mṛd eva dhatte
mṛd-gandhaṁ na hi kusumāni dhārayanti

A wicked man may develop saintly qualities in the company of a devotee, but a devotee does not become impious in the company of a wicked person. The earth is scented by a flower that falls upon it, but the flower does not contract the odor of the earth.

Commentary: The only religion of the pure devotee is *sanātana-dharma,* the "eternal religion." Service to God should not be confused with membership in a church congregation or religious society. We are all eternal servants of Lord Kṛṣṇa. This realization may come in an instant or it may take millions of lifetimes. The best way to become self-realized, as advised by Cāṇakya Paṇḍita in this verse and the next, is the association of those who are already situated upon the path of Kṛṣṇa consciousness. There is no better example of a wicked man developing saintly qualities through the company of a pure devotee than that of Dhṛtarāṣṭra through Vidura:

> Thus Mahārāja Dhṛtarāṣṭra, the scion of Ajamīḍha, firmly convinced by introspective knowledge, broke at once the strong network of familial affection by his resolute determination. Thus he immediately left home to set out on the path of liberation as directed by his younger brother Vidura. (SB 1.13.29)

ŚLOKA 12.8

साधूनां दर्शनं पुण्यं तीर्थभूता हि साधवः ।
कालेन फलते तीर्थं सद्यः साधुसमागमः ॥८॥

sādhūnāṁ darśanaṁ puṇyaṁ
tīrtha-bhūtā hi sādhavaḥ
kālena phalate tīrthaṁ
sadyaḥ sādhu-samāgamaḥ

Devotees are holy places personified and their darśana is in itself virtuous. By visiting the holy tīrthas, one becomes purified gradually, yet by seeing a devotee, one becomes purified instantly.

Commentary: For many neophytes, *tīrtha-yātrā* is a means by which to unload their sins and pray for forgiveness. Consequently, the *puṇya-bhūmis* (centers of piety) become burdened with the sins of the pilgrims. As one such pilgrim once confessed to us, "I went to Banaras and slept with a prostitute. But I washed away my sin in the Ganges."

The effect of genuine *sādhus* is to neutralize this weighty burden of sins left by neophyte devotees. Consequently, saintly devotees of the Lord are described as "walking holy spots." Indeed all sacred spots gather in the footprints of the pure devotee. In *Śrīmad-Bhāgavatam,* King Yudhiṣṭhira tells Vidura:

> My Lord, devotees like your good self are verily holy places personified. Because you carry the Personality of Godhead within your heart, you turn all places into places of pilgrimage. (SB 1.13.10)

The example of His Divine Grace A.C. Bhaktivedanta Swami Prabhupāda was even greater than Vidura's. Śrīla Prabhupāda displayed his spiritual potency by establishing transcendental holy places all over the world. Wherever his lotus feet touched the earth, that place became holy.

> Unless one takes the dust of the lotus feet of a pure Vaiṣṇava on one's head, one cannot understand what the Supreme Personality of Godhead is, and unless one knows the Supreme Personality of Godhead, one's life remains imperfect. (SB 4.21.43, purport)

ŚLOKA 12.9

विप्रास्मिन्नगरे महान्कथय कस्तालद्रुमाणां गणः
को दाता रजको ददाति वसनं प्रातर्गृहीत्वा निशि ।
को दक्षः परवित्तदारहरणे सर्वेऽपि दक्षाः जनाः
कस्माज्जीवसि हे सखे विषकृमिन्यायेन जीवाम्यहम् ॥९॥

viprāsmin nagare mahān kathaya kas tāla-drumāṇāṁ gaṇaḥ
ko dātā rajako dadāti vasanaṁ prātar gṛhītvā niśi
ko dakṣaḥ para-vitta-dāra-haraṇe sarve 'pi dakṣāḥ janāḥ
kasmāj jīvasi he sakhe viṣa-kṛmi-nyāyena jīvāmy aham

A stranger inquired of a brāhmaṇa, "Tell me, who is great in this city?" The brāhmaṇa replied, "The grove of palm trees is great!" Then the traveler asked, "Well then, who is charitable?" The paṇḍita replied, "The washerman is charitable because he returns the washed garments in the evening." The wanderer persisted,

"Then tell me who is most expert?" The brāhmaṇa responded, "In this city everyone is expert… at robbing others of their wives and wealth!" The traveler demanded, "Then how do you manage to dwell in such a place?" The wise vipra replied, "As a worm survives in poison, so do I survive here!"

Commentary: The devotee drinks the nectar of the holy name and prospers even while apparently residing in a world surrounded by sense gratifiers who themselves are drowning in a sea of poison. For the practitioner of *hari-nāma-saṅkīrtana,* this world becomes Vaikuṇṭha. The secret is to offer everything to Śrī Kṛṣṇa, and thereby turn *viṣa* (poison) into nectar.

ŚLOKA 12.10

न विप्रपादोदककर्दमाणि
न वेदशास्त्रध्वनिगर्जितानि ।
स्वाहास्वधाकारविवर्जितानि
श्मशानतुल्यानि गृहाणि तानि ॥१०॥

na vipra-pādodaka-kardamāṇi
na veda-śāstra-dhvani-garjitāni
svāhā-svadhā-kāra-vivarjitāni
śmaśāna-tulyāni gṛhāṇi tāni

The house in which the lotus feet of brāhmaṇas are not washed, in which Vedic mantras are not loudly recited, and in which the holy sounds of svāhā and svadhā do not resound is no better than a funeral pyre.

Commentary: *Svāhā* is chanted over the sacrificial flames of *agni-hotra* (fire sacrifice) as an offering to Lord Viṣṇu or Nārāyaṇa. *Svadhā* is chanted as an offering to the *pitṛs* (ancestors). A house void of religious activities is condemned by Cāṇakya Paṇḍita as no better than a *śmaśāna,* where the dead are burned. In a proper Vedic household God is not worshipped merely as an abstract thought, rather, the Personality of Godhead is considered the chief of the house and all who live there are His servants.

In *Śrīmad-Bhāgavatam* (2.9.31, 33–34), the Supreme Lord Nārāyaṇa appeared before Lord Brahmā to teach him the essence of knowledge:

> The Personality of Godhead said: Knowledge about Me as described in the scriptures is very confidential, and it has to be realized in conjunction with devotional service. The necessary paraphernalia for that process is being explained by Me. You may take it up carefully… It is I who existed before creation. When there was nothing, I was still there. I upon whom you are now gazing, the Supreme Lord, will also remain after the time of the universe has come to an end. O Brahmā, whatever appears to be of any value, if it is without relation to Me, has no reality. Know it to be My *māyā,* that reflection which appears to be in darkness.

Therefore, just as Lord Nārāyaṇa is the proprietor of the entire universe, in the same way He is the proprietor of every household. When this fact is recognized the place where we live is transformed from a burning ground of sense gratification into a temple of the Supreme Lord.

ŚLOKA 12.11

सत्यं माता पिता ज्ञानं धर्मो भ्राता दया सखा ।
शान्तिः पत्नी क्षमा पुत्रः षडेते मम बान्धवाः ॥११॥

satyaṁ mātā pitā jñānaṁ
dharmo bhrātā dayā sakhā
śāntiḥ patnī kṣamā putraḥ
ṣaḍ ete mama bāndhavāḥ

[A sādhu, when asked about his family, gently replied:] "Truth is my mother and realized knowledge is my father, righteousness is my brother, mercy is my friend, inner peace is my wife, forgiveness is my son. These six are my kinsmen."

Commentary: Herewith the great *paṇḍita* praises a *sādhu's* qualities of *satya* (truth), *jñāna* (realized knowledge), *dharma* (righteousness), *dayā* (mercy), *śānti* (inner peace) and *kṣamā* (forgiveness). Śrīla Prabhupāda once mentioned that he saw a saffron-clad *sādhu* mingling with some worldly householders in a Delhi *dharma-śālā* discussing day-to-day topics: "I realized that the '*sādhu*' was merely an ordinary man dressed as a *sādhu* only." A quality of a true *sādhu* is that he will take mundane chit chat and turn it into an opportunity to preach Kṛṣṇa consciousness.

Genuine renunciants are not much attracted to discussions regarding family matters, hence the *sādhu's* wise answer to a materialistic question. The greatest *sādhu* of the first half of the twentieth century, Śrīla Bhaktisiddhānta Sārasvatī Ṭhākura, emphasized that a *sādhu's* association is best understood through his speech which, abandoning social grace, cuts to the heart of the truth. He said:

> There is no doubt that the words of *sādhus* possess the power to destroy the evil propensities of one's mind. The *sādhus* in this way benefit everyone who associates with them. There are many things, which we do not disclose to the *sādhu.* The real *sādhu* makes us speak out what we keep concealed in our hearts. He then applies the knife. The very word *sādhu* has no other meaning than this. He stands in front of the block with the uplifted sacrificial knife in his hand. The sensuous desires of men are like the goats. The *sādhu* stands there to kill those desires by the merciful stroke of the keen edge of the sacrificial knife in the form of unpleasant language. If the *sādhu* turns into my flatterer, then he does me harm, he becomes my enemy. If he gives flattery, then we are led to the road that brings enjoyment, but no real well-being. (from *Shri Chaitanya's Teachings,* pp. 26–27)

The inspiring qualities possessed by a genuine *sādhu* are described in *Śrīmad-Bhāgavatam* by none other than the Supreme Lord Himself in His incarnation as a *sādhu,* Śrī Kapiladeva:

> The symptoms of a *sādhu* are that he is tolerant, merciful, and friendly to all living entities. He has no enemies, he is peaceful, he abides in the scriptures, and his characteristics are sublime. Such a *sādhu* engages in staunch devotional service to the Lord without deviation. For the sake of the Lord, he renounces all other connections, such as family relationships and friendly acquaintances within the world. Engaged constantly in chanting and hearing about Me, the Supreme Personality of Godhead, the *sādhus* do not suffer from material miseries because they are always filled with thoughts of My pastimes and activities. (SB 3.25.21–23)

ŚLOKA 12.12

अनित्यानि शरीराणि विभवो नैव शाश्वतः ।
नित्यं सन्निहितो मृत्युः कर्तव्यो धर्मसङ्ग्रहः ॥१२॥

anityāni śarīrāṇi
vibhavo naiva śāśvataḥ
nityaṁ sannihito mṛtyuḥ
kartavyo dharma-saṅgrahaḥ

This body is perishable, wealth is transient and death waits nearby. Therefore immediately engage yourself in dharma.

Commentary: The Sanskrit word *dharma,* as explained by Śrīla Prabhupāda in the introduction to his *Bhagavad-gītā As It Is,* comes from the verbal root *dhṛ*. *Dhṛ* means "to support or sustain" and refers only to the essential nature of a thing. The essence of fire is heat and light; water, its wetness; sugar, its sweetness. The everlasting sustenance of the soul is the eternal religion, *sanātana-dharma.* This highest meaning of *dharma* is quite different from the material *dharma* or the dogma into which we have somehow landed at birth.

Converting from Christian to Buddhist to Hindu and back again will never solve the search for a true conception of religion. Unless one becomes a devotee fixed in his unending relationship with the Absolute Truth, true *dharma* remains elusive. Actual devotees who become elevated to the platform of *sanātana-dharma,* the eternal religion of Kṛṣṇa consciousness, may find eternal life in the Lord's service. Then when this lifetime is finished, Kṛṣṇa's devotees go back to home back to Godhead, never to return to this miserable world of false values and temporary *dharmas.*

ŚLOKA 12.13

निमन्त्रणोत्सवा विप्रा गावो नवतृणोत्सवाः ।
पत्युत्साहयुता भार्या अहं कृष्ण रणोत्सवः ॥१३॥

nimantraṇotsavā viprā
gāvo nava-tṛṇotsavāḥ
paty-utsāha-yutā bhāryā
ahaṁ kṛṣṇa raṇotsavaḥ

Arjuna said, "Brāhmaṇas find joy in attending feasts, cows are delighted by chewing fresh grass, married ladies find pleasure in the company of their husbands, know O Bhagavān Kṛṣṇa, that in the same way I rejoice in battle."

Commentary: Since there is no specific mention of Arjuna in this verse, the origin of it is a bit of a mystery. However one reply to it is found in the *Gītā.* Śrī Kṛṣṇa tells Arjuna:

> O Pārtha, happy are *kṣatriyas* for whom an opportunity for battle comes unsought, opening for them the gate to Svarga. (Bg 2.32)

Another reading of the last line (*ahaṁ kṛṣṇa-raṇotsavaḥ*) yields a more neutral meaning of the whole verse—taking the word *raṇa* to mean delight or pleasure, the verse need not be attributed to the famous Pāṇdava:

> *Brāhmaṇas* find joy in attending feasts, cows are delighted by chewing fresh grass, married ladies find pleasure in the company of their husbands, but my festival is the pleasure found in the Supreme Personality of Godhead, Kṛṣṇa.

ŚLOKA 12.14

मातृवत्परदारेषु परद्रव्येषु लोष्ट्रवत् ।
आत्मवत्सर्वभूतेषु यः पश्यति स पण्डितः ॥१४॥

mātṛvat para-dāreṣu
para-dravyeṣu loṣṭravat
ātmavat sarva-bhūteṣu
yaḥ paśyati sa paṇḍitaḥ

He who looks upon another's wife as his mother, another's property as a lump of clay, and sees the spiritual unity of all creatures is a true paṇḍita.

Commentary: This was perhaps Śrīla Prabhupāda's most-frequently-quoted Cāṇakya *śloka.* As told in *A Transcendental Diary* of Hari Śauri Dāsa (vol. 2), when an Australian State Minister requested Śrīla Prabhupāda's help in educating the young, Śrīla Prabhupāda explained that real learning is condensed in the three principles contained in this verse. One does not become a qualified *paṇḍita* by the mere reading of books alone. It is the ornament of suitable behavior and not mere erudition that distinguishes a true *paṇḍita* from a mere scholar. Cāṇakya Paṇḍita's advice bears great similarity to these words Kṛṣṇa shared with Arjuna:

vidyā-vinaya-sampanne brāhmaṇe gavi hastini
śuni caiva śva-pāke ca paṇḍitāḥ sama-darśinaḥ

> The humble sage, by virtue of true knowledge, sees with equal vision a learned and gentle *brāhmaṇa,* a cow, an elephant, a dog and a dog-eater. (Bg 5.18)

The purport of Cāṇakya Paṇḍita's phrase *ātmavat sarva-bhūteṣu* ("sees the spiritual unity of all") or Lord Kṛṣṇa's explanation *paṇḍitāḥ sama-darśinaḥ* ("equanimity of vision") is this: The learned view all living entities as parts and parcels of the Supreme Personality of Godhead, regardless of the entity's present state of embodiment. Since God is the father of all creatures, therefore all living entities are brothers. The difference of the degree of consciousness from one life form to the next should not preclude our recognition of spiritual oneness in a world of differences.

In his purport to SB 9.10.27, Śrīla Prabhupāda gave this verse as exemplifying the mind of Śrīmatī Mandodarī, the chaste wife of Rāvaṇa:

> Thus Rāvaṇa was condemned not only by Lord Rāmacandra but even by his own wife, Mandodarī. Because she was a chaste woman, she knew the power of another chaste woman, especially such a wife as mother Sītādevī.

By disrespecting the chastity of a woman who he should have honored on an equal platform with his own mother, Rāvaṇa invited his own death. This verse was so important to Śrīla Prabhupāda that it was one of two verses from *Cāṇakya-nīti* he quoted in his letter to India's Prime Minister Nehru, as given in our commentary on CN 8.20.

ŚLOKA 12.15

धर्मे तत्परता मुखे मधुरता दाने समुत्साहता
मित्रेऽवञ्चकता गुरौ विनयता चित्तेऽतिगम्भीरता ।
आचारे शुचिता गुणे रसिकता शास्त्रेषु विज्ञानता
रूपे सुन्दरता शिवे भजनता त्वय्यस्ति भो राघव ॥१५॥

dharme tat-paratā mukhe madhuratā dāne samutsāhatā
mitre 'vañcakatā gurau vinayatā citte 'tigambhīratā
ācāre śucitā guṇe rasikatā śāstreṣu vijñānatā
rūpe sundaratā śive bhajanatā tvayy asti bho rāghava

Rāma, descendant of the Raghu dynasty! The love of dharma, sweet speech, an ardent desire for acts of charity, guileless dealings with friends, humility in the guru's presence, deep tranquility of mind, pure conduct, appreciation for virtues, realized knowledge of the śāstras, beauty of form and devotion to the Absolute Truth are all found in You.

Commentary: We have heard that these words were spoken by the great sage Vasiṣṭha Muni, the spiritual preceptor of the dynasty of the sun-god, to Lord Rāmacandra at the time of His return from *vana-vāsa* and subsequent coronation. The *Rāmāyaṇa* of *Vālmīki* (*Yuddha-kāṇḍa* 128.120) explains:

> Lord Rāma, who is none other than the Personality of Godhead Lord Viṣṇu, remains forever pleased with one who daily listens to or recites the *Rāmāyaṇa.* Śrī Rāma is none other than the Ādi-deva or primordial Lord Nārāyaṇa of powerful arms and remover of the sins of His devotees. He dwells upon the waters of the causal ocean and Lakṣmaṇa is none other than Lord Śeṣa, His couch.

In the *Sundara-kāṇḍa* of *Śrī Vālmīki Rāmāyaṇa,* Hanumān finds Sītādevī held prisoner in the kingdom of Śrī Laṅkā. So that Hanumān can verify his identity as the messenger of Rāma, Sītā requests Hanumān to describe her beloved husband, to which Hanumān replies:

> O Princess of Videha, Rāma has eyes that resemble lotus petals. He has broad shoulders and mighty arms, and His neck is shaped like a conch. His eyes are coppery and His voice is deep like the sound of a kettledrum. He is solid in three places: His breast, wrist and fist. He is elevated in three places: His chest, the rim of His navel and His abdomen. He is reddish in three places: His eyes, His nails and palms and the soles of His feet. He is deep of voice, His navel is

> deep and He walks swiftly. He has three folds of skin on His neck and belly. He is small in four places: neck, genitals, calves and back. He walks with four different gaits, like a lion, like a tiger, like an elephant and like a bull. Ten places on His body are like a lotus: His complexion, mouth, eyes, tongue, lips, palate, breast, nails, hands and feet. He is fine in four places: His bodily hair, skin, finger joints and perception. Indeed, He has all these features and many more. (*Rāmāyaṇa, Sundara-kāṇḍa,* chapter 35)[19]

Lord Rāma appeared in the Tretā-yuga. Next in the Dvāpara-yuga the Supreme Lord appeared in His original form as Kṛṣṇa. In the present age of Kali-yuga, Lord Kṛṣṇa again appeared but this time He accepted the simple dress of a *sannyāsī,* as Śrī Caitanya Mahāprabhu.

The *Bhāgavata Purāṇa* (1.3.26) declares:

> O *brāhmaṇas,* the incarnations of the Lord are innumerable, like rivulets flowing from inexhaustible sources of water.

The Supreme Lord appears personally or sends His expansions to this material world simply to attract us conditioned living entities back to home, back to Godhead. Although Lord Rāmacandra appeared along with His associates millions of years ago, He is worshipped throughout India and the world to this day. This is the all-attractive quality of the Personality of Godhead, and His everlasting influence still delivers the faithful to His abode. In this way that fortunate devotee who dedicates his or her life to the *saṅkīrtana* movement of Śrī Caitanya Mahāprabhu may never take birth here again.

ŚLOKA 12.16

काष्ठं कल्पतरुः सुमेरुरचलश्चिन्तामणिः प्रस्तरः
सूर्यस्तीव्रकरः शशी च विकलः क्षारो हि वारां निधिः ।

19. Quoted from the *Rāmāyaṇa* presented by Bhakti Vikāsa Swami, pages 297–98.

कामो नष्टतनुर्बलिर्दितिसुतो नित्यं पशुः कामगौ-
नैतांस्ते तुलयामि भो रघुपते कस्योपमा दीयते ॥१६॥

kāṣṭhaṁ kalpa-taruḥ sumerur acalaś cintāmaṇiḥ prastaraḥ
sūryas tīvra-karaḥ śaśī ca vikalaḥ kṣāro hi vārāṁ nidhiḥ
kāmo naṣṭa-tanur balir diti-suto nityaṁ paśuḥ kāmagaur
naitāṁs te tulayāmi bho raghu-pate kasyopamā dīyate

The kalpa-vṛkṣa [desire tree] is mere wood. Though made of gold, Mount Meru is motionless. The wish-fulfilling cintāmaṇi gem is but a mere stone. The sun is scorching, the moon is prone to waning and the boundless ocean is saline. The god of material love, Kāmadeva, lost his body [due to Śiva's wrath]. Bali Mahārāja was born into the clan of demons descended from Diti. Kāmadhenu, the wish-fulfilling cow, is a mere animal. O Lord of the Raghus [taking their merits into account], I cannot compare You to any one of these!

Commentary: Here Lord Rāma is addressed with great devotion with the words *bho raghu-pate* meaning "Oh, leader of the Raghu dynasty." Hence, this verse carries the thread of the last one. Although the Supreme Personality of Godhead incarnates in our midst for our deliverance, He remains untouched by any material quality because He is the Lord of the three worlds. Ultimately nothing of this world or the next can be compared to Him who created it. Neither does He covet any possession because He is the possessor of all opulences. When crowned regent of Ayodhyā, Lord Rāma gave the *brāhmaṇas* 300,000,000 gold coins along with innumerable other gifts. Cāṇakya Paṇḍita herewith worships Lord Rāmacandra in a mood of awe and reverence.

ŚLOKA 12.17

विनयं राजपुत्रेभ्यः पण्डितेभ्यः सुभाषितम् ।
अनृतं द्यूतकारेभ्यः स्त्रीभ्यः शिक्षेत कैतवम् ॥१७॥

vinayaṁ rāja-putrebhyaḥ
paṇḍitebhyaḥ subhāṣitam
anṛtaṁ dyūta-kārebhyaḥ
strībhyaḥ śikṣeta kaitavam

Courtesy should be learned from princes, the art of conversation from paṇḍitas, lying should be learned from gamblers and deceit from women.

Commentary: Paṇḍita Nārāyaṇa, echoing the *Pañca-tantra* says in his *Hitopadeśa,* "All the *nīti* of Uśanā (Śukrācārya) and Bṛhaspati exists in the mind of a woman." Indeed, for a man it is impossible to fathom the mind of a woman.

ŚLOKA 12.18

अनालोक्य व्ययं कर्ता अनाथः कलहप्रियः ।
आतुरः सर्वक्षेत्रेषु नरः शीघ्रं विनश्यति ॥१८॥

anālokya vyayaṁ kartā
anāthaḥ kalaha-priyaḥ
āturaḥ sarva-kṣetreṣu
naraḥ śīghraṁ vinaśyati

The spendthrift, the orphan, the quarrelmonger, he who is disturbed in all spheres of his activities—all these are swiftly ruined.

Commentary: Therefore the opposite would be proper *nīti:* be frugal in spending, seek a protector, be tolerant and avoid arguing uselessly, keep a cool outlook and consider one thousand times your every action. For better or worse we create our own destinies. Through the wisdom of *nīti-śāstra* correctly applied our lives will be happier, healthier and longer, and we may look forward to a better destination once this spot life is finished.

ŚLOKA 12.19

नाहारं चिन्तयेत्प्राज्ञो धर्ममेकं हि चिन्तयेत् ।
आहारो हि मनुष्याणां जन्मना सह जायते ॥१९॥

nāhāraṁ cintayet prājño
dharmam ekaṁ hi cintayet
āhāro hi manuṣyāṇāṁ
janmanā saha jāyate

He who is of high intelligence should not be anxious about his meals, but he should be concerned about dharma. Each man's food is determined at birth.

Commentary: Cāṇakya Paṇḍita summarizes the concept of fate in a nutshell. How much of which foods we will eat in this life is decided before we are born. Therefore our greatest concern must be not the maintenance of the temporary body, but the nourishment of the eternal soul on our path to realizing Kṛṣṇa consciousness.

ŚLOKA 12.20

जलबिन्दुनिपातेन क्रमशः पूर्यते घटः ।
स हेतुः सर्वविद्यानां धर्मस्य च धनस्य च ॥२०॥

jala-bindu-nipātena
kramaśaḥ pūryate ghaṭaḥ
sa hetuḥ sarva-vidyānāṁ
dharmasya ca dhanasya ca

As tiny droplets eventually fill a pot, so also are knowledge, virtue and wealth gradually accumulated.

Commentary: Gradually become learned one verse at a time, acquire *puṇya* one good deed at a time and mind your money dollar by dollar. Grow in Kṛṣṇa consciousness by daily chanting sixteen rounds of the *mahā-mantra,* pronouncing and listening to each *mantra* properly, one by one.

ŚLOKA 12.21

वयसः परिणामेऽपि यः खलः खल एव सः ।
सम्पक्वमपि माधुर्यं नोपयातीन्द्रवारुणम् ॥२१॥

vayasaḥ pariṇāme 'pi
yaḥ khalaḥ khala eva saḥ
sampakvam api mādhuryaṁ
nopayātīndra-vāruṇam

A wicked person remains wicked even in his old age just as the indra-vāruṇa fruit does not become sweet no matter how ripe it becomes.

Commentary: No fool will admit his foolishness and neither will a wicked person admit his wickedness. That rascal described here in this verse was too arrogant to follow the instructions of the previous verse. The Buddhists are fond of saying, "What has a front has a back." The tragic flipside of the "American Dream" is the old age home where doddering curmudgeons who have exhausted their lives while looking forward to their "golden years," now wait bleary-eyed in front of TV sets fearfully anticipating the last breath. Truly there is nothing worse than being a foolish rascal except for being an old one. The *indra-vāruṇa* fruit mentioned in this verse is also known in English as the colocynth or the bitter apple.

Thus Ends Chapter Twelve

CHAPTER THIRTEEN

ŚLOKA 13.1

मुहूर्तमपि जीवेच्च नरः शुक्लेन कर्मणा ।
न कल्पमपि कष्टेन लोकद्वयविरोधिना ॥१॥

muhūrtam api jīvec ca
naraḥ śuklena karmaṇā
na kalpam api kaṣṭena
loka-dvaya-virodhinā

A life of only a moment is successful if that moment is spent in auspicious activities. A life the length of a kalpa is useless if it is spent in bringing distress to the two worlds.

Commentary: Only in this human form of life do we have the opportunity to choose between *vikarma,* fruitive activities that are binding and sinful, and *śukla-karma* as recommended here by Cāṇakya Paṇḍita. And the most auspicious *śukla-karma* is selfless devotional service for the pleasure of the Supreme Lord Śrī Kṛṣṇa. Regarding a *kalpa,* the *Bhagavad-gītā* explains that it equals one day of Lord Brahmā or one thousand *yuga* cycles, and consists of Satya, Tretā, Dvāpara and Kali-yugas; or 43,200,000 times 1,000 years. (Bg 8.17) The two worlds mentioned herein—*loka-dvaya*—refer to this life and to the next one. Indeed, he who harms others by transgressing the laws of nature in this birth will be forced to suffer the same miseries he has caused here in the next. For the devotee engaged in Kṛṣṇa consciousness, the next world will be the eternal one. The Lord advises:

> Always think of Me and become My devotee. Worship Me and offer your homage unto Me. Thus you will come to Me without fail. I promise you this because you are My very dear friend. (Bg 18.69)

ŚLOKA 13.2

गते शोको न कर्तव्यो भविष्यं नैव चिन्तयेत् ।
वर्तमानेन कालेन वर्तयन्ति विचक्षणाः ॥२॥

gate śoko na kartavyo
bhaviṣyaṁ naiva cintayet
vartamānena kālena
vartayanti vicakṣaṇāḥ

We should not worry about the past nor should we be anxious about the future; men of discernment deal only with the present moment.

Commentary: The thread of 13.1 continues. Most people are optimistic about the future, although the only real certainty is either a six-foot hole in the ground or the burning *ghāṭas*. Prabhupāda used to call such blind optimism a "dog's attitude." The wit Ambrose Bierce put it this way, "*Future, n.* That period of time in which our affairs prosper, our friends are true and our happiness is assured."

The great-grandfather of the modern Hare Kṛṣṇa movement Śrīla Bhaktivinoda Ṭhākura advised:

Forget the past, it sleeps,
And ne'er the future dream at all.

Just act in times that are with thee,
And progress thee shall call.

ŚLOKA 13.3

स्वभावेन हि तुष्यन्ति देवाः सत्पुरुषाः पिता ।
ज्ञातयः स्नानपानाभ्यां वाक्यदानेन पण्डिताः ॥३॥

svabhāvena hi tuṣyanti
devāḥ sat-puruṣāḥ pitā
jñātayaḥ snāna-pānābhyāṁ
vākya-dānena paṇḍitāḥ

It is certainly the nature of the devatās, men of good character and one's father to be easily pleased. Near and distant relatives are pleased when they are hospitably received with bathing facilities and food and drink. Paṇḍitas are pleased with an opportunity for giving spiritual discourse.

Commentary: Kali-yuga is characterized as a time when even a devotee's own family members have capacity for limitless gossip yet look upon one sentence of spiritual discourse as torture. Therefore, when a devotee finds the opportunity to preach the glories of Kṛṣṇa consciousness, he should seize the opportunity by understanding it to be the Lord's causeless mercy.

ŚLOKA 13.4

अहो बत विचित्राणि चरितानि महात्मनाम् ।
लक्ष्मीं तृणाय मन्यन्ते तद्भारेण नमन्ति च ॥४॥

aho bata vicitrāṇi
caritāni mahātmanām

lakṣmīṁ tṛṇāya manyante
tad-bhāreṇa namanti ca

Oh, how wonderful is the character of the great souls. They consider the blessing of the goddess of fortune a mere straw and yet obtaining it they humbly bend down under its weight.

Commentary: The translation given above is the version of Kiśora Dāsa who comments that the acquisition of wealth does not make the *mahātmā* puffed up but he becomes all the more humble. And, although the *mahātmā* is not interested in wealth, he obtains it in abundance.

The translation of Śrī V. Badarayana Murthy given next carries quite another perspective:

> O how surprising: the activities of the great are strange! They treat the blessings of the goddess of fortune as light as a straw, yet obtaining it they bend under its weight.

Since we come to this life naked and take nothing with us when we leave, those who fail to understand that wealth is meant for the service of the Supreme Lord will be crushed by it. And those who use the blessings of Lakṣmī in the service of her husband Lord Nārāyaṇa are glorified.

ŚLOKA 13.5

यस्य स्नेहो भयं तस्य स्नेहो दुःखस्य भाजनम् ।
स्नेहमूलानि दुःखानि तानि त्यक्त्वा वसेत्सुखम् ॥५॥

yasya sneho bhayaṁ tasya
sneho duḥkhasya bhājanam
sneha-mūlāni duḥkhāni
tāni tyaktvā vaset sukham

He who is overly attached experiences fear and sorrow, for the root of all grief is attachment. Thus one should discard attachment and be happy.

Commentary: Cāṇakya Paṇḍita advises in line four, "Live happily through renunciation." Since everything is the energy of God, using that which He has lent us for His service is practical renunciation. Real renunciation means to understand that everything is Kṛṣṇa's energy and all that we have in our possession must be used for His service. Only the devotee who has eschewed all sense of false proprietorship over this material world by offering everything to Kṛṣṇa can hope to be promoted to the spiritual kingdom. As sung by Śrīla Bhaktivinoda Ṭhākura:

mānasa, deha, geha, yo kichu mora
arpiluṅ tuyā pade, nanda-kiśora

> Mind, body and family; whatever may be mine, I have surrendered at Your lotus feet, O youthful son of Nanda Mahārāja. (*Śaraṇāgati,* song 11)

Excessive attachment to family members is decried throughout the Vedic literatures as the inevitable pathway to further pain and delusion. As the *Bhāgavata* states:

> By such ignorance the living entity accepts the material body, which is made of five elements, as his actual identity. With this misunderstanding, he accepts nonpermanent things as his own and increases his ignorance in the darkest region. For the sake of the body, which is a source of constant trouble to him and which follows him because he is bound by ties of ignorance and fruitive activities, he performs various actions which cause him to be subjected to repeated birth and death. (SB 3.31.30–31)

ŚLOKA 13.6

अनागतविधाता च प्रत्युत्पन्नमतिस्तथा ।
द्वावेतौ सुखमेधेते यद्भविष्यो विनश्यति ॥६॥

anāgata-vidhātā ca
pratyutpanna-matis tathā
dvāv etau sukham edhete
yad-bhaviṣyo vinaśyati

He who is prepared for the future and he who deals cleverly with any situation that may arise are both happy. But the fatalist who totally depends upon luck is ruined.

Commentary: Once in India when examining the horoscope of a young marriageable lady, an astrologer noted that the stars revealed that it was time for her marriage. Her father challenged, "Then why is she not married?" The *paṇḍita* replied, "What time do you arise in the morning?" The son responded on behalf of his dad, "Ten o'clock, and he naps in the afternoon, too!" So the *paṇḍita* asked, "Without endeavor, how can you expect to obtain the results of good stars? A cow does not milk itself." That father who waits for Lord Indra to appear at his door bearing a new son-in-law will have a spinster for a daughter.

ŚLOKA 13.7

राज्ञि धर्मिणि धर्मिष्ठाः पापे पापाः समे समाः ।
राजानमनुवर्तन्ते यथा राजा तथा प्रजाः ॥७॥

rājñi dharmiṇi dharmiṣṭhāḥ
pāpe pāpāḥ same samāḥ
rājānam anuvartante
yathā rājā tathā prajāḥ

If the king is virtuous, the subjects are virtuous. If the king is sinful, the subjects become sinful. If he is mediocre, the subjects are mediocre. The subjects follow the king; as is the king, so are the citizens.

Commentary: In the *Bhagavad-gītā* Kṛṣṇa encouraged Arjuna to perform his duty and fight:

> Whatever action a great man performs, common men follow. And whatever standards he sets by exemplary acts, all the world pursues. (Bg 3.21)

Example is louder than precept. When the leader is a libertine and a philanderer, as commonly seen in today's society, then sinful activities spread across the land like cancer. Therefore, it is the example of the leader that determines the overall piety or impiety of the state. To follow the leader is human nature. Cāṇakya Paṇḍita raised Candragupta to the throne of Magadha since his incorruptible character would serve as an ideal example for the citizens at large. The great problem with the modern invention of democracy, as Prabhupāda used to say, is that "little dogs elect big dogs." Today there is no proper example of leadership, except how to become better two-legged dogs in a dog-eat-dog world.

ŚLOKA 13.8

जीवन्तं मृतवन्मन्ये देहिनं धर्मवर्जितम् ।
मृतो धर्मेण संयुक्तो दीर्घजीवी न संशयः ॥८॥

jīvantaṁ mṛtavan manye
dehinaṁ dharma-varjitam
mṛto dharmeṇa saṁyukto
dīrgha-jīvī na saṁśayaḥ

I consider him who does not act religiously as dead though living, but he who dies upholding dharma unquestionably lives long though dead.

Commentary: A favorite story of Śrīla Prabhupāda goes like this:

> Once a group of innocent villagers crowded around a wandering *sādhu* to seek his blessings. Among them was a prince, a *brahmacārī,* a Kṛṣṇa-*bhakta* and a butcher. The *sādhu* blessed the prince, "Live

long!" Looking to the *brahmacārī,* he said, "Die today." To the Kṛṣṇa-*bhakta* he said, "Live long or die now." To the butcher he said, "Don't live and don't die."

The villagers looked at the holy man in amazement. "What sort of *sādhu* could this be?" All previous *sādhus* had simply exclaimed, "May you enjoy a long life"—and then collected their alms and left. The *sādhu* explained, "I have blessed the prince with a long life because his only interest is enjoying the wealth of his father, and when he leaves this world he will be dispatched to the hellish regions. So it is best he lives and enjoys as much as possible here and now. As far as the *brahmacārī* is concerned, he is now performing penance and thinking of the Supreme Lord, but once he marries, who can say what will happen? Therefore if he dies now, he will obtain the ultimate destination. As far as this saintly Kṛṣṇa-*bhakta* is concerned, he is an unalloyed devotee of the Supreme Lord who has surrendered every thought, word and deed to Him. Since he has achieved the goal of life, it makes no difference whether he lives or dies. And lastly, although the butcher lives a life worse than death, his death will be even worse than a life worse than death. So he should neither live nor die." After that the villagers all returned home a bit wiser.

Those who live for the sake of sense enjoyment are simply decorating a dead body. Śrīla Prabhupāda writes:

Cāṇakya Paṇḍita says, *śarīraṁ kṣaṇa-vidhvāṁsi kalpānta-sthāyino guṇāḥ:* "The duration of one's life in the material world may end at any moment, but if within this life one does something worthy, that qualification is depicted in history eternally." (…) In the human form of life one should perform activities in such a way that at the end he goes back home, back to Godhead. This is self-realization. (SB 9.13.3, purport)

ŚLOKA 13.9

धर्मार्थकाममोक्षाणां यस्यैकोऽपि न विद्यते ।
अजागलस्तनस्येव तस्य जन्म निरर्थकम् ॥९॥

dharmārtha-kāma-mokṣāṇāṁ
yasyaiko 'pi na vidyate
ajā-gala-stanasyeva
tasya janma nirarthakam

He who has acquired in this life neither virtue, wealth, satisfaction of desires nor salvation lives a useless life like the "nipples" hanging from a goat's neck.

Commentary: In the first line Cāṇakya Paṇḍita identifies the four principles of material life: *dharma, artha, kāma* and *mokṣa.* Though cherished by common men, these four goals—namely religion, wealth, sense enjoyment and impersonal liberation—are not at all attractive to a devotee of the Lord. For the Vaiṣṇava, *dharma* means *sanātana-dharma. Mokṣa* is defined as coming to one's eternal loving relationship or *rasa* with God and not the futile attempt of trying to become "one" with God. The example of nipples on the neck of a goat is a famous one used in many *śāstras,* including *Śrī Caitanya-caritāmṛta* (2.24.93):

> With the exception of devotional service, all the methods of self-realization are like nipples on the neck of a goat. An intelligent person adopts only devotional service, giving up all other processes of self-realization.

ŚLOKA 13.10

दह्यमानाः सुतीव्रेण नीचाः परयशोऽग्निना ।
अशक्तास्तत्पदं गन्तुं ततो निन्दां प्रकुर्वते ॥१०॥

dahyamānāḥ sutīvreṇa
nīcāḥ para-yaśo 'gninā
aśaktās tat-padaṁ gantuṁ
tato nindāṁ prakurvate

The hearts of base men burn in the fire of others' fame, and thus they slander them, being unable to rise to such heights.

Commentary: The great must tolerate the envy of lesser minds. *The Devil's Dictionary* offers a back-handed agreement: "*Calamity, n.* Calamities are of two kinds: misfortune to ourselves and good fortune to others."

ŚLOKA 13.11

बन्धाय विषयासङ्गं मुक्त्यै निर्विषयं मनः ।
मन एव मनुष्याणां कारणं बन्धमोक्षयोः ॥११॥

bandhāya viṣayāsaṅgaṁ
muktyai nirviṣayaṁ manaḥ
mana eva manuṣyāṇāṁ
kāraṇaṁ bandha-mokṣayoḥ

The mind attached to sense gratification leads to bondage and the mind detached from sense gratification leads to liberation. Therefore it is the mind alone that is responsible for bondage or liberation.

Commentary: Kṛṣṇa advises Arjuna:

> A man must elevate himself by his own mind, not degrade himself. The mind is the friend of the conditioned soul, and his enemy as well. (Bg 6.5)

Life's pleasures and pains, which ebb and flow like the tides of the ocean, should be accepted by the devotee in a spirit of detachment. Because each one must alternatively suffer or enjoy according to his karmic destiny, becoming attached to this temporary life is a serious blunder. The sacred *Bhāgavata* therefore inquires:

> What mortal man, having achieved this human form of life, which is the very gateway to both heaven and liberation, would willingly

> become attached to that abode of worthless material property? (SB 11.23.23)

Attachment and detachment are actions of the mind. In the *Gītā,* Arjuna declares:

> For the mind is restless, turbulent, obstinate and very strong, O Kṛṣṇa, and to subdue it seems more difficult than controlling the wind. (Bg 6.34)

To which Kṛṣṇa responds:

> O mighty-armed, it is undoubtedly very difficult to curb the restless mind. But, O son of Queen Kuntī, it is possible by constant practice and detachment. (Bg 6.35)

Only when the mind finds repose in the service of the Supreme Personality of Godhead and the senses are engaged in His service is the door to liberation thrown wide open, as Cāṇakya Paṇḍita shows in the next verse.

ŚLOKA 13.12

देहाभिमाने गलिते ज्ञानेन परमात्मनि ।
यत्र यत्र मनो याति तत्र तत्र समाधयः ॥१२॥

dehābhimāne galite
jñānena paramātmani
yatra yatra mano yāti
tatra tatra samādhayaḥ

He who sheds bodily identification by means of knowledge of the Paramātmā will always be absorbed in meditative trance wherever his mind leads him.

Commentary: The Supreme Lord Kṛṣṇa in His feature as the indwelling Lord of the heart is called Paramātmā, which literally translates as the "Supreme Soul." Cāṇakya Paṇḍita's instruction is that *jñāna* (knowledge) of Paramātmā leads the devotee to fixed-mind consciousness or *samādhi,* the transcendental awakening of Kṛṣṇa consciousness. Kṛṣṇa tells Arjuna:

> A true *yogī* observes Me in all beings, and also sees every being in Me. Indeed, the self-realized see Me everywhere. (Bg 6.29)

ŚLOKA 13.13

ईप्सितं मनसः सर्वं कस्य संपद्यते सुखम् ।
दैवायत्तं यतः सर्वं तस्मात्सन्तोषमाश्रयेत् ॥१३॥

īpsitaṁ manasaḥ sarvaṁ
kasya saṁpadyate sukham
daivāyattaṁ yataḥ sarvaṁ
tasmāt santoṣam āśrayet

Who achieves all the pleasures that the mind desires? Everything is in the hands of Providence. Therefore, one should learn contentment.

Commentary: Cāṇakya Paṇḍita advises us to be satisfied in the knowledge that everything is under the control of the Supreme Lord. Real happiness is found as per Kṛṣṇa's statement:

> The *yogī* whose mind is fixed upon Me verily attains the highest happiness. By virtue of his identity with Brahman, he is liberated; his mind is peaceful, his passions are quieted, and he is freed from sin. (Bg 6.27)

ŚLOKA 13.14

यथा धेनुसहस्रेषु वत्सो गच्छति मातरम् ।
तथा यच्च कृतं कर्म कर्तारमनुगच्छति ॥१४॥

yathā dhenu-sahasreṣu
vatso gacchati mātaram
tathā yac ca kṛtaṁ karma
kartāram anugacchati

As a calf finds its mother among a thousand cows, so the [good or bad] deeds of a man follow him.

Commentary: Truly the effects of *karma* are inescapable. But they are certainly lightened and the reactions softened as the devotee increases his surrender at the lotus feet of the Lord. Full surrender to Śrī Kṛṣṇa alone utterly wipes out all karmic reactions, as the devotee qualifies himself for final liberation at last.

ŚLOKA 13.15

अनवस्थितकार्यस्य न जने न वने सुखम् ।
जने दहति संसर्गाद्वने सङ्गविवर्जनात् ॥१५॥

anavasthita-kāryasya
na jane na vane sukham
jane dahati saṁsargād
vane saṅga-vivarjanāt

He whose actions are disorganized has no happiness either in the midst of men or in a jungle. In the midst of men his heart burns by social contact, and his rejection of social contact burns him in the forest.

Commentary: Whether one's goals are material or spiritual, there must be some systematic plan for success.

ŚLOKA 13.16

खनित्वा हि खनित्रेण भूतले वारि विन्दति ।
तथा गुरुगतां विद्यां शुश्रूषुरधिगच्छति ॥१६॥

khanitvā hi khanitreṇa
bhū-tale vāri vindati
tathā guru-gatāṁ vidyāṁ
śuśrūṣur adhigacchati

As he who digs with a shovel obtains underground water, so the student through his service acquires the realized knowledge of his guru.

Commentary: As advised in all Vedic *śāstras,* it is incumbent upon any civilized person to voluntarily submit to initiation from a bona fide *guru,* the representative of the Supreme Absolute Truth, and render him unflinching service. Prabhupāda often said, "Without taking shelter of a qualified spiritual master, one cannot lay claim to being a gentleman." This process of spiritual initiation is clearly recommended in the *Bhagavad-gītā As It Is:*

tad viddhi praṇipātena paripraśnena sevayā
upadekṣyanti te jñānaṁ jñāninas tattva-darśinaḥ

Just try to learn the truth by approaching a spiritual master. Inquire from him submissively and render service unto him. The self-realized soul can impart knowledge unto you because he has seen the truth. (Bg 4.34)

Śrīmad-Bhāgavatam (6.3.19) emphasizes:

dharmaṁ tu sākṣād bhagavat-praṇītam

The path of religion is directly enacted by God.

The Supreme Lord Kṛṣṇa is the original spiritual master; therefore a genuine *guru* will have been initiated into one of the genuine *sampradāyas* or chains of disciplic succession descending directly from the Personality of Godhead. There are four bona fide *sampradāyas:* (1) Brahmā (Madhva), (2) Śrī (Rāmānuja), (3) Rudra (Viṣṇusvāmī) and (4) Kumāra (Nimbārka). It is not possible to manufacture some new-fangled process and label oneself a *guru* by behaving like a mad monk or *pāgala pūjārī.* A genuine *guru* has the capacity to deliver the sincere candidate back to home, back to Godhead. As implied by this important instruction, which Cāṇakya Paṇḍita has repeated from the *Manu-saṁhitā* (2.218), the genuine disciple must serve his spiritual master with every thought, word and deed. Through unflinching service to the spiritual master, the disciple gradually perfects his qualities, knowledge, renunciation and devotion. For the surrendered disciple, the *guru* is served on a platform equal to God Almighty.

ŚLOKA 13.17

कर्मायत्तं फलं पुंसां बुद्धिः कर्मानुसारिणी ।
तथापि सुधियश्चार्याः सुविचार्यैव कुर्वते ॥१७॥

karmāyattaṁ phalaṁ puṁsāṁ
buddhiḥ karmānusāriṇī
tathāpi sudhiyaś cāryāḥ
suvicāryaiva kurvate

Men reap the fruits of their deeds and their intellects bear the marks of deeds performed in previous lives. Even so, the wise act after due circumspection.

Commentary: It is the advice of *nīti-śāstra* to consider one thousand times what is to be done, and act after judging all sides. But, above all, be prepared to take responsibility for your decisions never relying on the whims of fate.

ŚLOKA 13.18

एकाक्षरप्रदातारं यो गुरुं नाभिवन्दते ।
श्वानयोनिशतं गत्वा चाण्डालेष्वभिजायते ॥१८॥

ekākṣara-pradātāraṁ
yo guruṁ nābhivandate
śvāna-yoni-śataṁ gatvā
cāṇḍāleṣv abhijāyate

Even that man who has taught the significance of just one syllable ought to be worshipped. He who does not revere such a guru is born as a dog one hundred times, and at last takes birth as a dog-eater.

Commentary: There is an old saying in India:

> For he who is ungrateful, what use has he for other sins?

Of ingratitude the *Manu-saṁhitā* says:

> The *guru-drohī,* or he who is ungrateful to his *guru,* will be born in the species of one of the larger insects. (MS 2.201)

ŚLOKA 13.19

युगान्ते प्रचलेन्मेरुः कल्पान्ते सप्त सागराः ।
साधवः प्रतिपन्नार्थान्न चलन्ति कदाचन ॥१९॥

yugānte pracalen meruḥ
kalpānte sapta sāgarāḥ
sādhavaḥ pratipannārthān
na calanti kadācana

At the end of the yuga, Mount Meru may shake; at the end of the kalpa, the waters of the seven oceans may be disturbed; but a sādhu will never swerve from the spiritual path.

Commentary: As discussed earlier, there are four *yugas* (great ages): Kali (iron), Dvāpara (copper), Tretā (silver) and Satya (gold). The length of Kali-yuga is 432,000 years; Dvāpara-yuga is twice as long, Tretā thrice and Satya-yuga four times as long. The time measurement of a *kalpa* is discussed in 13.1.

As far as the steady *sādhu* is concerned, Kṛṣṇa explains to Arjuna:

> What is night for all beings is the time of awakening for the self-controlled; and the time of awakening for all beings is night for the introspective sage. (Bg 2.69)

The entire world may fall victim to its own passions and attachments, but the devotee remains fixed in spiritual trance. By meditating upon the lotus feet of the Lord, the pure devotee remains unshaken because he is immersed in transcendental consciousness.

ŚLOKA 13.20

पृथिव्यां त्रीणि रत्नानि जलमन्नं सुभाषितम् ।
मूढैः पाषाणखण्डेषु रत्नसंज्ञा विधीयते ॥२०॥

pṛthivyāṁ trīṇi ratnāni
jalam annaṁ subhāṣitam
mūḍhaiḥ pāṣāṇa-khaṇḍeṣu
ratna-saṁjñā vidhīyate

There are three gems upon this earth: water, food and pleasing words. Fools consider pieces of rock as gems.

Commentary: Food and water in the form of *prasāda* are the most pleasing of all. The most pleasing words are those that glorify the Supreme Personality of Godhead. These include not only Kṛṣṇa-*kathā* but devotional *bhajanas* that glorify the holy names, features, pastimes, opulence and associates of the Supreme Personality of Godhead. The sixteen words of the *mahā-mantra* have liberated countless souls, while the dead weight of ornamentation, even up to the stolen Koh-i-Noor diamond, cannot liberate even the one who wears it.

Thus Ends Chapter Thirteen

CHAPTER FOURTEEN

ŚLOKA 14.1

आत्मापराधवृक्षस्य फलान्येतानि देहिनाम् ।
दारिद्र्यरोगदुःखानि बन्धनव्यसनानि च ॥१॥

ātmāparādha-vṛkṣasya
phalāny etāni dehinām
dāridrya-roga-duḥkhāni
bandhana-vyasanāni ca

Poverty, disease, sorrow, imprisonment and other calamities are the fruits borne by the tree of one's own sins.

Commentary: Who knows what evil lurks in the hearts of men? The god of death Yamarāja does! Suffering caused by sinful seeds planted long ago manifests in this life as the ripened fruits of our past impropriety.

Lord Yamarāja tells his *dūtas:*

> "My dear servants, please bring to me only those sinful persons who do not use their tongues to chant the holy names and qualities of Kṛṣṇa, whose hearts do not remember the lotus feet of Kṛṣṇa even once, and whose heads do not bow down even once before Lord Kṛṣṇa. Send me those who do not perform their duties toward

Viṣṇu, which are the only duties in human life. Please bring me all such fools and rascals." (SB 6.3.29)

ŚLOKA 14.2

पुनर्वित्तं पुनर्मित्रं पुनर्भार्या पुनर्मही ।
एतत्सर्वं पुनर्लभ्यं न शरीरं पुनः पुनः ॥२॥

punar vittaṁ punar mitraṁ
punar bhāryā punar mahī
etat sarvaṁ punar labhyaṁ
na śarīraṁ punaḥ punaḥ

Wealth, friends, wife and land, if lost, may all be regained. But once this body is lost, it can never be regained.

Commentary: Which is more valuable, the assets that belong to the body, or the body itself? Wisdom begins from the point of understanding that we are not this body. Yet the prudent sage maintains his body as a rare and precious gift of God because it is a temple of not only the individual *jīva* particle, but also of Paramātmā, Lord Viṣṇu, who resides within the body as the Supersoul. The human form of body is the rarest gift out of millions of species of life. The embodied living entity has the choice of elevating himself to transcendence and liberation or he may throw this opportunity away through sense gratification. If wasted through neglecting this rare opportunity to become Kṛṣṇa conscious, the precious boon of this human birth may not come again for millions of years of *saṁsāra.*

ŚLOKA 14.3

बहूनां चैव सत्त्वानां समवायो रिपुञ्जयः ।
वर्षधाराधरो मेघस्तृणैरपि निवार्यते ॥३॥

bahūnāṁ caiva sattvānāṁ
samavāyo ripuñjayaḥ
varṣa-dhārādharo meghas
tṛṇair api nivāryate

The enemy can be overcome by the union of large numbers, just as clumps of grass together prevent erosion in the season of the rains.

Commentary: Śrīla Prabhupāda gave the following example to illustrate how success in Kṛṣṇa consciousness can be achieved. Though grass is fragile, many strands woven together become a rope that can subdue an elephant. His Divine Grace admonished, "Demonstrate your love for me by working together." Humble blades of grass woven together have many practical uses. For millennia, grass roofs in tropical India have been an effective means of keeping the house dry during the wet monsoon season. Grass growing on a slope prevents soil erosion in wet weather.

Regarding *varṣā* (the monsoon rains) as mentioned in this verse, by Vedic calculation in the course of a year there are six two-month seasons, the *ṣaḍ-ṛtus*. These are *vasanta* (spring), *grīṣma* (summer), *varṣā* (rains), *śarat* (autumn), *hemanta* (winter) and *śiśira* (deep winter).

ŚLOKA 14.4

जले तैलं खले गुह्यं पात्रे दानं मनागपि ।
प्राज्ञे शास्त्रं स्वयं याति विस्तारं वस्तुशक्तितः ॥४॥

jale tailaṁ khale guhyaṁ
pātre dānaṁ manāg api
prājñe śāstraṁ svayaṁ yāti
vistāraṁ vastu-śaktitaḥ

Oil on water, a secret told to a base man, a gift to the deserving and scriptural instructions given to an intelligent man all have the tendency to spread according to their nature.

Commentary: Cast your seeds in season, but not your pearls before swine! Regarding the broad dissemination of scriptural instructions, just see the example of Śrīla Prabhupāda: A solitary saint arrived in America from India with only a few volumes of *Śrīmad-Bhāgavatam.* He then proceeded to reestablish a true conception of religion worldwide at a time when the very concept of *dharma* had been lost.

ŚLOKA 14.5

धर्माख्याने श्मशाने च रोगिणां या मतिर्भवेत् ।
सा सर्वदैव तिष्ठेच्चेत्को न मुच्येत बन्धनात् ॥५॥

dharmākhyāne śmaśāne ca
rogiṇāṁ yā matir bhavet
sā sarvadaiva tiṣṭhec cet
ko na mucyeta bandhanāt

By always retaining the state of mind experienced when hearing religious instruction, when at the burning ghāṭa, and in sickness, who would not achieve liberation?

Commentary: Buddhist monks are sometimes sent to penance at burning *ghāṭas* or the *śmaśāna,* as mentioned in this verse, just to keep such thoughts in mind. For the transcendentally aware Vaiṣṇava immersed in sublime Kṛṣṇa-*kathā,* realization of the fragility of life comes naturally.

ŚLOKA 14.6

उत्पन्नपश्चात्तापस्य बुद्धिर्भवति यादृशी ।
तादृशी यदि पूर्वं स्यात्कस्य न स्यान्महोदयः ॥६॥

utpanna-paścāt-tāpasya
buddhir bhavati yādṛśī
tādṛśī yadi pūrvaṁ syāt
kasya na syān mahodayaḥ

If one's intelligence were just as bright before sinning as it is during repentance, who then would not achieve perfection?

Commentary: In this verse, Cāṇakya Paṇḍita praises *tapasya,* voluntary acceptance of sense restraint for achieving a higher goal of life. All penance, learning, practice of *yoga* and austerities, fruitive and religious activities are ultimately meant for the satisfaction and attainment of Śrī Kṛṣṇa. This is clearly spelled out by Śrīla Sūta Gosvāmī:

vāsudeva-parā vedā vāsudeva-parā makhāḥ
vāsudeva-parā yoga vāsudeva-parāḥ kriyāḥ

vāsudeva-paraṁ jñānaṁ vāsudeva-paraṁ tapaḥ
vāsudeva-paro dharmo vāsudeva-parā gatiḥ

> In the revealed scriptures, the ultimate object of knowledge is Śrī Kṛṣṇa, the son of Vasudeva and Supreme Personality of Godhead. The purpose of performing sacrifice is to please Him. *Yoga* is for realizing Him. All fruitive activities are ultimately rewarded by Him only. He is supreme knowledge, and all severe austerities (*tapasya*) are performed to know Him. Religion (*dharma*) is rendering loving service unto Him. He is the supreme goal of life. (SB 1.2.28–29)

Like Hiraṇyakaśipu and Rāvaṇa, today's demonic politicians may also undergo *tapasya* for some material gain, but this is not genuine austerity. Only that penance which is undertaken for the pleasure of the Supreme Lord can have lasting results.

ŚLOKA 14.7

दाने तपसि शौर्ये वा विज्ञाने विनये नये ।
विस्मयो न हि कर्तव्यो बहुरत्ना वसुन्धरा ॥७॥

dāne tapasi śaurye vā
vijñāne vinaye naye
vismayo na hi kartavyo
bahu-ratnā vasundharā

We should not feel pride in our charity, austerity, valor, scriptural knowledge, modesty or morality for gems are found all over the earth.

Commentary: What is the need for pride when there will always be someone better at whatever we can do? No better example of this verse can be seen than Śrīla Prabhupāda who, finding no jewels in his homeland, set out with the shovel of his faith and determination to mine the jewels of Western shores. There he turned coal into diamonds and polished them into gemstones. Regarding the preservation of moral and spiritual assets as mentioned in this verse, the devotee ceaselessly cultivates humility, knowing well that all can be lost in a moment of unthinking pride.

ŚLOKA 14.8

दूरस्थोऽपि न दूरस्थो यो यस्य मनसि स्थितः ।
यो यस्य हृदये नास्ति समीपस्थोऽपि दूरतः ॥८॥

dūra-stho 'pi na dūra-stho
yo yasya manasi sthitaḥ
yo yasya hṛdaye nāsti
samīpa-stho 'pi dūrataḥ

He who lives in our mind is near though he may actually be far away, but he who is not in our heart is far though he may really be nearby.

Commentary: As Śrīla Prabhupāda wrote in dedicating his monumental *Śrīmad-Bhāgavatam:*

To Śrīla Prabhupāda Bhaktisiddhānta Sarasvatī Gosvāmī Mahārāja, my spiritual master, on the 26th annual ceremony of his disappearance day. He lives forever by his divine instructions, and the follower lives with him.

Just as no two snow flakes are alike, so each person is unique. It is this singular difference in individuality that is the springboard for relationships and interactions among different people. Individuality does not cease with the demise of the body. Indeed, the uniqueness of each material body is due to its having reflected its material identity and characteristics from the individual soul housed within. Every identity, whether judged materially or spiritually, is distinct because each one has emanated from the supreme individual, Lord Kṛṣṇa. Therefore each individual devotee's relationship with Kṛṣṇa is unique. Kṛṣṇa may be billions of light years away from the nondevotee, but for those fortunate souls who develop their relationships of loving reciprocal service with the Lord, He lives within their hearts and minds forever. Although Kṛṣṇa is far, far removed from the nonbeliever, for the devotee there is no one nearer.

ŚLOKA 14.9

यस्माच्च प्रियमिच्छेत्तु तस्य ब्रूयात्सदा प्रियम् ।
व्याधो मृगवधं कर्तुं गीतं गायति सुस्वरम् ॥९॥

yasmāc ca priyam icchet tu
tasya brūyāt sadā priyam
vyādho mṛga-vadhaṁ kartuṁ
gītaṁ gāyati susvaram

Speak that which will please him from whom you expect a favor, just as the hunter sings sweetly to shoot the deer.

Commentary: Although truth can be as sharp as an arrow, one who is expert in *nīti-śāstra* will present it palatably. Tactfulness is a basis for communicating and does not necessarily constitute dishonesty. Śrīla Prabhupāda cautioned that "politics means polite" just as "courteous" implies "manners of the court."

ŚLOKA 14.10

अत्यासन्ना विनाशाय दूरस्था न फलप्रदा ।
सेव्यतां मध्यभागेन राजवह्निगुरुस्त्रियः ॥१०॥

atyāsannā vināśāya
dūra-sthā na phala-pradā
sevyatāṁ madhya-bhāgena
rāja-vahni-guru-striyaḥ

It is ruinous to be excessively familiar with the king, fire, the religious preceptor and a woman. To stay too far in the background is to be deprived of the opportunity to benefit ourselves. Hence our association with them must be from a proper distance.

Commentary: Many an aspirant has wrecked his opportunity for salvation by considering himself to be equal or superior to the spiritual master. There was a would-be member who was not satisfied with the International Society for Krishna Consciousness; "international" did not go far enough for him. Hence he founded the Intergalactic Love-Trance Society, to carry the message even further, presumably into outer space. Rather than finding himself on the heavenly planets, this intergalactic love swami ended up with a seven year jail sentence for offering an excessive degree of his "love" to underage female disciples. Hence the sincere disciple must never consider himself equal to the spiritual master. He must never attempt to "improve," change, alter or criticize the teachings of the *ācārya* if he is serious about spiritual advancement.

ŚLOKA 14.11

अग्निरापः स्त्रियो मूर्खाः सर्पा राजकुलानि च ।
नित्यं यत्नेन सेव्यानि सद्यः प्राणहराणि षट् ॥११॥

agnir āpaḥ striyo mūrkhāḥ
sarpā rāja-kulāni ca
nityaṁ yatnena sevyāni
sadyaḥ prāṇa-harāṇi ṣaṭ

Always be cautious with fire, water, women, fools, serpents and members of the royal family. Any of these six may cause death.

Commentary: *Nīti-śāstra* advises wise circumspection at every step. Sudden desires and sensual urges can be so overwhelming that the *Manu-saṁhitā* advises:

> Do not be alone with even your mother, sister, or daughter. The senses can pull even a controlled man astray. (MS 2.215)

In the *Bhagavad-gītā As It Is* (6.34, purport) Śrīla Prabhupāda offers this analogy:

> The individual is the passenger in the cart of the material body, and intelligence is the driver. Mind is the driving instrument and the senses are the horses (touch, smell, hearing, sight and taste). The self is thus the enjoyer or sufferer in the association of the mind and the senses.

Genuine happiness is enjoyed only by the person of controlled senses, while the man of uncontrolled senses is the cause of his own ruin.

ŚLOKA 14.12

स जीवति गुणा यस्य यस्य धर्मः स जीवति ।
गुणधर्मविहीनस्य जीवितं निष्प्रयोजनम् ॥१२॥

sa jīvati guṇā yasya
yasya dharmaḥ sa jīvati
guṇa-dharma-vihīnasya
jīvitaṁ niṣprayojanam

Only he who is virtuous and pious shall be considered as living. He in whom there are neither good qualities nor dharma lives in vain.

Commentary: The *viṣayī* (sense gratifier) is like a corpse haunted by the ghosts of desire and wandering the graveyards of this world seeking temporary pleasures of the dead body.

Śrīla Prabhupāda wrote to a disciple in a letter dated 17 October 1967:

> As a man haunted by a ghost speaks so much nonsense, so also when a man is overpowered by the illusory energy—maya—he also speaks all sorts of nonsense. The last attack of maya upon the conditioned souls is impersonalism. There are four stages of the attack of maya:
>
> (1) a man wants to be a protagonist of religion,
>
> (2) the man neglects religiosity and tries to improve his economic development,
>
> (3) he tries to become a protagonist of sense enjoyment; and when a man is frustrated in the three above mentioned stages he comes to impersonalism,
>
> (4) the final stage is impersonalism wherein one thinks himself one with the Supreme. This last attack is very serious and fatal.

ŚLOKA 14.13

यदीच्छसि वशीकर्तुं जगदेकेन कर्मणा ।
पुरा पञ्चदशास्येभ्यो गां चरन्तीं निवारय ॥१३॥

yadīcchasi vaśī-kartuṁ
jagad ekena karmaṇā

purā pañcadaśāsyebhyo
gāṁ carantīṁ nivāraya

If you wish to gain control of the world by a single deed, then keep the roaming cow of fifteen faces under your control: the five sense objects, the five sense organs and the organs of activity.

Commentary: The five sense objects are: objects of sight, sound, smell, taste and touch. The five sense organs are eyes, ears, nose, tongue, and skin. The five organs of activity are hands, legs, mouth, genitals, and anus. The single act of controlling these fifteen and thereby "conquering the world" is to control the mind—and the means to do that is daily chanting of the *mahā-mantra.*

ŚLOKA 14.14

प्रस्तावसदृशं वाक्यं प्रभावसदृशं प्रियम् ।
आत्मशक्तिसमं कोपं यो जानाति स पण्डितः ॥१४॥

prastāva-sadṛśaṁ vākyaṁ
prabhāva-sadṛśaṁ priyam
ātma-śakti-samaṁ kopaṁ
yo jānāti sa paṇḍitaḥ

He is a paṇḍita who speaks that which is suitable to the occasion; who renders loving service according to his ability; and who exhibits his anger no more than his ability to influence.

Commentary: That *brāhmaṇa* who is learned in all *śāstras* yet does not know *nīti-śāstra* cannot be called a *paṇḍita.* The great Cāṇakya herewith reveals what it means to be a *paṇḍita,* as he also does in 12.14. As we can see at any college or university there is no dearth of learned fools. Without common sense all education is wasted. A true *paṇḍita* knows not only the *śāstras,* but how and when to practically apply his learning as well as his own strength in applying them. Anger should be applied only according to one's ability to influence. Anger can burn in both directions and how it is used depends upon a wise man's ability to handle the consequences.

ŚLOKA 14.15

एक एव पदार्थस्तु त्रिधा भवति वीक्षितः ।
कुणपं कामिनी मांसं योगिभिः कामिभिः श्वभिः ॥१५॥

eka eva padārthas tu
tridhā bhavati vīkṣitaḥ
kuṇapaṁ kāminī māṁsaṁ
yogibhiḥ kāmibhiḥ śvabhiḥ

A single object [a woman's body] appears in three different ways. To the yogī it is a corpse, to the lusty man it is a source of pleasure, to the dog it is a slab of flesh.

Commentary: *The Devil's Dictionary* notes: "*Bait, n.,* a preparation that renders the hook more palatable." Indeed, the physical beauty composed of blood, flesh, bones, etc. in the form of the female is the bait that keeps the male of the species hooked to the cycle of death and rebirth *ad infinitum.* Though temporary, the beauty found in this material world is actually real because it has been reflected from the supreme beauty. Therefore, because its source is real, it is also real. Our mistake lies in trying to enjoy temporary beauty in forgetfulness of the true beauty of Kṛṣṇa consciousness. All beauty has its origin in Śrī Kṛṣṇa, the possessor of all beauty.

The *Bhagavad-gītā* (15.1–3) explains that the material world is like a banyan tree reflected in a pool of water. The reflection of the tree has drawn its origin from an actual tree. But it remains the reflection—because it is not the real tree it offers no fruits, shade or wood—but neither is it false. Those who cannot differentiate between the original beauty and the reflected beauty drown while trying to embrace the reflection. The beauty we see here is no less genuine, but it is temporary, and is therefore called the "shadow energy." Shadows change with the movements of the sun. Since we are eternal beings, we are not meant to enjoy the flickering shadows of temporary pleasures.

Lust forms the shackles that keep us bound by *karma* to the jail of this saṁsāric world. Indeed the source of that never-ending, all-consuming lust is our own defiance of God's will. He who desires a ticket on the Back to Godhead Express must purchase it through surrender to Him who is the source of all that is genuinely beautiful: Śrī Kṛṣṇa. He is the sole enjoyer, and therefore all beauties of this world or the next are meant for His satisfaction alone. These secrets of personal transcendence elude even the world's great thinkers who are not favored by the Lord's pure devotee.

ŚLOKA 14.16

सुसिद्धमौषधं धर्मं गृहच्छिद्रं च मैथुनम् ।
कुभुक्तं कुश्रुतं चैव मतिमान्न प्रकाशयेत् ॥१६॥

susiddham auṣadhaṁ dharmaṁ
gṛha-cchidraṁ ca maithunam
kubhuktaṁ kuśrutaṁ caiva
matimān na prakāśayet

He who is wise should not divulge the formula of an effective medicine, pious acts which he has performed, domestic conflicts, his sexual activities, poorly prepared food he has been offered, or malicious rumors he may have heard.

Commentary: Men who discuss in detail the specific affairs of their household are not appreciated by the listener. As far as acts of charity are concerned, boasting about one's own magnanimity ruins the piety of the deed. As Cāṇakya Paṇḍita points out elsewhere, "one's food is decided for him at birth," hence complaining about what one has been offered is ultimately a criticism of one's own *karma-phala.*

This verse also warns of the evils of gossip which Śrīla Prabhupāda characterized as the disease of Kali-yuga.

ŚLOKA 14.17

तावन्मौनेन नीयन्ते कोकिलैश्चैव वासराः ।
यावत्सर्वजनानन्ददायिनी वाक्प्रवर्तते ॥१७॥

tāvan maunena nīyante
kokilaiś caiva vāsarāḥ
yāvat sarva-janānanda-
dāyinī vāk pravartate

Through several seasons the kokila birds remain silent, until their songs impart joy to everyone.

Commentary: Lawgiver Manu describes the art of conversation:

> Speak the truth, but that which is pleasant. Do not speak unpleasantness even if it is the truth, nor should one speak pleasant-sounding falsehood. This is a fixed law. (MS 4.138)

It is said that the *kokila* (cuckoo) sings only in the *vasanta-ṛtu* (spring season), when it will gladden the ears of all its listeners. Similarly, great saints preserve their power through *mauna* (the vow of silence) and speak only when their words will not be wasted. *Mauna* also means speaking only that which is necessary to the situation at hand, foregoing small talk and saving conversation for the glorification of the Supreme Lord and His elects.

ŚLOKA 14.18

धर्मं धनं च धान्यं च गुरोर्वचनम् औषधम् ।
सुगृहीतं च कर्तव्यमन्यथा तु न जीवति ॥१८॥

dharmaṁ dhanaṁ ca dhānyaṁ ca
guror vacanam auṣadham
sugṛhītaṁ ca kartavyam
anyathā tu na jīvati

Secure and keep the following: dharma, wealth, grains, the spiritual master's instructions and medicine. For him who does not, life becomes impossible.

Commentary: Cherish and preserve religious assets as you would put aside wealth or store grains. Money and foodstuffs are required in the Lord's service. And though we may have the eternal medicine of *guror vacanam*—the spiritual master's instructions—we should not neglect attending to our health. Common sense considers that unless we care for this body, how can we engage it in the Lord's service?

ŚLOKA 14.19

त्यज दुर्जनसंसर्गं भज साधुसमागमम् ।
कुरु पुण्यमहोरात्रं स्मर नित्यमनित्यताम् ॥१९॥

tyaja durjana-saṁsargaṁ
bhaja sādhu-samāgamam
kuru puṇyam aho-rātraṁ
smara nityam anityatām

Eschew the companionship of the wicked and associate always with devotees. By day and night acquire virtue. Meditate upon that which is eternal and keep in mind that life is temporary.

Commentary: This was one of Śrīla Prabhupāda's favorites, and he quoted it in many places, such as the purports to SB 7.5.37 and 10.1.44. In *Teachings of Lord Kapila,* he writes:

> All *śāstras* advise us to associate with a *sādhu.* Even Cāṇakya Paṇḍita, the great politician, recommended: *tyaja durjana-saṁsargaṁ bhaja*

> *sādhu-samāgamam.* One Vaiṣṇava householder asked Caitanya Mahāprabhu what the duty of a householder is, and Śrī Caitanya Mahāprabhu immediately replied, *asat-saṅga-tyāga—ei vaiṣṇava-ācāra:* "Don't associate with nondevotees, but search out a *sādhu.*" (Cc 2.22.87)
>
> At the present moment it is very difficult to avoid the company of *asādhus,* those who are not *sādhus.* It is very difficult to find a *sādhu* for association. We have therefore started this Kṛṣṇa consciousness movement to create an association of *sādhus* so that people may take advantage and become liberated. There is no other purpose for this society. Kṛṣṇa states in *Bhagavad-gītā* (6.47) that the first-class *sādhu* is one who is always thinking of Him. This process is not very difficult. (*Teachings of Lord Kapila,* ch. 11)

During a talk on *Bhagavad-gītā* 2.15 in Hyderabad, delivered on 21 November 1972, Śrīla Prabhupāda lectured on the last line of this verse as follows:

> My father was doing cloth business. So sometimes in his dreams he was quoting a price: "This is the price." So similarly it is all dreaming. This material existence, made of these five gross elements and three subtle elements, they're exactly like dream... Therefore Cāṇakya Paṇḍita says, *smara nityam anityatām.* This *anitya,* temporary... Dreaming is always temporary.
>
> So we must know that whatever we possess, whatever we are seeing, these are all dream, temporary. Therefore if we become engrossed with the temporary things, so-called socialism, nationalism, family-ism or this-ism, that-ism, and waste our time, without cultivating Kṛṣṇa consciousness, then that is called *śrama eva hi kevalam* (SB 1.2.8), simply wasting our time, creating another body. Our own business is that we should know that "I am not this dream. I am fact, spiritual fact. So I have got a different business." That is called spiritual life. That is spiritual life, when we understand that "I am Brahman. I am not this matter." *Brahma-bhūtaḥ prasannātmā.* (Bg 18.54) That time we shall be joyful.

Cāṇakya Paṇḍita emphasizes the association of *sādhus* over the company of *durjanas* (sense gratifiers) not only here but in 1.16, 4.2, 4.3, 9.11, 10.14, and 12.5. The company of saints is the key principle of devotional life. Kṛṣṇa defines such *sādhus* or *mahātmās* ("great souls") in the *Bhagavad-gītā* (9.13–14) as follows:

> O son of Pṛthā, those who are not deluded, the *mahātmās,* are under the protection of the divine nature. They are fully engaged in devotional service because they know Me as the Supreme Personality of Godhead, original and inexhaustible. Always chanting My glories, endeavoring with great determination, bowing down before Me, these great souls perpetually worship Me with devotion.

Kṛṣṇa specifically mentions to Arjuna, *satataṁ kīrtayanto mām:* "They are always chanting My glories." Therefore, in this age a true devotee is recognized by his attachment to chanting the *mahā-mantra:*

Hare Kṛṣṇa Hare Kṛṣṇa Kṛṣṇa Kṛṣṇa Hare Hare
Hare Rāma Hare Rāma Rāma Rāma Hare Hare

Thus Ends Chapter Fourteen

CHAPTER FIFTEEN

ŚLOKA 15.1

यस्य चित्तं द्रवीभूतं कृपया सर्वजन्तुषु ।
तस्य ज्ञानेन मोक्षेण किं जटाभस्मलेपनैः ॥१॥

yasya cittaṁ dravī-bhūtaṁ
kṛpayā sarva-jantuṣu
tasya jñānena mokṣeṇa
kiṁ jaṭā-bhasma-lepanaiḥ

For him whose heart melts with compassion for all living beings, what is the necessity of learning, liberation, matted hair on the head or smearing the body with ashes?

Commentary: One must come to the stage of seeing the Supreme Personality of Godhead in all creatures. Cāṇakya Paṇḍita's instruction of "compassion towards all mankind" echoes Kṛṣṇa's instruction (Bg 16.1) *dayā bhūteṣu* or "mercy to all living beings." Dressing as a *sādhu* adorned with *bhasma* (the ashes of Śaivites mentioned in this verse) does not make one a holy man any more than the mere act of putting on black robes makes one a high court judge. The devotee, who serves the father of all living entities Śrī Kṛṣṇa, soon learns to love all creatures as brothers. Inner qualities alone distinguish a true saint from a Bollywood holy man.

At the 1954 Kumbha-melā in Prayāga, a mob of so-called *sādhus* went riot as the shocked Prime Minister Jawaharlal Nehru watched helplessly from a boat. Thousands of pilgrims were injured and nearly a thousand were trampled to death or drowned. Such bogus *yogīs* only harm the religion they claim to serve. Cāṇakya's point is that qualities of the heart are more important than making a show of renunciation.

ŚLOKA 15.2

एकमप्यक्षरं यस्तु गुरुः शिष्यं प्रबोधयेत् ।
पृथिव्यां नास्ति तद्द्रव्यं यद्दत्त्वा सोऽनृणी भवेत् ॥२॥

ekam apy akṣaraṁ yas tu
guruḥ śiṣyaṁ prabodhayet
pṛthivyāṁ nāsti tad dravyaṁ
yad dattvā so 'nṛṇī bhavet

There is no treasure on earth that the disciple can offer his guru to repay his debt for teaching even a single syllable.

Commentary: Nonetheless, the *guru* is so kind that he is pleased with any sincere service, and continues offering his boundless blessings that leads the disciple to Kṛṣṇa consciousness. Unlike repaying borrowed money, the system of *guru-dakṣiṇā* is an eternally ongoing process. Indeed, service to the spiritual master or *ācāryopāsanam*—as described by Kṛṣṇa Himself in the *Gītā* 13.8—is the only means to reach the ultimate goal. Only a deluded fool thinks he can approach God directly. For more on the importance of revering Śrī Guru, see 13.19.

ŚLOKA 15.3

खलानां कण्टकानां च द्विविधैव प्रतिक्रिया ।
उपानन्मुखभङ्गो वा दूरतो वा विसर्जनम् ॥३॥

khalānāṁ kaṇṭakānāṁ ca
dvividhaiva pratikriyā
upānan-mukha-bhaṅgo vā
dūrato vā visarjanam

There are two ways to deal with thorns and evil-minded men: either stomp them down with your shoes [so they cannot rise up again] or keep them at a safe distance.

Commentary: The association of a fool is a thorn in the side and the company of a rascal is a knife in the heart. Cāṇakya Paṇḍita advises strict measures in dealing with blockheads and scoundrels. Avoiding the company of nondevotees, one should associate with gentle devotees and live happily in Kṛṣṇa consciousness.

ŚLOKA 15.4

कुचैलिनं दन्तमलोपधारिणं
बह्वाशिनं निष्ठुरभाषिणं च ।
सूर्योदये चास्तमिते शयानं
विमुञ्चति श्रीर्यदि चक्रपाणिः ॥४॥

kucailinaṁ danta-malopadhāriṇaṁ
bahv-āśinaṁ niṣṭhura-bhāṣiṇaṁ ca
sūryodaye cāsta-mite śayānaṁ
vimuñcati śrīr yadi cakrapāṇiḥ

The goddess of fortune forsakes him who wears unclean garments, has dirty teeth, is a glutton, speaks harshly and sleeps from sunrise to sunset, even if he is Cakrapāṇi Himself [Viṣṇu, the holder of the disc weapon].

Commentary: It does not take much money to be clean, eat in moderation, speak sweetly and control sleep. Only the self-controlled man will grow rich, either in wealth or in the wealth of devotional service. Since Lakṣmī turns her face from misers and disorganized urchins, their misfortune is boundless.

ŚLOKA 15.5

त्यजन्ति मित्राणि धनैर्विहीनं
पुत्राश्च दाराश्च सुहृज्जनाश्च ।
तमर्थवन्तं पुनराश्रयन्ति
अर्थो हि लोके मनुषस्य बन्धुः ॥५॥

tyajanti mitrāṇi dhanair vihīnaṁ
putrāś ca dārāś ca suhṛj-janāś ca
tam arthavantaṁ punar āśrayanti
artho hi loke manuṣasya bandhuḥ

He who loses his money is forsaken by his friends, his wife, his children and his acquaintances. Yet when he regains his riches they all return. Thus there can be no better relative than wealth.

Commentary: Bṛhaspati agrees:

> He who has riches has many friends and kinsmen. He alone is a real man and a scholar. (GP 1.111.17)

Indeed, at least for the materialist, dollar signs are the yardstick of merit and education. This verse echoes two very similar verses, CN 6.5 and 7.15.

ŚLOKA 15.6

अन्यायोपार्जितं द्रव्यं दश वर्षाणि तिष्ठति ।
प्राप्ते चैकादशे वर्षे समूलं तद्विनश्यति ॥६॥

anyāyopārjitaṁ dravyaṁ
daśa varṣāṇi tiṣṭhati
prāpte caikādaśe varṣe
sa-mūlaṁ tad vinaśyati

Wealth acquired sinfully may be enjoyed for up to ten years. But in the eleventh year it disappears with even the principal reserve.

Commentary: *Karma* (work) is of two types, (1) deeds performed in the past life and (2) those which are executed in this life. Here Cāṇakya Paṇḍita points out that legitimate assets gained due to past piety will be lost through illicitly acquired gains in the here and now. Thus the wise always choose the path of honesty if only to preserve what they rightfully have.

ŚLOKA 15.7

अयुक्तं स्वामिनो युक्तं युक्तं नीचस्य दूषणम् ।
अमृतं राहवे मृत्युर्विषं शङ्करभूषणम् ॥६॥

ayuktaṁ svāmino yuktaṁ
yuktaṁ nīcasya dūṣaṇam
amṛtaṁ rāhave mṛtyur
viṣaṁ śaṅkara-bhūṣaṇam

That powerful man who performs a wrongful deed is not denounced [because none can reproach him]. The low-class man who tries to benefit society is condemned [because none respect him]. Just see: the drinking of nectar is meritorious, yet it became the reason for Rāhu's death. The drinking of poison is deadly, but when Śaṅkara consumed halāhala, it became an ornament to his neck.

Commentary: Cāṇakya Paṇḍita herewith comments upon two different Purāṇic episodes, using them to impart pearls of common sense while encouraging scriptural study.

As *Śrīmad-Bhāgavatam* instructs:

> The place, the time, the activity and the ambition were all the same for both the demigods and the demons, but the demigods achieved one result and the demons another. Because the demigods are always under the shelter of the dust of the Lord's lotus feet, they could very easily drink the nectar and get its result. The demons, however, not having sought shelter of the lotus feet of the Lord, were unable to achieve the result they desired. (SB 8.9.28)

As explained in *Śrīmad-Bhāgavatam* 8.9.25, Rāhu attempted to drink the nectar produced of the churning of the ocean of milk, and as a result, achieved a swift decapitation. Yet, as shown in *Śrīmad-Bhāgavatam* 8.7.42–43, Lord Śiva, on the other hand, drank *halāhala* poison, and today he is glorified all over the world as Nīla-kaṇṭha, the "blue-throated one."

Since the beginning of creation there are two types of persons, devotees and demons. Of this conundrum, Śrīla Prabhupāda writes:

> In *Bhagavad-gītā* it is said *ye yathā māṁ prapadyante tāṁs tathaiva bhajāmy aham:* the Supreme Personality of Godhead is the supreme judge who rewards or punishes different persons according to their surrender unto His lotus feet. Therefore, it can actually be seen that although *karmīs* and *bhaktas* may work in the same place, at the same time, with the same energy, and with the same ambition, they achieve different results. The *karmīs* transmigrate through different bodies in the cycle of birth and death, sometimes going upward and sometimes downward, thus suffering the results of their actions in the *karma-cakra,* the cycle of birth and death. The devotees, however, because of fully surrendering at the lotus feet of the Lord, are never baffled in their attempts. Although externally they work almost like the *karmīs,* the devotees go back to home back to Godhead, and achieve success in every effort. The demons or atheists have faith in their own endeavors, but although they work very hard day and night, they cannot get any more than their destiny. The devotees however can surpass the reactions of *karma* and achieve wonderful results, even without effort. It is also said *phalena paricīyate:*

one's success or defeat in any activity is understood by its result. There are many *karmīs* in the dress of devotees, but the Supreme Personality can detect their purpose. The *karmīs* want to use the property of the Lord for their selfish sense gratification, but the devotee endeavors to use the property of the Lord for God's service. (SB 8.9.28, purport)

ŚLOKA 15.8

तद्भोजनं यद्द्विजभुक्तशेषं
तत्सौहृदं यत्क्रियते परस्मिन् ।
सा प्राज्ञता या न करोति पापं
दम्भं विना यः क्रियते स धर्मः ॥८॥

tad bhojanaṁ yad dvija-bhukta-śeṣaṁ
tat sauhṛdaṁ yat kriyate parasmin
sā prājñatā yā na karoti pāpaṁ
dambhaṁ vinā yaḥ kriyate sa dharmaḥ

A true meal consists of the remnants of a brāhmaṇa's meal. True friendship means to act for others. To abstain from sin is true wisdom. True dharma is action performed without ostentation.

Commentary: As it is said, "to the crow its child is golden." This indicates that offspring, as other family members, are natural objects of affection. But here Cāṇakya Paṇḍita points out that true love is selfless and is shown when offering compassion to strangers, or even to creatures in other species of life. It is common for Westerners to adopt Buddhism and speak of compassion towards all creatures. The prerequisite for universal love is a vegetarian diet, for as the Jains remind us, "If you love animals, why do you eat them?" Today it is common to see so-called Buddhists sermonizing about compassion while chowing down on delicacies prepared from the corpses of slaughtered animals. Genuine followers of *sanātana-dharma* do not need worldly recognition for their acts of devotion because they see the Supreme Lord everywhere and have faith that He is watching them.

ŚLOKA 15.9

मणिर्लुण्ठति पादाग्रे काचः शिरसि धार्यते ।
क्रयविक्रयवेलायां काचः काचो मणिर्मणिः ॥९॥

maṇir luṇṭhati pādāgre
kācaḥ śirasi dhāryate
kraya-vikraya-velāyāṁ
kācaḥ kāco maṇir maṇiḥ

Gems may lie at the feet and broken glass may be worn on the head, but when it comes to buying and selling, glass will be glass and gems will be gems.

Commentary: Paṇḍita Śrī V. Badarayana Murthy's translation of this verse is given here:

> For want of discernment, the most precious jewels lie in the dust at the feet of men, while bits of glass are worn on their heads. But we should not imagine that the gems have sunk in value, and the bits of glass have risen in importance. When a person of critical judgment shall appear, each will be given its right position.

Worthless baubles advertised as "real faux pearls" or "genuine diamelles" are sold to the gullible glued to their TV screens. The jeweler knows the difference between valuable gemstones and worthless imitations. Similarly, it takes the discrimination of a sage to understand the difference between a genuine *guru* and an imposter. Crucial differences between the bona fide religious doctrine or Kṛṣṇa consciousness and the wise-sounding truisms invented by self-styled New Age mental speculators must be understood through genuine spiritual guidance.

ŚLOKA 15.10

अनन्तशास्त्रं बहुलाश्च विद्याः
स्वल्पश्च कालो बहुविघ्नता च ।
यत्सारभूतं तदुपासनीयं
हंसो यथा क्षीरमिवाम्बुमध्यात् ॥१०॥

ananta-śāstraṁ bahulāś ca vidyāḥ
svalpaś ca kālo bahu-vighnatā ca
yat sāra-bhūtaṁ tad-upāsanīyaṁ
haṁso yathā kṣīram ivāmbu-madhyāt

Śāstric knowledge is unlimited and the branches of knowledge that must be mastered are many. There is but little time, and opportunities for study are beset by obstacles. Therefore learn that which is essential, just as a swan can extract milk from water.

Commentary: Swans are celebrated throughout the *śāstras* of ancient Bhārata for their ability to separate milk from water, as discussed earlier. The self-realized spiritual master is called a *paramahaṁsa,* or "supreme swan" for his ability to extract essential truths in a world of confusion. Our spiritual master, who introduced Cāṇakya Paṇḍita to the world, was a *paramahaṁsa* of the highest order. Through his efforts alone the movement of Śrī Caitanya Mahāprabhu grew from the confines of Bengal, Orissa and Vṛndāvana to every town and village of the globe. His Divine Grace Śrīla Prabhupāda thereby fulfilled the essence of this verse by freely distributing the cream of knowledge through his commentaries on *Bhagavad-gītā, Śrīmad-Bhāgavatam, Caitanya-caritāmṛta,* and other essential Vaiṣṇava litrature. Life is short and therefore the essence must be learned, while that which is unnecessary should be eschewed.

ŚLOKA 15.11

दूरागतं पथि श्रान्तं वृथा च गृहमागतम् ।
अनर्चयित्वा यो भुङ्क्ते स वै चाण्डाल उच्यते ॥११॥

dūrāgataṁ pathi śrāntaṁ
vṛthā ca gṛham āgatam
anarcayitvā yo bhuṅkte
sa vai cāṇḍāla ucyate

The host who enjoys his meal without honoring the tired stranger who has arrived from far away or even someone who has visited without a specific purpose is no better than an eater of dogs.

Commentary: Vedic civilization and culture lays great importance upon sharing food with guests, and those who eat without offering food to their guest are sent to the miser's hell. Manu adds:

> One should unhesitatingly give food to newly married daughters-in-law, children, those in ill health and pregnant women even before the guests. He who eats before them will become food for dogs and vultures. (MS 3.114–115)

The region of Naraka (hell) reserved for the miser who does not share his food is described in *Śrīmad-Bhāgavatam:*

> A person is considered no better than a crow if after receiving some food, he does not divide it among his guests, old men and children, but simply eats it himself, or if he eats it without performing the five kinds of sacrifice. After death he is put into the most abominable hell called Kṛmibhojana. In that hell there is a lake 100,000 *yojanas* (800,000 miles) wide and filled with worms. He becomes a worm (*kṛmi*) in that lake and eats (*bhojana*) on the other worms there, who also feed on him. Unless he atones for his actions before his death, such a sinful man remains in the lake of Kṛmibhojana for as many years as there are *yojanas* in the width of the lake. (SB 5.26.18)

The *Bhagavad-gītā* says:

> The devotees of the Lord are released from sin because they eat food that is first offered for sacrifice. Others who prepare food for personal enjoyment eat only sin. (Bg 3.13)

ŚLOKA 15.12

पठन्ति चतुरो वेदान्धर्मशास्त्राण्यनेकशः ।
आत्मानं नैव जानन्ति दर्वी पाककरसं यथा ॥१२॥

paṭhanti caturo vedān
dharma-śāstrāṇy anekaśaḥ
ātmānaṁ naiva jānanti
darvī pāka-rasaṁ yathā

He who studies the four Vedas and the dharma-śāstras yet remains void of spiritual realization, is no better than a ladle which does not know the taste of any dish it stirs.

Commentary: There was a favorite example of Śrīla Prabhupāda: Sometimes in old India a jar of fresh milk left by a window would become an invitation for a cobra to slither up the wall and have a drink. Tainted by venom, the milk would then cause death to whoever drank it. In the same way, there are many unqualified commentators who publish interpretations of the scriptures simply to increase their fame as knowers of *śāstras.* There are others who are far worse because they twist novel meanings out of the holy books with the intent of misleading the innocent public. Vedic wisdom obtained from such pretenders who themselves do not know the depth of the *śāstras* is equal to drinking milk that has been touched by the lips of a serpent. As shown in this verse, the purpose of scriptural study is found in realization of the *ātmā* or spiritual particle; which by implication means understanding how to engage the soul in Kṛṣṇa consciousness. It is also common for worldly politicians to write commentaries or to publicly read holy books simply for impressing the voters. Days after Bill Clinton was accused in the infamous Monica Lewinsky affair, the President was filmed going to church with a Bible in his hand. In India the *Bhagavad-gītā* has been similarly waved before TV cameras by politicians eager to appear devout. The closer looms election day, the more fervent and religious the politicians become.

ŚLOKA 15.13

धन्या द्विजमयी नौका विपरीता भवार्णवे ।
तरन्त्यधोगताः सर्वे उपरिष्ठाः पतन्त्यधः ॥१३॥

dhanyā dvija-mayī naukā
viparītā bhavārṇave
taranty adhogatāḥ sarve
upariṣṭhāḥ patanty adhaḥ

A qualified brāhmaṇa is like a toppled boat floating in the ocean of material existence. Those who hold on to the boat cross over to the other side, while those who climb up on its hull fall down into the water.

Commentary: Śrī Badarayana Murthy's translation for this verse is as follows:

> "Blessed are the passengers of the "boat" of the qualified twice-born *brāhmaṇa,* which floats against the current in the ocean of material existence. Those passengers who sit at the feet of the qualified *brāhmaṇa* cross easily, yet those who raise themselves above the ship's captain fall overboard and drown."

Through the analogy of a boat, this verse illustrates the dangers of a disciple displaying his arrogance in the presence of the *guru.* A genuine *brāhmaṇa* acts as the spiritual guide of society, ferrying the devotees across the currents of misunderstanding and around the whirlpools of atheism to the shore of spiritual realization. *Śrīmad-*

Bhāgavatam similarly conveys this example. When the sages of Naimiṣāraṇya welcomed Śrīla Sūta Gosvāmī, they proclaimed:

> We think that we have met Your Grace by the will of Providence, that we may accept you as the captain of the ship for those who desire to cross the difficult ocean of Kali, which deteriorates all the good qualities in men. (SB 1.1.22)

In this verse, the *brāhmaṇa* is referred to as a *dvija* (twice born). One's first birth is the material one, and the second is the birth into spirit or initiation by a qualified *guru*. Indeed, this is the same concept that Jesus Christ spoke of when he advised, "You must be born again." In this verse, the analogy of falling overboard and drowning refers to losing the *guru's* shelter, and falling back into the material ocean of birth and death. Spiritual salvation or Kṛṣṇa consciousness is assured for the devotee who, tolerating the waves of desire, humbly accepts as his life and soul the orders of the twice-born captain of his ship.

Had the British Raj likewise displayed humility before India's *brāhmaṇas* and *gurus*—rather than condemning the followers of the *Vedas* as heathens because they were not Christians—then an entirely different hand of history would have been dealt the Empire. Had the *pukka sahib* removed his crown and bowed before Lord Viṣṇu, the Koh-i-noor of Britain's "jewel in the crown" might be shining brightly upon India even today. It is an irony that the arrogance that propped up the British Raj for over two hundred years would also sink it like a concrete slab. Today open-minded Indians have accepted qualified *brāhmaṇas* of the International Society for Kṛṣṇa Consciousness who were born outside of India, and the same could have happened during the days of British India had the British qualified themselves through understanding *sanātana-dharma*.

Whoever would seek to rule mother India properly should realize the value of her ancient God-conscious culture, scriptures, religion and four-tiered society headed by her *brāhmaṇas*. Like King Candragupta, who bowed before Cāṇakya Paṇḍita, a proper king must give his obeisance unto the twice-born, and thereby set an example for society at large. India is the ancient cradle of civilization. Every truth mankind requires for a perfect life—both here and hereafter—is locked in the treasure chest of her Sanskrit texts, and humility is the key to opening that trove.

ŚLOKA 15.14

अयममृतनिधानं नायकोऽप्यौषधीनाम्
अमृतमयशरीरः कान्तियुक्तोऽपि चन्द्रः ।
भवति विगतरश्मिर्मण्डलं प्राप्य भानोः
परसदननिविष्टः को लघुत्वं न याति ॥१४॥

ayam amṛta-nidhānaṁ nāyako 'py auṣadhīnām
amṛta-maya-śarīraḥ kānti-yukto 'pi candraḥ
bhavati vigata-raśmir maṇḍalaṁ prāpya bhānoḥ
para-sadana-niviṣṭaḥ ko laghutvaṁ na yāti

Candra, the resplendent moon, who is the abode of immortal nectar and the presiding deity of medicines, loses the brilliance of his cool rays when he repairs to the abode of Bhānu the sun. Therefore will not an ordinary man be made to feel inferior by going to live in the house of another?

Commentary: The glow of self-respect is the monopoly of the self-reliant. As regards to the Vedic conception of the moon planet as seen in this verse, we find in the sacred *Bhāgavata Purāṇa* the following description:

> When the moon is waxing, the illuminating portion of it increases daily, thus creating day for the demigods and night for the *pitās*. When the moon is waning, however, it causes night for the demigods and day for the *pitās*. In this way the moon passes through each constellation of stars in thirty *muhūrtas*. The moon is the source of nectarean coolness that influences the growth of food grains, and

therefore the moon god is considered the life of all living entities. He is consequently called Jīva, the chief entity within the universe. Because the moon is full of all potentialities, it represents the influence of the Supreme Personality of Godhead. The moon is the predominating deity of everyone's mind, and therefore the moon god is called Manomaya. He is also called Annamaya because he gives potency to all herbs and plants, and he is called Amṛtamaya because he is the source of life for all living entities. The moon pleases the demigods, *pitās,* human beings, animals, birds, reptiles, trees, plants, and all other living entities. Everyone is satisfied by the presence of the moon. Therefore the moon is called Sarvamaya or all-pervading. (SB 5.22.9–10)

ŚLOKA 15.15

अलिरयं नलिनीदलमध्यगः
कमलिनीमकरन्दमदालसः ।
विधिवशात्परदेशमुपागतः
कुटजपुष्परसं बहु मन्यते ॥१५॥

alir ayaṁ nalinī-dala-madhya-gaḥ
kamalinī-makaranda-madālasaḥ
vidhi-vaśāt para-deśam upāgataḥ
kuṭaja-puṣpa-rasaṁ bahu manyate

This bumblebee used to sit inside the lotus flower, intoxicated with its nectar. Now, by the will of Providence, it finds itself in a foreign land and considers even the kuṭaja flowers very tasty.

Commentary: The *kuṭaja* flower is used in a number of Āyurvedic preparations and is more native to Sri Lanka (which may account for the comment "in a foreign land"). Just as the bee, forgetful of the lotus, thinks that a non-fragrant flower is a feast, so the sentimental religionist or impersonalist with his poor fund of knowledge mistakes dogma for devotion. Mental speculation is no substitute for śāstric wisdom, and neither can sentimentality replace transcendental realization (though in the absence of a bona fide spiritual master they might appear to do so). Social pressures calling for the political correctness of "interfaith" ask us to equate the mere act of being born into a material religion with a *brāhmaṇa's* years of Vedic study and austerity. Likewise, the soul fallen from the spiritual plane mistakes that he has found—in this body and that—lasting enjoyment in these temporary worlds of birth and death!

ŚLOKA 15.16

पीतः क्रुद्धेन तातश्चरणतलहतो वल्लभो येन रोषा-
दाबाल्याद् विप्रवर्यैः स्ववदनविवरे धार्यते वैरिणी मे।
गेहं मे छेदयन्ति प्रतिदिवसमुमाकान्तपूजानिमित्तं
तस्मात्खिन्ना सदाहं द्विजकुलनिलयं नाथ युक्तं त्यजामि ॥१६॥

pītaḥ kruddhena tātaś caraṇa-tala-hato vallabho yena roṣād
ābālyād vipra-varyaiḥ sva-vadana-vivare dhāryate vairiṇī me
gehaṁ me chedayanti prati-divasam umā-kānta-pūjā-nimittaṁ
tasmāt khinnā sadāhaṁ dvija-kula-nilayaṁ nātha yuktaṁ tyajāmi

[Lord Viṣṇu inquired of His spouse Lakṣmī why she does not dwell in the house of a brāhmaṇa, and she replied]: "O Lord, a ṛṣi named Agastya drank up my father [the ocean] in anger. Bhṛgu Muni kicked You. My competitor [Sarasvatī] rests in the throats of the best of the brāhmaṇas even from their very childhood. Finally they daily pluck the lotus, which is my abode, and therewith worship the husband of Umā. All this saddens me and that is why I refuse to live with the brāhmaṇas!"

Commentary: It is said that the Lord protects His *brāhmaṇas* from acquiring the blessings of His wife Lakṣmī in the form of wealth, lest their heads become turned by excessive material attachment. Voluntary poverty keeps the *brāhmaṇa* humble, and this is more important for one whose job is teaching society rather than becoming preoccupied with wealth. And this is why the goddess of learning Sarasvatī and the goddess of wealth Lakṣmī seldom dwell in the same household together.

In this verse, Lakṣmī recalls to her husband the story of the great Agastya Muni who, it is said, was "no larger than a thumb." As narrated in *Mahābhārata's Vana-parva* (chs. 101–105), despite his size Agastya swallowed the ocean because the *asuras* (demons) were hiding there from the wrath of the demigods. Once their hiding place was exposed, the demigods made short work of the demons. Goddess Lakṣmī arose from the ocean during its churning (SB 2.7.13), thus the disdain she holds for Agastya Muni. As stated in the *Bhāgavata:*

> Then there appeared the goddess of fortune, Ramā, who is absolutely dedicated to being enjoyed by the Supreme Personality of Godhead. She appeared like electricity, surpassing the lightning that might illuminate a marble mountain. (SB 8.8.8)

The episode of Bhṛgu Muni's placing his foot on the chest of Lakṣmī's husband Lord Viṣṇu is told by Śrīla Prabhupāda in his book *Kṛṣṇa, the Supreme Personality of Godhead,* chapter 34, entitled "The Superexcellent Power of Kṛṣṇa." Once at a gathering of *munis* beside the Sarasvatī River, a plan was devised to determine which of the so-called *tri-mūrti*—Brahmā, Viṣṇu and Śiva—is the Supreme Lord. The sages unanimously agreed that Bhṛgu should test each one of them. Bhṛgu first went to his father, Brahmā, whom he angered through a mental offense, failing to respect him properly. Then, proceeding to Lord Śiva's abode of Kailāsa, the sage insulted the husband of Pārvatī with a spoken offense, causing Lord Śiva to bristle.

Bhṛgu encountered Lord Viṣṇu who was deep in His trance called *yoga-nidrā.* Bhṛgu had angered Brahmā with thoughts, Śiva with words, and now he was determined to test Viṣṇu with physical actions, by placing his foot on the Lord's chest. Viṣṇu awoke and begged the *muni* for forgiveness, stating that His chest was too hard for the soft lotus-like foot of an exalted *brāhmaṇa.* Lord Viṣṇu began massaging the foot of Bhṛgu who silently wept tears of joy. Then the *ṛṣi* returned to the august assembly of sages and, relating his experiences, told his conclusion. All the *munis* there accepted the tolerant Lord Viṣṇu as the Supreme Lord.

ŚLOKA 15.17

बन्धनानि खलु सन्ति बहूनि
प्रेमरज्जुकृतबन्धनमन्यत् ।
दारुभेदनिपुणोऽपि षडङ्घ्रि-
र्निष्क्रियो भवति पङ्कजकोशे ॥१७॥

bandhanāni khalu santi bahūni
prema-rajju-kṛta-bandhanam anyat
dāru-bheda-nipuṇo 'pi ṣaḍ-aṅghrir
niṣkriyo bhavati paṅkaja-kośe

Out of so many ways of tying one up in this world, the bond of affection is the strongest. The bumblebee is expert in piercing hardened wood, yet he becomes caught in the embrace of the one he loves [as the bud of the lotus flower closes at dusk].

Commentary: In a man's home, his wife, children and relatives form a tight bond. Beyond the home the circle of friends, religious congregation, clubs, etc. tie the *karmī* to his false identity. Due to this invisible attachment the foolish materialist willingly sacrifices eternal bliss for temporary association amongst those with whom he shares no real relationship or even useful affinity.

ŚLOKA 15.18

छिन्नोऽपि चन्दनतरुर्न जहाति गन्धं
वृद्धोऽपि वारणपतिर्न जहाति लीलाम् ।

यन्त्रार्पितो मधुरतां न जहाति चेक्षुः
क्षीणोऽपि न त्यजति शीलगुणान्कुलीनः ॥१८॥

chinno 'pi candana-tarur na jahāti gandhaṁ
vṛddho 'pi vāraṇa-patir na jahāti līlām
yantrārpito madhuratāṁ na jahāti cekṣuḥ
kṣīṇo 'pi na tyajati śīla-guṇān kulīnaḥ

Although cut, sandalwood does not forsake its natural quality of fragrance, so also even in old age an elephant retains his love of sporting with his wives. Though crushed in a mill, sugarcane does not give up its sweetness. In the same way, a man of noble extraction does not lose his qualities no matter how pinched he is by poverty.

Commentary: Śrīla Prabhupāda was no different whether he lived in a tiny room in Delhi, or in a London manor house; on the mean streets of the Bowery, or chatting with prime ministers in their mansions. Virtue and character are inner qualities not conditioned by the patina of external situations.

ŚLOKA 15.19

उर्व्यां कोऽपि महीधरो लघुतरो दोर्भ्यां धृतो लीलया
तेन त्वं दिवि भूतले च सततं गोवर्धनोद्धारकः ।
त्वां त्रैलोक्यधरं वहामि कुचयोरग्रे न तद्गण्यते
किं वा केशव भाषणेन बहुना पुण्यैर्यशो लभ्यते ॥१९॥

urvyāṁ ko 'pi mahī-dharo laghutaro dorbhyāṁ dhṛto līlayā
tena tvaṁ divi bhū-tale ca satataṁ govardhanoddhārakaḥ
tvāṁ trailokya-dharaṁ vahāmi kucayor agre na tad gaṇyate
kiṁ vā keśava bhāṣaṇena bahunā puṇyair yaśo labhyate

[Śrīmatī Rukmiṇī, the most beloved wife of the Supreme Lord Śrī Kṛṣṇa, said to Him:] "Dear Keśava, with Your hands You playfully

lifted a very light hill and are therefore celebrated throughout the earth and heaven as Govardhana-dhārī. But although I hold You, the bearer of the three worlds, on the tip of my breasts, no one takes that into account. What is the use of saying this, the fact is that fame is gained only by sufficient accumulation of puṇya."

Commentary: This verse also appears in Śrī Bilvamaṅgala Ṭhākura's *Kṛṣṇa-karṇāmṛta* (2.106).

In this age of quarrel and discord, the highest *puṇya* is to glorify Śrī Kṛṣṇa, or Giridhārī, the lifter of Govardhana Hill by chanting:

Hare Kṛṣṇa Hare Kṛṣṇa Kṛṣṇa Kṛṣṇa Hare Hare
Hare Rāma Hare Rāma Rāma Rāma Hare Hare

Thus Ends Chapter Fifteen

CHAPTER SIXTEEN

ŚLOKA 16.1

न ध्यातं पदमीश्वरस्य विधिवत्संसारविच्छित्तये
  स्वर्गद्वारकपाटपाटनपटुर्धर्मोऽपि नोपार्जितः।
नारीपीनपयोधरोरुयुगलं स्वप्नेऽपि नालिङ्गितं
  मातुः केवलमेव यौवनवनच्छेदे कुठारा वयम् ॥१॥

na dhyātaṁ padam īśvarasya vidhi-vat saṁsāra-vicchittaye
svarga-dvāra-kapāṭa-pāṭana-paṭur dharmo 'pi nopārjitaḥ
nārī-pīna-payodharoru-yugalaṁ svapne 'pi nāliṅgitaṁ
mātuḥ kevalam eva yauvana-vana-cchede kuṭhārā vayam

Nearing the bitter end, an old man laments: We did not properly meditate on the lotus feet of the Lord which could liberate us from the cycle of birth and death, neither have we taken up the pious duties which open the door to heaven. Not even in a dream have we ever embraced the breasts and thighs of a woman. In this way we are nothing more than axes who have cut the forest of our mother's youth.

Commentary: Cāṇakya Paṇḍita's backhanded remark about courting a beautiful lady should be taken as tongue-in-cheek. His point is, hey, if you cannot be a spiritual success at least do something here and now! Cāṇakya Paṇḍita was a celibate and his sense of humor should be understood. Of course courtship of a young lady should be understood in the proper sense of Vedic civilization and culture in which there is no tolerance for illicit sex. Marriage is a *gṛhastha's* lifelong commitment, and that is why they call it "wedlock."

ŚLOKA 16.2

जल्पन्ति सार्धमन्येन पश्यन्त्यन्यं सविभ्रमाः ।
हृदये चिन्तयन्त्यन्यं न स्त्रीणामेकतो रतिः ॥२॥

jalpanti sārdham anyena
paśyanty anyaṁ sa-vibhramāḥ
hṛdaye cintayanty anyaṁ
na strīṇām ekato ratiḥ

The affection of a woman is not one-pointed, it is divided. While talking with one man, she glances winsomely at another and thinks of a third, the one in her heart.

Commentary: This verse is quite famous. The *nīti-śāstras* in some places praise women to the sky and in other places criticize the fair sex as though they are she-devils. Some *paṇḍitas* suggest that opinions in these complex matters hinge upon personal experiences that color a man's outlook. The debate over women has been raging since time immemorial, with happily married men on one side and unfortunate misogynists soured by unrequited love on the other. And as *nīti-śāstra* continually reminds us, personal experiences rest largely upon our own *karma.* For the record, here are a few quotes about the Xanthippes, which are bound to ruffle some feathers:

> Women are incorrigible; they can never be brought round by making a gift, or offering respect, or through straight-forward dealings, or repeated service. They can never be threatened with a weapon nor quieted by citing scriptural codes. (GP 1.109.45)

As blazing fire cannot be satisfied with sufficient fuel, the ocean can never be filled by all the rivers of the world flowing into it, and as Yamarāja is not satisfied by any number he carries away, so a passionate woman is never satisfied with a man. (GP 1.109.40)

A woman who is devoid of love, terrifying in appearance, ferocious by nature, more horrible than a serpent entwined about the neck, tiger-like, and red-eyed should never be approached. (GP 1.108.27)

The following activities ruin the chastity of women: association with the base, long separation from the husband, too much consideration and love (from a would-be seducer) and residence in another man's house. (GP 1.109.16)

Just as it is impossible to overcome sleep by sleeping, smother a flame by adding fuel or quenching thirst by drinking wine, so it is impossible to satisfy a woman. (GP 1.109.34)

Both rivers and women enjoy choosing their own courses. The river undermines its own banks and women undermine their own families. Both are wayward and cannot be checked. (GP 1.109.38–9)

If a husband has to leave home, he should not let his young wife be independent. A woman in the company of other men is the root of all misfortune, especially if she is young. (SN 2.127)

Begging and death are better than being a householder with a bad wife. (SN 3.288)

The true *paṇḍita* is not bewildered by such seemingly contradictory *ślokas*. The great sages of the Vedic age were mostly all householders. What is sure and certain is that horoscopes must be matched according to the *jyotiṣa-śāstra* before the knot is tied. That will assure a marriage that is as happy as possible.

ŚLOKA 16.3

यो मोहान्मन्यते मूढो रक्तेयं मयि कामिनी ।
स तस्यां वशगो भूत्वा नृत्येत्क्रीडाशकुन्तवत् ॥३॥

yo mohān manyate mūḍho
rakteyaṁ mayi kāminī
sa tasyāṁ vaśago bhūtvā
nṛtyet krīḍā-śakunta-vat

The fool who fancies that a charming young lady loves him becomes her slave and dances like a śakunta bird tied to a string.

Commentary: Cāṇakya Paṇḍita uses the word *mūḍha* (ass) for the hopelessly attached victim of *moha* (infatuation). It is said that the bow of Kāmadeva (Cupid) has five arrows. These are *harṣaṇa* (happiness), *rocana* (attraction), *mohana* (infatuation), *śoṣaṇa* (dwindling) and *maraṇa* (death). Hence he who is attracted to mundane sex life does nothing more than court his own slow death.

In His instructions to Śrīla Sanātana Gosvāmī, Lord Śrī Caitanya Mahāprabhu quoted the words of Śrīla Kapiladeva:

> By association with worldly people, one becomes devoid of truthfulness, cleanliness, mercy, gravity, spiritual intelligence, shyness, austerity, fame, forgiveness, control of the mind, control of the senses, fortune and all opportunities. One should not at any time associate with a coarse fool who is bereft of the knowledge of self-realization and who is no more than a toy animal in the hands of a woman. The illusion and bondage that accrue to a man from attachment to any other object are not as complete as that resulting from association with a woman or with men who are too attached to women. (Cc 2.22.88–90)

ŚLOKA 16.4

कोऽर्थान्प्राप्य न गर्वितो विषयिण: कस्यापदोऽस्तं गता:
स्त्रीभि: कस्य न खण्डितं भुवि मन: को नाम राजप्रिय: ।
क: कालस्य न गोचरत्वमगमत्कोऽर्थी गतो गौरवं
को वा दुर्जनदुर्गमेषु पतित: क्षेमेण यात: पथि ॥४॥

ko 'rthān prāpya na garvito viṣayiṇaḥ kasyāpado 'staṁ gatāḥ
strībhiḥ kasya na khaṇḍitaṁ bhuvi manaḥ ko nāma rāja-priyaḥ
kaḥ kālasya na gocaratvam agamat ko 'rthī gato gauravaṁ
ko vā durjana-durgameṣu patitaḥ kṣemeṇa yātaḥ pathi

Who having attained riches has not become haughty? Which slave of lust is free from woe? Which man has never been conquered by women? Who is ever the favorite of the king? Who has not been overcome by the ravages of time? Which beggar is glorious? Who has become happy by taking on the vices of the wicked?

Commentary: *Strībhiḥ kasya na khaṇḍitaṁ manaḥ?* Cāṇakya Paṇḍita inquires which man has not been conquered by women, but elsewhere he asks which man has ever conquered a woman? Indeed, it is becoming common now in California for husbands to take on the last name of their brides. The term "tying the knot" for marriage refers to the act of the groom ceremoniously tying his *chādar* to the wife's sari in a Vedic wedding ceremony. But it may also be applied to the knot of false ego or false sense of proprietorship that tightens at the time of union.

This verse summarizes many of the various *nīti-śāstra's* observations including the endless battle of the sexes; associating with materialists; and wealth or the lack of it. The conclusion is that one should always avoid the company of materialists and associate with devotees of the Supreme Lord. Genuine devotees are oceans of good qualities. While instructing Śrīla Sanātana Gosvāmī, Lord Caitanya quoted the *Kātyāyana-saṁhitā:*

> It is better to accept the miseries of being encaged within bars and surrounded by burning flames than to associate with those bereft of good Kṛṣṇa consciousness. Such association is a very great hardship. (Cc 2.22.91)

ŚLOKA 16.5

न निर्मिता केन न दृष्टपूर्वा
न श्रूयते हेममयी कुरङ्गी ।
तथापि तृष्णा रघुनन्दनस्य
विनाशकाले विपरीतबुद्धिः ॥५॥

na nirmitā kena na dṛṣṭa-pūrvā
na śrūyate hema-mayī kuraṅgī
tathāpi tṛṣṇā raghunandanasya
vināśa-kāle viparīta-buddhiḥ

No one has ever made, seen, or heard of a golden deer and yet, without a second thought, Raghunandana was attracted to it. In times of adversity intelligence becomes deluded.

Commentary: Fate is discussed from many angles throughout *nīti-śāstra.* This verse refers to the *līlā* of kidnapping Queen Sītā when Mārīca, the agent of the demonic King Rāvaṇa, took the form of a golden deer to lure Lord Rāma into the jungle. Mother Sītā is the wife of Lord Rāma, and Sītā-Rāma are expansions of Śrī Lakṣmī-Nārāyaṇa. In fact, Rāvaṇa could abduct only a "Māyā Sītā," hence Their *līlā* (pastimes) as recorded in the *Rāmāyaṇa* of Vālmīki, were enacted for our benefit. The Lord's *avatāras* appear just to attract devotees back to home, back to Godhead. Devotees of the Lord never mistake that the Lord succumbs to His deluding potency, *māyā,* which affects us conditioned souls. Cāṇakya Paṇḍita here shows that even the great of this world will be conquered by their own destinies sooner or later, and in the next several verses describes the qualities that separate the supposed "greats" from the truly great. Cāṇakya has taken the example of a golden deer from the *Mahābhārata;* spoken by Yudhiṣṭhira when he was called by Duryodhana for the second, fateful gambling match.

ŚLOKA 16.6

गुणैरुत्तमतां याति नोच्चैरासनसंस्थिताः ।
प्रासादशिखरस्थोऽपि काकः किं गरुडायते ॥६॥

guṇair uttamatāṁ yāti
noccair āsana-saṁsthitāḥ
prāsāda-śikhara-stho 'pi
kākaḥ kiṁ garuḍāyate

One attains greatness by his merits, not by sitting on an exalted āsana. Can a crow become Garuḍa just by perching atop a palace?

Commentary: A mosquito sits upon the same throne as the king, but while the king rules the country the mosquito only sucks the blood of the king. Cāṇakya Paṇḍita herewith advises: look to the character of the man, not to his throne. Śrīla Prabhupāda made a similar wry comment about *sādhus* who parade around the Kumbha-melās sitting atop elephants.

The Tenth Canto of the *Bhāgavata Purāṇa* narrates the story of King Pauṇḍraka who tried to convince the world that he was Lord Nārāyaṇa by having an extra pair of arms mounted to his shoulders! Needless to say, the fate of the foolish Pauṇḍraka was not a happy one. *Yogīs* who claim to be God should take a lesson from the life of Pauṇḍraka. A neophyte devotee should wisely avoid ascending the *vyāsāsana* prematurely and proclaiming himself as a world *ācārya* or even an *ācārya* for any particular part of the world. The symbols of the *paramahaṁsa* are meant for the *paramahaṁsa.* For a neophyte to usurp such symbols is to draw his own disgrace and destruction very near.

ŚLOKA 16.7

गुणाः सर्वत्र पूज्यन्ते न महत्योऽपि सम्पदः ।
पूर्णेन्दुः किं तथा वन्द्यो निष्कलङ्को यथा कृशः ॥७॥

guṇāḥ sarvatra pūjyante
na mahatyo 'pi sampadaḥ
pūrṇenduḥ kiṁ tathā vandyo
niṣkalaṅko yathā kṛśaḥ

Qualities, not wealth, make a man worthy of respect everywhere. Is the full moon ever glorified as much as the moon on the second day of its waxing phase when it does not have any spots?

Commentary: The moon planet is a favorite subject of both Vedic poets as well as the *ṛṣis* of ancient Bhārata. Modern scientists claim to have gone to the moon, a boast which has been repeatedly dismantled as a total fabrication. What is certain is that they could learn more about Candraloka from reading the Vedic literatures than building rocket ships.

The full moon on *pūrṇimā* clearly exhibits all its spots (which are considered blemishes) while the moon on the Dvitīyā *tithi,* when it is just beginning to wax, hides them and is thus more worthy of glorification. And so it is that a young man full of enthusiasm is always praised as he begins his new journey, while when that same fellow becomes old only his faults will be noticed.

ŚLOKA 16.8

परैरुक्तगुणो यस्तु निर्गुणोऽपि गुणी भवेत् ।
इन्द्रोऽपि लघुतां याति स्वयं प्रख्यापितैर्गुणैः ॥८॥

parair ukta-guṇo yas tu
nirguṇo 'pi guṇī bhavet
indro 'pi laghutāṁ yāti
svayaṁ prakhyāpitair guṇaiḥ

He whose glories are sung by others is regarded as great though he is really without merit. But he who vaunts his own merit lowers

himself in the estimation of others even if he is Indra, the king of heaven.

Commentary: This is why ordinary men who desire cheap fame hire "press agents" to toot their horns for them. Even so, the newspaper that carries their picture on Sunday is carted away by the garbage men on Monday. Practically every day another ordinary rascal burdened by artificial celebrity finds fame to be his downfall. Those who wish to be celebrated in this temporary world are like the insignificant ant who longs to be the king of the anthill.

ŚLOKA 16.9

विवेकिनमनुप्राप्ता गुणा यान्ति मनोज्ञताम् ।
सुतरां रत्नमाभाति चामीकरनियोजितम् ॥९॥

vivekinam anuprāptā
guṇā yānti mano-jñatām
sutarāṁ ratnam ābhāti
cāmīkara-niyojitam

If good qualities should characterize a man of discrimination, the brilliance of his qualities will be recognized just as a gem which is essentially bright really shines when fixed in an ornament of gold.

Commentary: *Viveka* (discrimination) is the essential ingredient that separates man from animal. It is therefore a twist of irony that within today's "modern, liberated and classless" society; discrimination is condemned as a form of prejudice to the extent that the definition of the word has been rewritten in modern dictionaries. Human life minus discrimination is no better than a hog's, whose diet consists of comestibles that have been pre-processed in the intestines of other hogs. One scientist suggested a plan to turn sewage into food proving that even two-legged Dr. Hogs can have PhD's.

ŚLOKA 16.10

गुणैः सर्वज्ञतुल्योऽपि सीदत्येको निराश्रयः ।
अनर्घ्यमपि माणिक्यं हेमाश्रयमपेक्षते ॥१०॥

guṇaiḥ sarvajña-tulyo 'pi
sīdaty eko nirāśrayaḥ
anarghyam api māṇikyaṁ
hemāśrayam apekṣate

Even he who by his qualities is celebrated as all-knowing suffers without patronage. The gem, though precious, requires a gold setting.

Commentary: *Paṇḍitas* whose talents remain unappreciated are better off becoming renunciants. Bṛhaspati instructs:

> A man should be like the *mālatī* blossom. Either he should be worn on the head of the king, or fade away in oblivion in the woods. (GP 1.110.13)

In Vedic India the kings employed monies collected as taxes to maintain *brāhmaṇas* whose activities were aimed at the upliftment, welfare and preservation of society. The study of Vedic arts, Sanskrit, dissemination of Vedic literature, building of temples and schools, cow protection and the sponsoring of *yajñas* directed at worshipping the Supreme Lord: all these and more enjoyed royal support. In the sixty years since India's so-called independence, and in the name of secularism, the government has done absolutely nothing to revive the brahminical glory of ancient Bhārata. If there ever was a missed opportunity, it occurred on August 15, 1947 when India was granted *svarājya* (self-rule). At that time India should have reverted to its former Kṛṣṇa conscious glory. An India that is no longer Vedic, but is shackled by foreign conceptions of imperfect social organization cannot be considered independent.

Today, the old land of India is becoming a world leader due not to the "leadership" of the government, but by the determination of many individual citizens. As India emerges, let mother India's leaders remember the great precedents held sacred by the great kings of the Vedic era who upheld Vedic civilization and culture. It is a great mistake to blindly imitate the doomed hodge-podge-podgery of modern Western education, politics, science, cinema, entertainment or religion. Undoubtedly India is a land of uncountable problems, but through the re-emergence of *sanātana-dharma,* including governmental support of the *saṅkīrtana* movement of Śrī Caitanya Mahāprabhu, all problems will be solved. It is the promise of the *ācāryas* that the great social experiment of applying ancient truths to these modern times will meet with sure success, bringing glory to India and the world.

ŚLOKA 16.11

अतिक्लेशेन ये अर्था धर्मस्यातिक्रमेण तु ।
शत्रूणां प्रणिपातेन ते ह्यर्था न भवन्तु मे ॥११॥

ali-kleśena ye arthā
dharmasyātikrameṇa tu
śatrūṇāṁ praṇipātena
te hy arthā na bhavantu me

Let me not possess wealth which is to be attained by enduring much hardship, by transgressing rules of virtue, or by submitting to an enemy.

Commentary: In verses six through ten above, Cāṇakya Paṇḍita establishes that qualities, not wealth, make the man. Here he points out that a man of good qualities does not compromise his character to obtain money. Truth and dignity should never be made to bow to riches. This verse is from the *Garuḍa Purāṇa* (1.109.28).

ŚLOKA 16.12

किं तया क्रियते लक्ष्म्या या वधूरिव केवला ।
या तु वेश्येव सामान्या पथिकैरपि भुज्यते ॥१२॥

kiṁ tayā kriyate lakṣmyā
yā vadhūr iva kevalā
yā tu veśyeva sāmānyā
pathikair api bhujyate

What is the use of money locked up and protected like the wife? Money should be used in the service of everyone, just like a street woman is enjoyed by any traveler who happens by.

Commentary: By comparing money to a prostitute, the author of the *Artha-śāstra* reveals his opinion of hoarded wealth that is not used for social welfare activities. Therefore, a man of moral fiber should not sacrifice his qualities for obtaining funds any more than he should by patronizing prostitutes. While appreciating the brilliant point made, V. Badarayana Murthy called this "Cāṇakya's dirtiest example."

ŚLOKA 16.13

धनेषु जीवितव्येषु स्त्रीषु चाहारकर्मसु ।
अतृप्ताः प्राणिनः सर्वे याता यास्यन्ति यान्ति च ॥१३॥

dhaneṣu jīvitavyeṣu
strīṣu cāhāra-karmasu
atṛptāḥ prāṇinaḥ sarve
yātā yāsyanti yānti ca

No man whether of the past, present or the future has ever been or will ever be satisfied with his wealth, living conditions, wife and food.

Commentary: He who has found ultimate satisfaction with material forms of so-called enjoyment is yet to be born. Therefore, one's efforts should be invested in the salvation of his eternal soul through Kṛṣṇa consciousness. As Bṛhaspati says:

> All have the same destination. All are proceeding there. If one goes more quickly, why should that be lamented? (GP 1.113.46)

ŚLOKA 16.14

क्षीयन्ते सर्वदानानि यज्ञहोमबलिक्रियाः ।
न क्षीयते पात्रदानमभयं सर्वदेहिनाम् ॥१४॥

kṣīyante sarva-dānāni
yajña-homa-bali-kriyāḥ
na kṣīyate pātra-dānam
abhayaṁ sarva-dehinām

Yajñas, homas and charity [performed for fruitive gains] bring only temporary results, but acts of charity offered to deserving persons and protection offered to all creatures never perish.

Commentary: The *saṅkīrtana yajña* of Lord Śrī Caitanya Mahāprabhu is the prescribed method of imperishable religious sacrifice for this age. In Kali-yuga, the proper way to offer everlasting protection to the world is to worship God through public congregational chanting of the *mahā-mantra:*

Hare Kṛṣṇa Hare Kṛṣṇa Kṛṣṇa Kṛṣṇa Hare Hare
Hare Rāma Hare Rāma Rāma Rāma Hare Hare

ŚLOKA 16.15

तृणं लघु तृणात्तूलं तूलादपि च याचकः ।
वायुना किं न नीतोऽसौ मामयं याचयिष्यति ॥१५॥

tṛṇaṁ laghu tṛṇāt tūlaṁ
tūlād api ca yācakaḥ
vāyunā kiṁ na nīto 'sau
mām ayaṁ yācayiṣyati

A blade of grass is light, cotton is lighter still, yet far lighter than either is the beggar. Why then does not Vāyu blow him away? Because the wind god fears that the beggar will ask him for alms.

Commentary: It is said that:

> Facial contortions, a low pleading voice, perspiration and a frightened appearance are features that beggars have in common with people who are on their death bed. (GP 1.115.77)

An important lesson of *nīti-śāstra,* especially as contained here in chapter sixteen, is self-reliance. One should earn with dignity by one's own efforts, and be satisfied with one's own destined allotment. By taking from others and doing nothing in return, a karmic cycle is continued from which extraction is difficult. Consider the following:

> O misers of this world! The beggar requesting your charity with the words 'please give' is really teaching by his example the result of not giving. Do not become like them. (GP 1.109.25)

Verses fourteen and fifteen illustrate the difference between an offering to a learned *brāhmaṇa,* which infinitely blesses the donor, and money uselessly thrown away on a habitual beggar. When devotees of the International Society for Kṛṣṇa Consciousness collect alms from willing givers, and use those funds as per the directions of the *ācārya,* then not only the donor but the entire world is benefited.

ŚLOKA 16.16

वरं प्राणपरित्यागो मानभङ्गेन जीवनात् ।
प्राणत्यागे क्षणं दुःखं मानभङ्गे दिने दिने ॥१६॥

varaṁ prāṇa-parityāgo
māna-bhaṅgena jīvanāt
prāṇa-tyāge kṣaṇaṁ duḥkhaṁ
māna-bhaṅge dine dine

Death is preferable to a life of dishonor and infamy. The loss of life causes but a moment's pain, but disgrace brings grief day after day.

Commentary: This is the same logic—and *nīti*—that Lord Śrī Kṛṣṇa presented to Arjuna, thereby inciting the bewildered warrior into battle. Kṛṣṇa said:

> If you do not fight, people will always speak of your infamy. For an honorable man, dishonor is worse than death. (Bg 2.34)

Śrī Īśopaniṣad gives this direction for longevity in Kṛṣṇa consciousness:

> Everything animate or inanimate that is within the universe is controlled and owned by the Lord. One should therefore accept only those things necessary for himself, which are set aside as his quota, and one should not accept other things, knowing well to whom they belong. One may aspire to live for hundreds of years if he continuously goes on working in that way, for that sort of work will not bind him to the law of *karma*. There is no alternative to this way for man. (SI 1–2)

ŚLOKA 16.17

प्रियवाक्यप्रदानेन सर्वे तुष्यन्ति जन्तवः ।
तस्मात्तदेव वक्तव्यं वचने का दरिद्रता ॥१७॥

priya-vākya-pradānena
sarve tuṣyanti jantavaḥ
tasmāt tad eva vaktavyaṁ
vacane kā daridratā

Words imbued with love are pleasing to all creatures. There is no question of poverty when it comes to sweet words. Why then speak words devoid of pleasantness?

Commentary: Neither does *priya-vākya,* sweetly spoken speech, cost anything.

ŚLOKA 16.18

संसारविषवृक्षस्य द्वे फले अमृतोपमे ।
सुभाषितं च सुस्वादु सङ्गतिः सज्जने जने ॥१८॥

saṁsāra-viṣa-vṛkṣasya
dve phale amṛtopame
subhāṣitaṁ ca susvādu
saṅgatiḥ saj-jane jane

There are two nectarean fruits hanging from the poisonous tree of this world. The first is pleasant conversation, and second is the company of saintly men.

Commentary: A devotee fulfills the requirements of verses 16.17 and 16.18 by speaking from the vantage point of these three: *guru, sādhu, śāstra.*

ŚLOKA 16.19

जन्मजन्मनि चाभ्यस्तं दानमध्ययनं तपः ।
तेनैवाभ्यासयोगेन देही चाभ्यस्यते पुनः ॥१९॥

janma-janmani cābhyastaṁ
dānam adhyayanaṁ tapaḥ
tenaivābhyāsa-yogena
dehī cābhyasyate punaḥ

The good habits of charity, learning and austerity practiced during many past lives continue to be cultivated in this birth by virtue of the link of this life to the previous.

Commentary: As past good deeds provide the propellant for this birth, so any evil deeds performed here and now can ruin future lifetimes.

ŚLOKA 16.20

पुस्तकस्था तु या विद्या परहस्तगतं धनं ।
कार्यकाले समुत्पन्ने न सा विद्या न तद्धनम् ॥२०॥

pustaka-sthā tu yā vidyā
para-hasta-gataṁ dhanaṁ
kārya-kāle samutpanne
na sā vidyā na tad dhanam

Knowledge sitting in books and wealth in the hands of others can not be used at the time of need.

Commentary: This verse describes modern education based upon volumes of impractical subjects stored on dusty shelves, and modern wealth based upon credit. *The Devil's Dictionary* defines: "*Erudition, n.* Dust shaken out of a book into an empty skull."

Wealth that has been hijacked by creditors like the government, usurious banks and greedy in-laws is as useful as learning that has no practical value. Perhaps this verse is the best description of modern civilization wherein people are helplessly forced to waste their precious lives learning things they'll never use so they can go into debt to the banks and government forever. The ultimate wisdom of *nīti-śāstra* is to keep one eye on a practical, useful, honest, responsible, fulfilled and constructive life; while the other eye is focused upon spiritual development or Kṛṣṇa consciousness. "Live wisely both here and hereafter."

Thus Ends Chapter Sixteen

CHAPTER SEVENTEEN

ŚLOKA 17.1

पुस्तकप्रत्ययाधीतं नाधीतं गुरुसन्निधौ ।
सभामध्ये न शोभन्ते जारगर्भा इव स्त्रियः ॥१॥

pustaka-pratyayādhītaṁ
nādhītaṁ guru-sannidhau
sabhā-madhye na śobhante
jāra-garbhā iva striyaḥ

The scholar who has acquired knowledge through studying innumerable books but has not studied in the presence of a bona fide spiritual master does not shine in an assembly of learned men, just as the mother of illegitimate children is not honored in society.

Commentary: What better description of modern academia than this verse? Herewith Cāṇakya Paṇḍita underscores the importance of spiritual initiation, comparing unauthorized scholars to mothers without legitimate husbands. As a bee cannot taste the honey sealed within a glass jar, so one who studies the *śāstras* without the guidance of a bona fide spiritual master cannot understand their meaning. Many so-called Indologists arose during the late nineteenth century, but their

Sanskrit studies only served to enhance their own prejudice against Vedic culture. The blessings of a self-realized soul are absolutely necessary to illuminate the depth of the revealed *śāstras* culminating in genuine spiritual realization. Without the sanction of the spiritual master the secrets of *śāstra* will remain locked tight, and studies will end in useless dry speculations. Those who are without any link to the *paramparā* system of disciplic succession, yet try to comment on the Vedic *śāstras,* only offend the very texts they claim to illuminate.

Since time immemorial, this authorized system of transmitting knowledge from *guru* to disciple has been acknowledged by all genuine authorities. Even Lord Kṛṣṇa accepted Sāndīpani Muni as His spiritual master, and resided at his *guru's* Avantikā *āśrama* as a young *brahmacārī.* Likewise, Śrī Caitanya Mahāprabhu accepted initiation from Śrī Īśvara Purī at Gayā. This method is explained by Lord Kṛṣṇa Himself in the *Bhagavad-gītā:*

evaṁ paramparā-prāptam imaṁ rājarṣayo viduḥ
sa kāleneha mahatā yogo naṣṭaḥ parantapa

> This supreme science was thus received through the chain of disciplic succession, and the saintly kings understood it in that way. But in course of time the succession was broken, and therefore the science as it is appears to be lost. (Bg 4.2)

Our spiritual master without whose blessings and guidance this work would not have been possible, was not only a great scholar but he could recall countless thousands of *ślokas* from memory. He is recognized as the current *ācārya* in his disciplic line. He was the leading disciple of his spiritual master Śrī Śrīmad Oṁ Viṣṇupāda Bhaktisiddhānta Sārasvatī Gosvāmī Mahārāja, the *ācārya* of the Gauḍīya Vaiṣṇava *sampradāya* in the first half of the twentieth century. In his Bhaktivedanta purport to *Śrīmad-Bhāgavatam* (6.3.20–21) Śrīla Prabhupāda states:

In the *Padma Purāṇa* it is said, *sampradāya-vihīnā ye mantrās te niṣphalā matāḥ*: if one does not follow the four recognized disciplic successions, his *mantra* or initiation is useless. In the present day there are many *apasampradāyas,* or *sampradāyas* which are not bona fide, which have no link to authorities like Lord Brahmā, Lord Śiva, the Kumāras or Lakṣmī. People are misguided by such *sampradāyas.* The *śāstras* say that being initiated in such a *sampradāya* is a useless waste of time, for it will never enable one to understand the real religious principles.

ŚLOKA 17.2

कृते प्रतिकृतिं कुर्याद्धिंसने प्रतिहिंसनम् ।
तत्र दोषो न पतति दुष्टे दुष्टं समाचरेत् ॥२॥

kṛte prati-kṛtiṁ kuryād
dhiṁsane prati-hiṁsanam
tatra doṣo na patati
duṣṭe duṣṭaṁ samācaret

The favors of others should be repaid by acts of kindness. Likewise cruel behavior may be returned with cruelty. There is no sinful reaction if a wicked fellow is remunerated in his own coin.

Commentary: Cāṇakya Paṇḍita set the example by repaying the corrupt Nanda kings in their own currency, and by installing King Candragupta Maurya on the throne of Magadha. The great Cāṇakya saved the entire sub-continent of India through this ideology, one which is superior to transforming oneself into a docile sheep for slaughter by turning the other cheek. As Śrīla Prabhupāda writes:

> One should act to satisfy the Supreme Lord. For example, Arjuna was a *kṣatriya.* He was hesitating to fight the other party. But if such fighting is performed for the sake of Kṛṣṇa, the Supreme Personality of Godhead, there need be no fear of degradation. (Bg 18.47, purport)

In the Age of Kali, however, the Lord is more merciful than ever before as shown by the deliverance of Jagāi and Mādhāi. Therefore, we are attempting to follow the example of Śrīla Rūpa Gosvāmī who upon meeting Mahāprabhu at Prayāga prayed:

namo mahā-vadānyāya kṛṣṇa-prema-pradāya te
kṛṣṇāya kṛṣṇa-caitanya-nāmne gaura-tviṣe namaḥ

> O most munificent incarnation! You are Kṛṣṇa Himself appearing as Śrī Kṛṣṇa Caitanya Mahāprabhu. You have assumed the golden color of Śrīmatī Rādhārāṇī, and You are widely distributing pure love of Kṛṣṇa. We offer our respectful obeisances unto You. (Cc 2.19.53)

ŚLOKA 17.3

यद्दूरं यद्दुराराध्यं यच्च दूरे व्यवस्थितम् ।
तत्सर्वं तपसा साध्यं तपो हि दुरतिक्रमम् ॥३॥

yad dūraṁ yad durārādhyaṁ
yac ca dūre vyavasthitam
tat sarvaṁ tapasā sādhyaṁ
tapo hi duratikramam

That which is distant, that which appears impossible, and that which is far beyond our reach can easily be brought into our hands by tapasya, for nothing can defeat religious austerity.

Commentary: The *Bhāgavata* describes the *tapasya* of Dhruva Mahārāja. Pleased with the boy's austerities, Lord Nārāyaṇa appeared before him and spoke:

> My dear Dhruva, I shall award you the glowing planet known as the polestar which will continue to exist even after the dissolution at the end of the millennium. No one has ever ruled this planet, which is surrounded by all the solar systems, planets and stars. All the

luminaries in the sky circumambulate this planet, just as bulls tread around a central pole for the purpose of crushing grains. Keeping the polestar to their right, all stars inhabited by the great sages like Dharma, Agni, Kaśyapa and Śukra circumambulate this planet, which continues to exist even after the dissolution of all others. (SB 4.9.20–21)

ŚLOKA 17.4

लोभश्चेदगुणेन किं पिशुनता यद्यस्ति किं पातकैः
सत्यं चेत्तपसा च किं शुचि मनो यद्यस्ति तीर्थेन किम् ।
सौजन्यं यदि किं गुणैः सुमहिमा यद्यस्ति किं मण्डनैः
सद्विद्या यदि किं धनैरपयशो यद्यस्ति किं मृत्युना ॥४॥

lobhaś ced aguṇena kiṁ piśunatā yady asti kiṁ pātakaiḥ
satyaṁ cet tapasā ca kiṁ śuci mano yady asti tīrthena kim
saujanyaṁ yadi kiṁ guṇaiḥ sumahimā yady asti kiṁ maṇḍanaiḥ
sad-vidyā yadi kiṁ dhanair apayaśo yady asti kiṁ mṛtyunā

What vice could be worse than covetousness? What is more sinful than slander? For one who is truthful, what need is there for religious austerity? For one who has a clean heart, what need for pilgrimage? For a person with a good disposition, are other virtues required? For he who has fame, will other ornaments be required? For he who has practical knowledge, can there be any superior wealth? And if you have lost your reputation, what could there be worse in death?

Commentary: Regarding the last line, there is a saying:

> If you lose your wealth you've lost nothing. If you lose your health you've lost something. But if you lose your character, you've lost everything.

Śrī Kṛṣṇa advises Arjuna:

> If, however, you do not fight this religious war, then you will certainly incur sins for neglecting your duties and thus lose your reputation as a fighter. People will always speak of your infamy, and for one who has been honored, dishonor is worse than death. (Bg 2.33–34)

ŚLOKA 17.5

पिता रत्नाकरो यस्य लक्ष्मीर्यस्य सहोदरा ।
शङ्खो भिक्षाटनं कुर्यान्न दत्तमुपतिष्ठते ॥५॥

pitā ratnākaro yasya
lakṣmīr yasya sahodarā
śaṅkho bhikṣāṭanaṁ kuryān
na dattam upatiṣṭhate

The ocean, abode of precious jewels, is the father of the conch shell. The sister of the conch is the goddess of fortune Lakṣmī. Still, the conch must go from door to door seeking alms [in the hands of a beggar]. It is true, therefore, that we cannot rely on what has been given to us at birth.

Commentary:

> One's happiness, sorrow, or even the womb selected for him, are all in accordance with the actions of his previous life. (GP 1.113.19)

In old India, alms were often collected by holy men carrying a conch shell. Indeed this tradition of charitable solicitation is still observed by disciples, as in the case of your commentator who was trained as a *brahmacārī* collecting alms with a conch shell for the *guru's āśrama* with the *saṅkīrtana* party led by Brahmānanda Prabhu on the streets and parks of New York City in 1968–69. The example given here infers that even if one is born into a wealthy family, he may not be able to enjoy that wealth if such enjoyment is not ordained by destiny.

ŚLOKA 17.6

अशक्तस्तु भवेत्साधुर्ब्रह्मचारी वा निर्धनः ।
व्याधितो देवभक्तश्च वृद्धा नारी पतिव्रता ॥६॥

aśaktas tu bhavet sādhur
brahmacārī vā nirdhanaḥ
vyādhito deva-bhaktaś ca
vṛddhā nārī pati-vratā

He who is devoid of virility becomes a sādhu. He who is without means must become a brahmacārī. He who is ill becomes the Lord's supplicant. As a woman becomes old she becomes devoted to her husband.

Commentary: Those who act without desire and self-motivation are rare.

ŚLOKA 17.7

नान्नोदकसमं दानं न तिथिर्द्वादशी समा ।
न गायत्र्याः परो मन्त्रो न मातुर्दैवतं परम् ॥७॥

nānnodaka-samaṁ dānaṁ
na tithir dvādaśī samā
na gāyatryāḥ paro mantro
na mātur daivataṁ param

There is no offering equal to food and drink. There is no day of the month like Dvādaśī. There is no mantra like the Gāyatrī. There is no devatā worthy of worship like one's own mother.

Commentary: Śrī Kṛṣṇa declares:

gāyatrī chandasām aham

Of poetry I am the Gāyatrī verse, sung daily by *brāhmaṇas.* (Bg 10.35)

Śrīla Prabhupāda comments:

> Because the Gāyatrī *mantra* is especially meant for God realization, it represents the Supreme Lord.

In Vedic culture and civilization the offering of food and drink to guests is a must. In line two Cāṇakya Paṇḍita praises the Dvādaśī *tithi* or twelfth day of the lunar month, a day when the Ekādaśī fast of the previous day has ended for most. However, many continue the *vrata* (vow) by taking only milk on Dvādaśī.

The Vedic calendar measures lunar days in increments of twelve degrees or *tithis*. When the sun and moon are conjoined the presiding phase is the dark moon day, or Amāvasyā. As the quicker moon moves ahead of the sun in waxing mode, the first day or *tithi* of the lunar month called Pratipat becomes manifest. Next, when the moon crosses the distance measuring twelve degrees from the sun, from twelve to twenty-four degrees, the Dvitīyā *tithi* or second day of the moon is in force. There are fifteen *tithis* during the waxing fortnight or *śukla-pakṣa* (literally, "bright wing") and fifteen *tithis* during the waning period or *kṛṣṇa-pakṣa* ("dark wing"). These *tithis* are as follows: Amāvasyā (dark moon), Pratipat, Dvitīyā, Tṛtīyā, Caturthī, Pañcamī, Ṣaṣṭhī, Saptamī, Aṣṭamī, Navamī, Daśamī, Ekādaśī, Dvādaśī, Trayodaśī, Caturdaśī, and Pūrṇimā (full moon). Some calendars, especially in North India and the Gauḍīya calendar, end the month at the full moon. This is the system called *pūrṇimānta.* In the South generally, and in Maharashtra and Gujarat, the month is ended with Amāvasyā, or the *amāvasyānta* system.

This lunar system of monthly measurement still followed in India today is the actual source of the modern calendar. Vedic *ṛṣis* scientifically understood the significance and unique effect of each lunar *tithi* according to each particular month and thus gave daily guidance to the world. This system of lunar influence regarding festival dates, travel, conception of children, opening a business, etc. is based upon *tithi* (lunar day), *nakṣatra* (constellation), *vāra* (day), *yoga* (conjunction of planets) and *kāraṇa* (half of a *tithi*). This science of *pañcāṅga,* or dividing a day into these "five parts," should be understood by devotees.

Regarding one's mother, Vedic culture and civilization insists that she be offered respect as one would respect the Supreme Lord. Indeed the very body we have is a gift from her, and Śrīla Prabhupāda said that in this world there is no purer example of selfless love than that of one's mother. In Vedic society, the parents are cared for in their old age. Unfortunately for the parents nowadays the children are too busy with their own lives so they conveniently lock them away in old age homes. Still other ungrateful offspring become advocates of euthanasia, which is no solution at all since it only shoves the bad *karma* of this body onto the next birth, and implicates the son in the heinous crime of medically-sanctioned murder.

ŚLOKA 17.8

तक्षकस्य विषं दन्ते मक्षिकायास्तु मस्तके ।
वृश्चिकस्य विषं पुच्छे सर्वाङ्गे दुर्जने विषम् ॥८॥

takṣakasya viṣaṁ dante
makṣikāyās tu mastake
vṛścikasya viṣaṁ pucche
sarvāṅge durjane viṣam

Poison is found in the fang of the serpent, in the head of the fly and in the tail of the scorpion, but the wicked are thoroughly saturated with it.

Commentary: Vipers, stinging flies and scorpions are all good company, at least when compared to the envious. *Sarvāṅge durjane viṣam:* "Every limb of the crooked man is poisonous." In fact, due to enviousness of the Supreme Lord such *durjanas* sometimes pen śāstric commentaries claiming that the individual *jīva* soul can become God. Hence books written out of envy of the Supreme Lord must be avoided by serious devotees.

While lecturing from *Śrīmad-Bhāgavatam* (7.9.14) in Māyāpur on 21 February 1976, Śrīla Prabhupāda, quoting a similar verse from *Cāṇakya-śloka,* dilated on this point.

> So (we are discussing) two living creatures. One is the snake, and the other one is a jealous or envious person. So Cāṇakya Paṇḍita said, *sarpāt krūrataraḥ khalaḥ:* 'This envious man is more dangerous than the snake. Than the snake.' Why? He's a human being. Yes, because he's human being and he has got developed consciousness and he has practiced to use the developed consciousness for becoming jealous, he's more dangerous than the snake. So therefore he concludes, *mantrauṣadhi-vaśaḥ sarpaḥ khalaḥ kena nivāryate.* The snake, although by nature he is so [deadly], still, he can be controlled by *mantras* and some herbs. In India they still do that. But this *khalaḥ,* the jealous person, he cannot be pacified any means. Therefore he's more dangerous than the snake. A person who has become jealous and envious, he cannot be controlled either by *mantra* or by bribe or this or that. No.

ŚLOKAS 17.9–10

पत्युराज्ञां विना नारी ह्युपोष्य व्रतचारिणी ।
आयुष्यं हरते भर्तुः सा नारी नरकं व्रजेत् ॥९॥
न दानैः शुद्ध्यते नारी नोपवासशतैरपि ।
न तीर्थसेवया तद्वद्भर्तुः पादोदकैर्यथा ॥१०॥

patyur ājñāṁ vinā nārī
hy upoṣya vrata-cāriṇī
āyuṣyaṁ harate bhartuḥ
sā nārī narakaṁ vrajet

na dānaiḥ śuddhyate nārī
nopavāsa-śatair api
na tīrtha-sevayā tadvad
bhartuḥ pādodakair yathā

The wife who fasts and observes religious vows without the permission of her husband shortens his life and goes to hell. A woman becomes holy not by offering charity, by observing hundreds of fasts, or by going on pilgrimage as by sipping water that has washed her husband's feet.

Commentary: Vedic society, as all other ancient cultures of the earth, prescribes that the husband must dutifully behave as the head of the household. In Vedic culture a chaste wife is honored as the *gṛha-lakṣmī,* or the "goddess of fortune in the home," because in her is invested the home's devotional atmosphere. Blind or heartless restriction of women was never a part of Vedic society.

When women are forced to work in a competitive society that artificially rubber stamps all workers as equals, then the atmosphere of the abandoned home is rendered sterile. Further, whatever the would-be *gṛha-lakṣmī* makes as her salary, the sly government, mortgage holder or landlord blithely steal by raising the taxes, rates and monthly household payments. Neither does it hurt the wife to offer a little respect to the husband who cares for her despite the opinions heard on liberated women's TV talk shows. Today the Western world is overflowing with literally millions of lovelorn divorcees who bitterly regret not having respected the man who years earlier walked away from a relationship of artificially forced equality.

ŚLOKA 17.11

पादशेषं पीतशेषं सन्ध्याशेषं तथैव च ।
श्वानमूत्रसमं तोयं पीत्वा चान्द्रायणं चरेत् ॥११॥

pāda-śeṣaṁ pīta-śeṣaṁ
sandhyā-śeṣaṁ tathaiva ca
śvāna-mūtra-samaṁ toyaṁ
pītvā cāndrāyaṇaṁ caret

That water which remains after washing the feet, after drinking or after the performance of sandhyā is equal to dog's urine. He who drinks it should perform a cāndrāyaṇa-vrata.

Commentary: The twice-born recite the Gāyatrī *mantra* in adoration of the sun god at the *sandhyā* (meeting points) of: (1) night with day (sunrise), (2) morning with afternoon (noon), and (3) day with night (sunset). According to our Guru Mahārāja:

> The meaning of Gāyatrī *mantra* is *gāyat. Gāyat* means 'sin,' and *trī* means 'deliverance.' Gāyatrī. And *mantra, man*—means 'mind,' *tra* means 'deliverance.'(Letter, 21 October 1968)

Hence that water used in the prayer is considered contaminated through expiation. Cāṇakya Paṇḍita praises the Gāyatrī *mantra* in 17.7.

The *cāndrāyaṇa-vrata* is the *vrata* (vow) regulated by the moon. It involves the penance of fasting on the Amāvasyā day, eating one mouthful on the Pratipat day, two on the next and so on until the full moon when fifteen mouthfuls are allowed. The next day, Caturdaśī of the *kṛṣṇa-pakṣa,* fourteen mouthfuls are allowed, then thirteen until the dark of the moon when the fast is ended after thirty days.

The intended meaning is that if such a great vow must be undertaken for the relatively mild offenses mentioned above, then what of other offenses common to Kali-yuga, namely illicit sex, meat eating, gambling and intoxication. Lord Caitanya knew the difficulty of the situation and prescribed one *mantra*—the *mahā-mantra*—as the only remedy for people hopelessly adrift in this iron age of quarrel and hypocrisy. Therefore to remain free from sinful reactions, devotees must always chant:

Hare Kṛṣṇa Hare Kṛṣṇa Kṛṣṇa Kṛṣṇa Hare Hare
Hare Rāmā Hare Rāmā Rāmā Rāmā Hare Hare

ŚLOKA 17.12

दानेन पाणिर्न तु कङ्कणेन
स्नानेन शुद्धिर्न तु चन्दनेन ।
मानेन तृप्तिर्न तु भोजनेन
ज्ञानेन मुक्तिर्न तु मण्डनेन ॥१२॥

dānena pāṇir na tu kaṅkaṇena
snānena śuddhir na tu candanena
mānena tṛptir na tu bhojanena
jñānena muktir na tu maṇḍanena

Golden ornaments do not adorn the hand as do acts of charity. The body is cleansed by bathing, rather than smearing sandalwood pulp [or other scents] upon it. One is more satisfied with an offering of respect than an offer of dinner. Realized knowledge is the key to salvation, not dressing in fine clothes.

Commentary: One must realize what *mukti* (salvation) actually is. Lord Kṛṣṇa is known as Mukunda, the giver of liberation. *Śrīmad-Bhāgavatam* (3.29.13) lists five types of liberation, which are:

(1) *sāyujya* (or *ekatva*): impersonal liberation or merging into the spiritual rays of the *brahma-jyoti* effulgence which emanate from the all-transcendental body of the Supreme Personality of Godhead Viṣṇu; (2) *sārūpya:* obtaining a spiritual form resembling the Supreme Lord; (3) *sāmīpya:* association with the Supreme Lord; (4) *sālokya:* dwelling upon the same spiritual planet as the Lord Himself in Vaikuṇṭha, "the world of no fear;" and (5) *sārṣṭi:* having spiritual opulence equal to that of the Lord.

The first, or *sāyujya,* might be achieved by impersonalists after many births. Because remaining desireless is very difficult, even once achieving the immortal bliss of Brahman, the impersonalist *jñānī* may still fall from the *sāyujya* platform and return here to the *mṛtyu-loka* planets where birth and death follow in short order.

The forms of liberation numbered as two to five above are termed Vaiṣṇava or "personalist" liberation. In a word, the difference between impersonalism and personalism is this: to think of oneself as spirit is impersonal, to act as spirit is personal. Devotional service at Śrī Kṛṣṇa's lotus feet or *bhakti-yoga* is the personalist's sure and certain key to liberation. Thus liberation is not achieved by one's own efforts alone, it is offered by the Lord to qualified *bhaktas.* Nor does liberation mean that the infinite *jīva* particle becomes God, rather to achieve liberation it is required that the separated and disenfranchised living entity free himself from *māyā* through surrender unto his eternal constitutional position of devotional service as subordinate to Kṛṣṇa. In the four forms of Vaiṣṇava liberation, rather than extinguishing all desires, a devotee dovetails his individual identity and personal traits in the Lord's loving devotional service.

ŚLOKA 17.13

नापितस्य गृहे क्षौरं पाषाणे गन्धलेपनम् ।
आत्मरूपं जले पश्यञ्शक्रस्यापि श्रियं हरेत् ॥१३॥

nāpitasya gṛhe kṣauraṁ
pāṣāṇe gandha-lepanam
ātma-rūpaṁ jale paśyañ
śakrasyāpi śriyaṁ haret

He who has his hair shaved in a barber's shop, spends time grinding sandalwood paste for his own forehead, or admires his own reflection in water, will have his prosperity taken away, even if he is Indra himself.

Commentary: Immediately after shaving, Vedic standards of cleanliness demand taking a bath. Sandalwood pulp is meant for adorning the Deities of the household, and afterwards that which remains may be accepted as *prasāda.* Vanity and self-love are the downfall of the miser, and Cāṇakya Paṇḍita has elucidated upon the fate of the miser in several earlier *ślokas.* The so-called beauty of the body gradually fades away with the daily rising and setting of the sun. All opulence attached to the physical body, even that which belongs to the demigods, is swept away by the tide of time. However, activities performed in Kṛṣṇa consciousness yield eternal merit.

ŚLOKA 17.14

सद्यः प्रज्ञाहरा तुण्डी सद्यः प्रज्ञाकरी वचा ।
सद्यः शक्तिहरा नारी सद्यः शक्तिकरं पयः ॥१४॥

sadyaḥ prajñā-harā tuṇḍī
sadyaḥ prajñā-karī vacā
sadyaḥ śakti-harā nārī
sadyaḥ śakti-karaṁ payaḥ

Eating the tuṇḍī gourd deprives a man of his sense, while administering the vacā root revives his reasoning immediately. A woman robs a man of his vigor while milk restores it in an instant.

Commentary: It is said that many mouthfuls of food must be processed by the body to produce a drop of blood. Many drops of blood are required for a man's body to create a drop of semen. A man should protect his luster, strength and health by avoiding illicit or excessive sexual contact. Not only does moral decline produce unwanted population, the bane of any society, but illicit sex is directly responsible for impotence and venereal epidemics, the feared STDs. In some parts of the world today, especially Africa, as much as thirty per cent of the virile men are afflicted with deadly AIDS. Śrīla

Prabhupāda specified that sex should be restricted to husband and wife, and therein employed solely for procreative purposes.

Tuṇḍī, the ivy gourd, also known as *Cephalandra indica* or *Goccinia grandis,* is sometimes identified with the *kundru* plant. The *vacā* is an aromatic root also called *Acorus calamus,* known for its ability to improve mental acumen.

ŚLOKA 17.15

परोपकरणं येषां जागर्ति हृदये सताम् ।
नश्यन्ति विपदस्तेषां सम्पदः स्युः पदे पदे ॥१५॥

paropakaraṇaṁ yeṣāṁ
jāgarti hṛdaye satām
naśyanti vipadas teṣāṁ
sampadaḥ syuḥ pade pade

He who nurtures benevolence for all creatures within his heart overcomes difficulty and receives many types of riches step by step.

Commentary: Not only does the naturally kind-hearted person accrue good *karma,* but he becomes blessed by the Supreme Lord to advance towards devotional service. Kṛṣṇa tells Arjuna:

> One who is not envious but is a kind friend to all creatures, who does not think himself a proprietor, who is free from false ego and equal both in happiness and distress, who is always satisfied and engaged in devotional service with determination, and whose mind and intelligence are fixed upon Me—he is very dear to Me. (Bg 12.13–14)

ŚLOKA 17.16

यदि रामा यदि च रमा यदि तनयो विनयगुणोपेतः ।
तनये तनयोत्पत्तिः सुरवरनगरे किमाधिक्यम् ॥१६॥

yadi rāmā yadi ca ramā
yadi tanayo vinaya-guṇopetaḥ
tanaye tanayotpattiḥ
sura-vara-nagare kim ādhikyam

What is there to be enjoyed in the world of Lord Indra for one whose wife is loving and virtuous, who possesses wealth, who has a well-behaved son endowed with good qualities and who has grandchildren born of his son?

Commentary: Since such a fortunate person as described here has Nandana (the garden of Indra) on earth, what is the use of hankering after the enjoyments of Svarga? *Śukra-nīti* advises:

> One should be a gentleman with women and speak sweetly to them without becoming a slave.

It is therefore best to be satisfied with this life, never hankering for increased sense pleasures. Our time and efforts should be aimed towards going back to home, back to Godhead by engaging in Kṛṣṇa-*bhakti.*

According to Kiśora Dāsa, this peculiar verse form with an uneven number of syllables in each line is known as the *āryā* meter.

ŚLOKA 17.17

आहारनिद्राभयमैथुनानि
सामान्यमेतत्पशुभिर्नराणाम् ।

ज्ञानं नराणामधिको विशेषो
ज्ञानेन हीनाः पशुभिः समानाः ॥१७॥

āhāra-nidrā-bhaya-maithunāni
sāmānyam etat paśubhir narāṇām
jñānaṁ narāṇām adhiko viśeṣo
jñānena hīnāḥ paśubhiḥ samānāḥ

Mankind has eating, sleeping, fearing and mating in common with the lower animals. That in which man excels the beasts is discretionary knowledge. Hence indiscreet men who are without knowledge should be regarded as beasts.

Commentary: A stray mutt mates with a bitch in the street while the film hero "makes love" in a fancy bed. Wild animals bare fangs at one another, while a nuclear superpower saturates a defenseless country with bombs. A royal family enjoys a banquet of fillet served on silver while a jungle predator rips his victim to shreds with claws and fangs. In Kali-yuga, there is actually very little difference between men and animals, other than the leg count and "polish" on the bodies. In CN 3.7 Cāṇakya Paṇḍita refers to such men as *dvipadaḥ paśuḥ.* Quite simply, human life is meant for self-realization, without which man remains a manicured beast.

The *Gītā* advises that the tight knot of lust that binds the individual to the cycle of *saṁsāra* must be cut loose with the sword of discrimination and knowledge. As stated, *nīti-śāstra* is useful in helping man center his life both here and hereafter. The *Śukra-nīti* (1.5–6) advises:

> The *nīti-śāstra* is the root of *dharma, artha* and *kāma* as well as the bestower of *mokṣa.* Therefore rulers should carefully put its lessons into practice.

There is a similar verse in the *Hitopadeśa:*

āhāra-nidrā-bhaya-maithunaṁ ca
sāmānyam etat paśubhir narāṇām
dharmo hi teṣām adhiko viśeṣo
dharmeṇa hīnāḥ paśubhiḥ samānāḥ

> Both animals and men share the activities of eating, sleeping, mating and defending. But the special property of the humans is that they are able to engage in spiritual life. Therefore without spiritual life, humans are on the level of animals.

Regarding *maithuna* or sex life, mentioned in this verse, *Śrīmad-Bhāgavatam* (7.9.45) famously states: *yan maithunādi-gṛhamedhi-sukhaṁ hi tucchaṁ.* "Sex and the so-called pleasures of the envious householder are insignificant." In his purport to that verse, Śrīla Prabhupāda comments,

> Prahlāda Mahārāja therefore advises one not to be misled by this civilization of sense gratification, and especially not by sex life. Rather, one should be sober, avoid sense gratification and be Kṛṣṇa conscious. The lusty person, who is compared to a foolish miser, never gets happiness by sense gratification. The influence of material nature is very difficult to surpass, but as stated by Kṛṣṇa in *Bhagavad-gītā* (7.14), *mām eva ye prapadyante, māyām etāṁ taranti te:* if one voluntarily submits to the lotus feet of Kṛṣṇa, he can be saved very easily.

ŚLOKA 17.18

दानार्थिनो मधुकरा यदि कर्णतालै-
दूरीकृताः करिवरेण मदान्धबुद्ध्या ।
तस्यैव गण्डयुगमण्डनहानिरेषा
भृङ्गाः पुनर्विकचपद्मवने वसन्ति ॥१८॥

dānārthino madhukarā yadi karṇa-tālair
dūrī-kṛtāḥ kari-vareṇa madāndha-buddhyā

tasyaiva gaṇḍa-yuga-maṇḍana-hānir eṣā
bhṛṅgāḥ punar vikaca-padma-vane vasanti

If the bees which seek the liquid oozing from the head of a lust-intoxicated elephant are driven away by the flapping of his ears, then it is the elephant who has lost the ornament of his temples, while the bees are quite happy in a lake filled with blooming lotuses.

Commentary: Just as a bee collects nectar, so a devotee draws out the essence of life. Therefore, if *bhaktas* are chased away by the narrow-minded, they will drink nectar elsewhere. The *sādhu* does not approach materialists for his own personal benefit. The presence of a *sādhu* in society is a blessing for the entire society, whether the narrow-minded appreciate him or not.

ŚLOKA 17.19

राजा वेश्या यमश्चाग्निश्चौरो बालकयाचकौ ।
परदु:खं न जानन्ति अष्टमो ग्रामकण्टक: ॥१९॥

rājā veśyā yamaś cāgniś
cauro bālaka-yācakau
para-duḥkhaṁ na jānanti
aṣṭamo grāma-kaṇṭakaḥ

These seven cannot understand the sufferings of others: the king, the prostitute, Yamarāja, fire, a thief, a young boy and a beggar. The eighth of this category is the tax collector.

Commentary: Add to this list the parking meter maid and the usurer known as the loan officer at the bank. In Kali-yuga there is no dearth of heartless people milling here and there waiting patiently to increase your misery. It is fruitless to seek sympathy from the materialist. Therefore, one must associate with genuine devotees to alleviate suffering caused by past *karma*. In contrast to the *karmī* who is described here as *para-duḥkhaṁ na jānanti* (unable to feel another's pain), the Vaiṣṇava is *para-duḥkha-duḥkhī* or even willing to take upon himself the reactions of the sins of others to relieve their suffering. *Grāma-kaṇṭaka* (lit. "thorn in the village"), aside from denoting a tax collector, can also be a term that the local council (*panchayat*) would use to censure a village resident who misbehaves.

ŚLOKA 17.20

अधः पश्यसि किं बाले पतितं तव किं भुवि ।
रे रे मूर्ख न जानासि गतं तारुण्यमौक्तिकम् ॥२०॥

adhaḥ paśyasi kiṁ bāle
patitaṁ tava kiṁ bhuvi
re re mūrkha na jānāsi
gataṁ tāruṇya-mauktikam

"Lady, why do you gaze downward? Has something of yours dropped to the ground?" [She replies:] "You fool! Can you not understand that the pearl of my youth has fallen away?"

Commentary: Truly, life is fleeting. All that we call ours now will soon be lost by the influence of the all-powerful time factor. Here Cāṇakya Paṇḍita reminds us of this fact before he draws his *nīti-śāstra* to a close. The spot life we now occupy has the power to make or break our destiny. Proper use of this human form of life can save us from serving our time like prisoners for billions and billions of years in this material jail. The lessons contained herein should be seriously weighed while we still enjoy the facility of the human form of life. The choice is ours. By the grace of Śrī Guru and Gaurāṅga, we can go back to home, back to Godhead in this very life.

ŚLOKA 17.21

व्यालाश्रयापि विफलापि सकण्टकापि
वक्रापि पङ्कसहितापि दुरासदापि ।
गन्धेन बन्धुरसि केतकि सर्वजन्तो-
रेको गुणः खलु निहन्ति समस्तदोषान् ॥२१॥

vyālāśrayāpi viphalāpi sakaṇṭakāpi
vakrāpi paṅka-sahitāpi durāsadāpi
gandhena bandhur asi ketaki sarva-jantor
eko guṇaḥ khalu nihanti samasta-doṣān

O ketakī flower! Serpents live in your midst, you bear no edible fruits, your leaves are covered with thorns, your stature is crooked, you thrive in mud and you are not easily accessible. Still for your exceptional fragrance you are as dear as a kinsman to others. Hence, a single excellence overcomes a multitude of blemishes.

Commentary: We reflect upon this *śloka* when visiting the *agarbaṭṭi-wālās* in Bombay because they have some of the best *ketakī* (or *kewra*) incense in the world. Why does Cāṇakya Paṇḍita end his great *nīti-śāstra* with this verse? If we can improve ourselves by absorbing one lesson at a time from this great book of learning, as a pleasant aroma is inhaled slowly, then our time studying these words will be well spent!

Thus Ends Chapter Seventeen

APPENDIX I

Cāṇakya-śloka

As a young student, Śrīla Prabhupāda studied a Sanskrit/Bengali version of *Śrī Cāṇakya-nīti* called *Cāṇakya-śloka.* Several of the *ślokas* that His Divine Grace would recall from that version are not found among the verses of the standard Sanskrit or English editions that we have come across. Gathered hereunder are several of those *ślokas,* or even just significant lines from them, along with Śrīla Prabhupāda's lucid explanations.

Text: Teachings of Queen Kuntī, ch. 22

pṛthivī-bhūṣaṇaṁ rājā nārīnāṁ bhūṣaṇaṁ patiḥ
śarvarī-bhūṣaṇaṁ candro vidyā sarvasya bhūṣaṇam

Translation: The earth is beautified by a good king; a woman appears beautiful in the presence of her husband; the moon is the ornament of the world; learning beautifies everything.

Śrīla Prabhupāda's comments: There are certain particular marks on the feet of the Lord which distinguish the Lord from others. The marks of a flag, thunderbolt, and instrument to drive an elephant, and also an umbrella, lotus, disc, etc., are on the bottom of the Lord's feet. These marks are impressed upon the soft dust of the land where the Lord traverses. The land of Hastināpura was thus marked while Lord Śrī Kṛṣṇa was there with the Pāṇḍavas, and the kingdom of the Pāṇḍavas thus flourished by such auspicious signs. Kuntīdevī points out these distinguished features and is afraid of ill luck in the absence of the Lord.

In the *Cāṇakya-śloka,* the instructions of the great moralist Cāṇakya Paṇḍita, there is this very nice verse:

pṛthivī-bhūṣaṇaṁ rājā nārīnāṁ bhūṣaṇaṁ patiḥ
śarvarī-bhūṣaṇaṁ candro vidyā sarvasya bhūṣaṇam

Everything looks beautiful when one is intimately related with it. The sky, for example, becomes beautiful in relationship with the moon. The sky is always present, but on the full-moon night, when the moon and stars shine brilliantly, it looks very nice. Similarly, the state looks very well if there is a good government, with a good king or president. Then everyone is happy, and everything goes on nicely. Also, although girls are naturally beautiful, a girl looks especially beautiful when she has a husband. *Vidyā sarvasya bhūṣaṇam:* but if a person, however ugly, is a learned scholar that is his beauty. Similarly, everything will look beautiful when Kṛṣṇa is present.

Therefore Kuntīdevī thinks, "As long as Kṛṣṇa is with us, everything in our kingdom and our capital, Hastināpura, is beautiful. But when Kṛṣṇa is absent our kingdom will not be beautiful." She says, "Kṛṣṇa, You are now walking in our kingdom, and the impressions of Your footprints are making everything beautiful. There is sufficient water and fruit, and everything looks beautiful, but when You leave us it will not look beautiful."

Lecture: Śrīmad-Bhāgavatam 5.5.3—Stockholm, 9 September 1973

ajā-yuddhe muni-śrāddhe prabhāte megha-garjane
dāmpatya-kalahe caiva bahv-ārambhe laghu-kriyā

Translation: That which appears great but which does not produce much can be compared to either the *śrāddha* ceremony of *munis,* the fighting of goats, clouds in the morning or a quarrel between a husband and wife.

Śrīla Prabhupāda's comments: What is the use of keeping big, big paraphernalia? *Bahv-ārambhe laghu-kriyā. Ārambha.* Although the arrangement is very big no work is going on. What is the use of keeping a useless machine? So that is going on in the material world where everything is *bahv-ārambhe laghu-kriyā.* That has been spoken by Cāṇakya Paṇḍita. *Ajā-yuddhe muni-śrāddhe. Ajā-yuddhe. Ajāḥ* means goats. Have you seen goats fighting? It is as if two great heroes are fighting. But as soon as somebody comes and says: "Hut!" they'll go away. Have you seen, experienced? Goats and lambs, they'll fight: "*Onh, onnh.*" Like this. But, but as soon somebody comes: "Hut!"

So this is one of the examples of *bahv-ārambhe laghu-kriyā. Ārambha.* As if something very serious going to happen... But actually it is insignificant. *Ajā-yuddhe muni-śrāddhe. Muni,* in the jungle, in the forest there are *munis.* So they are arranging for some festival to offer oblations to the forefathers called *śrāddha.* So what do they have? Some fruits and leaves, that's all. So the arrangement may be that "Tomorrow, we are going to have this festival." But the festival means some leaves and some water. That's all. No utensils, no gold, no jewels, nothing of the sort. So this is another *bahv-ārambhe laghu-kriyā.* The arrangement is very big, but in fact nothing happens.

Dāmpatya-kalahe caiva: fighting between a husband and wife. In India, there is no question of divorce. So nobody takes it very seriously when there is a fight between a husband and wife. They may say, "I'm going to immediately leave you... going to kill you...." So many things. But after an hour, everything is finished. No more quarrel. *Dāmpatya-kalahe caiva prabhāte megha-garjane.*

And in the morning, if you see big clouds assembling and hear thunder, then rest assured, there will be no rain. So these things are *bahv-ārambhe laghu-kriyā. Ārambha,* the beginning is very gorgeous. But in the end is there is nothing. So that is not good, *bahv-ārambhe laghu-kriyā.*

So here it is suggested that in this human form of life you have two choices. Either you will again go to hell or you can go back to home, back to Godhead: two choices only. By the evolutionary process you have come to the human form of life after going through eight million forms of lower-grade life. Now you have arrived at this human form of life and your consciousness is developed. You are not exactly like the animals. The animal propensities are there, but it is decent because you have an advanced consciousness. The animals eat; we also eat. But our eating process is more decent than the animals. We have a nice kitchen. We can prepare varieties of foodstuffs by mixing so many ingredients. Because we have a higher intelligence, we can do what the animals cannot do. Similarly, sleeping; the animals sleep and we also sleep. But our apartment is very nice; we have a nice bed and we sleep in an improved way."

Lecture: Śrīmad-Bhāgavatam 7.6.1—San Francisco, 15 March 1968

āyuṣaḥ kṣaṇa eko 'pi na labhyaḥ svarṇa-koṭibhiḥ
na cen nirarthakaṁ nītiḥ kā ca hānis tato 'dhikā

Translation: Do not waste even a second of your life. A single moment which has been wasted cannot be purchased back for ten thousand gold coins. He who wastes his life for no profit becomes the greatest loser.

Śrīla Prabhupāda's comments: So (Prahlāda Mahārāja) was agitating in the school amongst his class fellows to become Kṛṣṇa conscious. So he was preaching. Just in the *tiffin* hour, in the recess hour, as soon as the teacher left, he took the opportunity and stood up on the bench and began to agitate his friends, "My dear friends," *kaumāra ācaret prājñaḥ,* "now we must become Kṛṣṇa conscious from childhood. Do not wait for your old age." Generally, people think, "When we become old, we shall take care of becoming Kṛṣṇa conscious. We shall become God conscious by going to the church or temple. For the present let us play and enjoy life." So Prahlāda Mahārāja says, "No." *Kaumāra ācaret prājñaḥ. Prājñaḥ* means "intelligent." And intelligent means "he who does not waste time." Time is very valuable. You Americans know very well how to utilize time. That time is very valuable is also accepted in Vedic civilization.

There is a very nice verse in *Cāṇakya-śloka* from which you will understand how valuable time was considered. By this verse, you will know. Cāṇakya Paṇḍita was a great politician. He was once the prime minister of the emperor of India. So he says, *āyuṣaḥ kṣaṇa eko 'pi na labhyaḥ svarṇa-koṭibhiḥ.* He says that "A moment's time of the duration of your life, just a moment..." Not to speak of hours and days, but moments. He was considering moment to moment. Just like today, 15th March, 1968. Now it is half past seven or seven thirty-five. Now this 1968, 7:35 will be gone as soon as it is 7:36. You will not be able to bring back that 1968, 15th March, evening, 7:35 ever again. Even if you pay millions of dollars. "Please come back again." No, it is finished. So Cāṇakya Paṇḍita says that "Time is so valuable that even if you pay millions of golden coins, you cannot get back even a moment." What is lost is lost for good. *Na cen nirarthakaṁ nītiḥ:* "If such valuable time is spoiled for nothing, without any profit," *na ca hānis tato 'dhikā,* "just imagine how much you are losing, what a great loser you are." The thing which you cannot get back by paying millions of dollars; if that thing is lost for nothing then how much have you lost? Just imagine.[20]

Lecture: Bhagavad-gītā As It Is 6.4–12—New York City, 4 September 1966

na kaścit kasyacin mitra na kaścit kasyacid ripuḥ
vyavahāreṇa jāyante mitrāṇi ripavas tathā

Translation: Nobody is a born enemy and nobody is a born friend. But by our mutual behavior, somebody becomes my friend and somebody becomes my enemy.

Śrīla Prabhupāda's comments: Nobody is anybody's friend and nobody is anybody's enemy. It is only by one's behavior by which one can understand who is our friend and who is our enemy. Similarly, just as we deal with ordinary daily affairs I have my own dealings with

20. For more on this verse see CN 4.1.

myself. Myself. If I deal with myself as a friend, then I am my friend. And if I deal with myself inimically… Then what is that friendship or enmity? The friendship is that I am soul. Somehow or other, I have been in contact with this material nature. So I have to get myself out of the entanglement of this material nature. If I act in that way, then I am my friend. But even after getting this opportunity, if I do not act in that way, then I am my own enemy. So *ātmaiva hy ātmano bandhur ātmaiva ātmano ripuḥ.* So I am either my own friend or I am my own enemy.

Lecture: Bhagavad-gītā As It Is 16.4—Honolulu, 30 January 1975

sarpaḥ krūraḥ khalaḥ krūraḥ sarpāt krūrataraḥ khalaḥ
mantrauṣadhi-vaśaḥ sarpaḥ khalaḥ kena nivāryate

Translation: Of the two types of cruel serpents, the envious man is worse. A snake can be controlled by mantras but an envious man can never be controlled.

Śrīla Prabhupāda's comments: Cāṇakya Paṇḍita says, *sarpaḥ krūraḥ khalaḥ krūraḥ sarpāt krūrataraḥ khalaḥ.* "Two kinds of *krūraḥ,* envious animals, are there. One is the snake and the other is the envious man." So Cāṇakya Paṇḍita says, "Both of them are envious but the envious man is more dangerous than the envious snake." Why? "Because the snake can be brought into submission by herbs and *mantra.*" There are snake charmers who can chant *mantras,* apply some herb, and bring the snake under subjugation. But *khalaḥ kena nivāryate:* "The snake-like man, he cannot be subdued at any cost."[21]

Purport: Śrīmad-Bhāgavatam 6.11.4

ko 'rthaḥ putreṇa jātena yo na vidvān na dhārmikaḥ
kāṇena cakṣuṣā kiṁ vā cakṣuḥ pīḍaiva kevalam

21. Similar themes are echoed in CN 3.4 and 17.8.

Translation: What is the use of a son who is neither glorious nor devoted to the Lord? Such a son is like a blind eye, which simply gives pain but cannot help one see.[22]

Lecture: Śrīmad-Bhāgavatam 1.16.21—Los Angeles, 11 July 1974

mātā yasya gṛhe nāsti bhāryā cāpriya-vādinī
araṇyaṁ tena gantavyaṁ yathāraṇyaṁ tathā gṛham

Translation: A person who has no mother at home and whose wife is not agreeable with him should immediately renounce his family life and go away to the forest. For such a person, living at home and living in the forest are equal.

Śrīla Prabhupāda's comments: In a family where there is a good mother and good wife, then that is a happy family. And one who has no good mother and good wife, then it is hell. This is Vedic culture. So Cāṇakya Paṇḍita said, *mātā yasya gṛhe nāsti.* If somebody has no mother at home, *bhāryā cāpriya-vādinī,* and the wife is very harsh, dealing with the husband not very properly, *araṇyaṁ tena gantavyam,* he immediately give up that house and go to the forest. This is Cāṇakya Paṇḍita. Then what is the use of such a nonsense house? For him the home is as good as forest. Therefore there is no family system. Everything finished. So only this Kṛṣṇa consciousness movement is trying to bring back Vedic culture so that people may be very happy. It is not a business; it is not a religious sentiment. It is a program to make everyone happy. *Sarve sukhino bhavantu.* This is Vedic culture.[23]

22. For Prabhupāda's comments on this verse see CN 3.15.

23. See also CN 4.16.

Lecture: Śrīmad-Bhāgavatam 1.5.24—Vṛndāvana, 5 August 1975

nirguṇeṣv api sattveṣu dayāṁ kurvanti sādhavaḥ
na hi saṁharate jyotsnāṁ candraś caṇḍāla-veśmani[24]

Translation: Candra does not refuse to shed his rays even on the place where the dog-eaters dwell.

Śrīla Prabhupāda's comments: Just like Kṛṣṇa, He is open to everyone. Kṛṣṇa says *sarva-dharmān parityajya mām ekaṁ śaraṇaṁ vraja.* (Bg 18.66) It is not that Kṛṣṇa is meant for only Arjuna. Just like sunlight is available to everyone; everyone can enjoy it. But if you keep your doors closed then what can the sun do? The sun is *tulya-darśanaḥ.*[25]

There is a verse by Cāṇakya Paṇḍita, *na hi harate jyotsnāṁ candraś caṇḍāla-veśmani. Caṇḍāla. Caṇḍāla* means the lowest caste, lower than the *śūdras.* The meat-eaters in India are called *caṇḍāla,* especially pig-eaters. Still you will see that in villages the sweeper class will capture a pig. They maintain the pigs for selling as well as for eating. So to this day they publicly burn the living pig in the fire. Although it cries like anything, they are still allowed to do it. So, *caṇḍāla-veśmani.* Their place is very polluted and sinful place, but that does not mean that the moonlight is refused there. The moonlight is not refused. Neither the moon nor the sun considers that because it is the residence of a *caṇḍāla* they should be refused. No. Sunlight is equally distributed. *Na hi harate jyotsnāṁ candraś caṇḍāla-veśmani. Candra* means the moon. Similarly, neither Kṛṣṇa nor His devotees

24. Śrīla Prabhupada quoted only the second part of the verse. We quote the entire verse and herewith provide the translation for it:

"Just as the moon does not refuse to shed its light upon the homes of *caṇḍālas,* the saintly persons bestow their mercy even to those who have no good qualities."

25. *Lit.* equally visible to all.

are reluctant to bestow mercy upon anyone. *Tulya...* That is called *tulya-darśanaḥ,* mercy that is available to everyone.

Lecture: Śrīmad-Bhāgavatam 5.5.9—Vṛndāvana, 31 October 1976

dhanāni jīvitaṁ caiva parārthe prājña utsṛjet
san-nimitte varaṁ tyāgo vināśe niyate sati[26]

Translation: Whatever you have will be destroyed. You cannot remain together. Either your riches will leave you, or you will have to leave them.

Śrīla Prabhupāda's comments: So, one has to do it. If he does not do it for God, then he will have to do it ultimately for the dog. Therefore it is better that as long you have money, spend it for God. *San-nimitte varaṁ tyāgo vināśe niyate sati.* It is the instruction of Cāṇakya Paṇḍita that whatever money you have, it will be spent. You cannot keep it. Either the money will leave you or you will have to leave the money. You cannot stay together. That is not possible. If you don't spend the money for Kṛṣṇa, if you keep it, thinking "I shall see it. I shall lick up this money and become happy, then..." The *kṛpaṇas,* misers, hoard their money and do not spend it for Kṛṣṇa.

Therefore this has become a problem for us: how to spend the money? Our policy is how to spend the money for Kṛṣṇa. We do not want to keep money. We cannot keep it; that is not possible. Somebody will take it. Ultimately the government will take it. Better to spend it for Kṛṣṇa. Spend it for Kṛṣṇa—that is the correct use. *San-nimitte varaṁ tyāgo vināśe niya...* Cāṇakya Paṇḍita—he was a great politician and

26. Śrīla Prabhupāda quoted, translated and commented upon the second half of the verse. We quote the entire verse and herewith provide the translation for it:

"A wise man gives up his wealth and even his life for a higher purpose. It is better to renounce it for a good cause than wait for destiny to take it away."

he advises that if you have money, spend it for Kṛṣṇa. Don't keep it. Spend it for Kṛṣṇa. Why? It will be spoiled. Today or tomorrow it will be spoiled. Somebody will take it and spoil it. Better, if you spend it for Kṛṣṇa, at least your service will be recognized. Kṛṣṇa will see that this man is spending his hard-earned money for Me.[27]

Conversation: Vṛndāvana, 25 May 1977

durjanaḥ parihartavyo vidyayālaṅkṛto 'pi san
maṇinā bhūṣitaḥ sarpaḥ kim asau na bhayaṅkaraḥ

Translation: An evil man should be avoided, even though he may be decorated with great knowledge. He is just like a venomous serpent adorned with a jewel on his hood. Is not such a snake fearful?

Śrīla Prabhupāda's comments: Cāṇakya Paṇḍita says, *maṇinā bhūṣitaḥ sarpaḥ kim asau na bhayaṅkaraḥ:* "If a snake has a jewel on his hood, he can find his way in the darkness by the light of the jewel." Then if somebody thinks, "Oh, here is a snake with jewel. Let me embrace him." No, no, no, it is very ferocious. Even if a jewel is there, it is ferocious. Similarly, these people are envious. Although they have become so-called Vaiṣṇavas, they are ferocious. They have not acquired the qualifications of Vaiṣṇavas.

Purport: Śrīmad-Bhāgavatam 9.13.3

śarīrasya guṇānāṁ ca dūram atyantam antaram
śarīraṁ kṣaṇa-vidhvāṁsi kalpānta-sthāyino guṇāḥ[28]

27. For additional comments on this verse see CN 5.9.

28. Śrīla Prabhupāda quoted and translated only the second half of the verse in the purport to SB 9.13.3. We added the first half and herewith provide the translation for the whole verse:

"There is a gulf of difference between the body and one's virtues. The body perishes in a moment but one's virtues remain (in the memory of others) until the dissolution of the material world."

Translation: The duration of one's life in the material world may end at any moment, but if within this life one does something worthy, that qualification is depicted in history eternally.[29]

APPENDIX II

Cāṇakya's ślokas quoted most often by Śrīla Prabhupāda

Are you adept at memorizing *ślokas?* These are Śrīla Prabhupāda's most-often quoted *ślokas* from *Śrī Cāṇakya-nīti:*

— 12.14: "All women are your mother…" (quoted 37 times)[30]
— 4.6: "Moon dispels darkness…" (quoted 29 times)
— 14.19: "Associate with devotees…" (quoted 15 times)
— 1.15: "Women and politicians…" (quoted 14 times)
— 4.14: "Without a son, household life is void…" (quoted 10 times)
— 4.16: "Reject the frowning wife…" (quoted 9 times)[31]
— 3.21: "Where husband and wife do not quarrel…" (quoted 7 times)
— 1.16: "Take gold from an unclean place…" (quoted 6 times)
— 8.20: "A learned man is honored everywhere…" (quoted 6 times)[32]
— 1.5: "Like a serpent in the house…" (quoted 5 times)
— 3.9: "Ugly man's beauty is learning, cuckoo bird…" (quoted 4 times)
— 6.11: "Father in debt, wife too beautiful…" (quoted 4 times)

---

29. See also CN 13.8.

30. This data is culled from the latest version of the Bhaktivedanta Vedabase.

31. The actual verse quoted by Śrīla Prabhupāda is a similar verse from the *Cāṇakya-śloka.* See CN 4.14, commentary.

32. The actual verse quoted by Śrīla Prabhupāda is a similar verse from the *Cāṇakya-śloka.* See CN 8.20, commentary.

— 3.18: "Indulge your son till fifth year..." (quoted 4 times)
— 1.9: "Do not stay for a day..." (quoted one time)
— 6.20: "Learn even from a dog..." (quoted one time)

The following are the *ślokas* which were quoted by Śrīla Prabhupāda but no records of that are found in the archives available at present:

— 1.17: "Women have..."
— 2.11: "Mother and father become enemies..."
— 2.11: "As a stork among swan..."
— 3.7: "Two legged beast..."
— 3.14: "Good son like flowering tree..."
— 3.15: "Bad son like withered tree..."
— 3.16: "Need only one moon..."

APPENDIX III

Principal Nīti-śāstras

Every scripture of the Vedic culture and civilization—from Vālmīki's *Rāmāyaṇa* to thc vast works of Śrīla Vyāsadeva—have scattered elements of morality or *nīti* built in. Following is a list of texts that have been cited or quoted in this volume. Each of the following, except *Manu-saṁhitā,* deals exclusively with *nīti,* and therefore each one is famous today as a *nīti-śāstra.* Abbreviations in parentheses indicate how each is cited in this volume.

1. *Manu-saṁhitā* (MS)—Though not specifically recognized as a *nīti-śāstra,* the *Manu-saṁhitā*—or *Manu-smṛti*—is also filled with common sense advice making it a *nīti-śāstra* of sorts. Known as "the law book for mankind," *Manu-saṁhitā* lays down the codes of behavior or duties for the various classes of society. It is a very ancient text spoken by Manu, whom Lord Kṛṣṇa calls the "father of mankind" in the *Bhagavad-gītā* (4.1).

2. ***Śukra-nīti*** **of Śukrācārya (SN)**—Śukra is celebrated as the *asura-guru* or spiritual master of the demons. Called the presiding deity of planet Venus, Śukra is mentioned in the *Bhagavad-gītā* (10.37) under the name of Uśanā.

3. ***Bṛhaspati-nīti-sāra*** **(GP)**—Bṛhaspati, the *deva-guru* or spiritual master of the demigods, is mentioned in the *Bhagavad-gītā* (10.24). He is the presiding deity of planet Jupiter. His *Nīti-sāra* ("essence of *nīti*") is found in the *Garuḍa Purāṇa.*

4. ***Vidura-nīti*** **(VN)**—Vidura was the incarnation of Lord Yamarāja. Vidura's common sense counsel to his half brother King Dhṛtarāṣṭra went unheeded and thus the Battle of Kurukṣetra had to take place. His instructions to King Dhṛtarāṣṭra, as recorded in the *Mahābhārata,* constitute *Vidura-nīti.*

5. ***Pañcatantra*** **of Paṇḍita Viṣṇuśarmā**—Viṣṇuśarmā was a court *paṇḍita* of King Amaraśakti (c. 400 BC) who had five duds for sons. Through the medium of animal tales, the *paṇḍita* instilled in the princes keener intelligence, wisdom and common sense. *Pañcatantra* became the source of the Greek *Aesop's Fables.*

6. ***Cāṇakya-nīti-śāstra*** **(CN)**—It is mostly derived from older Sanskrit classics and was compiled around 300 BC.

7. ***Nīti-śataka*** **of Bhartṛhari (NS)**—Bhartṛhari was brother to King Vikramāditya of Ujjain, ancient Avantikā. Hindu India still measures years in Vikram Samvat just as the Christian world measures their years from the advent of Jesus Christ (2012 AD = 2068 VS). Bhartṛhari wrote three *śatakas* or "collections of one hundred verses," viz., the *Śṛṅgāra-śataka, Nīti-śataka* and the *Vairāgya-śataka.*

8. ***Hitopadeśa*** **of Nārāyaṇa**—This is a later retelling of moral fables. (c. 1675 AD)

GLOSSARY

A

Ācārya—a *guru* who has realized the import of sacred scriptures. It is often used as a title for the head of a religious institution.

Ādityas—a group of demigod-descendants of sage Kaśyapa and his wife Aditi.

Ādi-deva—the primeval Lord, Supreme Personality of Godhead.

Advaita Ācārya—an incarnation of the Supreme Lord and intimate associate of Lord Caitanya.

Agarbaṭṭi-wālā—a seller of incense.

Age of Kali (Kali-yuga)—the last in the universal cycle of four ages (*yugas*), characterized by an increase in irreligion. It began five thousand years ago. *See:* **Yuga.**

Agni—the fire god. Vedic sacrificial offerings are made to him and are accepted by the other *devas* through him.

Ajāmila—a *brāhmaṇa* (described in *Śrīmad-Bhāgavatam*) who deviated from his prescribed duties but at last attained salvation by calling out the name of his son, Nārāyaṇa, in the moments before his death.

Akbar (1542–1605)—the most influential among the Mogul emperors. The Mogul dynasty dominated parts of India from the sixteenth century until the middle of the nineteenth century.

Anasūyā—the wife of sage Atri, who was known for her chastity. She was tested by the demigods and emerged victorious.

Annapūrṇā(-devī)—(a form of goddess Durgā) a benevolent motherlike figure who feeds all of her dependents.

Aṅkuśa—an elephant goad (usually a metal stick with a sharp tip and a hook), used to control elephants by pressing it on soft spots on their body.

Anuloma—a proper Vedic marital match, wherein the husband is socially superior to the wife.

Apsarā—any heavenly nymph whose primary function is to dance in the court of Lord Indra.

Arcā-vigraha—the Deity form of the Lord or His consort that is worshipped in temples.

Arjuna—a confidential friend of Lord Kṛṣṇa and most famous of the five Pāṇḍava brothers, who were sons of Mahārāja Pāṇḍu and his two queens, Kuntī and Mādrī.

Artha—economic development (one of the four goals of human life according to Vedic scriptures). *See also:* **Dharma, Kāma, Mokṣa.**

Artha-śāstra—the science of politics and economics from the perspective of a Vedic ruler. This compendium was written by Cāṇakya Paṇḍita (also known as Kauṭilya) and even today remains a famous textbook of political science.

Aryan invasion theory—a dubious construct in Indology that posits that the origins of Vedic culture lay outside India and that the race of Aryans moved into India from abroad and subjugated the subcontinent.

Asat—that which is not eternal, true or spiritual. This may refer to matter itself or to persons who are either disinterested in spiritual life or who improperly practice spiritual disciplines.

Āśrama—(1) any of the four orders of Vedic spiritual life: *brahmacarya* (celibate student life), *gṛhastha* (regulated married life), *vānaprastha* (celibate retirement), *sannyāsa* (celibate renounced life); (2) a hermitage or a residential facility for renunciants.

Aṣṭāṅga-yoga—the eightfold *yoga* system, consisting of meditative postures, controlling the breath, concentration, meditation and so on, leading to full absorption (called *samādhi,* or yogic trance).

Asura—a demon.

Asura-guru—the spiritual master of the demons, Śukrācārya.

Ātmā—the spirit soul.

Atharva Veda—one of the four *Vedas,* collections of hymns meant for worshipping demigods. (The other three are the *Ṛg, Sāma* and *Yajur Vedas.*)

Avantikā—an ancient Indian city (now known as Ujjain) in Madhya Pradesh.

Ayodhyā—the capital of King Daśaratha and his son, Lord Rāmacandra, who ruled over the land of Kośala.

Āyur-veda(-śāstra)—the ancient Vedic science of medicine. (*Āyur* refers to longevity.)

B

Bābājī—a reclusive saint who lives away from society and embraces a life of extreme austerity.

Baladeva Vidyābhūṣaṇa—a prominent eighteenth-century Gauḍīya Vaiṣṇava *ācārya.*

Banaras—Vārāṇasī, a holy city in northern India on the bank of the Ganges.

Bazaar—market.

Bhagavad-gītā—a portion of the great epic *Mahābhārata,* and one of the central sacred scriptures of Vaiṣṇavism.

Bhagavān—the Supreme Lord.

Bhāgavata (Purāṇa)—the most prominent of the eighteen *Purāṇas* (ancient histories) and especially relevant to Vaiṣṇavas.

Bhajana—(1) a musical rendering of a devotional poem; (2) intense personal spiritual practice.

Bhajanānandī—"one who takes pleasure in *bhajana*"; a devotee who withdraws from the world and focuses on spiritual practice.

Bhakta—a devotee of the Supreme Lord. *See also:* **Vaiṣṇava.**

Bhakti—*See:* **Devotional service.**

Bhaktisiddhānta Sarasvatī Ṭhākura (1874–1937)—the powerful preacher of the message of Kṛṣṇa consciousness all over India during the first half of the twentieth century, and the spiritual master of His

Divine Grace A. C. Bhaktivedanta Swami Prabhupāda.

Bhaktivinoda Ṭhākura (1838–1915)—the inaugurator of the modern-day Kṛṣṇa consciousness movement and father of Śrīla Bhaktisiddhānta Sarasvatī Ṭhākura.

Bhārata—an ancient name for modern India.

Bhāryā—a common Sanskrit word for *wife.*

Bhīma—the strongest of the five Pāṇḍava brothers (sons of King Pāṇḍu and his two queens, Kuntī and Mādrī).

Bhīṣma, Grandfather—a senior member of the Kuru dynasty who forfeited his claim to the throne upon the request of his father's second wife.

Bihar—(traditionally known as Magadha) one of the states of present-day India. Its capital city is Patna.

Brahmā—the demigod who is in charge of secondary creation within each universe.

Brahmacārī—a celibate student, a member of the first order of Vedic spiritual life (*brahmacarya*).

Brahma-jyoti—the impersonal effulgence of the Supreme Lord's body.

Brahmaloka— the highest planet in each universe, the abode of Lord Brahmā.

Brahman—the impersonal all-pervasive aspect of the Absolute Truth.

Brahma-saṁhitā—a collection of prayers to Lord Govinda (Kṛṣṇa) composed by Lord Brahmā.

Brāhmaṇa—a priest or scholar who is fixed in *sattva-guṇa* and well versed in spiritual understanding, thus qualifying as a member of the first occupational division of Vedic society.

Bṛhaspati (Brihaspati)—the spiritual master of the demigods.

British Raj—(from the Sanskrit word *rājya,* kingdom) the domination of India by the British from 1858 until 1947.

C

Caitanya-caritāmṛta—a biography of Lord Caitanya composed in Bengali and Sanskrit by Śrīla Kṛṣṇadāsa Kavirāja Gosvāmī.

Caitanya Mahāprabhu, Lord (1486–1534)—the most recent incarnation of Lord Kṛṣṇa, who appeared in this form as His own devotee to spread the chanting of the holy names of the Lord. He is the originator of the Gauḍīya Vaiṣṇava *sampradāya.*

Caṇḍāla, **cāṇḍāla**—(usually translated as "dog-eater") a member of a community that lives on the brink of society, has abhorrent habits and a lowly status.

Candragupta (Maurya)—a young *kṣatriya* who was adopted and educated by Cāṇakya Paṇḍita and enthroned in Pāṭaliputra (the capital of the Magadha empire) after the successful coup-d'état, masterminded by Cāṇakya, that caused the downfall of the corrupt Nanda dynasty.

Cātaka—(*Cucculus melanoleucus*) a bird that drinks only raindrops directly from the sky.

D

Damayantī—a princess from Vidarbha (an ancient Indian kingdom) who was exceptionally devoted to her husband Nala despite his bad luck in gambling, which resulted in their being banished from their kingdom into the forest. This story is narrated in the great epic *Mahābhārata.*

Darśana—(1) audience of the Supreme Lord or His Deity in the temple; (2) a meeting with a saint.

Daśaratha, King—an ancient ruler of the province of Kośala (in northern India), and the father of Lord Rāma.

Deva(tā)—may refer either to the Supreme Lord or to any demigod.

Deva-gaṇa—humans who have celestial traits ascertained in their horoscope.

Devahūti—the saintly wife of Kardama Muni and mother of Kapila-deva, the famous incarnation of Lord Viṣṇu. Her life and the teachings of her son are described in *Śrīmad-Bhāgavatam.*

Devotional service—the process of worshipping the Supreme Lord as described in sacred scriptures: dedication of one's words, thoughts and actions to Him in loving submission. *See also:* **Kṛṣṇa consciousness.**

Dhāma—a transcendental territory in this world that has been sanctified by the appearance and pastimes of the Supreme Lord in any of His incarnations.

Dharma—(1) religiosity (the first of the four Vedic goals of human life); (2) religious duty. *See also:* **Artha, Kāma, Mokṣa.**

Dharma-śālā—a charitable lodge for pilgrims.

Dharma-śāstra(s)—codes (written by Manu and other Vedic sages) that regulate human life and also form the basis of the ancient Vedic judicial system.

Dhṛtarāṣṭra, King—the blind king who ruled in Hastināpura (ancient Delhi) five thousand years ago. His son Duryodhana had caused a colossal war between the two groups of cousins (Kurus and Pāṇḍavas). This conflict is the central theme of the epic *Mahābhārata.*

Dhruvaloka—the polestar, given by the Supreme Lord to prince Dhruva as his residence.

Diti—one of the wives of sage Kaśyapa and mother of the race of demons (the Daityas).

Draupadī—the daughter of King Drupada and wife of the five Pāṇḍava brothers.

Droṇa, Droṇācārya—the military instructor who taught both the Pāṇḍava brothers and the sons of Dhṛtarāṣṭra. The two groups later fought with each other, even involving their common teacher in the battle.

Durgā—the predominating deity of material nature and consort of Lord Śiva.

Durvāsā Muni—a powerful *yogī* and mystic who is often mentioned in the *Purāṇas* and *Śrīmad-Bhāgavatam.*

Duryodhana—the evil-minded eldest son of King Dhṛtarāṣṭra.

Dvādaśī (tithi)—the twelfth day of both the waxing and the waning phase of the moon.

Dvija—(*lit.* "twice-born") another Sanskrit term for a *brāhmaṇa.* "Second birth" refers to initiation into chanting of sacred Vedic *mantras.*

E

Ekādaśī (tithi)—the eleventh day of both the waxing and the waning phase of the moon, a particularly holy fast-day for Vaiṣṇavas.

G

Gāndhārī—a celebrated princess from Gandhāra (present-day Afghanistan) who, upon learning that she had been betrothed to the blind King Dhṛtarāṣṭra, blindfolded herself for her entire life so as to never feel superior to her husband.

Gaṅgā—the river Ganges.

Gauḍīya Maṭha—the religious institution founded by Śrīla Bhaktisiddhānta Sarasvatī Ṭhākura, consisting of numerous *maṭhas* (temples cum ashrams) all throughout India that were dedicated to the spreading of Kṛṣṇa consciousness.

Gauḍīya sampradāya—the disciplic succession of Gauḍīya Vaiṣṇavas.

Gauḍīya Vaiṣṇava—a follower of the teachings of Śrī Caitanya Mahāprabhu and His associates.

Gaurakiśora Dāsa Bābājī—the spiritual master of Śrīla Bhaktisiddhānta Sarasvatī Ṭhākura.

Gautama Ṛṣi—an ancient sage and the husband of Ahalyā.

Gayā—a sacred city in Bihar that has been celebrated since ancient times as the best place for performing *piṇḍa* (offerings to the forefathers).

Gāyatrī—the most prominent Vedic *mantra,* recited thrice daily by *brāhmaṇas.*

Giri Govardhana—a sacred hill in Vṛndāvana that is nondifferent from Lord Viṣṇu.

Ghāṭa—stone steps built on a riverbank or around lakes to facilitate easier access to the water for bathing.

Ghee—butter that has been cooked and strained to remove the milk protein and thus can be used even as a medium for frying. An age-old traditional ingredient in cooking, it is most healthy and tasty.

Gopāla Bhaṭṭa Gosvāmī—one of the Six Gosvāmīs (direct disciples of Śrī Caitanya Mahāprabhu who recorded His teachings).

Gopī—a cowherd damsel in Vṛndāvana and the prototype form of those souls who are the most advanced and surrendered to Lord Kṛṣṇa.

Gośālā—(1) a cowshed; (2) a traditional dairy farm where cows are protected from slaughter.

Goṣṭhy-ānandī—(*lit.* "one who takes pleasure in associating with fellow devotees") a devotee who is committed to preaching and associating with other devotees (in contrast to the *bhajanānandī,* who prefers solitary *bhajana*).

Gotra—a line of descent from one of the great Vedic sages.

Gṛhamedhī—a householder who is excessively attached to home and family.

Gṛhastha—a married person who follows the Vedic religious principles for the purpose of spiritual advancement.

Gṛhastha-āśrama—regulated married life, the second *āśrama* of Vedic spiritual life.

Grim Reaper—death personified.

Guṇas—(the three modes of material nature) the three general influences that are discernible in a person's character, behavior, and occupation, in the environment, in food, and so on: (1) goodness, or *sattva,* (2) passion, or *rajas,* and (3) ignorance, or *tamas.* All three *guṇas* are extensively described in the *Bhagavad-gītā.*

Guñjā—(*Abrus precatorius*) a small white or red berry that is dried for the purpose of stringing into a simple necklace.

Guru—spiritual master, teacher. The three kinds of *gurus* are: *dīkṣā-guru* (who initiates the disciple), *śikṣā-guru* (who instructs the disciple), and *vartma-pradarśaka-guru* (*lit.* "he who shows the way"; who first directs one toward spiritual life).

Guru-dakṣiṇā—a donation given by the disciple to the *guru* at initiation or other occasions.

Guru-mahārāja, Guru Mahārāja—an honorific title for one's spiritual master.

H

Haṁsāvatāra, Lord—an ancient incarnation of Lord Viṣṇu.

Hari, Lord—a common name for Lord Viṣṇu, meaning "He who takes away (obstacles to spiritual life)."

Hari-bhakti-vilāsa—a treatise on rules, regulations and rituals for Gauḍīya Vaiṣṇavas that was composed in the sixteenth century by two prominent disciples of Śrī Caitanya Mahāprabhu.

Haridāsa Ṭhākura—a celebrated follower of Lord Caitanya who was born of Muslim parents. Caitanya Mahāprabhu conferred upon him the title Nāmācārya out of high regard for his incessant chanting of the holy names of the Lord.

Hayagrīva, Lord—one of the ancient incarnations of Lord Viṣṇu.

Himavat—another name for the Himalayan mountains.

Hindu—a Persian misspelling for the Sanskrit word *sindhu,* which was used by Muslim invaders to denote the original inhabitants of India and then later appropriated as the general term for followers of Vedic practices (hence termed "Hinduism"). However, the terms Hindu and Hinduism are in many ways inadequate.

Hiraṇyakaśipu—an evil demon of ancient times (whose son Prahlāda was a devotee of Lord Viṣṇu) who was killed by Lord Nṛsiṁha, an incarnation of Lord Viṣṇu.

Hlādinī—the pleasure-potency, one of the three features of the Supreme Lord's internal energy. *See also:* **Saṁvit, Sandhinī.**

I

Indra, Lord—the king of heaven (Svargaloka).

Īśopaniṣad—one of the principal *Upaniṣads,* Vedic philosophical treatises.

J

Jaḍa-yoga—(also called "python *yoga*") the austerity of not endeavoring for survival but accepting whatever comes of its own accord.

Jaipur—the capital of Rajasthan, one of the present-day Indian states.

Jagāi and Mādhāi—two infamous drunkards and criminals in the town of Navadvīpa (where Śrī Caitanya Mahāprabhu and Śrī Nityānanda Prabhu began the movement of public chanting of the holy names). These two locals got into a skirmish with Nityānanda Prabhu and even wounded Him, but when Mahāprabhu angrily confronted them they both relented and surrendered. They became sincere devotees, wholly remorseful about their past misdeeds.

Jagannātha Dāsa Bābājī—a great Gauḍīya Vaiṣṇava *ācārya* from the eighteenth century.

Jamadagni—an ancient Vedic sage and the father of Paraśurāma, an incarnation of Lord Viṣṇu.

Japa—the soft or silent recitation of Vedic *mantras* on a string of prayer beads that resembles a rosary.

Jayadratha—the king of the Sindhu province (in present Western India and Eastern Pakistan) and an opponent of the Pāṇḍava brothers in the great Battle of Kurukṣetra.

Jīva—spirit soul.

Jñāna—realized knowledge or spiritual knowledge, distinguished from mere *vidyā* (acquired learning, material knowledge).

Jñāna-yoga—the path of abstruse philosophical speculation as one of the three ways to attain the Absolute Truth (the other two being *karma-yoga,* the path of fruitive work, and *bhakti-yoga,* the path of devotional service to the Supreme Lord).

Jyotiṣa-śāstra—the Vedic science of astronomy and astrology.

K

Kāla—time.

Kāla-cakra—the wheel of time.

Kali-yuga—the Age of Kali, the last in the universal cycle of four ages (*yugas*), characterized by an increase in irreligion. It began five thousand years ago. *See:* **Yuga.**

Kalki, Lord—the incarnation of Lord Viṣṇu who appears at the end of Kali-yuga and is the last of the cyclically recurring incarnations.

Kalpa—a day in the life of Lord Brahmā, comprised of a thousand cycles of all four *yugas* (Satya, Tretā, Dvāpara and Kali). One *kalpa* lasts 4,320,000,000 earth years.

Kāma—(1) satisfaction of sense desires (one of the four Vedic goals of human life); (2) lust, or desire for sense gratification. *See also:* **Artha, Dharma, Mokṣa.**

Kapila(deva), Lord—an incarnation of Lord Kṛṣṇa who appeared as the son of sage Kardama and Devahūti. He instructed His mother extensively on the principles of spiritual life (recounted in *Śrīmad-Bhāgavatam*).

Karma—(1) action or activity; (2) ritual activities, performed under the direction of the *karma-kāṇḍa* portion of the Vedic literature, aimed at achieving a higher birth or the heavenly realm; (3) the principle governing material action and reaction; (4) destiny, the effect of previous activity.

Karma-phala—(*lit.* "the fruit of activity") destiny.

Karma-yoga—the lowest of the three processes of spiritual upliftment; ritualistic activities recommended in the *Vedas* to be performed without a sense of proprietorship or expectation of reward.

Karṇa—one of the celebrated *kṣatriya* warriors of the epic *Mahābhārata,* the son of Sūrya (the sun god) and Queen Kuntī. He was forced to side with Duryodhana against his own brothers, the Pāṇḍavas.

Kāśī—another name for Vārāṇasī (Banaras), an ancient holy city in northern India.

Kaśyapa Muni—one of the great ancient sages and progenitor of the races of demigods and demons through his thirteen wives.

Kauśalyā, Queen—the wife of King Daśaratha and mother of Lord Rāma.

Khālsā—the Sikh community.

Krishnadeva Raya, King—the emperor of the Vijayanagara empire in South India in the beginning of the sixteenth century.

Kṛṣṇa, Lord—the Supreme Personality of Godhead in His original, most attractive form.

Kṛṣṇa consciousness—the path of linking oneself with Lord Kṛṣṇa through devotional service to Him, and subsequent saturation of one's consciousness with His name, form, qualities and pastimes.

Kṛṣṇadāsa Kavirāja Gosvāmī—the author of *Śrī Caitanya-caritāmṛta,* the biography of Śrī Caitanya Mahāprabhu.

Kṛṣṇa-kathā—narrations of Lord Kṛṣṇa's teachings or pastimes.

Kṛṣṇa-prasāda—remnants of food that has been ritually offered to the Deity of Lord Kṛṣṇa.

Kṛṣṇa-saṅkīrtana—the practice of congregational chanting of the holy names of Lord Kṛṣṇa.

Kṣatriya—(a member of the second occupational division in Vedic society) a ruler, administrator or soldier.

Kulaśekhara, King—a South Indian king and one of the Alvars (great Vaiṣṇava devotees in South India), who was famous for his poetry.

Kumāras—the four celibate sons of Lord Brahmā.

Kumbha-melā—the greatest religious gathering on earth, occurring every twelve years at Prayāga (Allahabad), near the confluence of the sacred rivers Gaṅgā, Yamunā and the mystical Sarasvatī. Anyone who bathes in the confluence at the stipulated time is guaranteed liberation from material bondage.

Kuntī, Queen—the wife of King Pāṇḍu, the emperor in Hastināpura, who was cursed to die if he ever attempted to conceive offspring. As a young princess, Queen Kuntī had received a boon from Durvāsā Muni that she could summon any demigod to do her bidding, and hence the royal couple availed of this boon to beget five celestial sons (the Pāṇḍavas).

Kūrma, Lord—an incarnation of Lord Viṣṇu in the form of a giant tortoise.

Kurukṣetra—an ancient holy place north of Delhi, the site of the historical battle described in the *Mahābhārata.*

Kuṭīra—a simple hut used by renunciants.

L

Lakh—100,000.

Lakṣmaṇa—Lord Rāmacandra's younger brother.

Lakṣmī—the goddess of fortune, the eternal consort of Lord Viṣṇu.

Lakṣmī-Nārāyaṇa—a pair of Deities (the Supreme Lord and His consort) who are worshipped by Vaiṣṇavas as the transcendental Divine Couple.

Lakṣmīpati—"the Lord of Lakṣmī," a common name for Lord Viṣṇu.

Liberation—(in Sanskrit: *mokṣa*) extrication of the spirit soul from material bondage and its subsequent return to the spiritual realm (the last of the four Vedic goals of human life).

Līlā—pastime(s) of the Supreme Lord and His associates.

Loi Bazaar—the main market in the town of Vṛndāvana.

M

Madhya Pradesh—a state in central India.

Magadha—the ancient Sanskrit name for the territory of the present state of Bihar, in northeastern India.

Mahābhārata—the longest epic in the world, describing the history, religion and culture of ancient India in one hundred thousand Sanskrit verses.

Mahājana—(1) a title for twelve exceptional devotees who are considered authorities in devotional service to the Supreme Lord; (2) a great soul or an exalted devotee.

Mahārāja—title for a king, ruler or *sannyāsī.*

Mahā-mantra—Hare Kṛṣṇa, Hare Kṛṣṇa, Kṛṣṇa Kṛṣṇa, Hare Hare/ Hare Rāma, Hare Rāma, Rāma Rāma, Hare Hare.

Mahā-samādhi—a great soul's departure from this world.

Mākhana-cora—Lord Kṛṣṇa as the child butter thief.

Malaya Mountains—the southern portion of the Western Ghats, on the West coast of India.

Mandir—temple.

Mantra—(1) a pure sound vibration; (2) a Vedic incantation that frees the mind from material attachments and illusion.

Manu—the father of mankind and author of the *Manu-saṁhitā,* the most ancient *dharma-śāstra.*

Manu-saṁhitā, Manu-smṛti—the most important among the twenty different *dharma-śāstras* (the body of ancient Vedic laws and codes of social and religious conduct).

Manuṣya-gaṇa—persons with human traits as ascertained by their horoscope.

Martyaloka—"the world of the mortals," the earthly plane.

Mathurā—the ancient city, close to Vṛndāvana, in the greater area called Vraja-*maṇḍala.* Lord Kṛṣṇa appeared in Mathurā and was then taken to Vraja.

Matsya, Lord—the famous incarnation of Lord Viṣṇu in the form of a giant fish.

Mauryas—the dynasty established by Candragupta Maurya.

Māyā—illusion (*lit.* "that which is not").

Māyādevī—the personification of the Lord's illusory potency.

Māyā Sītā—the apparition of (the real) Sītādevī that was abducted by Rāvaṇa.

Māyāvāda—the faulty philosophy of oneness, or monism, that claims that the *jīva* (soul) is equal to God in all respects and has simply forgotten this "fact." This stand was widely propagated throughout India by the great Śaṅkarācārya during the seventh and the beginning of the eighth century AD.

Māyāvādī—(1) a renunciant who has been initiated into one of Śaṅkarācārya's orders; (2) one who believes in monism.

Menakā—a celestial nymph (Apsarā) who was sent to earth by Indra to disturb the meditation of sage Viśvāmitra.

Mitra—a friend.

Mleccha—a person born outside of Vedic culture and not raised according to Vedic standards of behavior.

Modes of material nature—*See:* **Guṇas.**

Mogul Empire—the portions of India that had been subjugated by a dynasty of Muslim invaders who were in power from the sixteenth century until the middle of the nineteenth century.

Mohinī-mūrti—an incarnation of Lord Viṣṇu in the form of an alluring goddess.

Mokṣa—liberation (the fourth Vedic goal of human life). *See also:* **Artha, Dharma, Kāma.**

Mount Meru—a celestial golden mountain the top of which is the residence of the demigods.

Mṛdaṅga—a clay drum used in *kīrtana.*

Mṛtyu-loka—"the world of the mortals," Earth.

Muhūrta—(a Vedic time unit) forty-eight minutes.

Mūrti, śrī-mūrti—the deity form of the Lord or of an *ācārya.*

N

Nakṣatra—one of the twenty-seven stars.

Nāmācārya—"the *ācārya* of chanting the holy names," a title conferred upon Śrīla Haridāsa Ṭhākura by Śrī Caitanya Mahāprabhu.

Nandagrāma—the hill in Vraja that hosts the palace of Lord Kṛṣṇa's foster father, Nanda Mahārāja.

Nanda Mahārāja—Lord Kṛṣṇa's foster father in Vraja and the husband of Queen Yaśodā.

Nandas, the Nanda dynasty, the Nanda kings—the nine successive kings who ruled over the ancient province of Magadha a few hundred years before Cāṇakya. The last of them was overthrown by Cāṇakya and Candragupta.

Nārada Muni—a great sage and preacher of devotional service to Lord Viṣṇu.

Naraka—hell.

Nārāyaṇa—Lord Viṣṇu.

Narottama Dāsa Ṭhākura—a prominent preacher of the Gauḍīya Vaiṣṇava *sampradāya* in Bengal after the time of Śrī Caitanya Mahāprabhu. He had been studying under the tutelage of the Gosvāmīs of Vṛndāvana and then returned to Bengal to preach.

Nindaka—one who is excessively prone to criticize.

Nīti—moral teachings.

Nīti-śāstra—collections of ethical and moral instruction.

Nivṛtti-mārga—the path of detachment (as opposed to *pravṛtti-mārga,* the path of material enjoyment).

Nṛsiṁha(deva), Lord—a celebrated incarnation of Lord Viṣṇu who appeared in an unusual half-man, half-lion form to uphold the boon that Lord Brahmā had given to the demon Hiraṇyakaśipu. Lord Nṛsiṁhadeva killed Hiraṇyakaśipu for having tortured his son Prahlāda, who was a great Vaiṣṇava.

O

Orissa (now Odisha)—a state on the eastern coast of India.

P

Pāṇḍavas—Yudhiṣṭhira, Bhīma, Arjuna, Nakula and Sahadeva, the five pious *kṣatriya* brothers who were sons of King Pāṇḍu and his two queens, Kuntī and Mādrī.

Paṇḍita (pandit)—a traditional Vedic scholar.

Pān-wālā—a seller of betel.

Paramātmā—the "Supersoul," an expansion of the Supreme Lord who is localized in the heart of each embodied living being and in every atom of the creation.

Parāśara Muni—a great sage and author of a *dharma-śāstra* named after him, and the father of Vyāsadeva, the main compiler of the Vedic literature.

Paraśurāma, Lord—an incarnation of Lord Viṣṇu who reduced the population of haughty *kṣatriyas* on the earth.

Parīkṣit, King—the king of the Kuru dynasty who was enthroned after King Yudhiṣṭhira decided to renounce his position as emperor of the world. He was the son of Arjuna's son Abhimanyu.

Pārtha—(*lit.* "son of Pṛthā [Kuntī]") another name for Arjuna.

Pātāla(loka)—the nether regions of the universe.

Pativratā—a pious married woman whose vow is chastity to her husband.

Piṇḍa-dāna—an offering to one's deceased forefathers for their benefit.

Pitās—deceased forefathers.

Pracetās—the ten saintly sons of the ancient king named Prācīnabarhi, who were instructed by Lord Śiva how to worship and thus please Lord Viṣṇu.

Prācīnabarhi—an ancient Vedic emperor.

Prahara—(a Vedic unit of time) three hours.

Prahlāda (Mahārāja)—the saintly son of the demonic king Hiraṇyakaśipu.

Prajalpa—worthless talk.

Pralaya—universal devastation, annihilation of the material universe at the end of a *kalpa.*

Pratiloma—a Vedic marital match that is not ideal due to the husband's being socially inferior to the wife.

Pravṛtti-mārga—the path of material enjoyment (in contrast to *nivṛtti-mārga,* the path of detachment).

Prayāga—an ancient holy city (presently named Allahabad) at the confluence of the Gaṅgā, Yamunā and the mystical Sarasvatī.

Pṛthu, King—an ancient Vedic king who was an incarnation of Lord Viṣṇu.

Pūjārī—a priest who performs regular worship of Deities in a temple.

Puṇya-bhūmi—(*lit.* "pious land") place of pilgrimage, or an abode of the Lord.

Purāṇas—ancient histories that are enriched with narrations of the pastimes of Lord Viṣṇu's many incarnations and of the lives of His devotees.

Purī—any of the holy cities glorified in the *Purāṇas* (such as Jagannātha Purī or Vārāṇasī).

Purohita—a priest.

R

Rādhā-Kṛṣṇa—Lord Kṛṣṇa and Śrīmatī Rādhārāṇī worshipped together as the transcendental Divine Couple.

Rādhārāṇī, Śrīmatī—the divine consort of Lord Kṛṣṇa and personification of His pleasure-potency.

Raghus—the dynasty of *kṣatriyas* in which Lord Rāma descended.

Rajas, rajo-guṇa—passion, one of the three *guṇas* or modes of material nature. *See also:* **Guṇas.**

Rākṣasas—a race of powerful evil-minded creatures.

Rākṣasa-gaṇa—humans who have lower traits in their character, as ascertained by their horoscope.

Rāma(candra), Lord—a prominent incarnation of Lord Viṣṇu who appeared in Tretā-yuga as the son of King Daśaratha of Kośala.

Rāmāyaṇa—a sacred narration of Lord Rāma's exploits by the sage Vālmīki.

Rāvaṇa—the ancient king of Rākṣasas who was killed by Lord Rāma.

Ṛṣi—a sage.

Ṛtvik—a priest.

Rūpa Gosvāmī—the foremost of the Six Gosvāmīs (direct disciples of Śrī Caitanya Mahāprabhu who recorded His teachings).

S

Sādhu—a saint or devotee.

Sādhu-saṅga—association of saintly devotees.

Samādhi—meditative trance, the highest stage of *yoga.*

Sampradāya—a chain of spiritual masters and disciples.

Saṁsāra—the whirlpool of material life, the cycle of repeated birth and death.

Saṁskāra—Vedic purificatory rituals, such as marriage and last rites.

Saṁvit—the potency of omniscience, one of the three features of the Supreme Lord's internal energy. *See also:* **Hlādinī, Sandhinī.**

Sanātana-dharma—"the eternal duty of the soul," an ancient Vedic concept of religion.

Sanātana Gosvāmī—one of the Six Gosvāmīs (direct disciples of Śrī Caitanya Mahāprabhu who recorded His teachings) and the elder brother of Śrī Rūpa Gosvāmī.

Sandhinī—the existence-expanding potency in both the material and the spiritual world, one of the three features of the Supreme Lord's internal energy. *See also:* **Hlādinī, Saṁvit.**

Sāndīpani Muni—the spiritual master of Lord Kṛṣṇa and Lord Balarāma, who educated Them in the sixty-four Vedic arts.

Sandhyā-vandana—silent recitation of the Gāyatrī *mantra* by *brāhmaṇas* thrice daily.

Śaṅkarācārya (686–718)—a great South Indian philosopher who established the doctrine of monism, or Māyāvāda.

Saṅkīrtana—congregational chanting of the holy names of the Lord, especially the *mahā-mantra* (q.v.).

Saṅkīrtana devotee—a devotee who performs public chanting or distributes spiritual literature for the benefit of all.

Saṅkīrtana-yajña—the sacrifice of congregationally chanting the holy names, greater even than ancient Vedic sacrifices meant to benefit the entire world.

Sannyāsa(-āśrama)—the stage of renunciation, the fourth *āśrama* of the Vedic social system.

Sannyāsī—a person in the renounced order of life.

Sanskrit—the sacred language (used in the Vedic scriptures) that appeared from Lord Nārāyaṇa. It is the oldest and original language, from which all other languages developed.

Śakti—(1) power, potency; (2) the consort of any of the demigods or of the Supreme Lord.

Śālagrāma-śilā—Lord Viṣṇu in the form of a particular blackish stone that is worshipped by many *brāhmaṇas.*

Sāma Veda—one of the four *Vedas,* the original sacred scriptures, which are known to be eternal and of superhuman origin.

Śambhu—another name for Lord Śiva.

Sarayū—a river that flows through the city of Ayodhyā, the capital of the Kośala kingdom.

Śāstra—a sacred scripture.

Śāstrī—one who has mastered the scriptures.

Śatapatha Brāhmaṇa—one of the auxiliary Vedic scriptures.

Sat—real, spiritual, not false (as opposed to *asat*).

Sat-saṅga—association of saintly devotees.

Sattva(-guṇa)—goodness, one of the three *guṇas* or modes of material nature. *See* **Guṇa.**

Sāvitrī—an ancient celebrated chaste woman who was able to bring her husband Satyavān back from the dead by a sagacious argument with Yamarāja.

Śeṣa—one of the first expansions of Lord Viṣṇu, and His transcendental rcsting placc.

Śikhā (shikha)—a tuft of hair tied at the back of the head, traditionally kept by male members of Vedic society (especially *brāhmaṇas*).

Śikṣāṣṭaka—eight verses by Śrī Caitanya Mahāprabhu about the glories of chanting the holy names of the Lord.

Sītā(devī)—the divine consort of Lord Rāma and adopted daughter of King Janaka of Mithilā.

Sītā-Rāma—Lord Rāma and Śrīmatī Sītādevī, who are worshipped as the Divine Couple.

Śiva, Lord—the demigod in charge of the destruction of the material world and famous as the best of Vaiṣṇavas.

Śiva-liṅga—the form of Lord Śiva that is worshipped in his temples.

Śloka (shloka)—a Sanskrit verse with thirty-two syllables in four equal lines, or a Sanskrit verse in general.

Soma—the moon god, also known as Candra.

Śrāddha—offerings to the forefathers.

Śrī, Śrīla, Śrīmad, Śrīmān, Śrīmatī—honorific prefixes to individual names.

Śrīla Prabhupāda—an honorific and endearing title for His Divine Grace A. C. Bhaktivedanta Swami Prabhupāda.

Śrīmad-Bhāgavatam—(also known as the *Bhāgavata Purāṇa*) an ancient history of the universe interspersed with narrations of different incarnations of the Supreme Lord, and the most outstanding of the eighteen *Purāṇas*.

Śuddha-bhakta—a pure devotee.

Śūdra—a laborer, a member of the fourth class of the Vedic social system.

Śūdra-mahājana—a great soul who is respected as a devotee despite being a *śūdra* by birth.

Śukadeva Gosvāmī—the son of Vyāsadeva and great self-realized sage who spoke the *Śrīmad-Bhāgavatam.*

Sukanyā—a celebrated chaste woman of Vedic times, who agreed to marry and serve an elderly and irritable sage, thus pleasing him.

Śukla-pakṣa—the bright fortnight.

Śukra, Śukrācārya (Shukracharya)—the spiritual master of the demons and author of a *nīti-śāstra* by his name.

Sura—a demigod.

Svarga(loka)—heaven.

Svātī—one of the twenty-seven stars, or *nakṣatras.*

Śyāmānanda Prabhu—a prominent preacher in the Gauḍīya Vaiṣṇava *sampradāya* after the time of Śrī Caitanya Mahāprabhu. After studying under the tutelage of the Six Gosvāmīs in Vṛndāvana, he returned to his native Odisha and preached with amazing success.

T

Tamas, tamo-guṇa—ignorance, one of the three *guṇas* or modes of material nature. *See* **Guṇa.**

Tapasya—religious austerity.

Tilaka—an auspicious clay-marking on the forehead of a person that signifies his adherence to a particular *sampradāya.*

Tithi—a lunar day.

Tīrtha—a holy place.

Tīrtha-yātrā—pilgrimage.

Tri-kāla—the three phases of time: past, present and future.

Tulasī—a pious plant worshipped by devotees of Lord Viṣṇu.

Tulasī Dāsa—a poet who retold the *Rāmāyaṇa* for Hindi-speaking devotees.

U

Uddhava—Lord Kṛṣṇa's cousin, minister, and great devotee.

Upaniṣads—auxiliary Vedic texts that are philosophical treatises.

Uttar Pradesh—a state in present North India.

V

Vaikuṇṭha—the spiritual abode of Lord Viṣṇu.

Vaiṣṇava—a devotee of Lord Viṣṇu. *See also:* **Viṣṇu-bhakta.**

Vaiśya—a farmer or merchant, a member of the third occupational division of Vedic society.

Vaitaraṇī—the river that divides material and spiritual worlds.

Vālmīki—an ancient sage and author of the *Rāmāyaṇa,* the pastimes of Lord Rāma.

Vāmana, Lord—an incarnation of Lord Viṣṇu in the form of a *brāhmaṇa* boy.

Vānaprastha—(the third stage, or *āśrama,* in the Vedic social structure) celibate retirement from family life in preparation for complete renunciation.

Vana-vāsa—(*lit.* "living in the woods") a euphemism for Lord Rāma's exile to the forest for fourteen years.

Varāha, Lord—an incarnation of Lord Viṣṇu in the form of a gigantic boar.

Varṇāśrama—the Vedic social system of four occupational divisions (*varṇas*) and four spiritual orders or stages of social involvement (*āśramas*).

Vasiṣṭha—an ancient sage who was the family priest of the dynasty of King Daśaratha.

Vedānta-sūtra—aphorisms compiled by Śrīla Vyāsadeva that summarize the essence of Vedic knowledge.

Vedas—the four original sacred scriptures of the Vedic canon: the *Ṛg Veda, Sāma Veda, Atharva Veda* and *Yajur Veda.*

Vidura—a great devotee of Lord Kṛṣṇa who was a senior member of the Kuru dynasty and a brother of King Dhṛtarāṣṭra.

Viṣṇu, Lord—(*lit.* "one who pervades everything") one of the most common Sanskrit names denoting the Supreme Lord.

Viṣṇu-bhakta—a devotee of Lord Viṣṇu. *See also:* **Vaiṣṇava.**

Viṣṇudūtas—eternal associates of Lord Viṣṇu in Vaikuṇṭha who serve as His messengers.

Viśrāma-ghāṭa—a famous bathing *ghāṭa* with a stone staircase on the bank of the river Yamunā in Mathurā.

Viśvambhara—the Supreme Lord who sustains and supports everything.

Viśvāmitra—a celebrated ancient sage whose determination in performing austerities frightened even Lord Indra, the king of heaven.

Viśvanātha Cakravartī—a great *ācārya* of the Gauḍīya *sampradāya* in the seventeenth century.

Viśvanātha Mandira—the main temple of Lord Śiva in Vārāṇasī.

Vraja(-maṇḍala)—"the area of Vraja," the surroundings of the town of Vṛndāvana and the city of Mathurā.

Vṛndāvana—the present town of Vrindavan (south of Delhi) and also the surrounding area, where Lord Kṛṣṇa performed His childhood pastimes some five thousand years ago and which is now a sprawling place of pilgrimage.

Vṛndāvana-līlā—the pastimes of Lord Kṛṣṇa and His devotees in Vṛndāvana at the time of His appearance in this world approximately five thousand years ago.

Vyāsa(deva)—the literary incarnation of God who compiled and divided the Vedic scriptures.

X

Xanthippe—an argumentative woman named after Socrates's famous wife, who was known to have been of difficult temper.

Y

Yadupati—"the leader of the Yadu dynasty," a name for Lord Kṛṣṇa.

Yajamāna—the person who pays for a sacrifice and organizes its performance.

Yajña—a Vedic sacrifice for satisfying the Supreme Lord or demigods.

Yajñapati—"the Lord of all sacrifices," a name of Lord Viṣṇu.

Yajña-śālā—a pavilion wherein a sacrifice takes place.

Yamadūta—the servants and messengers of Yamarāja who come to claim the sinful at death.

Yamarāja—the lord of death.

Yavana—a Sanskrit word for the Greek race and others outside of the Vedic culture.

Yaśodā, Mother—the foster mother of Lord Kṛṣṇa in Vṛndāvana and wife of Nanda Mahārāja.

Yoga—a Vedic path for linking oneself with the Supreme Lord in any of His aspects.

Yogī—one who practices *yoga,* primarily *aṣṭāṅga-yoga* (mystic *yoga*).

Yudhiṣṭhira, King—the eldest among the five Pāṇḍava brothers, who was crowned the king of Bhārata-varṣa after the fateful Battle of Kurukṣetra.

Yuga—one of the four ages (Satya, Tretā, Dvāpara, Kali) in the cyclic history of the universe. A thousand cycles of four *yugas* are known as a *kalpa* and are equal to one day of Lord Brahmā.

Z

Zamindar—a landowner, aristocrat.

Made in the USA
Thornton, CO
03/21/24 16:36:41

f4a8ddbe-8389-4ea3-9e97-e3da22bf1336R01